Ingo Berensmeyer
Literary Culture in Early Modern England, 1630–1700

Ingo Berensmeyer

Literary Culture in Early Modern England, 1630–1700

Angles of Contingency

DE GRUYTER

This book is a revised translation of *"Angles of Contingency": Literarische Kultur im England des siebzehnten Jahrhunderts*, originally published in German by Max Niemeyer Verlag, Tübingen 2007, as vol. 39 of the *Anglia Book Series*.

ISBN 978-3-11-099517-6
e-ISBN (PDF) 978-3-11-069137-5
e-ISBN (EPUB) 978-3-11-069140-5
DOI https://doi.org/10.1515/9783110691375

This work is licensed under a Creative Commons Attribution-NonCommercial-NoDerivatives 4.0 International License. For details go to http://creativecommons.org/licenses/by-nc-nd/4.0/.

Library of Congress Control Number: 2020934495

Bibliographic information published by the Deutsche Nationalbibliothek
The Deutsche Nationalbibliothek lists this publication in the Deutsche Nationalbibliografie; detailed bibliographic data are available from the Internet at http://dnb.dnb.de.

©2022 Ingo Berensmeyer, published by Walter de Gruyter GmbH, Berlin/Boston
This volume is text- and page-identical with the hardback published in 2020.
The book is published with open access at www.degruyter.com.

Cover image: Jan Davidszoon de Heem, Vanitas Still Life with Books, a Globe, a Skull, a Violin and a Fan, c. 1650. UtCon Collection/Alamy Stock Photo.
Typesetting: Integra Software Services Pvt. Ltd.
Printing and binding: CPI books GmbH, Leck

www.degruyter.com

Preface to the Revised Edition

This book was first published in German in 2007 as volume 39 of the *Anglia* Book Series. In returning to it for this English version, I decided not simply to translate but to revise it thoroughly in order to correct mistakes, bring it up to date, and make it a little more reader-friendly by discarding at least some of its Teutonic baggage. The German text was my *Habilitationsschrift* (the monograph whose main purpose is to demonstrate one's eligibility to a professorship in Germany), and this may explain, though not excuse, its lengthy footnotes and occasionally arcane expressions. In fact, this German version already *was* a translation – required by academic rules and regulations – from the English original I had first written in 2003 and 2004, in blissful ignorance of the rules at my then home university of Siegen, which required it to be submitted in German. I have since returned to this English version now and then in my teaching and come to regret the fact that it was not available in English for a wider readership. This new book, then, is – for me – a recovery as much as a revision.

Over the years, I have incurred many debts of gratitude to friends and colleagues in many countries, as well as numerous research institutions and libraries whose generosity contributed to the making of this book. Its beginnings owe much to J. Hillis Miller, who invited me to spend a year at the University of California at Irvine in 2002, and to the late Richard Kroll, whose wit and expertise helped foster many ideas for this project. I miss his disagreement. In Germany, K. Ludwig Pfeiffer knows how much of his inspiration is in this book. I would also like to thank Nicola Glaubitz for an amazing co-teaching experience that has left distinct traces in these pages.

Also, over the years, conversations with colleagues have indirectly contributed to the reworking of this book. I would like in particular to thank Andrew Hadfield, Margaret Ezell, and the late Herbert Grabes. Obviously, any remaining mistakes should be laid firmly at my door. Speedy revision was made possible by a research sabbatical generously granted by LMU Munich in the summer of 2018. Finally, thanks – as ever – to my family: Hella, Henrik, Niklas, and Talea.

Contents

Preface to the Revised Edition —— V

List of Figures —— IX

List of Abbreviations —— IX

"Seeking the Noise in the Depth of Silence": A Naval Prelude with Spectators, 1665 —— 1
    The Sensibility of Dissociation —— 6

1 Historicising Literary Culture: Communication, Contingency, Contexture —— 13
    Communication —— 13
    Contingency —— 15
    Contexture —— 18
    Literary Culture —— 23

2 Literary Cabinets of Wonder: The 'Paper Kingdomes' of Robert Burton and Sir Thomas Browne —— 28
    Early Modern Knowledge Technologies —— 28
    Reading the Theatre of Writing: Burton's *Anatomy of Melancholy* —— 34
    "Collaterall Truths" in the "Multiplicity of Writing": Sir Thomas Browne —— 47

3 Writing, Reading, Seeing: Visuality and Contingency in the Literary Epistemology of Neoclassicism —— 70
    Literary Epistemology —— 70
    "Not Truth, But Image, Maketh Passion": Optics and the Force of Reading in Milton and Hobbes —— 77
    "The Conquests of Vertue": Mimesis and Strategic Visuality in Davenant's *Preface to Gondibert* (1650) —— 96
    Visuality and Imagination between Science and Fiction: Margaret Cavendish's *Observations upon Experimental Philosophy* and *The Blazing World* (1666) —— 104
    Literary Worldmaking —— 114

4 Literature as Civil War —— 117
    Ciceronian Moments: State of Nature and Natural Law in the Cultural Imaginary —— 117
    Words as Weapons: Rhetoric and Politics in Hobbes and Milton —— 124

Pastoral Politics: Crypto-Royalism in Izaak Walton's *The Compleat Angler* (1653–1676) —— **134**
Between *Astræa Redux* and *Paradise Lost*: Cultural Memory and Countermemory in the Restoration —— **144**
Contingency, Irony, Sexuality: Nature, Law, and Kingship in *Absalom and Achitophel* (1681) —— **161**
Spaces of Distinction —— **176**

5 Private Selves and Public Lives: Neoclassical Perspectives —— 179
Inwardness, Probability, and Wit —— **179**
The 'Rhetoric of Love': Inwardness, Reading, and the Novel in Aphra Behn's *Love-Letters Between a Nobleman and His Sister* (1684–87) —— **184**
'This Deed of Trust': Law, Literature, and the Unbearable Politeness of Being in Congreve's *The Way of the World* (1700) —— **200**

The Augustan Angle: Civilised Contingency and Normative Discourse —— 214

Bibliography —— 225

Index —— 249

List of Figures

Fig. 1 Robert Burton, *The Anatomy of Melancholy,* title page (detail), London 1676. Wellcome Collection. CC BY —— 38
Fig. 2 Frontispiece by William Marshall and title page of *Eikon Basilike*. Beinecke Rare Book & Manuscript Library, Yale University. Wikimedia Commons —— 78

List of Abbreviations

AM *Anatomy of Melancholy*
EL *Elements of Law*
L   *Leviathan*

. . . humbly pursuing that infallible perpetuity,
unto which all others must diminish their diameters,
and be poorly seen in Angles of contingency.

Sir Thomas Browne, *Urne-Buriall*

"Seeking the Noise in the Depth of Silence":
A Naval Prelude with Spectators, 1665

John Dryden opens his *Essay of Dramatick Poesie* (1668), one of the birth documents of English literary criticism, with a scene of naval warfare that establishes a connection between an event of the utmost political and economic importance and the effect that such an event has on the public as it occurs:

> It was that memorable day, in the first Summer of the late War, when our Navy ingag'd the *Dutch:* a day wherein the two most mighty and best appointed Fleets which any age had ever seen, disputed the command of the greater half of the Globe, the commerce of Nations, and the riches of the Universe. While these vast floating bodies, on either side, mov'd against each other in parallel lines, and our Country men, under the happy conduct of his Royal Highness, went breaking, by little and little, into the line of the Enemies; the noise of the Cannon from both Navies reach'd our ears about the City: so that all men, being alarm'd with it, and in a dreadful suspence of the event, which they knew was then deciding, every one went following the sound as his fancy led him; and leaving the Town almost empty, some took towards the Park, some cross the River, others down it; all seeking the noise in the depth of silence. (Dryden 1971, 8)

'The public' as a site of social observation and self-reflection, theatrical in its flexible formations of actors and spectators, has only recently emerged as a dimension of collective awareness among the upper ranks of Restoration London's population, expressing itself in patriotic terms, mediated by newspapers, coffee-house conversations, and plays (Schweikart 1986, 63–70; Frank 1961; Pincus 1995). Public curiosity about the Battle of Lowestoft (3 June 1665), a naval engagement that remains invisible because it happens offshore and is yet barely audible in London, is motivated by a patriotic impulse, registered in Dryden's use of the first person plural in reporting and even in recording sense perceptions ("our Navy", "our Country men", "our ears"). This impulse is the result of a new social awareness outside of traditional notions of court and commonwealth that articulates itself in nationalist and incipiently imperial terms ("the riches of the Universe").[1] The disintegration of the traditional social order in the violent upheavals of Reformation, Civil War, and the English Republic seems all but forgotten in this new language of national unity after 1660.

But Dryden's text does more than observe the common and unifying impulse of public curiosity; it also registers a social reality of disintegration, dissociation, dispersal, and individualisation contingent upon it. As a consequence of the public desire of news, "the Town" – centre stage for dramatic events and public communication – is left "almost empty". This depletion of the public sphere is noted in a series of subtle

---

[1] On Dryden's fusion of the aesthetic and the political in the *Essay*, see Docherty 1999; on his careful manipulation of discursive levels, see Gelber 1999, 44–45.

linguistic shifts, first to the third person plural ("they knew") and then to the third person singular ("every one went following the sound as his fancy led him"). The effect of dissociation into smaller groups ("some [. . .], some [. . .], others"), is just barely compensated for at the end in the word "all" that emphasises a common goal of "seeking the noise in the depth of silence".

This short extract anticipates some of the topics and concerns of this study. Dryden's paragraph can be read as a *mise en abyme* of seventeenth-century English culture and its fundamental problems. Not only does it point to the interdependence of literary and current political events and more long-term historic developments, namely the impending globalisation of economically motivated imperialism; it also reflects an awareness of the *public* dimension of political processes. To open an essay on the theatre with a modern variant of teichoscopy (the witnessing of an offstage event in ancient Greek literature) is to associate theatrical and political culture in more than a simple analogy. From the very beginning, Dryden problematises the relation of a performance (political as well as theatrical) to its intended audience; indeed, drama at this time could still be presented as a predominantly aural rather than visual form (Milhous 1984, 42). He knows that a battle has more dimensions than two ("Country men" vs. "Enemies") and that its interpretation crucially depends on the spectator's or listener's perspective. The situation of his public battle-listeners resembles the *topos* of curiosity as analysed by Hans Blumenberg (1991, 1996). He also knows that a public audience is fragmented into many smaller groups who are driven by individual interests and subjective, perhaps irrational motivations ("fancy"). The essay as a whole is constructed in a dramaturgical manner that casts the reader in the role of a spectator who follows the movements and the dialogue of four disputants: Eugenius, Crites, Lisideius, and Neander. Rhetorically, the first paragraph attempts to include the contemporary reader in a network of shared values and interests by appealing to a shared memory: "It was that memorable day [. . .]", and by including the reader in the first person plural, imputing to him (and, by 1668, increasingly to *her* as well[2]) a shared nationality and shared experiences, which in their turn serve as a postulated common ground supporting Dryden's argument, in the *Essay*, for a specific national taste. Literary and political matters are thus inextricably, yet strategically, intertwined.

But the paragraph not only contains a patriotic appeal to a new sense of Englishness as a unifying attribute transcending minor issues of disagreement and division, modelled in contrast to perceptions of foreigners – Dutch, French – as insurmountably different. In its indecisive use of pronouns and grammatical persons, as well as in its shifting narrative focalisation, the text also implicitly reflects on the problems that arise in understanding and describing public opinion as a basis of modern politics and a modern conception of the state. Most importantly, such an

---

[2] Female literacy grows significantly in the late sixteenth and throughout the seventeenth century. See, for example, Cressy 1980, 176–77; Pearson 1996; Wheale 1999, 105–31; Zwicker 2003, 311.

understanding has to grapple with the philosophical and political problem of reconciling the one and the many, unity and multitude, private and public interest (Gunn 1969; Schweikart 1986). How must a political order be constructed and maintained that is capable of uniting the separate and distinct bodies of individuals and groups of individuals, each motivated by distinct interests or irreducible passions, "every one [. . .] as his fancy led him", in a single body politic – defined by Hobbes as "the union of many men" (1994, 167; 2.27.7) – propelled and stabilised by a single sovereign purpose?

Hobbes famously attempts to solve this problem by means of a language of representation (1996, 114; 1.16):

> A Multitude of men, are made *One* Person, when they are by one man, or one Person, Represented; so that it be done with the consent of every one of that Multitude in particular. For it is the *Unity* of the Representer, not the *Unity* of the Represented, that maketh the Person *One*. And it is the Representer that beareth the Person, and but one Person: And *Unity*, cannot otherwise be understood in Multitude.

This problem of the multitude and its unity – or otherwise – is one of the key issues of seventeenth-century English politics and culture. As Dryden well knew, a centralised, hierarchical social order could work very efficiently in military operations ("our Country men, under the happy conduct of his Royal Highness"), but it was much harder to maintain when a public 'we' was prone to disintegration into ever smaller divisions, when people were running in different directions even as they seemed to be pursuing a common goal. This difficulty would become manifest in the subsequent fate of "his Royal Highness", the Duke of York and later King James II, who was forced to abandon his throne and flee the country in 1688, an escape that was later reinterpreted as an act of abdication in order to legitimise the new monarch, William of Orange, as King William III.

What role do literature and rhetoric play in the formation of the body politic? Dryden does not expressly address this question, but his self-conscious use of rhetorical figures (which call attention to themselves, to their own mode of operation) can be taken as eloquent on this issue. The *Essay of Dramatick Poesie* stages a discussion about literary theory against the background of the Battle of Lowestoft, the most decisive victory of the English in all three Dutch Wars in the seventeenth century, thus connecting international politics to national poetics and loosely suggesting the advantages of (English) heterogeneity and mixed modes over (French) absolutism in literature as well as politics (Kroll 2002, 25–26). Like many authors of his time, Dryden could take for granted the decipherability of many levels of allusion, could trust in his reader's ability to seek out the "noise in the depth of silence", that place where the text reflects on its own operative conditions and strategies.

The necessity and rationality of such strategic language use and its reflection is indirectly established by the last paragraph of the essay, which completes its narrative frame. The battle is over, but the process of dispersal that the first paragraph wished to contain is intensified rather than stopped, as the text ends with the abrupt dissolution of the quartet of disputants: "Walking thence together to the *Piazze* they parted there; *Eugenius* and *Lisideius* to some pleasant appointment they had made, and *Crites* and *Neander* to their several Lodgings" (Dryden 1971, 81). The Italian word *piazza* was a common name for the North and East sides of Covent Garden. Its choice as the final scene of Dryden's essay underscores the modernity of his setting and his literary-political thought. Covent Garden had been built in 1631 outside the City limits, signalling the spread of a newly elegant lifestyle of conspicuous consumption (McKendrick et al. 1982, Burke 1993), and the demise of the older social order in which rich and poor had been living side by side in the City parishes. It virtually embodied the economic force of secularisation because the site on which it was erected was the site of Westminster Abbey's convent garden. As Simon Jenkins explains (1975, 28), "[t]he Convent Garden piazza was an instant success and it immediately led to the development of the surrounding streets. [. . .] Leading courtiers poured in applications for the gracious houses overlooking the square." The *piazza* is a theatrical space for social self-presentation and self-reflection, emblematic of a new understanding of society that is capitalist both in its economic, consumerist outlook and in its focus on the capital of London as a social stage. Its neoclassical Palladian architecture, designed by Inigo Jones, is a result of urban planning, not of haphazard growth: "elegant, uniform façades, instead of [. . .] fiercely idiosyncratic and 'misshapen' houses" (Picard 1997, 24). Covent Garden is the fit emblem of Neander's (and Dryden's) dramatic ideals as well as of the social ideals of its time, praising elegant uniformity above 'ugly' idiosyncrasy in spectatorial, theatrical, and aesthetic (but above all *visual*) terms.

Strikingly, Dryden's use of the Italian word for 'square' – following popular usage – also resonates with an allusion to Italian Renaissance humanism and republican political thought, which may well sound ironic in the political climate of later Stuart England: a typical witticism that downplays its challenge to royal prerogative, but which, despite its tongue-in-cheek mockery of democratic politics, does not fail to register the rise in political power of public opinion and early modern media in the second half of the seventeenth century – which was to come into its own in the Exclusion Crisis and the ravages of the Popish Plot scare of the late 1670s and early 1680s.

While the public square (*forum, piazza*) is a place of meeting, of contact, transit, exchange and trade, it is also, as Dryden's essay accentuates, a place of separation, distinction, and individualisation. Milton, in *Areopagitica* (1644), uses it to describe the public nature of printed texts and to make fun of the baroque licensing practices of the Catholic church: "Sometimes 5 *Imprimaturs* are seen together dialogue-wise in the Piatza of one Title page" (Milton 1953b, 504). The printed text is a public square (or rectangle). For the theatre – and, by extension, for any text understood as a cultural event or performance occurring in a 'public sphere' (Habermas 1989) – this duality is important, perhaps decisive for understanding the role of media, and the relations between authors, texts, and readers in early modern culture. The public sphere is a place of difference as well as unity, a place – in more theoretical terms – that embodies the unity of different observations and representations. It creates distance and enables a more flexible management of distinctions (see Luhmann 1984, 597). From a Luhmannian perspective, one could describe the early modern public sphere as a first step towards the evolution of social systems. It is a place where public and private discourses, shared values and contested agreements, representations and figurations of social reality, mediations of power and lived lives meet, perhaps to intersect or intertwine, perhaps to differentiate and dissociate again, "to their several Lodgings"; but none of them will remain completely unchanged in the process. The public sphere emerges in the mid-seventeenth century as the very opposite of earlier representations of social coherence as a 'commonwealth' or 'common-weale' that postulated a "central fusion in an ultimate unity" (Luhmann 1984, 599).

Although Jürgen Habermas locates the emergence of a public sphere in the eighteenth century, there are good arguments for placing it in the seventeenth – even though not necessarily on Habermas's rationalist terms (see Pincus 1995; Achinstein 1994, 9). Despite its limitations, Habermas's model of the public sphere has the merit of connecting political theory with literary history and media studies, broaching a wider perspective on "phenomena that have been underplayed in revisionist historiography" (Norbrook 1994, 6) while "complicating the stereotyped notions of Renaissance individualism and bourgeois humanism that are still found in many current narratives of early modern subjectivity" (8). Early modern tensions between unity and disunity in the public sphere are prominent, for instance, in the conflict between commerce and virtue in republican theory (as analyzed by J. G. A. Pocock), but they can also be made visible in the lack of "clear-cut distinctions [. . .] between a 'modern' rationality, the classical discourse of civic *phronesis,* and the apocalyptic Protestant belief in progressive revelation" (Norbrook 1994, 10).[3]

In the emergence of the early modern public sphere and in the socio-cultural transformations of the republic of letters, all kinds of text (whether handwritten, scribally published, printed, spoken, recited or staged) functioned as key media of social exchange and reflection. Inasmuch as they reflect on the consequences of new technologies of public communication, they also become contributing factors in these transformations and media upheavals. But before we can come to a historical outline of these transformations, we need first to establish a more general methodological perspective as a firmer ground on which to base such 'contextural' readings of historical texts as this study aims to provide.

---

3 On the concept of 'commonwealth' before Hobbes, see Sharpe 2000b, 38–123.

The Sensibility of Dissociation

From today's perspective, the world of seventeenth-century England is strange and distant. It is, in the resonant phrase of Peter Laslett (1973), a "world we have lost", accessible only by means of documentary evidence and its interpretations. The preferences and dislikes of that world, its spotlights of attention and penumbra of neglect, its idioms and languages, problems and entertainments, even its material conditions of writing and reading are not ours (Goldberg 1990, Johns 1998, Brayman Hackel 2005), even though we may sometimes recognise (or imagine) suggestive familiarities and continuities. Furthermore, even though we may be able to locate the conceptual or material origins of modern cultural and political topics, values and obsessions in early modernity (e.g., Shakespearean drama; political economy; opera), to understand those origins requires historical analysis and an intellectual reconstruction of their conditions and contexts.

In a period as disturbed by violent religious and political conflict as the seventeenth century, what William Paulson (1988) has called the "noise of culture" (those elements that, for us today, are not easily translatable into information) must needs be greater than during less troubled historical periods. Although in many respects very different from our own time, the world and its descriptions that emerge from this noise still appear recognisable or at least amenable to reconstruction. It may be an audacious claim that, with the publication of Hobbes's *Leviathan* – certainly one of the 'noisiest' texts to appear in seventeenth-century England –, "the basic character of Enlightenment politics [and thus of modern politics] was already in place" (Tuck 1993, 348). But such statements, whatever their truth value, assert the importance of seventeenth-century English (in connection with Welsh, Scottish and Irish) developments for the history of modern European ideas and mentalities without simply confirming the Whiggish truism of England's role as a forerunner of modernisation. It is the very complexity of the picture that results from a closer inspection, this peculiar combination of familiarity and strangeness, that makes the English seventeenth century so difficult to label as a literary period – late Renaissance, early baroque, neoclassicism? – and so fascinating in its multifaceted developments (Ezell 2018).

One of the challenges of this period is the fact that the later seventeenth century has no single genre that could aspire to the overarching cultural function of the novel in the nineteenth century, or of drama in the Elizabethan and Jacobean periods. What we find instead is an energetic, turbulent, and noisy multiplicity, a fascinating disorder and an unceasing circulation of different discourses. Between these discourses, there may be some contact, exchange, or overlap, but they never cohere or collapse into some form of unity. Literary communication and intellectual exchange in the seventeenth century are highly agonistic and full of conflict, transforming humanist reading habits of "admiring, annotating and absorbing texts" into "acts of contest and combat" (Zwicker 2003, 300). In this respect, Michel de Certeau's suggestions for "a *polemological* analysis of culture", in its situational interaction between tactics and strategies (articulated by the operations of rhetoric) have proved a valuable theoretical asset for my approach (de Certeau 1984, xvii; cf. 34–42). In such a combative framework, literature is to a considerable extent a continuation of warfare by other means. Literary communication originates and emerges from a multiplicity of idioms and forms, some readily available, others newly minted, bringing into contact and conflict a dynamic variety of discourses from religion, politics, rhetoric, and science to economics and eroticism. The results of this turbulence may at times be mere noise, at times rich in information.

I proceed, then, from a model of literary communication that is based on the observation that speakers (or writers) can "frame" their own speech but in which "the utterance cannot wholly determine the response" (Pocock 1985, 34). In such a configuration, observations of reality are indexed as contingent, as subject to dissent and revision, as soon as (or even before) they are made. If contingency – social as well as epistemic – can be understood as a decisive defining attribute of modernity (Luhmann 1998), then this attribute may lend added significance to the description of the seventeenth century as 'early modernity'. What distinguishes its literary culture from previous configurations is that it manages to integrate observations of contingency into "a self-conscious procedure" of literary writing and reading (Patey 1984, 179), transforming contingency into a structural element as well as a subject matter of textual communication. Contingency – the sense that things might as well be different – becomes the epistemological foundation for a "politics of utterance" that sets forth a method of discourse (as well as a number of discourses *on* method), a set of "operational rules determining the relational usage of a language that has become uncertain of the real" (de Certeau 1986, 91). In other words: writers begin to come to terms, more systematically than before, with the uncertainty of putting reality into words, by making this uncertainty a pre-condition for writing and reading (Blumenberg 1979; see also Aarsleff 1982 and Kroll 1991 on the changing understanding of language and signification in the seventeenth century).

This development, of which English neoclassicism is a decisive stage, traces a trajectory from images of stability, coherence, and certainty towards a conceptual rhetoric of mobility, circulation, contingency, and probability. The description of this passage from late humanism to English neoclassicism between 1630 and 1700 is the predominant concern of this book. Without unduly claiming a teleological development, I think it is safe to say that these seventy years are an important chapter in the history of literature as aesthetic communication, marked off from other kinds of discourse as "a sharply defined and autonomous realm of written objects that possess an 'aesthetic' character and value" (McKeon 1987b, 36). T. S. Eliot famously described this historical process of separation and distinction as a "dissociation of sensibility" (1951 [1921], 288) – as the prehistory of what he inevitably understood as the fragmentation of the modern world. Yet, quite anachronistically, this "dissociation" presupposes a previously unified, undissociated sensibility.[4] In contrast to Eliot, I see the prehistory of modern literature not as a unified field of discourse but as structured by manifold exchanges, circulations, and conflicts among different kinds of text, different situations of utterance, and different contexts of communication. The multiplicity of contingent perspectives that emerges from a closer examination of seventeenth-century discourse is better described as a sensibility of dissociation than as an undissociated sensibility.

The problem with Eliot's reading of metaphysical poetry not only illustrates the difference between New Critical and historicist readings (he is, after all, making a historical argument); it helps to envisage the wider problems of historical studies in framing access to texts from the past. As an initial theoretical presupposition, I see the necessity to conceptualise and historicise not only the concept of 'literature' but the modes of *production* and of *access to* literary texts, modes that are determined by what I call cultural *contextures*. As I will explicate below, these contextures can be described as functionally determined embeddings of situations of writing and reading in their material cultural surroundings. These surroundings, needless to add, are often no longer materially available to us; they are not less in need of interpretation than the literary texts themselves, and often not less subject to traditional distortions of perspective. Texts, contexts, and contextures form a continuum from which one must inevitably make critical selections and place one's own emphases. Moreover, these selections can only occur from 'angles of contingency', tied as they are to the inevitability of perspective, to the interpreter's own historical moment.

Taking as his cue a few verses from *Hamlet* (5.2.324–28), Stephen Greenblatt (2002, 19) sums up the New Historicist ideal of a non-teleological cultural history: "To write cultural history we need more a sharp awareness of accidental judgments than a theory of the organic; more an account of purposes mistook than a narrative of gradual emergence; more a chronicle of carnal, bloody, and unnatural acts than a story of inevitable progress from traceable origins." With regard to the seventeenth century, this emphasis on material contingencies rather than theoretical or ideological coherence seems particularly apt – whatever one may otherwise think of the benefits and drawbacks of the New versus Old Historicism (cf. Hume 1999). Various directions of historicism, both old and recent, have contributed to a critical examination of the scholarly vocabulary, enhancing awareness of the historical shifts in the meaning of key concepts such as 'humanity', 'nature', or 'taste'. Such awareness may help to indicate the limits of understanding the past in modern terms. The term 'culture', "one of the two or three most complicated words in the English language" (Williams 1983, 87), applied to the seventeenth century, cannot have the same elevated meaning that it had for the

---

4 For a critique of Eliot's position, see Kermode 1975. According to Kermode, Eliot applies what is essentially a modern theory of the poetic image, recognising or rather constructing in the metaphysical poets of the early seventeenth century precursors of an ideal 'undissociated' poet who unifies thought and feeling. See also now Collini 2019.

nineteenth- and early twentieth-century bourgeois: a realm of ideas and ideals separate from the crude realities of class conflict. For the Victorian sage and critic Matthew Arnold, culture famously was the opposite of anarchy (1971 [1869]). Early modern English culture, by contrast, requires a more comprehensive, flexible, and plural, even somewhat anarchic definition that opens it up to encompass a variety of geographical, historical, mental, and political factors.

In *The Interpretation of Cultures*, Clifford Geertz (1973, 49) argued for a symbolic anthropology that defines culture, in cybernetic terms, as "a set of control mechanisms [. . .] for the governing of behaviour." For Geertz, as for Kenneth Burke (1957), cultural representations (artefacts, rituals, social display) ought to be read as signifying structures that embody sociopolitical norms, values, and codes. More recently, both literary critics like Greenblatt and (post-)revisionist historians like Kevin Sharpe have proposed a "cultural turn" in early modern literary and social history in terms similar to Geertz's (see Sharpe 2000b, 19, 392–414). This can be supplemented by a systems-theoretical perspective (Luhmann 1995, 31–54), interpreting cultural media (including literary texts) not merely as ideological vehicles of "power-knowledge" (Foucault 1980) but as objects that "talk back" (Bal 1999) because they are instruments of analysis and reflection in their own right.

Such a perspective cannot rely merely on the presumed factuality of historical evidence to interpret literary texts from the past in and on their own terms. Facts are not enough; they are the *explanandum*, not the *explanans*. "Theory", as R. S. Crane put it (1953, xiii), "is inescapable", and so each generation of historians and critics needs to make its own selections and interpretations of the cultural archive. The archive is inert, passive; it requires what Aleida Assmann calls a "working memory" (2008, 100) in order to activate it for the present.

Very broadly speaking, literature can be examined from two different aspects: as product or process. To view literature as product is to look at the results of literature, by reading texts or reading authors' biographies where the text is understood as a self-enclosed work, an entity, a work of art maybe, which is autonomous from the rest of the world or other social systems. This autonomy of literature, meaning that literature is governed by its own rules and not by politics or other social codes, arises around 1800, in connection with ideas about the freedom of art and of speech. In the seventeenth century, by contrast, there is still censorship, and there are battles about state censorship of what is published, especially in print – this may be another reason why manuscript circulation was still a viable alternative (Love 1993). Literature in the seventeenth century is closely involved with other aspects of life; it is not just the final product of an author's individual efforts. Here, I am more interested in the processes of writing and reading these works; I am of course also interested in how the works themselves are shaped by the very situations from which they arise, but my main interest is in the workings of the literary system of the time; mine is a kind of systematic, if not systems-theoretical, approach to literary history as not just a series of masterpieces, but the result of numerous acts of human and sometimes non-human interaction or engagement.

I think that the multiplicity of communicative settings, situations, and media needs to be taken seriously and not to be hidden away by forcing such anachronistic concepts upon it as the modern distinction between 'fictional' and 'non-fictional' or between 'literary' and 'non-literary' texts (or contexts of utterance). Those distinctions arguably emerge in the professionalisation of a literary marketplace, beginning in the late seventeenth to early eighteenth century, but their imposition on an earlier period constitutes an unjustified simplification. Notwithstanding the fact that distinctions between 'kinds' of literary communication were very well known in early modern Europe, those distinctions were only very rarely used for meta-communicative reflection but were productive of "highly complex and flexible [. . .] uses of literary forms" (Lewalski 1986, 1; see also Colie 1973, Fowler 1982).

In other words, even scholars (like myself) attracted by a systems-theoretical vocabulary will have difficulties adapting their terminology to the period before 1700. Before what they call 'the autonomy of a literary system' begins to be socially established, systems theorists have severe difficulties seeing anything of note in the way of 'literature'. But literary history of course begins long before 1700. It would certainly be a special challenge to develop such a theoretical access, but – like other scholars in this field – I have come to the conclusion that systems theory in its most familiar form is too rigid to do justice to the multifariousness of literary-cultural phenomena in the early modern period, where the boundaries among social 'subsystems' or separate fields of discourse (e.g. politics, religion, history, economics) are far from clearly drawn. I have therefore mostly discarded the technical vocabulary of 'literary systems theory' while retaining certain basic assumptions about communication and contingency.

In framing a theoretical and historical perspective from which to describe and analyse seventeenth-century literary culture, I have concentrated on a number of focal areas. To give a very general outline, I have chosen to describe the emergence of English neoclassicism, a cultural formation – arguably the first one in modernity – that explicitly, in theory as well as practice, establishes functional boundaries of literary communication in relation to other media, other performative dimensions of culture. But its significance is far from exclusively and narrowly 'literary' in this respect: it is indeed the fundamental and coherent cultural orientation of eighteenth-century civility and sociability, and thus a formative condition of what has come to be known as the Enlightenment. To sketch the early history of this cultural formation in England, I have concentrated on four main areas of concern. First, there is the early history of neoclassicism in the vestiges of European humanism (chapter 2). Here, my focus is on the different literary strategies developed by Robert Burton and Sir Thomas Browne in response to their altered communicative situation. What are the forms in which contingency is envisaged; what is the cultural background against which these forms become visible; and in what ways do these writers respond to its cultural challenge? Chapters 3 and 4 then proceed to look (from different angles) at the moments of origin of neoclassical discourse in England, between Civil War and Restoration. First, I examine the embattled, polemic, and polemogenic distinction between literary and visual modes of cognition and communication in texts by Milton, Hobbes, Davenant, and Margaret Cavendish. This is followed by an enquiry into the problem of *social* (rather than epistemic) contingency, a problem that becomes visible in chapter 3 but needs to be dealt with in a wider historical context: the Civil War and its disruptions of older notions of commonwealth, and their progressive replacement by the conceptual idiom of the state. Here, in chapter 4, I give an outline of the intricate relations between literary culture and early modern politics, beginning with the cultural fiction of the 'state of nature' and the role of rhetoric as efficacious speech; this involves a critical reappraisal of the differences and commonalities between Milton and Hobbes. This is followed by an analysis of political allegory in pastoral discourse (Izaak Walton's *Compleat Angler*), and by an analysis of 'literary politics' in and around the cultural moment of the Restoration, an analysis which concentrates on the crucial issues of cultural memory, countermemory, and orchestrated acts of oblivion; my examples here are Dryden's *Astræa Redux*, Tuke's *Adventures of Five Hours*, and Milton's *Paradise Lost*. The crisis of cultural memory and literary politics in the Restoration is presented in a reading of Dryden's *Absalom and Achitophel*, a reading that sums up the concerns of chapter 4 by relating allegorical narrative (and its failure) to temporality and contingency.

The final chapter traces the neoclassical response to the problems of inwardness and individuality in relation to civility and social norms in the early modern public sphere. This chapter sets out to retrieve and sum up the major concerns of this study: first by providing a paradigmatic example of the evolution of contingent individuality in connection with politics, history, and textuality that sheds new light on the early history of the novel (Aphra Behn's *Love-Letters between a Nobleman and His Sister*); then tracing the consequences of the Lockean foundation of politics (in the second *Treatise of Government*) on potentially retractable principles of trust, agreement, and contract, principles which remain open to revision, in Congreve's *The Way of the World*. With an unsurpassed lightness of touch, this play, on the cusp of the eighteenth century, captures the neoclassical, polite 'angle of contingency' that is the new, post-1688 cultural standard. The cultural norm of politeness as a way of managing contingency (now both epistemic and socio-political) can then be gauged in its effectiveness by its presence even in the writings of dissenters (Bunyan, Defoe) who use it to avoid being classified as irrational enthusiasts – even religious dissent now comes to accept the Lockean "degrees of assent" (Locke 1979, 657–68; 4.16).

In sum, these enquiries into several paradigmatic examples of late seventeenth-century English literary culture from Milton to Congreve and from Hobbes to Locke intend to provide an outline of the spectrum of neoclassical discourse and of the different "angles of contingency" of which literary culture in seventeenth-century England was capable – outlining a period that was to become formative in English and, indeed, European cultural history.

Some readers will find my selections and their relative proportion unusual, surprising, or somewhat arbitrary; others may find them already too conventional. I do share these readers' regret at having to omit any extended discussion of – for instance – Shakespeare, Jonson, Donne, Herbert, Marvell, and Otway on the one hand or of John Taylor, Lucy Hutchinson, Anne Conway, Phineas Fletcher, and Nathaniel Lee on the other hand (both lists could be extended almost indefinitely), and it is sad to see even the better-known names – almost all except Shakespeare – slowly but steadily vanishing from undergraduate curricula. The period between Shakespeare and Swift or Defoe may not be under-researched, but it is definitely under-taught. But this book is not intended as another literary history of the seventeenth century, and lack of completeness – never to be achieved or desirable in any event – needs to be carefully weighed against the advantages of distinctive selections. Generally, I have chosen paradigmatic texts from a variety of genres for more detailed scrutiny instead of a 'complete works' approach to a single author or a structural historical description of the development of individual genres.

The theoretical grounds of this book will be laid out in the next chapter. They follow recent reconstructive and revisionist movements in the humanities, movements that have brought historical perspectives back into literary studies. Beyond the New Historicism, this study has been inspired by the somewhat unlikely combination of Cambridge School intellectual history, German media studies, and Luhmannian systems theory – although I hope this will not be too obvious as the book progresses. Readers averse to theory are encouraged to proceed directly to chapter 2.

1 Historicising Literary Culture: Communication, Contingency, Contexture

Communication

In order to understand early modern literary culture, we need to reconstruct the conditions of literary communication *prior* to the modern concept of literature as aesthetic (fictional) discourse. How did literature work? What were the functions of reading and writing in seventeenth-century England? My suggestion is to describe literary forms in relation to, and at times in conflict with, socio-cultural formations or arrangements in which these forms are negotiated, modified, and continued. The aesthetic, then, is not an independent realm that can be taken for granted or posited as given. If we want to come closer to an idea of what literary communication might mean, we will have to question and explore more closely the (historically specific) *modes of access* to (literary) texts.

For a long time, this question of access was deemed unproblematic: either literature was mere appearance and had no genuine knowledge to offer, or it dealt in pseudo-statements with no truth value. As Sir Philip Sidney famously wrote in his *Defence of Poesie* in c. 1579: "Now, for the poet, he nothing affirms, and therefore never lieth" (Sidney 1973, 102). Literature as fictional discourse cannot lie, cannot *not* tell the truth, because telling the truth is not the point of fiction. Because literature makes no truth claims, it cannot be judged according to the "fact convention" (Schmidt 1982, 87) that dominates real-life communication. Literary language, in this view, would be a special kind of language, a purely fictional mode of utterance.

In order to go beyond these conventional models, it is necessary to conceptualise and historicise the modes of access to literary texts. It may be useful to begin doing so in terms of a theory that does not conceive of media as message-bearers or carriers of information but as complex sensory arrangements that can trigger a range of experiences. These experiential effects are very difficult to rationalise or to describe either in a clear-cut definition of media or in traditional theories of aesthetics. They are more readily analysed in a communications-oriented approach. In Niklas Luhmann's systems theory, communication is a process that consists of three elements: 'information', 'utterance', and 'understanding'. Each of these operational units – (1) the possible intention of an origin, however inferred; (2) the verbal, material utterance, and (3) what a recipient takes the utterance to mean – can then be thematised, marked or underscored in follow-up communications. Communication, according to this theory, always *happens*, and its initial intent (the 'information') can never determine or control its possible outcome (understanding, misunderstanding, response) (Wilden 1987). Other perspectives on the theory and history of discourse, though not sharing these theoretical foundations, do share the assumption that the world they look at is "a world in which [...] the utterance cannot wholly determine the response" (Pocock 1985, 34). In media-theoretical terms, one would have to say that the effects of media on their recipients or participants, as the case may be, are incalculable. They can range from absolute fascination, heightened awareness or experiences of "flow" (Csikszentmihalyi 1990) to lack of interest or absolute boredom. If recipients attribute their emotional responses or aesthetic judgements to intrinsic qualities of what they have seen or heard, they may be subject to a familiar delusion.[5]

But even though there is a certain fixity about the written page so that, provided one knows the meaning of the signs, one should be able to know what a text *is* – "these words in this order" (Grabes 2013, 44, quoting Cameron 1962, 145) –, languages and contexts of utterance are unstable and subject to change, so that an utterance – even if it consists of the same words – need not, in fact will not stay the same when it is repeated. Texts, understood as utterances, do not remain the same over time but have a performative character. Two initial conclusions to be drawn from this, now commonplace in literary theory, are: firstly, that verbal constructs, such as literary texts, have no intrinsic univocal meaning, but, because of their linguistic nature, are ambiguous or multivalent: the sense of the words in the text has to be constructed by reference to a particular "universe of discourse" (Ogden and Richards 1927, 102) and their relation to the whole of a given text. In reading, then, we should pay attention to the "intratextual interaction of words" (Grabes 2013, 41). The second conclusion, following from this, is that any reading is not merely the reconstruction of a given verbal arrangement but a performative act, "intended to give rise to something else" (Jardine and Grafton 1990, 30). Reading, too, has a history (see, among many others, Darnton 1991, Chartier 1994).

It is the specific and different uses to which texts have (or might have) historically been put that constitutes the focal point of such criticism. For example, the habit of reading Virgil's *Aeneid* as a work of fiction is only one option among many; in former times, it was widely put to a rather more practical use as a medium of prophecy (the *sortes Virgilianae*). The communicative function of a text thus depends on a set of decisions made before, during, or after the actual experience of reading, and these decisions themselves depend on an array of factors (political, social, personal) that determine the reader's criteria.

Because all texts are essentially geared towards some kind of reader (even in cases when this reader is merely the author him- or herself), no 'actualisation' of a text's potential meaning, no interpretative act can be conceptualised without at least a hazy understanding of the reader's role. This role is embedded in historical and

---

5 Cf. Wimsatt and Beardsley 1954 for the New-Critical strategy of removing any personal or emotional responses from critical discourse for the sake of objective, formally 'correct' readings of literary texts.

social contexts, depending on a wide range of variables from psychology to media history. In their effects on different audiences, geographically or historically, media, including texts – including those texts we have become used to calling 'literary' – are extremely diverse. It could be said that each act of reading is a unique and unrepeatable historical event. A famous short story by Borges illustrates this: a modern author who rewrites Cervantes's *Don Quijote,* though using exactly the same words, produces a completely different novel because he is writing it at a different time (Borges 1962). The meanings and functions of texts are subject to change in different historical or cultural contexts and in varying media arrangements.[6]

Yet a text usually is a determinant of those acts that ascribe meaning to it, so that there is a danger not only of *under-* but also of *over*estimating the importance of readers for the generation of meaning. The relation of texts, their language(s), and their contexts is subject to change; this includes earlier responses to a text, which may trigger re-evaluations of individual or communal readings that modify the perception of a text. Certainly, the concept of text would be meaningless without a concept of reading; but it would be an oversimplification to claim that a text consists merely and exclusively of its readings (cf. Fish 1980). After all, reading is not situated outside the historical process but is embedded in and modified by it. The cultural practice of reading is itself subject to change, and so are the ways in which access to literary communication has been and is being codified. A reading is never merely the reconstruction of something given in the text, but an interaction between texts and readers, a process of communication that cannot be controlled completely by any of its constituents: not by the author, nor by the reader alone, nor by the text. To quote J. G. A. Pocock (1985, 17), "when action and response are performed through the medium of language, we cannot absolutely distinguish the author's performance from the reader's response." What one can try to do, however, is reconstruct the unique set of conditions and assumptions involved in the actual performances of writing and reading, or of media experience, in a particular time and place.[7]

Contingency

In order to gain a better sense of literary culture in relation to media and social knowledge formations, I suggest the concepts of communication and contingency as fundamental to understanding how seventeenth-century literature 'works' and to account for the way it develops and changes. What do I mean by 'contingency' as a framing concept? In the past decades, the concept of contingency has become an increasingly

---

[6] For a radical illustration of this, see Bohannan 1966; cf. Schwab 1996, 1–9.
[7] I am thinking along the lines of reconstructive efforts like those of Wallace 1974–75; see also Jardine and Grafton 1990.

central term in the humanities. From its classical roots in modal logic[8] to its redefinitions in action theory, phenomenology, and systems theory,[9] the concept of contingency has now advanced to the status of a key descriptive and explanatory category, if not *the* "defining attribute" (Luhmann 1998), for understanding *modernity*. Modernity, in this perspective, is characterised by an increased social awareness of contingency, by a knowledge that implies the knowledge of alternative possibilities to a given reality: the fact that 'things might as well be different'. This awareness has a dual nature in that it can focus, on the one hand, on the observation that things as they are might just as well be otherwise (contingency as possibility), and on the other hand on the observation that whatever occurs, even if it appears random and is caused by what Shakespeare calls "the shot of accident" and the "dart of chance" (in *Othello* 4.1), is nonetheless real and needs to be dealt with as such (contingency as destiny). The concept of contingency, in Luhmann's now classic formulation (1984, 152),

> signifies something given (experienced, expected, thought, imagined) with regard to the observation that it may possibly be different; it signifies objects in the horizon of possible alterations. Because it presupposes the given world, it does not signify the possible in general but that which, seen from the point of view of reality, may possibly be different.

This definition can be related to descriptions of modern concepts of reality as variable and plural (Blumenberg 1979). "A new form of order that we can call *modern*," writes Bernhard Waldenfels (1990, 18), "makes headway when the suspicion is aroused that the order that seemed so steadfast and all-encompassing might only be one among other possible orders." It can also be connected, in more socio-political terms, to what has been described as the specific "constructive strategic disposition" of a modern social order, a rational form of social management that "limits contingency through the goal-oriented use of contingencies", responding to its aspects of indeterminacy by putting its aspects of possibility to good use (Makropoulos 1998, 71; cf. Makropoulos 1997). Modern civilisation can thus be described as a culture of contingency, characterised by the productive duality of indeterminacy and possibility even to the point at which it forms the very basis on which society and social structure are seen to evolve, the point where traditional descriptions of society in terms of custom and grace give way to the political language of fortune (see Pocock 1975).

Beside its philosophical, sociological, and historical significance, the concept of contingency has communicative and epistemological implications. The indeterminacy or unpredictability of the future belongs first and foremost to the dimension of knowledge. In a sociological view, indeterminacy as the "cognitive correlate of contingency"

---

8 For the classical definitions (*contingens est quod nec est impossibile nec necessarium; quod potest non esse; quod potest aliud esse*), see Graevenitz and Marquard 1998, xi; Scheibe 1985, 5–6.
9 Cf. Bubner 1984, 35–36; Blumenberg 1981, 23, 47–48; Luhmann 1984, 148–90. In the development of Luhmann's theory, contingency advances from an action-theoretical to a radically constructivist concept.

(Hahn 1998, 518, my translation) structures social interaction and produces necessities, inevitabilities, by establishing links between contingencies in communication and thus compensating for the lack of mutual understanding between communicants. This knowledge of contingency – or, more precisely, "this teleologically determined non-knowledge" (Simmel 1968, 259, my translation) – is a motivating force in modernity not only in the formation and evolution of societies, but also in the area of culture, not least in the formation and evolution of literary writing. Early modern forms of narrative, for example, become affected by the possibility that any one story might be told in many different ways, and – perhaps even worse – might be understood, or misunderstood, in as many or even more different ways. Again, there is a dual aspect of contingency that, on the one hand, opens up possibilities for telling many stories in many different ways but, on the other hand, also imposes limiting constraints on the forms in which stories can be told. In the process, narrative is increasingly forced to develop, justify, and defend its own discursive foundations (see Greiner and Moog-Grünewald 2000; Lobsien 2000). This becomes particularly evident in the literary culture of the seventeenth century.

In early modernity, the role of the audience and their understanding is increasingly regarded as the most difficult and unpredictable instance in the communication process; hence all those "peritexts" (Genette 1997) – dedications, prefaces, title pages, frontispieces, errata lists, prologues, and epilogues – that surround the main text and often provide some form of guidance for the reader in an attempt to reduce the number of possible interpretations. There is a growing awareness in this process of the irreducible individuality (or incalculability) of readers and of the concomitant contingency of reading (Kroll 1991, 72–73, 77, 85).

This new predicament of writers in the early modern public sphere calls for new strategies in literary communication. Prefaces, epilogues, frontispieces, and other peripheral texts become strategic sites of debate, if not of intellectual warfare. They are the battlegrounds on which writers engage their colleagues and readers over the functional specifics of texts and their role as media of communication (as well as instruments of propaganda). The preface in particular becomes "so popular with the reading public that, it was said, books sold less well without them" (Sharpe 2000a, 56; cf. Dunn 1994). New forms of textual presentation, distribution, and marketing emerge. The outcome of this dynamic is the stabilisation, in the late seventeenth and early eighteenth century, of an "isomorphism of knowledge, literary structure, and implied procedures of interpretation" (Patey 1984, 175; cf. Shapiro 1983, van Leeuwen 1963, Hacking 1975). This isomorphism, or parallelism – which is also, I shall argue, the result of a successful socio-cultural compromise expressed in aesthetic terms as 'neoclassicism' – hinges on the concept of probability and its attendant tropes: inference, conjecture, circumstances, casuistry, sagacity, verisimilitude, so that "all knowing, all learning" becomes "a process of inference from signs", a process that creates structures which "require the exercise of that very judgment which the author wishes to teach" (Patey 1984, 179). Such a world of probable signs, which is explored in the emerging literary form of the novel, is none other than a world of contingency. The earliest novels deal with the lack of access to the inner lives of others, the insight that "all we know of others we know by signs: all our knowledge is irremediably *mediate*" (188).

To sum up: for literary communication (on its several levels of production, performance, and reception) in modernity, contingency is at once an enabling and a constraining factor – enabling inasmuch as it offers new possibilities of literary form, constraining inasmuch as these new forms are not free-floating and self-enclosed entities but are situated in a setting of contextual determinants, comprising forms that already exist as well as other areas of social communication. As a decisive attribute of modernity, contingency can thus become part of a "self-conscious procedure" (Patey 1984, 179) of literary writing and reading, the epistemological foundation of what I term, with Michel de Certeau (1986, 91), a "politics of utterance."

Contexture

As Michael McKeon has observed, "the very access to an abstract category 'literature' is to some degree anachronistic at this time, referring either backward to a broadly inclusive idea of *litterae humaniores* or forward to our modern notion of a sharply defined and autonomous realm of written objects that possess an 'aesthetic' character and value" (1987b, 36; cf. Reiss 1992). In other words, "'literature' did not become associated with specifically imaginative writing, as opposed to historical or scientific writing, until much later" (MacLean 1995, 7–8). This does not preclude the observation of the growing cultural and social importance of literature in this sense in the period: "by 1660, literature had established its own irreversible authority as a socially constitutive field of public activity" (13). Distinctions between textual 'kinds' were handled in a complex and flexible manner rather than as explicit demarcations among different genres. Logic, rhetoric, and poetic discourse were related and not strictly isolated forms of communication.[10] They are, to use a word that is part of the early modern vocabulary, bound up in a 'contexture', in a continuum of mutual influence that affects the form, content, and meaning of individual texts. In contrast to a text-context duality, 'contexture' emphasises the connections and the competition between different texts, largely regardless of genre. The word "contexture" can refer to the completion of a work, the act of tying together its

---

10 Cf. Howell 1956, 4: "Englishmen of these two centuries [1500–1700] did not waste their time in the vain effort to deny to poetry a primarily communicative function. Nor had the science of aesthetics yet been invented to insulate poetry from any contact with logic and rhetoric. Instead, poetry was considered to be the third great form of communication, open and popular but not fully explained by rhetoric, concise and lean but not fully explained by logic."

"parcells" (Davenant 1971, 24), con-texturing it for its first readers and thus weaving it into the web of public discourse.

Whereas the term 'context' is often seen to imply a hierarchy of value and/or a determinism of agency between texts and their 'background',[11] 'contexture' connotes a controlled levelling of such a hierarchy because it emphasises the discursive and public status of textuality in general and the competitiveness of texts, largely regardless of genre, in the early modern public sphere. This levelling is not to be confused with a poststructuralist notion of *écriture* or a simplistic reading of culture-as-text. It does not preclude the observance, and the observation, of genre distinctions in textual engagements and, in this respect, it is not a complete levelling of all discourse. *Contextural* rather than merely contextual reconstitution implies a continuum of semantic connections and effects, a mutual give and take between situations of writing, textual structures, and processes of response. For example, as I shall argue below in ch. 3 and 4, seventeenth-century literary theory, natural philosophy, and political thought are bound up in such a contexture of overlap and exchange between ideas, keywords, and tropes.

Contextures depend on the circulation of texts and ideas. Stephen Greenblatt's well-known metaphor of "the circulation of social energy" (1988), coined in the heyday of the New Historicism, is an apt description here also because the seventeenth century was itself obsessed with the language of circulation, a foundational vocabulary in descriptions of physiological, political, economic, and literary 'systems' from Edward Misselden's *The Circle of Commerce* (1623) and the "boundless Circles" of empire in Dryden's *Astræa Redux* (1956, 30, l. 299) to William Harvey's works on the motion of the heart (*De Motu Cordis*, 1628) and the circulation of the blood (*De Circulatione Sanguinis*, 1649) (Rogers 1996, 16–27; Kroll 2000, 104–11; Kroll 2007).

In order to reconstruct early modern literary culture, one needs a concept of literary production as a form of social action and of literary reception as performative rather than merely reconstitutive (Todorov 1976–77; Jauss 1970–71). The word 'contexture' emphasises the active, performative component of linking and intertwining elements into a structure, composition or texture: it underlines the operational aspects of discourse as process. The texts themselves often display an awareness of their performative nature: we get a glimpse of this process of negotiation in Dryden's naval scene at the beginning of the *Essay of Dramatick Poesie*, a glimpse of the crucial question how to address an audience that is always prone to disintegration, and how

---

11 Cf. Culler 1988, xiv on context: "But the notion of context frequently oversimplifies rather than enriches discussion, since the opposition between an act and its context seems to presume that the context is given and determines the meaning of the act. We know, of course, that things are not so simple: context is not fundamentally different from what it contextualizes; context is not given but produced; what belongs to a context is determined by interpretive strategies; contexts are just as much in need of elucidation as events; and the meaning of a context is determined by events. Yet when we use the term *context* we slip back into the simple model it proposes."

to use communication in such a way that it can transform this "dividuall" (Milton 1953b, 544)[12] audience into a unity.

As historically contingent performances, acts of writing and reading circumscribe the 'event horizon' of texts and therefore allow us to describe the functional change of literary communication. The concept of functional change requires a concept of reading that is not located outside or beyond historical processes but one that is embedded in the media history of writing and reading as cultural practices. Through investigating functional change, we can hope to arrive at a "thick description" (Ryle 1971, Geertz 1973) or even a mapping of the points of intersection between *literary* and *cultural* forms of knowledge.

Variability, dissociation, even disorder, can be regarded as keywords in the description of early modern literary culture, which is a literary culture *before* 'literature', before the codification of literary communication into a functionally specific (and socially much less problematic) medium but one that is already "deeply imbued with literate habits of mind" (Fox 1996, 90), a culture deeply affected by the social impact of writing and its various cultural uses. A recognisably 'modern' configuration of literary culture emerges from the dissolution of the closed medieval world picture, accompanied by a vast array of new discoveries in natural science, economics, and geographical exploration, from Copernicus to Columbus, resulting in a new concept of reality as "open context" (Blumenberg 1979; see also Reiss 1982a, Mahler 2019). The circulation of texts is increasingly uncoupled from direct interpersonal contexts of interaction. They become part of a more general endeavour to increase knowledge about a world that is now realised as still largely undiscovered, and to deal with the problems that arise from this increase – leading, in many cases, to an aesthetics of "unevenness" and "uncertainty" (Augustine 2018, 2).

When an older cultural formation erodes and is slowly superseded by a new one, there is a time of overlap between residual, dominant, and emergent structures (Williams 1977), an overlap that will create frictions or crises. It appears that only a form of communication that is not system-specific can address these overlaps without necessarily privileging one possible solution over others. This form of communication would have to be significantly different from others in its function. If science and other organisational institutions carve up reality in a certain way (determined by their need for specific solutions to specific problems) and thus reduce complexity,

---

12 In this context of his *Areopagitica*, Milton uses the word to denote the dissociation of external "piety" from genuine religious faith: "So that a man may say his religion is now no more within himself, but is becom a dividuall movable" (1953b, 544). Yet its semantic range can perhaps be extended to a more general socio-psychological description of dissociation in early modernity, a description that comprises both social processes and 'psychological' notions of substantial (individual) vs. accidental (dividual) elements of 'selfhood'. Cf. *Paradise Lost* 12.82–84, where Milton argues in political terms for a moral psychology in which "true liberty" and "right reason" should have "no dividual being" (1998, 651).

this other form of communication will address these disciplinary or systemic exclusions, creating a virtual contact zone for the encounter and the testing of other possible solutions (Berensmeyer 2003).

Literary communication before 1700 is less concerned with legitimising its fictionality vis à vis other forms of communication than with thematising ongoing transformations. Early modern literary culture, under the influence of humanist skepticism, often displays a proto-constructivist awareness of the fact that different discourses, rhetorics, and media can shape perceptions of what reality is or appears to be in very different ways. In the light of this awareness, texts explicitly overstep their generic limits (conventions) and play with (anticipate and then counteract) their readers' expectations. Shakespeare's plays, for example, engage in a sophisticated, highly reflexive, and at the same time highly entertaining dissolution and recombination of different discourses (see e.g. Iser 1993).

The open context which, according to Blumenberg (1979), is the key concept of reality in the early modern period, has a material correlate not only in the expansion of the known world through the 'discovery' of America, but also in the introduction of print culture and the massive circulation of written and printed matter, because the increasing production of knowledge not only expands the communicative range of written words but also creates an enormous complexity and openness of situations of communication. It also contributes to diagnoses of increasing uncertainty and disintegration. This is a radical change because textual utterances are uncoupled from the physical presence of human bodies and from immediate personal interaction (Gumbrecht 1985). New strategies have to be invented to make the connection between texts and their possible readers less susceptible to irritations. Among these texts, it appears that a certain type develops a paradoxical convention of its own: the convention of being in a strict sense unconventional, by allowing a heterogeneous multiplicity of perspectives and thematising possible clashes between other conventions, other organisational forms of carving up reality. Such texts may have appeared before, but now they no longer occupy merely a marginal place as they did in the high middle ages, for instance with troubadour poetry. Now, there is an increasing number of "texts with a negating character", which question the established sense-making proposals of social norms or conventions and do so by presenting literary "counter-worlds" (Gumbrecht 1980, 127, my translation).

The printed book in particular is geared towards an audience that could and probably would be much more diffuse than that of a speaker who addressed a gathering of listeners in person. The former certainty, or at least high probability, of a shared horizon of meaning can thus no longer be guaranteed. According to many critics, this structural change intensifies the sense of a "polarization between the spaces of everyday meaning and fictional meaning" and "the experience of a clear-cut boundary between these two spheres" (Gumbrecht 1990, 177, 181, my translation).[13] Early modern readers acknowledge the benefits as well as uncertainties inherent in print communication. The institutions of censorship in early modern Europe, however efficient or inefficient they may have been in practice (see Patterson 1984), provide evidence enough for the awareness of such uncertainty and for the social need to deal with it in some way. The effects of printed texts on their potential recipients were sometimes presented in terms of risks and even potentially lethal consequences; these dangers required a reader's active participation and watchfulness to the point of resistance. As the Canon of Toledo explains in his famous speech in book 1, chapter 47 of *Don Quijote,* "lying fictions must be wedded to the intelligence of those who read them" (Cervantes 1987, 1: 906–7; my translation). Adrian Johns has noted a similar "culture of discredit surrounding printed books" in seventeenth-century England, with the concomitant emphasis on the necessity of readers employing their critical faculties in order to produce "safe and true knowledge" (Johns 1998, 423). In early modernity, the 'fictionality' of a text thus depends to a great extent on its readers' acceptance. Not only Don Quijote took novels literally. For instance, at least one early reader of William Baldwin's *Beware the Cat* (1584) mistook it as a libellous slander against Gregory Streamer, the story's – fictional – protagonist and narrator. But if early modern fictionality is to such a high degree subject to the perspective of observers, then it cannot be maintained as the essential characteristic of a certain text type or genre; on the contrary, it appears to have been a highly unstable function attributed to texts by observers in certain circumstances and according to certain – and sometimes maybe less certain – rules.

Rather than being compartmentalised into separate categories, public discourse in the seventeenth century proceeds from, and is indeed constituted by, a mixture of media, genres, and languages, a fertile (and cross-fertilising) criss-crossing of different idioms and modes of signification. The central feature of textuality in the seventeenth century is its emerging public nature. Literature in the first age of print is argumentative, hortatory, cautionary or deliberative, but always involved and enveloped in the public arena of which it is a part and which it helps constitute. Early modern readers do not seek the meaning of a poem, for example, in relation to its author's individuality, unless typified as the 'I' of "the constant lover" or "the lover unhappy" in *Tottel's Miscellany,* but in the argument it presents (in and to the public) and in the quality of this presentation.[14] Seventeenth-century literary culture is

---

[13] On the media change from oral to written to printed texts, next to the classic studies by Eisenstein 1979, Ong 1982, Finnegan 1988, Elsky 1989, Giesecke 1991, see also Luhmann 1992, Wellbery 1992, Marotti 1995, Johns 1998, Bohn 1999, Cochran 2001, Ezell 2003, McKitterick 2003.
[14] Cf. Winn 1987, 1: "[P]oetry in his [Dryden's] culture was a public act: the attention paid to a new poem was far more likely to focus on its success as an argument and its quality as an artifact rather than on its overt or covert revelation of its author's soul; the fascination with childhood we find in Wordsworth and his contemporaries reflects a radically changed view of creativity."

still a highly rhetorical culture in its orientation towards a classical image of the *forum* as a public sphere in which social and political life emerges and is negotiated by the participants of public discourse. Given the political ideals of civic humanism and its indebtedness to classical rhetoric, it is no surprise that the spoken and written word is favoured in education over more sensuous forms of communication like the visual arts or music (see Winn 1987, 42–46; Skinner 1996, 19–40). There is a real sense in the seventeenth century that aesthetic decisions (e.g. whether to write in blank verse or heroic couplets) or theoretical programmes of literary writing (e.g. the neoclassical observation of the unities in drama) carry a direct political significance as well as claims to socially normative validity.[15] Another fundamental feature of this public discourse is its competitive rather than conciliatory or consolidating nature. There is a strong sense of the divisions that characterise the public realm and the 'republic of letters'. What did this republic of letters look like, and what was it based on?

Literary Culture

Most people in the seventeenth century were still unable to read or write. Probably about seventy percent of the male population were illiterate, and almost the entire female population. However, those who did learn to read and write had a decent chance of proceeding to higher education (one in fifteen),[16] and those who entered Oxford or Cambridge could not only expect a very good education – largely in Latin, which was still treated as a living language – but also professional opportunities after completing their studies. Furthermore, education in England was not entirely a privilege of the upper classes but was regularly open to boys of the middling sort (yeomen, artisans, tradesmen) and, in some cases, to talented children among the poor who could work their way through college as servants. Like today, education could open opportunities for upward social mobility. Yet the career opportunities opening up for these well-educated people were not academic. There was no professionalisation of philosophy, let alone literature, as an academic discipline. Those who published philosophical works did not do so because they thought of them as products of academic research. Likewise, those who produced what we may be tempted to call 'imaginative literature' did not do so because they considered writing

---

15 Cf. Hardison 1989, 219–25 (on Davenant's choice of the decasyllabic quatrain as a 'rational' form) and 258–76 (on rhyme vs. blank verse in Dryden and Milton). On the correlation between classical literary learning and contemporary politics in seventeenth-century England, see also Patterson 1986.
16 Tuck 1993, 2, whose calculation is based on information in Wrigley and Schofield 1981 and Stone 1964. Literacy was considerably higher in London (sixty percent of adult males); see Achinstein 1994, 12.

their profession or because they could hope to make a living from the sale of their literary property. Although there was no difficulty in getting published, because publishing houses were flourishing, books were still quite expensive, not least because of the high cost of paper.[17] The first edition of Hobbes's *Leviathan* cost eight shillings, "more than most ordinary laborers earned in a week" (Malcolm 1996, 14). Furthermore, the modern system of royalties did not exist, and any profits from print publication would accrue to the printer rather than the author, who had sold his or her work for a flat fee. The patronage system, as part of an early modern gift economy (see Fumerton 1991, Scott 2006, Heal 2014), enabled writers to profit more indirectly from dedicating their work to a patron. For the rest of their time, they had to rely on income from other sources, often as secretaries to a public official (like Spenser) or tutors in a private household (like Hobbes), positions that offered financial security, access to a well-stocked library, writing materials, and (not least) political protection or preferment.

The seventeenth-century 'republic of letters' is a very colourful and highly volatile place, "inhabited equally by churchmen, physicians, noblemen, officers of state, schoolmasters, and even, in the case of [. . .] Sir Kenelm Digby, a one-time amateur pirate" (Malcolm 1996, 14). There is great diversity and an "enormous variety of intellectual positions" (Tuck 1993, 4). Early modern culture, then, in the words of Richard Tuck (1993, 4), "was one where the way of looking at the world which anyone adopted depended very much on what kind of activity they were committed to." In this period, the idea of an 'autonomy' of literary texts in relation to other specified genres, or the idea of a 'literary' reading of certain texts as opposed to 'non-literary' or 'non-fictional' readings of certain other texts would have made no sense. Rather, what mattered to readers was the pragmatic, action-oriented use value of texts, including poetic texts. In the seventeenth century there were no professional readers of literature, no literary critics or literary magazines. Literary culture was part of a more general cultural layering of relational determinants of communication and action; a part that could be specified by its particular effects or by its utility for other forms of behaviour and activity, but a part that could not be observed as an independent, autonomous entity. It was a spider's web among other spider's webs.

Then as now there were of course no guaranteed recipes for literary success. But the insecurity of print communication – still, after all, a fairly new medium – was an experience that triggered an increased reflection on the specific differences of literary communication compared to other, more immediate forms of social interaction. Committing his translation of the Greek historian Thucydides to print (a work that expressly addresses the connection between language and the public sphere), Thomas Hobbes notes in 1628 that "there is something, I know not what, in the

---

17 Paper had to be imported from Europe, mostly from France and Italy, since the English paper industry was slow in developing. Around 1600, a ream of paper (500 sheets) would have cost between two and seven shillings. See Coleman 1958, 1–18; Daybell 2012, 30–52.

censure of a multitude, more terrible than any single judgment, how severe or exact soever" (Hobbes 1975, 6). For this *je ne sais quoi* of print culture, contemporaries – even if they were as eloquent as Hobbes – lacked a definite term. Print culture in early modernity extended but also weakened literary authorship as well as political authority to the point of their depersonalisation (see Sharpe 2000a, 28–29; Hobbes 1996, 1.16). As the unease about communicating to, and being judged by, complete strangers across vast distances of space and perhaps even time increased, so did the development of authorial strategies in response to this predicament – strategies "to contain the hermeneutic liberties of readers" (Sharpe 2000a, 44).[18] Writers could never be quite certain whether what they committed to print would be understood 'correctly', the way they wanted it to be understood. They could never be quite sure of reaching their target audience and establishing a bond of communication – in the sense of a communal understanding – with their readers. Readers, in turn, had to learn to decipher signs of manipulation and propaganda, to develop their own terms for interpretation, and to read texts 'against the grain', especially during the Civil War, when a flood of pamphlets – more than 22,000 according to some estimates (Achinstein 1994) – incited them to political action.

Public opinion on the cultural importance of the gradual shift from manuscripts to printed books appears to have been divided (see Love 1993, Marotti 1995, Beal 1998, Ezell 2003). Bacon, in 1620, aligns "printing, gunpowder, and the magnet" as three inventions that "have changed the whole face and state of things throughout the world" (*New Organon*, aphorism 129; in Bacon 1965, 373). In his later work, Hobbes prefers to downplay the impact of print when he calls the "Invention of *Printing*, though ingenious, [. . .] no great matter" compared to the invention of letters as such (1996, 1.4; cf. Hobbes 1990, 109, 115–17). Others show greater concern and argue passionately against the effects of print culture, in texts which they nevertheless publish in print. In the late 1630s and early 1640s, Sir Thomas Browne sees quite clearly that the printing press has become an important weapon in English political and religious conflict, an invention that resembles the compass and the gun in its military use and its "incommodities" or destructive potential, which he deplores (Browne 2012, 30, *Religio* 1.24). Yet his political opponent John Milton understands the new predicament very well and engages in the production and distribution of republican propaganda by means of print. For those who justify their actions on the basis of Scripture, the availability of relatively cheap printed Bibles means more than a blessing for the individual benefit of the faithful – it is ammunition in the collective armed struggle of the godly against their less godly antagonists. In a letter of advice written for the future Charles II in 1659 by William Cavendish, the Earl of Newcastle, the point is made quite clearly that

---

18 Cf. Sharpe 2000a, 55: "The explosion of print during the 1640s created an audience more remote and anonymous, as well as numerous, than any before; an audience harder to read and define or to address from the pulpit of dedication. Moreover, the speed with which claims to truth were exposed by events or other publications undermined the rhetoric of dedications [. . .]."

"controversey is a Civill warr with the Pen, which Pulls out the sorde soone afterwards." Cavendish sees increased literacy rates undermining governmental and ecclesiastical authority as well as social hierarchy: "The Bible In English under Every weavers, & Chamber maids Armes hath Done us much hurte", he notes, adding nostalgically that "when Moste was Unletterd, it was much a better world, both for Peace & warr" (Cavendish 1984, 21, 19, 20). Both sides in the Civil War, image-breakers as well as image-builders, appreciate and fear the transformative power of the printed word, for very good reasons (see also Scribner 1988, Watt 1991).

In a long-term perspective, the changes in early modern English literary culture can be read as a gradual and progressive disentanglement of different discourses. In this process, literary communication is increasingly understood as a medium of entertainment, associated with leisure rather than labour. But this new function of literature could be argued to emerge as a rather accidental side-effect because it is, and remains, to a large extent determined by external factors. The rules that specify how to read a text are not fixed by the texts themselves, however strongly such authorial control may be desired and asserted in prefaces and dedications. Literary history before 1700 is necessarily a history before 'literature' in the narrower modern sense because its object as we know it and have known it since Romanticism – literature as autonomous aesthetic communication – does not yet exist. This is not to say that readers did not appreciate aesthetic effects, or that imaginative writing was not supposed to give 'pleasure' – a key term in Renaissance as in classical literary theory – but this did not demarcate a particular kind of writing from other kinds of texts. In a wider European context, the proto-systemic differentiation of discourses belongs to the prehistory of Enlightenment attitudes towards public communication. It marks the basic intellectual trajectory traced in this study from humanism to neoclassicism and empiricism. The rationalism of the dawning 'age of reason' is based on a communicative ideal that is incompatible with the humanist literary strategies of persuasive rhetoric: to be acceptable, a proposition is not allowed to admit that it uses rhetorical strategies of adornment in order to convince others of its truth value.

Henceforth, literary techniques had to be banished from the court of philosophy like Hobbes from the court of Charles II: they would be protected and pensioned, but officially disregarded and kept within the bounds of a critical *cordon sanitaire*.[19] In Dryden's satires of the 1680s, the priorities of literary *decorum* and socio-political observation have noticeably shifted in comparison with his earlier Restoration panegyrics, shifted towards a substantial weakening of the communicative bond between political and literary discourse that had formerly (e.g. in Davenant and Milton) been mutually inclusive. Other writers (e.g. Behn, Congreve, and Defoe) are keen to exploit

---

19 This thesis of a separation of discourses does not necessarily conflict with the observation that discursive norms can be relativised and parodied as soon as they have been established (e.g. in Cavendish, Shaftesbury or Swift); rather, the fact that they can be parodied and playfully treated asserts and confirms the general validity of a fairly stable system of discursive norms.

this very weakness of connection, exploring the gaps that were opened up by this separation of discourses and developing new literary strategies from different 'angles of contingency' – literary strategies that, as I argue in chapter 5, coalesce into a prehistory of the eighteenth-century novel. This is not an accidental culmination of a proto-literary history from Burton to Behn, even though it is not the only possible one; but since the novel is one of the most fascinating cultural objects to emerge from the discursive turmoil of the seventeenth century, it is a special challenge to trace the intellectual and cultural foundations on which its literary epistemology is based.

2 Literary Cabinets of Wonder: The 'Paper Kingdomes' of Robert Burton and Sir Thomas Browne

Early Modern Knowledge Technologies

The writings of Robert Burton (1577–1640) and Sir Thomas Browne (1605–1682) are usually discussed as canonic examples of early modern English non-fictional prose, but they are rarely read comparatively. Yet they share a number of characteristics that can make such a comparison meaningful. Under the influence of continental humanism, most notably the Erasmian ideal of *copia* and Montaigne's introspective skepticism (see Cave 1979, Kahn 1985, Lobsien 1999), their texts are highly rhetorical and often playful. In Browne, such linguistic fireworks seem even to increase from one text to the next until they almost become the focus of attention. Their writings exceed any conventional boundaries of genre. What makes them highly *literary* are the ways in which they address and deal with the problem of the contingency of writing in the age of print. Their coping strategies, their literary epistemologies, are very different, almost contrary, and yet related. In Burton's case, the problem of contingency leads to a quasi-theatrical staging of the author-image, accompanied by an overt distrust of the reader's capacity for understanding. Browne's solution, as we shall see, is the exploration of the new possibilities opened up by print culture.

Both writers are transitional figures on the threshold of a new configuration of discourse. Burton can be seen as the culmination point of a long tradition of medieval and humanist literature, a copious compiler whose compulsive urge towards inflationary writing is incapable of stopping the erosion of the order of knowledge that he wishes to generate. Similarly, Browne's writing no longer fits the mould of a late medieval, Aristotelian scholasticism. In spite of his "expansive curiosity" (Willey 1965, 42) and his familiarity with the scientific achievements of his time, he is no experimental scientist in the modern sense; when he performs an experiment, it is merely to replicate what others have tried before, and he would never be a member of the Royal Society. Among Browne's "divided and distinguished worlds" (Browne 2012, 40, *Religio* 1.34) are allusions to Neoplatonic solar mysticism but also a professed belief in the geocentric world picture; a rather liberal understanding of religion combined with an unbroken belief in the existence of witches. Coleridge once described him as a "dramatic" rather than a "metaphysical" writer (Coleridge 1955, 438).

Both are provincial figures: Burton as an Oxford theologian, Browne as a physician in Norwich. Both devote their lives to the almost perpetual writing and rewriting of a single gargantuan work of natural philosophy: in Burton's case, the famous *Anatomy of Melancholy* (first ed. 1621, five subsequent editions 1623, 1628, 1632,

1638, 1651); in Browne's, the less famous *Pseudodoxia Epidemica: or, Enquiries into Very many received Tenents, and commonly presumed Truths* (also known as *Vulgar Errors*, first ed. 1646, sixth enlarged ed. 1672), whose modern edition runs up to more than six hundred pages. In its range of allusions and stylistic multiplicity, their prose offers a bewilderingly complex paradigm of early modern intertextuality and interdiscursivity.

It would be too easy to disqualify their writing as odd or quaint. After all, despite the rise of experimental science, early seventeenth-century styles of thinking and writing remain rooted in an "earlier conceptual world" (Talmor 1981, 12). Scientific writing has not yet developed its own distinctive rules and standards of expression. Furthermore, treatises in natural philosophy share the same space of the fluid and noisy republic of letters with a heterogeneous multiplicity of other types of text: political pamphlets, sermons, how-to-books, poems, and plays. As noted above, the writings of Milton, Donne, Bunyan, and others cannot easily be separated from the religious debates and the struggle of various sectarian movements before, during, and after the Civil War in which these texts originate and take shape. The same is true for other forms of writing, for Bacon, Hobbes, and Boyle as well as for the Cambridge Platonists, regardless of subsequent readers who see them as mainly scientific, political or philosophical in character (Gascoigne 1989; Vickers 1984; Kroll, Ashcraft, and Zagorin 1992).

In the seventeenth century, the overall cultural 'climate of opinions'[20] has few or no problems with such hybrid literary blends that transcend narrow boundaries of genre and that are not (yet) fully functionally specified. But this does not at all mean that these different worlds of discourse (science, religion, philosophy, politics, entertainment) are reconciled and harmonised. On the contrary, texts and opinions, as well as their authors, live "in divided and distinguished worlds." When these worlds collide – often within the work of a single author or within a single text – there is bound to be a burst of energy, not only cultural but at times political, visceral, or even lethal for the bodies and minds involved. The greatest problem for these texts and their authors is a problem of contingency: they lack the formal equipment with which they could effectively tackle the totality of different discourses that are in the process of drifting further apart and whose representation as a unified whole still constitutes the unattainable ideal.[21] As I shall argue, it is only in the second half of the seventeenth century that a relatively coherent and comprehensive solution to this problem of contingency begins to materialise when, in what I call 'neoclassical discourse', a predominantly rationalist, moderate attitude towards the competitive pressures of metaphysics, politics, and epistemology is developed and established. This attitude is at the same time a discursive technique of mediating between competing

---

20 This phrase originates with Joseph Glanvill, whose *The Vanity of Dogmatizing* (1661) is itself an interesting hybrid between philosophy, religion, and science.
21 The Cambridge Platonists (John Smith, Ralph Cudworth, Henry More) are a good case in point. See Tulloch 1874, Cassirer 1953.

dimensions of experience (including their humanist, neostoic, and Christian interpretations) and theoretical (philosophical, political, moral) concepts. Contingency is then relocated onto a communicative level that precedes this competitive division of discourses, and its potentially damaging effects can be cushioned by certain forms of refined sociability and politeness. Neoclassical discourse thus transforms contingency from an experiential mode of existential insecurity into a culture, into a communicative norm of intersubjectivity.

In contrast to the later formation of neoclassicism, English humanism in the early seventeenth century is still a very scholarly culture. The dense and orotund style cultivated in the writings of Burton and Browne, but also in those of Hooker or Cudworth, is the very opposite of a polite coffee-house conversation that relies on articulations of politeness and common sense. The cultural space of late humanist scholars is not the coffee-house but the cabinet of wonder. Their communicative ideal is not gentlemanly politeness but humanist erudition and eloquence; scholarship and wisdom, not 'virtue' in the dynamic political sense that this term connoted at that time, both as Ciceronian *virtus* or Machiavellian *virtù*. Its particular energies are not social and active but individual and contemplative.

The working hypothesis that grounds my reading of Burton and Browne is that the stylistic and formal peculiarities of their writings can be explained through their relation to two contemporary dispositives of cultural knowledge: the private library and the cabinet of wonder. As an intersection of macro- and microcosm, of public admiration and private curiosity, the cabinet of wonder is a physical embodiment of the order of knowledge characteristic of early seventeenth-century natural philosophy – an order of knowledge that wishes to be understood as a reflection of the order of reality as seen by the prime observer: "This World is as a Cabinet to GOD, in which the small things (however to vs hidde and secret) are nothing lesse keeped, than the great" (Drummond 1973 [1623], 77) This order of knowledge and its spatial arrangement are centred around the colourful figure of the *virtuoso*, who embodies the ability of replicating the totality of knowledge by means of *wit*. Once we have outlined the concrete social, spatial, and media-technological foundations on which their literary performances are based, we can understand the peculiarities of Burton's and Browne's texts as *funtional*: as attempts to solve certain epistemological problems that result from a changed communicative situation. I read their texts as exemplary instances of the development of epistemic virtuosity as a media phenomenon. Contextural preconditions of this phenomenon are the early modern 'knowledge technologies' (Rhodes and Sawday 2000) of print, the library, and the cabinet of wonder. Of these three, print contributes the most to the collapse of late medieval forms of knowledge and being. With its multiplication and dissemination of texts, print makes knowledge less exclusive but also more unstable, more subject to revision. Among other things, it gradually replaces "wisdom" with "information" as a "new form of communication" (Benjamin 2000, 79–80). It also complicates the relationship between writers and readers.

Browne has often been read as a virtuoso of learning, a type of scholar that is also embodied by his contemporaries Sir Kenelm Digby and John Evelyn (Löffler 1972). But in some respects, this concept can also be applied to Burton. The virtuoso is a cultural figure characterised by boundless curiosity and an insatiable hunger for knowledge of all kinds: biological, geological, physical, anthropological, historical, theological, spiritual. However, he is less a scientist than a collector: less interested in the systematic presentation of a body of knowledge than in a discontinuous, pleasant, and sometimes playful arrangement of individual knowledge-objects; less interested in scientifically exploring and explaining connections than in appealing to his spectators' faculty of wonder and admiration of the contiguous and surprising 'curiosities' that are prompted by the "answerings or analogies of beings" (Fairfax 1674, 2, qtd. in Preston 2000, 175) in a certain arrangement of objects in space (in the cabinet as well as in the textual space of the encyclopedia). The virtuoso is neither a mere amateur or dilettante nor a 'true scientist' in the modern sense.[22] The universal width of his knowledge is combined with a distinct lack of any unifying method. His attention is therefore likely to be attracted to the outlandish, the rare, the curious, and the marginal. If his method is eclectic, so are his reading and writing. The social scope of the virtuoso's erudition is limited to certain circles of friends and acquaintances; virtuosity is largely an elite phenomenon and a private gentlemanly pursuit. It owes its existence to the still recent developments of print culture and the phenomenon of private libraries, often in combination with collections of other rarities in the "virtual theater" (Agamben 1999, 32) of a cabinet of wonder: "a chamber stuffed from floor to ceiling with ivory, old iron, broken pots, urns, unicorns' horns, and magic glasses full of emerald lights and blue mystery" (Woolf 1994 [1925], 59), collected by noblemen but also frequently by physicians like Browne.[23] In these new spaces, more private than public, a huge assembly of various forms of information, either immediately appealing to the senses or in the form of pictures and texts, is readily available to a curious mind at the touch of a hand. They are representational, theatrical spaces whose world-content is also meant to express their owners' status; however, their prime concern is not conspicuous consumption but the preservation and display of rare possessions.

Both the cabinet of wonder and the library are actual spaces that contain knowledge about the world – knowledge that is removed from its original contexts but that can be recontextualised by an informed observer. These spaces facilitate an intersection of private experience with the world about which they purport to present a near-encyclopedic – albeit necessarily incomplete – knowledge. Implied in this encyclopedic urge is the notion that the coherence and harmony of creation, occluded by error since the Fall of Man, can be reconstructed and amended by certain techniques

---

[22] Löffler (1972, 47) mentions Chalmers 1936 as one of the few scholars who have tried to claim Browne as a Baconian.
[23] For a number of contemporary illustrations, see Rhodes and Sawday 2000, 152–54, figs. 45–49. See also Impey and MacGregor 1985, Daston and Park 1998.

of knowledge (collection, comparison, and correction). By finding hidden signatures or 'matches', one can discover analogies between objects, allowing a superior structure of order to appear beyond "the apparent disarray of the phenomenal world" (Preston 2000, 170) – a technique that is most evident in Browne's *Garden of Cyrus* (see Foucault 2002, 19–49 for a reconstruction of the Renaissance episteme of resemblance).

The library and the cabinet of wonder are prime instances of an early modern "knowledge technology" (Rhodes and Sawday 2000) based on a new European communications network. In theory at least, thanks to the convenience of printed reading matter, curiosity can now be satisfied at home without extensive travel. The seventeenth century becomes the first age of the private library; notably, the boundaries between libraries and cabinets of curiosities are still fluid. Knowledge becomes a kind of art all of its own: no longer pursued for reasons of application or for sheer necessity or survival, but as a form of recreation, something to be enjoyed and to be displayed for the enjoyment of others. This intersection of private and public, local and global aspects is mirrored in the writings of Burton and Browne. In the cabinet of wonder, knowledge becomes a media phenomenon eliciting reflection but also, and perhaps more prominently, admiration, fascination, sensual appeal. The literary configuration of late humanism, of which Burton and Browne are instances, depends on these epistemic novelties as it combines an amazing degree of intertextuality with a fascination for other media, other ways of communication, other possibilities of acquiring and transmitting knowledge. It is a library phenomenon in the spirit of a cabinet of wonder. The isolated and insulated context of the study, removed from the turmoil and drama of life, enables a distanced and depragmatised observation of a multiplicity of ideas and objects. Rearranging disparate objects results in contingent, improbable, and surprising perspectives. This experience is meant to be shared with the reader, although the reader's response is extremely uncertain and needs to be anticipated in one way or another by the author. It is at least doubtful if the reader can respond to the text with the same 'idleness' (Burton) or 'leisurable ease' (Browne) as the author, and this doubt has to be articulated and cushioned in some way in the text. Various solutions to this problem of addressability are suggested and practiced, ranging from the Burtonian extreme of self-deprecation and irony, in which the reader is implicated, to less strict and less harsh forms of reader-response anticipation. For Burton, learning, writing, and reading are therapeutic cures against melancholy; for Browne, to reconstruct a cabinet of wonder on the literary page is to open up an imaginary space of 'recreation' in the sense of a contemplative reshaping of the author's as well as the reader's self.

In the virtual contact zones of the library and its reconstruction *en miniature*, the encyclopedic book, the observer position of the writer in relation to the reader becomes increasingly problematic. In Burton, the ever-accumulating palimpsest of references and quotations is hardly manageable, making the self-reflection and self-dissection of the observer-writer ever more complex until it leads towards the theatrical self-staging and self-distancing of "a meere spectator" (*AM* 1: 4) in the role of Democritus Junior. In this process, knowledge is cast as a more or less contingent array of epistemological and emotional dualities (wisdom/folly, utopia/dystopia, mask/authenticity, crying/laughing, etc.) against the background of universal melancholy. The reverse happens in Browne, where a flexible stance of observation (indebted to humanist *curiositas*) discovers and reflects on many contingencies of perspective, and new knowledge is generated through these contingencies. For Browne, the world becomes a globe that can be handled and looked at from any point of view: "The world that I regard is my selfe, it is the Microcosme of mine owne frame, that I cast mine eye on; for the other, I use it but like my Globe, and turne it round sometimes for my recreation" (2012, 82; *Religio* 2.11).

Burton's and Browne's writings can thus be read as two distinct responses to the same predicament: the spread and differentiation of knowledge in modernity, which leads to the collapse of an order of knowledge and being that they feel most familiar with, to which they still feel the tie. They respond to the pressures and constraints that this spread and differentiation exert upon literary form and on the rhetorical strategies of authorial presentation, but they also begin to explore the horizon of possibilities that opens up for them. In such a situation, it is the *rapport* between writers and their readers that becomes extremely important, because it is that aspect of literary communication that best illustrates how problematic (complex and contingent) the epistemological foundations of literary communication have become in early modernity. In a more and more differentiated print culture, the distance (both spatial and mental) between author and audience is considerably extended, and hence the precise communicative function of writing in relation to different situations of reading is no longer self-evident. The possibility of understanding textual structures in many different ways, without hope of post-publication intervention by the author (at least until the next edition), makes it increasingly necessary or desirable for writers, who might fear the consequences of being misunderstood, but who might also begin to exploit and play with the literary surplus that semantic polyvalence had to offer, to build implicit or even explicit thematisations of the problematic reader-writer relationship into their texts. Rhetorical strategies of indirectness, irony, self-consciousness, and a cascade of authorial masks – techniques and devices that one would normally associate with the conventions of modern fiction – are employed in texts whose communicative purposes are not 'literary' in the conventional (aesthetic) sense. They appear even more prominently here than in texts whose primary function of story-telling can be taken for granted. By *staging* the very processes of production and reception on which their precarious structural balance depends, these 'proto-literary' texts (Pfeiffer 2002) gain an additional level of reflection.

Reading the Theatre of Writing: Burton's *Anatomy of Melancholy*

Robert Burton's *Anatomy of Melancholy* is a paradigmatic example of an encyclopedic text confronted with a set of transformations in early modern media culture. It is produced at a point in history when the encyclopedic method of knowledge compilation "was becoming virtually impossible to apply" (Bamborough 1989, xxvi), paradoxically at the same time as libraries began to promise an almost unlimited access to the knowledge of the past and present (on the *Anatomy* as a "postencyclopedic book", see also Grose 2002, 87, and Schmelzer 1999). Burton's writing needs to cope both with the crisis of universalism and the heightened contingency of textual communication that follows from the growing number and widening distribution of printed books. Indeed, the *Anatomy* can be read as a response to the effects of early modern print culture: a media configuration that encourages alternative and comparative observations of reality because anything that is given can now be questioned in terms of alternative possibilities. Using an elaborate array of textual and visual strategies, Burton engages with the vicissitudes of early modern literary communication, attempting to compensate for the lost immediacy of audience appeal – so prevalent in oral discourse, but also in manuscript coteries – by means of print. My focus therefore is on Burton's rhetorical strategies of authorial presentation and reader address, concentrating on the prefatorial matter that continued to grow around the main text through six editions printed during Burton's lifetime.

Many critics have observed that, in the case of the *Anatomy*, the peritexts are not hierarchically subordinate to the main text so as to support its authority but fulfil a more independent function of commentary and critique, even of contradiction.[24] My analysis is focused on these liminal texts because it is here, in the margins of his gigantic work, that Burton's staging of a literary epistemology most prominently and explicitly takes place. It is here that conditions and conventions of reading and writing, and the impossibility of securing a stable foundation on which author and reader can communicate, are addressed. In the peritexts, and in the different framing devices they present, author and reader can observe themselves, and each other, as performers of textual roles.[25] When I use the term 'author' in this analysis, it should be understood that I am referring to a textual function equivalent to the narrator in a work of fiction. As I am going to elucidate, the *Anatomy* is extremely concerned with the possibilities of complexity that can be generated by doubling the author into the

---

[24] For the term 'peritext', see Genette 1997. For Genette, the paratext is the sum total of individual peritexts (title, dedication, preface, etc.) and epitexts (author's commentary, interviews) to a given work. Genette's classification is strictly hierarchical, subordinating paratext to main text; Wagner-Egelhaaf (1997, 94) has pointed out the inapplicability of such a rigid notion of paratextuality to Burton's *Anatomy*. See also Maclean 1991.

[25] For an attempt to define authorship as (cultural) performance, see Berensmeyer, Buelens, and Demoor 2012.

personae of 'Democritus'/'Burton' and allowing him (it?) to inhabit and control the empty space between them as 'No-body'.

Burton's mode of presentation in the *Anatomy* is characterised by two major features: *enumeration* and *intertextuality*. Both relate to his encyclopedic approach to knowledge. The 'dissection' of the *Anatomy* proceeds by way of an unfolding, layer upon layer, "of divers things fore-knowne" (*AM* lxix), and this unfolding entails a constant increase of material that is kept from disintegraton only by a "vast superstructure of divisionary procedures" (Sawday 1995, 2). Through the parallel procedures of constant division and subdivision, as well as perpetual revision, refinement, and accretion, the text grows from about 350,000 words in the first edition to more than 500,000 in the sixth, comprising "the greatest anatomical encyclopedia of the age" in the form of "a textual investigation of the world and all that it contained" (Sawday 1995, 108, 135; Sawday 1997). Its ideal is to give an encyclopedic account of human knowledge, a carefully orchestrated and calculated enumeration of bits and pieces of knowledge approved by authorities, organised by principles derived from anatomy,[26] although Burton's interest in radically new advances in anatomical and medical knowledge is very limited, and he prefers to adhere to the conventional wisdom of Hippocrates, Galen, and Paracelsus (Bamborough 1989, xxi).

A consequence of this reliance on received wisdom, including obscure references and, at times, absurd contradictions, is a strong, sometimes extreme degree of *intertextuality*. Burton's abundance of sources is exposed and made visible on every page. Because he has no clear and distinct 'scientific' criteria that might have determined what to include and what to exclude, which received opinion to believe and which to discredit, he is forced to attempt the impossible and to include 'everything' anybody has ever written on the topic. This striving for totality results in his own author position with regard to this totality and its sources becoming unstable and insecure. Another factor for this instability is that the author diagnoses himself as being affected by the disease he examines in his book, effectively dividing himself into both doctor and patient, and that he presents writing as a curative, therapeutic act: "I write of Melancholy, by being busie to avoid Melancholy" (6), "*to exercise my selfe*" and "[t]o doe my selfe good" (7).[27]

Because it is impossible for human perception to process 'everything', this perception can easily switch over to the absolute negation of everything: "*Omne meum, nihil meum*" (11). Even this phrase, a confession of epigonality, is, as Burton

---

[26] At least this appears to be the standard opinion in modern criticism; cf. Babb 1959, Frye 1957, Hodges 1985. It has been rejected by some critics who regard the whole *Anatomy* as Menippean satire (Korkowski 1975) or a monstrous "epistemological aberration" (Williams 2001, 594).

[27] The best analysis of the self-reflexive, text-generating role of melancholy for Burton is in Wagner-Egelhaaf 1997, 93–158. Wagner-Egelhaaf analyzes the paradoxical way in which writing, as a therapy for melancholy, produces the very object that therapy is intended to cure (93, 118), a configuration that resembles a Moebius strip (108–9).

acknowledges, derived from someone else.[28] To a greater extent than usual, Burton's author position depends on the reader's respect, difficult to gain "in this scribling age, [...] wherein *the number of Bookes is without number* [...] and out of an itching humor, that every man hath to shew himselfe, desirous of fame and honour [...] he will write no matter what, and scrape together it bootes not whence" (8). If nearly everyone desires to be an author and the monarch of "a Paper-Kingdome" (9), the true distinction of authorship will disappear.

Thus Burton wavers between assertions of his originality of method and denigrations of his inevitable epigonality and triviality, referring to his book as a "*Cento* out of divers Writers" and as "this my *Maceronicon*" (11), terms that emphasise the intertextual and interlingual aspects of his book, but also, in their etymology – the latter derives from macaroni, a pasta dish – allude to physiological processes of nourishment, digestion, and consumption. These processes serve as metaphors of Burton's writing beyond the anatomical divisions of the text: "which nature doth with the aliment of our bodies, incorporate, digest, assimulate, I doe *conquoquere quod hausi,* dispose of what I take" (11). Writing is a process of digestion, and the writer, for Burton, is first of all a reader who 'digests' and then transforms what he has read into his own matter, into a 'digest'.

In the process, he has to develop a strategy of presentation that anticipates readers' potentially negative reactions to the totality they are confronted with. The reader's role in the text is at least as insecure as the author's. Burton's strategy consists in a procedure of authorial doubling and mirroring, on the thematic as well as on the textual level. Thematically, the author doubles himself into both doctor and patient: he writes a book on melancholy in order to cure himself of melancholy. By casting the reader also in the role of a patient, he presents him or her with the mirror of self-knowledge: his goal is to enable readers to become their own physicians. On the textual level, there is another doubling and mirroring, as the author presents himself both as a (copious) writer and as a (voracious) reader. The projected reader of the *Anatomy* is encouraged to identify with the double position of a voracious reader who is also a copious writer and who will digest the digest he is proffered by Burton. The text stages reading as an embodied experience.

This duality of writing and reading is well captured, in the 1628 edition, in the image of a writer seated within, and framed by, the decorative initial "G" that constitutes the first letter of the words "Gentle Reader" at the beginning of the extensive

---

28 Burton claims it is derived from Macrobius; his modern commentator proves him wrong and traces the phrase "omnia nostra, & nihil" to the sixteenth-century humanist Justus Lipsius, author of a cento of political writings; cf. commentary in *AM* 4: 26. It even served as the motto to the entire *Anatomy* until Burton chose a more conventional Horatian phrase; see commentary in *AM* 4: 2.

"Satyricall Preface" "Democritus Junior to the Reader."[29] The reader is addressed by an image of the author who resides in the space delineated by the initial. But author-reader communication is not unidirectional: the relationship between writer and reader is complicated when we realise that the writer in this image is also at the same time a reader, looking at a written page, a page he is either just writing or correcting. The author is staged in this image as a scholar in the act of writing (and reading), which is presented as an incomplete process still ongoing at the moment when the reader arrives at this point. The letter's opening towards the right, in the direction of reading, enhances the impression of openness and a forward-looking dynamic. The shape of the letter G encloses the writer and his desk but points to the direction where the text is going to travel, to the unknown and invisible space of the "Gentle Reader". By showing the author at work on a manuscript, the image also suggests a more immediate contact between author and reader, which the printed text cannot provide. It asserts the writer's authority and control over the text, rather than the printer's. It also mirrors the author as a reader and the reader as a potential author.

Despite this visual link between author and reader, their association in the text of the *Anatomy* remains difficult. Another, even more complex textual and visual engagement with the author-reader relation is enacted in the illustrated frontispiece by Christof Le Blon the elder, which first appears in the 1628 edition. It presents an engraving of Burton holding a closed book, as if proffering it to the viewer, surrounded by (clockwise) a coat of arms, an astrolabe, a ruler, and another, open book (Fig. 1). The image is subscribed "Democritus Junior", Burton's pseudonym, which securely identifies the image as a portrait of the book's alleged author. In 1632, Burton adds a poem to the title page, entitled "The Argument of the Frontispeice [sic]," which significantly complicates the image of the author giving his book to the prospective reader:

> *Now last of all to fill a place,*
> *Presented is the* Authors *face;*
> *And in that habit which he weares,*
> *His Image to the world appeares.*
> *His minde no art can well expresse,*
> *That by his writings you may guesse.* (lxii)

Presented "to fill a place" – a laconic but incisive comment on the contingency of authorship and on the need to find a representative placeholder for this position outside the text, the "zero point of discourse" (Iser 2013, 122) – the author's "Image" is distinguished from "His minde", access to which is only possible indirectly, through "his writings". An exterior public appearance is separated from an interiority that eludes secure knowledge. Mindreading through textual interpretation, Burton leaves

---

[29] The first page of the 1628 "Democritus Junior to the Reader" is reproduced as a frontispiece to the Faulkner/Kiessling/Blair edition. The words "Satyricall Preface" are from the title page as reproduced on p. lxiii. The image is dropped from the 1632 edition; see the facsimile on p. lxxii.

Fig. 1: Robert Burton, *The Anatomy of Melancholy,* title page (detail), London 1676. Wellcome Collection. CC BY.

no doubt, is nothing but guesswork. Image and text fulfil different functions at cross purposes. Whereas the image depicts an exterior world, the interior meaning of a text (here understood as the depiction of authorial consciousness, "minde") is lost in contingencies that do not allow certainty but produce new insecurities. Yet the text also has an effect upon the portrait, rendering it ambiguous: Burton's image may not be offering but withdrawing his book (i.e. according to the poem, his inwardness) from the reader. Furthermore, the book he his holding may not be the *Anatomy* at all, because its format seems too small (it had been changed from quarto to folio as early as the second edition, 1624; see *AM* xxxvii). Perhaps the *Anatomy* is the open book shown beside his likeness, detached from him, outside the frame – extending the distance between author (-image) and text. Moreover, the open pages appear to be empty – the book does not depict its author's inwardness, it rather demands to be filled and actualised by the reader. It challenges readers to use the book as the mirror of their own selves. The book in Burton's hand may be a Bible.[30] There is no way of knowing. The portrait, like the pseudonym 'Democritus Junior', is an elaborate mask that conceals more than it reveals.

---

30 Cf. Wagner-Egelhaaf 1997, 99–100. Mueller (1949, 1087) assumes the open book on the left to be a copy of the *Anatomy,* but there is of course no way to prove this; all that remains to be stated is the (perhaps deliberate) ambiguity of visual signs that opens up a "space between" image and meaning (Wagner-Egelhaaf 98), ultimately directing the readers' attention to their own curiosity in deciphering sign constellations.

The poem goes on to explain that the author did not have his likeness engraved on the frontispiece because of "pride" or "vaineglory" but – "if you must know" (again, the reader is accused of being overly curious) – because "The Printer would needs haue it so." It is the printer who demands the author's portrait precisely because he has 'an empty space to fill' on the page, presumably as part of a marketing strategy meant to increase his sales by drawing attention to, and inviting identification with, the author. The strategy of including a picture of the author on the title page may be read as a compensation for the physical distance that print places between writers and readers. Burton does not simply refuse such a *rapprochement* between the two, but he complicates the process of identification by inserting a textual commentary on the image, which draws the reader's attention to the technological conditions of production and the strategic necessities of print culture: "The Printer would needs haue it so." He further complicates the situation by inviting the reader to engage actively in this process of identification. This invitation, as it continues and even radicalises the 'magical' implications of the author-image in the eyes of the reader, also comments on the uneasy and perhaps irresolvable power relation between reader and author:

> *Then doe not frowne or scoffe at it,*
> *Deride not, or detract a whit.*
> *For surely as thou dost by him,*
> *He will doe the same againe.*
> *Then looke upon't, behold and see,*
> *As thou likest it, so it likes thee.*
> *And I for it will stand in view,*
> *Thine to command,* Reader *Adew.* (lxii)

The portrait is offered as a dynamic reflection of the reader's response. If the reader does "frowne or scoffe", so will the portrait, whose pokerface is indeed ambiguous, concealing any expression of emotion underneath a well-trimmed beard. The pun on 'like' implies physical resemblance but also affection. The penultimate line promises a replacement of the portrait by the author in person ("I for it"), encouraging the reader to identify "it" with the real author, "I", who "will stand in view", both passively and actively, seeing as well as being seen, looking back at the reader. Instead of the unusual substitution "I for it", readers might have expected the more conventional 'it for me' (i.e. 'the engraving represents me', and not, as here, 'I will stand in for my engraved portrait'). The final line is ultimately ambiguous because of a lacking comma. Are we to construe it as "Thine to command, Reader: 'Adew'", meaning "I, the author, will stand by so that you, the reader, can say 'Adieu' to me" (i.e. "so that you have someone to say goodbye to when you put away this book"), or as "Thine to command: 'Reader Adew'", i.e. "I will be there for you to see, instead of my portrait, so that I can say goodbye to you" – or perhaps even "so that you can say goodbye to me as if I were you"? Furthermore, if the reader reads this aloud, she is inevitably forced to assume the position of the "I" and to lend her voice to a farewell addressed to herself, so that the two positions of reader and author are ultimately conflated. The missing comma and this uncanny readerly/writerly ventriloquism make it impossible to decide between the different possible interpretations of the poem. Its recitation, however, is performative: it worries the stable roles and habits of readers and reading in the fluid role-play of reader, author, and author-image, thus anticipating the communicative strategy of the *Anatomy*, which aims at the curative transformation of its readers.

As in the other prefatory matter, readers are alternately invited and repelled. Their desire for identification with Burton's persona and his book (one, after all, 'stands in view' for the other) is encouraged and denied by the elaborate masquerade Burton stages in his text. Once established, the relation between the author's and reader's roles is far from stable and can tilt over in the next textual segment, 'dialogically', just as the binary emotional states of sadness and joy (or depression and mania) alternate in "*The Authors Abstract of Melancholy* Διαλογικως" (lxix–lxxi). The game of hide-and-seek between author and reader is taken to extremes in the actual preface, "Democritus Junior to the Reader". Continuing the metaphor of reading as a form of nourishment and digestion, Burton invites the reader as his guest: "Our writings are as so many Dishes, our Readers Guests" (13). He seems to accept the inevitable difference between readers' tastes and understandings ("that which one admires another rejects", 13; "Some understand too little, some too much", 14), but then he turns around and decides to play "a Dutch Host" to his reader: "As a Dutch Host, if you come to an Inne in Germany, & dislike your fare, diet, lodging, &c. replies in a surly tone, aliud tibi quaeras diversorium, if you like not this, get you to another Inne; I resolve, if you like not my writing, goe read something else" (14).

As in the case of Burton's engraved portrait, invitation gives way to repulsion. What the reader-as-guest is served by the author-as-("Dutch"-)host may even turn out to be the final excremental product of digestion: "a Rapsody of Rags gathered together from severall Dung-hills, excrements[31] of Authors, [. . .] harsh, raw, rude, phantasticall, absurd, insolent, indiscreet, ill-composed, vaine, scurrile, idle, dull and dry" (12). Again, Burton/Democritus turns the tables on the reader by addressing him as a potential writer and casting himself in the reader's role: "I should bee [. . .] loth my selfe to read him or thee" (12). This specular doubling initiates an interminable process of alternating self-justification and self-deprecation. Burton, in the mask of Democritus Junior, alternately flirts with and jilts the reader, courts and mocks him (Burton's reader is usually presumed to be male). What is ultimately at stake in this process is an epistemological perspective on the instability of literary communication in print culture. The preface to the *Anatomy* dramatises the

---

31 Although the commentary asserts that "excrements" is to be understood "in the sense of 'cast-off or rejected pieces'" (4: 29), the more drastic meaning is supported both by the pervasive metaphors of food and digestion and the close presence of the adjective "indigested" in this paragraph.

positions of author and reader in a form of textual theatre that stages the acts of writing and reading – acts that cannot become present in the text as such.[32] Both author and reader are transformed into actors in the process, conscious role-players who have a reflexive distance to the purposes and limits of their actions and desires. Readers are challenged to inquire into the foundations of their own curiosity by experiencing successive invitations and rebuffs from the author:

> Gentle Reader, I presume thou wilt be very inquisitive to know what Anticke or Personate Actor this is, that so insolently intrudes upon this common Theater, to the worlds view, arrogating another mans name, whence hee is, why he doth it, and what he hath to say? [. . .] I am a free man borne, and may chuse whether I will tell, who can compell me? [. . .] Seeke not after that which is hid, if the contents please thee, *and be for thy use, suppose* the Man in the Moone, *or whom thou wilt to be the Author*; I would not willingly be knowne. (1)

The mask of 'Democritus Junior' is not merely a pseudonym to conceal the author's identity – he almost immediately unmasks himself when he names his college (3) and, at least in the first edition, places his name and that of his college at the book's end[33] – but a strategic element in staging the processes of writing and reading. The assumed name of Democritus refers to the story of Hippocrates' visit to the city of Abdera, where he finds the philosopher Democritus dissecting animals in order to discover the seat of 'black bile' and to write a book on the causes and cures of melancholy, a book "now lost" which Burton, who tells this story in the preface, intends to "prosecute and finish" (6). In a figure of reversal that is fundamental for the textual strategies of the *Anatomy* itself, Hippocrates announces that it is not Democritus but the people of Abdera who are mad. The use of a mask may be, as Burton notes, a traditional medium for satire: "to assume a little more liberty and freedome of speech" (5). But here, too, Burton is turning the tables on the reader, unmasking the "anticke Picture" (cf. the engraving on the title page) as a marketing ploy, a lure for the unwary; indeed, "the market" for Burton is "a trappe" (50): "Howsoever it is a kinde of pollicie in these daies, to prefixe a phantasticall Title to a Booke which is to bee sold: For as Larkes come downe to a Day-net, many vaine Readers will tarry and stand gazing like silly passengers, at an anticke Picture in a Painters shop, that will not looke at a judicious peece" (6).

Never relinquishing his metaphors of visuality, Burton conceives of both reading and authorship as acts of seeing and observation: "*ipse mihi Theatrum* [A theatre to myself], [. . .] *Et tanquam in speculâ positus* [And like one placed on a watch-tower]

---

[32] As Wolfgang Iser argues (1992, 881): "what is staged is the appearance of something that cannot become present. Since every appearance, however, is imbued with an element of determinacy – otherwise it could not appear – it inevitably pales into areas of indeterminacy, which on the one hand point to what eludes the grasp and on the other stimulate the desire to lure into presence what has been excluded."

[33] Cf. Bamborough 1989, xxxi. Bamborough also notes that, in placing his family arms on the title page Burton "might as well have signed his name" (ibid.), and concludes that "[h]e was certainly not trying to cover his tracks" (n. 78).

[. . .] in some high place above you all, [. . .] I heare and see what is done abroad [. . .]. A meere spectator of other mens fortunes and adventures, and how they act their parts, which me thinkes are diversly presented unto me, as from a common Theater or Sceane" (4). This theatre, staged for the benefit of the onlooker, he explains in a lengthy enumeration, is made possible by modern media, which deliver world events even to those ensconced in a quasi-monastic scholarly life (4–5). Presenting this barrage of information as a form of theatre is Burton's way of assuring himself and the reader that the exploding world of media does not really affect him and his way of life: "I rub on *privus privatus* [an independent and private person], as I have still lived, so I now continue" (5). His critique of modern media belongs to the strategy, pervasive in the preface, of presenting the world as a "ship of fooles" (59) from which he desires his work to be salvaged – it is, after all, the Abderites and not Democritus who are mad. This is a strategy of totalisation with which to offset and justify the totalising strategy of his book: "*totus mundus histrionem agit*, the whole world plaies the Foole, we have a new Theater, a new Sceane, a new Commedy of Errors, a new company of personate Actors, *volupiæ sacra* [rites of pleasure] [. . .] are celebrated all the World over, where all the Actors were Mad-men and Fooles, and every houre changed habites, or tooke that which came next" (37). As in a theatre, "the world alters every day" (39). The *topos* of theatricality, traceable to John of Salisbury's twelfth-century saying quoted here and famously adapted by Shakespeare in *As You Like It* as "All the world's a stage" (2.7.138), is united to the *vanitas* motif. The world according to Democritus Junior is decidedly proto-Hobbesian: "A vast *Chaos*, a confusion of manners, as fickle as the Ayre, *domicilium insanorum*, a turbulent troope full of impurities, a mart of walking Spirits, Goblins, the Theater of hypocrisie, [. . .] the Academy of vice; a warfare, [. . .] in which kill or be kill'd" (51). It seems as if, for Burton as for Nietzsche (1988, 1: 47), the world is 'eternally justified' only in the form of theatre, as an aesthetic phenomenon. Only the unaffected, stoic spectator can stand apart and enjoy imagining himself free from "folly and madnesse" (107).

But again, Burton turns the theatrical trope inside out by pointing out that the spectator may "bee ridiculous to others, and not [. . .] perceive or take notice of it" (57). In a world of fools, not even the wise are safe from folly, and the only way to promote wisdom is to promote self-knowledge of one's own foolishness: "*mutato nomine, de te fabula narratur*", he cites Horace (57) – echoing his earlier appeal to the reader, "Thou thy selfe art the subject of my Discourse" (1). The result is well-nigh mathematical: "If none honest, none wise, then all Fooles" (61). Self-knowledge is presented as the only solace against this totality of folly. Slowly but steadily, as Burton hurls an ever growing avalanche of references and judgements, conceits and anecdotes at the reader, including more than ten pages that delineate a utopian community in the manner of Thomas More and Campanella (86–97), it may slowly but surely dawn upon the reader that the satirical purpose of this farrago is to unmask the "folly and madnesse" (107) of the very acts of writing and reading in print culture and to make him realise the double contingency inherent in the relation between author and reader – to force him to take the role of the other.[34] The text is self-referential in two ways: it includes itself in its disparagement of modern textuality, and it refers readers to their own preferences and delusions in reading: "hee was a madman that said it, and thou peradventure as mad to read it" (106). Only those who remain silent can escape from folly (107).

In the diagnostic frame of reference provided by the subject of melancholy – which the preface extends even further to include all kinds of "folly and madnesse" (107) – author, text, and reader are all placed within a global framework of (multiple) contingency, and the relations between them can therefore not be stabilised. The author defends himself by pointing to his literary mask, by what one could call the strength of his author position: "If I have overshot my selfe in this [. . .] you must consider what it is to speake in ones owne or anothers person, an assumed habit and name" (110; again, an appeal to the reader's powers of identification and self-reflection). Another strategy of defence is his emphasis on the intertextual nature of his work: "it is a *Cento* collected from others, not I, but they that say it" (110) – what one could call the weakness of Burton's author position. Strength and weakness are kept in an uneasy balance; the speaker is not in a position to decide, and therefore he begins once more to waver between them. First, strength: "I owe thee nothing, (Reader) I looke for no favour at thy hands, I am independent, I feare not" (112). Then – next sentence, next paragraph – weakness: "No, I recant, I will not, I care, I feare, I confesse my fault, acknowledge a great offence, [. . .] I have overshot my selfe, I have spoken foolishly", culminating in the promise of a new contract with the reader: "I promise you a more sober discourse in my following Treatise" (112).

Of course, as Burton admits early on ("'tis partly affected" [12]), the preface is an elaborate strategic venture, but it takes the conventional rhetorical manoeuvres of *captatio benevolentiae* to their very limits, and somewhat beyond these limits, by laying them open and unmasking them as strategies. To stretch the generic boundaries of the "satyricall preface" too far is a wilful and deliberate injury to the reader at the hands of the author, amounting to a breach of contract. But what the anatomist does in the anatomical theatre is, after all, cutting: "If hereafter anatomizing this surly humor, my hand slip, as an unskilfull Prentise, I launce too deep, and cut through skin and all at unawares, make it smart or cut awry, pardon a rude hand"

---

34 On role-taking, see Mead 1934, 254, 354–56. The concept of 'double contingency' derives from Talcott Parsons; see Parsons and Shils 1951, 16, and Parsons 1968, 436. I use it here with a glance at Niklas Luhmann's analysis of modern communication as giving rise to unavoidably complex problems in interaction; a solution, according to Luhmann, is provided by "the expression of *respect* and the communication about conditions of mutual respect" (1978, 46, my translation). What Burton attempts, then, is to establish a way of communicating about the conditions of respect between author and reader, to be as impertinent as possible without losing the reader's respect, by making the reader identify with the author's role.

(113). Here as elsewhere, Burton is extremely conscious and cautious of the injury that words alone can inflict. They can "hurt" and do the reader "harme" (24), having a material quality that can be hard as rock: "*Lapides loquitur* (so said *Agrippa de occ. Phil.*) & *caveant Lectores ne cerebrum iis excutiat* [He speaks stones, and readers should take care lest he beat out their brains with them]" (24).[35]

He continues with an appeal to the reader's "good favour and gratious acceptance" (113), which can only be 'presumed' by the author, whereas his true reaction ("excuse" or "accuse") cannot be controlled. The author's "last refuge" is the ultimate potential of ironic discourse: everything can always be retracted, can always be understood differently. This polyvalence is increased in print culture through the inevitable absence of the author from the text. Rant as he will, the author has no chance of explaining moot points after the fact of publication, no chance of correction and apology – until the next edition is printed. The only possible speaker position that can simulate the transcendence of these limitations, by staging the overstepping of the interplay of reflexive doublings (Burton/Democritus, author/reader, I/thou), is 'Nobody'. This ontological impossibility is not merely "the ultimate mask" (Fox 1976, 232), personified as "*Nicholas nemo*, or Mounsieur *no-body*" (*AM* 107), but the ultimate shedding of all masks in the act of negation. 'Nobody' is the first in Burton's list of exceptions from universal madness, and he is declared to be the author of the preface: "I writ this and published this οὖτις ἔλεγεν [No-one was speaking], it is *neminis nihil* [nothing by No-one]" (111–12). In the form of a declaration of absence, this is the ultimate staging of authorial irony as transcendent negativity.

Through his stagings of authorial doubling, mirroring, and negativity in the preface, Burton refers the reader to the media conditions that underlie the *Anatomy*. He encourages readers to question their motivations in reading a text on melancholy, and in particular a lengthy preface that, depending on one's point of view, is either a brilliant invitation to readerly self-questioning or a very immodest lecture on writerly modesty. Deciphering this double-edged, duplicitous text, readers can realise that they really are "the subject" of Burton's "Discourse" (1), in the triple sense of being its theme, its master, and its servant. After this realisation, they can indeed see themselves reflected in the author's mirror image, as "The Argument of the Frontispeice" promises, and "*command*, Reader *Adew*". If readers are willing to enter into Burton's game, they will learn that irony is "a way of controlling melancholy through play",

---

35 Burton is quoting Agrippa von Nettesheim, *De occulta philosophia*; cf. *AM* 4: 49. The motif of words as weapons is very widespread in early modernity and probably reflects a wider cultural concern with the 'magic' and uncanny powers of language and communication, even at a distance, through books. Thus Milton, in *Areopagitica*, famously asserts that "Books are not absolutely dead things, but doe contain a potencie of life in them" (1953b, 492) – although he then twists this argument around to declare that 'killing' a book through pre-publication censorship may be worse than killing a man. In a Burtonian vein, he later calls books "usefull drugs and materialls wherewith to temper and compose effective and strong med'cins, which mans life cannot want" (521).

and they will use irony themselves "to control [their] own melancholy" (Vicari 1989, 191). In this respect, the preface is not just an oddity but an integral part of the *Anatomy*: it teaches readers to focus their attention on their own experiences in reading the text, and on the conditions underlying these experiences, perhaps in order to facilitate what some critics have seen as Burton's homiletic intention in writing the *Anatomy*: a religious conversion.[36]

But one of the main problems with the play of authorial negativity is that, once it has been set in motion, it is virtually unstoppable. Thus, in the third edition of 1628, to which the emblematic title page and the two prefatory poems are added, Burton also inserts a Latin exhortation "*Lectori malè feriato*" (114), 'To the idle and frivolous reader', after the preface (the phrase is taken from Horace, *Odes* 4.6.14; see commentary in *AM* 4: 168–69). Before the *Anatomy* proper can begin, as he still promises at the end of "Democritus Junior to the Reader", Burton tackles the reader again, this time with a series of commands, prohibitions, and warnings, providing a kind of summary or abstract of the satirical import of the preface. The "gentle" (1, 113) "friendly" (16) or "good Reader" (23) is now exposed, and then dismissed, as the 'idle and frivolous' reader, in a final assertion of authorial superiority. I quote the English translation of this passage provided in the commentary:

> But to you, whoever you may be, I make proclamation that you be pleased not to rebuke the author of this work at a venture, nor mock him with fault-finding. No indeed, do not silently abuse him (to put it in a word) because of other people's criticism, nor be fool enough to express superior and sarcastic disapproval, nor accuse him falsely. For if it really is the case that Democritus Junior is what he professes to be, and is akin to his elder namesake, or indeed ever so little of the same kidney, then it is all up with you; he will be both censor and accuser ("being of a mischievous spleen"), will blow you apart into jests, crush you into salty witticisms, and sacrifice you, I may add, to the God of Mirth. Again I warn you not to cavil, lest while you insultingly defame or dishonourably disparage Democritus Junior, who has no quarrel with you, you should hear from some judicious friend the same thing that once upon a time the people of Abdera heard from Hippocrates, when they held that Democritus, their worthy townsman and fellow citizen, was a madman: "It is you, Democritus, who are wise, and the people of Abdera who are fools and madmen." *You have no more sense than the people of Abdera.* Having given you this warning in a few words, Reader who employ your leisure in idle frivolity, I bid you farewell.   (4: 168–69, emphasis original)

---

36 Being cured of melancholy would thus be a step on the way to salvation. Burton was, after all, a priest, and the much expanded Third Partition of the *Anatomy* on love melancholy and religious melancholy resembles a sermon in many respects. See Vicari 1989, 80–148, 186–87. Burton's book, Vicari explains, "does not teach its conclusions magisterially [. . .] because they can only be possessed authentically by being worked out through experience" (145).

In other words: "Reader *Adew.*" All these farewells are addressed to a traveller (and, if the reader is reading them aloud, also spoken *by* the traveller to himself) before he has even begun the journey proper.³⁷

Yet again, despite all the farewells, there is no finality to the author-reader relationship. Even after he has declared, in the third edition, that "I am now resolved never to put this Treatise out againe, *Ne quid nimis,* I will not hereafter adde, alter, or retract, I have done" (20), Burton keeps adding to the *Anatomy*, though he retains the somewhat paradoxical statement just cited in all subsequent editions (*AM* xxxix). In the fourth edition, which sees the first appearance of "The Argument of the Frontispeice", he adds another Latin poem following "*Lectori malè feriato*" (115), yet another text about doubling, this time about the duality of laughter and crying, as embodied in the philosophers Democritus and Heraclitus. In the fifth edition, he even manages to insert another appeal to the reader, again in Latin, physically situated "above the errata list on the last leaf" (xxxix). I quote the translation provided in the Oxford edition:

> TO THE READER
>
> Listen, good friend! This edition was begun not very long ago at Edinburgh, but was suppressed on the spot by our Printers. Subsequently, it was continued at London with their permission, and at last it was completed at Oxford; now for the fifth time it comes into the light as whatever kind of an edition it is [!]. In truth, if the first part does not indeed fit, nor the middle part with either the beginning or the end, on account of the frequent mistakes and omissions, whom do you blame? The Corrector, the Printer, this man, that man, everyone? I allow you to blame whomever you wish, this man, or that man, everyone. Meanwhile, I, the author, having been almost ignored by these men, am vexed in this manner. I am punished for their impudence. On account of their judgment I now sink into the depths, now again I am lifted up onto the stage, fastened to gates and door-posts, and to anyone you please I stand exposed as a slave put up for sale. But it is better, I suppose, to remember Harpocrates, lest I say something more serious against these men here, my masters; however irritated I am, I restrain myself, and as it is more fair, I here correct their mistakes and errors. (xl)

The perpetual wavering between authorial omnipotence and impotence cannot be brought to an end, unless by death. The very last, and now indeed final, note "To the Reader" is penned by Burton's printer and appended to the last leaf of the sixth edition: "Be pleased to know (Courteous Reader) that since the last Impression of this Book, the ingenuous Author of it is deceased, leaving a Copy of it exactly corrected, with severall considerable Additions by his own hand" (xliii). Thus the author of the

---

37 Readers are invited to imagine themselves as travellers, with the author as their guide, at p. 18: "if you vouchsafe to read this Treatise, it shall seeme no otherwise to thee, then the way to an ordinary Traveller, sometimes faire, sometimes foule [. . .]. I shall lead thee *per ardua montium, & lubrica vallium, & roscida cespitum, & glebosa camporum* [over steep mountains, through hazardous valleys, dewy lawns, and ploughed fields], through variety of objects, that which thou shalt like and surely dislike." Here, traditional concepts of the world as book and the book as landscape are brought together. Curiously, in the first edition, this passage was to be found in the "Conclusion of the Author *to the Reader*" which was dropped from subsequent editions (*AM* 3: 471).

Anatomy stages for the reader's benefit both the technical process and the epistemological conditions of making a book (as a commodity for the market, as a physical object produced by a collaboration of various people). He does so in the form of a game with multiple and changing roles. What is at stake in this game is ultimately nothing else than the changing ways in which knowledge can be communicated. Burton's theme in the peritexts to the *Anatomy* is the futility and at the same time the inevitability of attempts to bridge the gap between authors and readers in print culture. The discontents of theatricality are still clearly inscribed in Burton's author position, which wavers between affirmation and negation, apology and accusation; he regrets what he regards as a loss of authenticity in communication. Burton's author-image frequently tilts over into a grotesque figure, a victim of modernity: "lifted up onto the stage, fastened to gates and door-posts, and to anyone you please I stand exposed as a slave put up for sale" (xl). For Burton, the continuous reflection on the insecurity and the irresolvable contingency of the author-reader relationship leads to an unceasing oscillation between the poles of a double figure against the background of unpresentable negativity. We will meet this double figure again in the writings of Sir Thomas Browne, though with different values.

"Collaterall Truths" in the "Multiplicity of Writing": Sir Thomas Browne

The amount of critical attention paid to Sir Thomas Browne is extraordinary. Both his life and his writings have become and continue to be objects of persistent scrutiny, even though Browne's life appears to have been far from eventful or exceptional.[38] For a long time, style, or rather his plurality of styles, was the central aspect of reading Browne's writings as literary art. Browne's style has been valued as "the most artificial and literary of anyone of his century" (Cunningham 1996, 47), and he has even been credited with coining the word 'literary' (Huntley 1962, 169), if only in the now obsolete sense of "pertaining to the letters of the alphabet" (*OED*). Given such hyperbolic claims, it may be advisable to historicise those qualities said to be 'literary' in Browne's writings and to explicate his 'style' as a series of strategic responses to specific communicative situations.

As a brief glance at the *Oxford English Dictionary* shows, neither Burton nor Browne would have understood their writings or their style as 'literary' in the modern sense. A 'literary' reading of Browne, one that proceeds from the assumption that his texts have "value on account of [their] qualities of form" (*OED*), is a

---

38 Lytton Strachey is as usual reliably severe in his disparagement: "Everyone knows that Browne was a physician who lived at Norwich in the seventeenth century; and, so far as regards what one must call, for want of a better term, his 'life,' that is a sufficient summary of all there is to know" (1922, 31). The standard biography is now Barbour 2013.

thoroughly modern phenomenon. All attempts at defining his range of styles are retrospective constructions. While the critical debate on Browne as a stylist has not led to a final agreement, a stylometric study (Havenstein 1999, 201–202) has demonstrated that too rigid ideas of a 'baroque' style (Croll 1966) do not stand the test of quantitative methods. The relation of intellectual history to the history of style in the sixteenth and seventeenth centuries is still open to debate. The label 'baroque' has stuck to Browne, perhaps because it is sufficiently unspecific to connote many striking and sometimes conflicting tendencies in his writing: movement, spontaneity, gravity, a ceremonial tone, lack of logical progression, loose syntax, unconventional word choice and figurative language, abrupt transitions and mood changes (Havenstein 1999, 88–103, 118). Attempts to characterise Browne's writing with a single, if vague, descriptive label overlook its stylistic variety. As Austin Warren noted in 1951, "Browne has at least three styles", which Warren referred to as high, middle, and low and which he saw as represented by *The Garden of Cyrus*, *Religio Medici*, and *Pseudodoxia Epidemica* respectively (qtd. in Havenstein 1999, 94–95). A closer inspection would probably show that not only is there no unity of style in Browne as a writer but also no such unity within a single work, and what we observe instead is a fluid variability – a flexible, albeit controlled, range of expression. There may be some justification in calling this very flexibility 'baroque', but this issue of labelling loses much of its urgency if the question is shifted from a purely descriptive account of formal qualities to a historical account of his situatedness in seventeenth-century England and the social and cultural function(s) that his writings were thought to fulfil.

Browne has become an author of imaginative writing only in retrospect. To later generations of readers, the immediate functional and historical contexts of his writings are no longer evident without extensive research and commentary, which may have led to increasing attention being paid to aspects of "mere style" (Pater 1901, 158) and to the artfully contrived nature of his prose. But even if Browne would certainly have rejected the title of an author of "idle fictions" (1981, 57; *Pseudodoxia* 1.9), there is no doubt that he was a confident stylist. We know that he took great care to achieve an ornate literary style in his published work, quite in contrast to his personal letters. It is safe to assume that he regarded aspects of rhetoric and style as integral to the communicative purposes of his writings and that he adapted them to specific situations.

Burton's response to the contingency of modern knowledge is to create a textual maze surrounded by a complex and cumbersome machinery of peritextual evasions, implicating and activating each individual reader. Browne's response is to realign reader and author on a shared quest for knowledge that proceeds from an awareness of contingency and leads towards a programme of self-observation and self-cultivation. He responds to the existing "multiplicity of writing" by multiplying it even further: as he says in the *Garden of Cyrus*, "Of old things we write something new" (1964a, 86). The success of this multiplicatory function of writing, proceeding by means of "excursions [. . .] and collaterall truths" (ibid.), depends to a large extent on a programme of stylistic experiment and formal self-reflection. It is in this sense that Browne's writing could be said to embody a particular historical form of *literary knowledge,* not merely a literary approach to objects of knowledge. The means by which this knowledge is gained and communicated are twofold: on the one hand, linguistic *stylisation,* a controlled and reflected deviation from communicative normalcy, and on the other hand an *epistemology of contingency,* a method of observation and thought that, in the absence of certainty and reliable authority, concentrates on the probable, the "collaterall" and the individual, and views its objects from "Angles of Contingency", meaning "poorly" or from "the least of Angles" (Browne 2012, 138; *Hydriotaphia,* ch. 4).

Some of Browne's earliest compositions, Latin writings of an undergraduate at Broadgates Hall (later Pembroke College, Oxford), are humanist essays in style and rhetoric. As one of his modern editors comments (Keynes 1964, xvi), "Browne seems to have amused himself by bringing into his compositions every catch phrase and idiom related to his subject that he could think of, and the result has sometimes been so allusive as to be almost untranslatable." This accumulation of commonplaces notwithstanding, in one of these pieces, "Amico Opus Arduum Meditanti" ("To a Friend Intending a Difficult Work"), Browne recommends the following precepts:

> Force not your theme into narrow circuit, run not on with prolix trail in small matters to fill a thousand pages. [. . .] So be neither diffuse with damp and slippery words nor blunt the edge of your discourse by abruptness of style. Study in particular the purest period of style, that those who move only to Cicerionian rhythm call you not a Celt. [. . .] Only let your language match your subject, then it will be shapely and free; but take care all the time not to overwhelm your work [*rem*] in a spate of words [*verborum cataclysmo*] [. . .]. (1964b, 3: 154–55)

Browne's intricate Latin phrasing indicates a penchant for rhetorical style but also for its theoretical reflection. However, the verbal overkill (*verborum cataclysmus*) that he warns against in this text also betrays a tendency towards images, metaphors, and conceits that threaten to overwhelm the subject matter. For example, at the end of a meditation on life, death, and the possibility of attaining virtue, full of stoic commonplaces, the classical image of "the play of life" (*mimus vitae*) is transformed into a spectator sport observed from two perspectives simultaneously, that of the actors and spectators. The result is two paragraphs that read like Kafka translated into Latin (or English, the language in which I cite them here):

> Let me speak in terms of sport: our life is a race to which we are summoned by lot from fate's stable, set high or low in the car, and we drive our trace-horses badly. Often we crash before reaching the dolphins, we seldom pass the turning point, we mostly stop before the circuit-marks are finished, the course is hardly ever completed.
>
> We pour into the theatre of life in a great rabble, there are not enough entrances, gangways, rows, or sections for this silly show [*inanibus spectaculis*]. From top to bottom of the theatre few are satisfied with their seats. The knights get into the senators' seats, the populace into the knights'. No-one takes notice of Lectius, hardly anyone considers Oceanus. From the ceiling to the floor everyone watches comic and savage acts [*ludicra juxta ac saeva*] with the same expression, few protest, more applaud. We ourselves in the end on the field of death

> [*arena mortis*] repay in all seriousness the price of folly, mangled by disease, wounded by many darts, without hope of release, we are dragged away into the pit of hell. (3: 174)

Even the moralistic finale of this text is dominated by the image of the circus arena; the hyperbolic concreteness of the setting undermines the moral earnestness of the statement. Moral urgency is jettisoned for visual and imaginative effects of style. Already in this early text, observation becomes contingent: perspectival and performative. Browne cannot or will not decide what perspective to follow, the participants' or the spectators', and therefore attempts to integrate both – which leads to a jarring conflation of points of view.

The consequences of such stylistic self-consciousness are highly problematic. Is the comic effect of an increased 'literariness' intentional or involuntary? Is he deliberately playing with language? How are we to read his engagements with serious religious questions, his allusions to mystic experiences and esoteric knowledge (like the Kabbalah and alchemy) when his artistic prose deflects our attention away from them? It has been affirmed, for instance, that Browne's uniqueness consists in presenting *himself* instead of merely the conclusions he arrived at (Wiley 1952, 144), but this self is not merely eloquent but ultimately elusive – there is always more than 'self', or, in Browne's own words, "every man is not onely himselfe" (2012, 10; *Religio* 1.6). Language, for Browne as for Burton, is not a transparent medium or vehicle of knowledge, but has a material and palpable object quality. There is an aspect of resistance in language that intervenes between reality and semiotic representations. Rhetoric as a cultural technique uses this predicament to transform it into an advantage: its fundamental assumption is the uncertainty, contingency, and non-totalisability of knowledge, representation, and communication. With regard to Browne, a reading that focuses on rhetoric will follow and expand on Coleridge's injunction that Browne's writings, especially the *Religio Medici*, "ought to [be] considered [. . .] in a *dramatic* & not in a metaphysical View" (Coleridge 1955, 438). What rhetoric, as the performative, action-oriented, and political aspect of communication establishes, or hopes to establish, is not a stable epistemology (based on transtemporal identity, for instance on the eternal verities of Scripture), but a provisional, contingent, or 'collateral' access to truth, a truth that is admittedly imperfect and subject to revision (see Blumenberg 1981, 104–36; cf. Kroll 1991, 3–8).

The ambiguous rhetorical stance, most noticeable in *Religio Medici*, its shifting between the presentation of an intimate personal confession and the dramatic or ironic staging of a persona, between self-description and self-distancing, forces the reader time and again to change perspective and, as in Burton's case, "to see 'round' the offered persona" (Mulryne 1982, 65). It becomes impossible to focus only on the identity of the person behind the persona, or on the persona in front of the person. The result is not an expression of the self, nor a mimetic mirroring of reality, but neither is it "mere style" (Pater) or "spiritual gymnastics" (Dunn 1950, 42). Dramatic modes of presentation, in Browne as in Burton, are inconclusive, momentary and tactical, a "kinetic" (Straznicky 1990, 212) wavering between different modes of presentation, several viewpoints, multiple epistemological orientations.

Browne's rhetoric is conciliatory and non-violent, often rather passive and careful, even evasive. "These opinions", he states in *Religio Medici* (1.7), "I never maintained with pertinacity, or endeavoured to enveagle any mans beliefe unto mine" (2012, 11). His "dislike" of the name 'Protestant' (5, *Religio* 1.2) is eloquent testimony both of his non-sectarian attitude as well as to the close attention he pays to words. In *Religio Medici*, this non-aggressive rhetoric is made possible by the speaker's unusual discursive position, which remains ambiguously semi-private and semi-public. In the preface "To the Reader", prefixed to the 1643 edition, one year after its first unauthorised printing, Browne emphasises his anti-persuasive attitude:

> He that shall peruse that worke, and shall take notice of sundry particularities and personall expressions thererin, will easily discerne the intention was not publick: and being a private exercise directed to my selfe, what is delivered therein was rather a memoriall unto me then an example or rule unto any other: and therefore if there bee any singularitie therein correspondent unto the private conceptions of any man, it doth not advantage them; or if dissentaneous thereunto, it no way overthrowes them. (4)

Here as elsewhere the text teems with signal words that emphasise individuality: "particularities", "personall expressions", "private exercise", "my selfe", "unto me", "singularitie", "private". In a letter to Digby, Browne calls this text "an exercise unto my self, rather then exercitation for any other" (qtd. in Browne 1964a, 76). At the same time, the author distances himself from "that worke" – referring to the unauthorised 1642 edition in the past tense, as though it were a completely different text. The preface deflects what the main text continuously celebrates. Here, Browne indeed "protest[s]" (2012, 4) but only to apologise for the individuality of his discourse by referring first to a lack of books ("the assistance of any good booke") and then to his youth at the time of writing, "seven yeares past". Browne is thirty-seven when the authorised edition is printed; in the text, he states that he is still under thirty: "nor hath my pulse beate thirty yeares" (47; *Religio* 1.41). Clearly, the Civil War that began in 1642 has left its traces in this preface; any text with the word 'religion' in the title is now a potential threat, and Browne's writing from the mid-1630s needs to be carefully presented to accommodate the changed climate. It can no longer be read with the same "leisurable" (3) ease in which it was composed. Taking responsibility for it, after it had been circulating in manuscript and "was most imperfectly and surreptitiously published" (3), Browne is now forced to engage in a strange rhetorical manoeuvre that transcends the usual prefatory apologies and appeals to benevolence. In making "publick" what is actually and of its own nature "private", but what has already been forced out of its private context, he attempts to reclaim it for himself and to reinstate, if only rhetorically, its original condition.

The preface casts the Civil War itself in terms of a conflict and confusion between public and private spheres of experience. Its social upheaval is eclipsed in Browne's writings – in the letter to Digby, he merely refers with casual understatement to "the liberty of these times" (1964a, 76) – but it is subtly mirrored in the fate of his book as described in the preface. Here, the confusion about the book's private or public quality becomes a metonymy for the condition of England during the war. The Senecan cliché of its beginning already introduces a contrast between private and public sphere whose collapse is imminent:

> Certainly that man were greedy of life, who should desire to live when all the world were at an end; and he must needs be very impatient, who would repine at death in the societie of all things that suffer under it. Had not almost every man suffered by the presse; or were not the tyranny thereof become universall; I had not wanted reason for complaint: but in times wherein I have lived to behold the highest perversion of that excellent invention; the name of his Majesty defamed, the honour of Parliament depraved, the writings of both depravedly, anticipatively, counterfeitly imprinted; complaints may seeme ridiculous in private persons, and men of my condition may be as incapable of affronts, as hopelesse of their reparations.
> (Browne 2012, 3)

Here the "excellent invention" of the printing press indeed figures as an 'agent of change' (Eisenstein 1979), inducing suffering and – via the rhetorical connection between the two occurrences of the word 'suffer' – even death. This metaphor would become literally true when the "defamed" king was executed in 1649. The allusion here is to the breakdown of censorship in 1640, but the printing press is only one instance of the general upheaval. As Browne is well aware, the social effects of change are irreversible, "hopelesse", and the book he is publishing in order to guarantee textual fixity can no longer be quite the same book he once wrote.[39] Seeing his book in print without having given his *imprimatur* was disconcerting for Browne, who everywhere in his text praises the value of handwriting over the ambiguous nature of print. God needed no printing press to publish his work. Using the traditional metaphor of the world as book, Browne calls nature "that universall and publik Manuscript" (2012, 19; *Religio* 1.16). In another passage, the "hand of God" is interpreted as a writing hand: "the line of our dayes is drawne by night, and the various effects therein by a pencill that is invisible; wherein though wee confesse our ignorance, I am sure we doe not erre, if wee saye, it is the hand of God" (48, *Religio* 1.43). The printing press, on the other hand, is likened to a deadly weapon, being one of those "inventions in *Germany* [. . .] which are not without their incommodities, and 'tis disputable whether they exceed not their use and commodities" (30, 1.24) – the other inventions being the compass and guns (a triad

---

[39] Although there are few substantive changes to extant manuscript versions or to the two editions of 1642, Browne's minor revisions and excisions are sometimes significant, mostly avoiding too unambiguous references to what radical Protestants would have regarded as 'popery' or as heretical. Cf. the textual notes in the edition by L. C. Martin, Browne 1964a, 261–68, and for a more detailed critical assessment Post 1985. Critics have for a long time ignored the political implications of Browne's writing. Michael Wilding (1987, 95, 99–100) deserves credit for being the first to read the changes in the 1643 version of the *Religio* as political commentaries; see also Berensmeyer 2006.

derived from Bacon's *Novum Organon*). In a rare moment of invective, Browne complains about the abundance of printed books and recommends book-burning as an antidote to the scribblings of religious enthusiasts: "to condemne to the fire those swarms and millions of *Rhapsodies*, begotten onely to distract and abuse the weaker judgements of Scholars, and to maintain the Trade and Mystery of Typographers" (ibid.).

Having seen his opinions made public, publicly to apologise for them as private does not relieve them from their now altered, publicised state – even less so in a time and country that finds the very distinction between private and public increasingly difficult to uphold. Therefore, in a final rhetorical twist, Browne lets the distinction collapse and invokes the public as a congeries of individuals: "Lastly all that is contained therein is in submission unto maturer discernments, and as I have declared [cf. 1.60] shall no further father them then the best and learned judgements shall authorize them; under favour of which considerations I have made its secrecie publike and committed the truth thereof to every ingenuous Reader" (4).

Here, Browne professes not to be interested in swaying public opinion but in the individual *ingenium* or 'discernment' of the reader who will understand "all that is contained therein" better than the author himself. This important declaration of purpose – the text's intended effect is not public but personal – needs to be related to the preceding sentence. This is one of Browne's very few direct statements on style and language, here also in the apologetic vein: "There are many things delivered Rhetorically, many expressions therein meerely Tropicall, and as they best illustrate my intention; and therefore also there are many things to be taken in a soft and flexible sense, and not to be called unto the rigid test of reason" (2012, 4). Again, rhetoric is not understood primarily as a persuasive use of language but is located on the private side of the equation ("my intention"). The function of rhetorical-tropical language is to enable individual insights into the most incommunicable, private "secrecie" of a person. By a subtle rhetorical move, both "reason" and "truth" lose at least some of their "rigid" nature as concepts that belong to the public side of the distinction; if readers are benevolent, they will tolerate the "soft and flexible sense" and thereby discern *their own* "truth" in the text. ("I have committed the truth thereof to every ingenuous Reader.") Tolerance of the other's truth implies the admitted relativity of knowledge and the indeterminacy of at least some 'indifferent' aspects of religion. As he formulates in the main text, "every mans owne reason is his best *Oedipus*" (9, 1.6). We should bear in mind that Browne himself imposes social restrictions on intellectual latitude, excluding "those vulgar heads that looke asquint on the face of truth" (7, 1.3). In this respect, he echoes the Canon of Toledo in Cervantes's *Don Quijote* for whom it is also of primary importance to 'wed' the reader's understanding to whatever is being read; but this injunction is now reinterpreted into a license for latitude for those happy few who can claim to possess such a refined understanding: they can use their own reason without being harmed by what they read or think.[40]

Browne's implicit theory of reading and interpretation also becomes relevant whenever he addresses the question of literal vs. tropological readings of Scripture. On this hotly debated issue, he takes a position that corresponds to what he states in the preface: "unspeakable mysteries in the Scriptures are often delivered in a vulgar and illustrative way, and being written unto man, are delivered, not as they truely are, but as they may bee understood" (2012, 51, *Religio* 1.45). The reader who returns to the preface from such passages of the main text is invited to draw an analogy between Browne's reading of Scripture and the "soft and flexible" understanding he demands for his own text. Metaphorical latitude is also his solution to the problem of reconciling reason, passion (or affection) and faith, a problem posed by all those queries that arise in literal readings of the Bible and instil doubt in the believer. This, Browne opines, is the devil's way of tempting the curious:

> There are, as in Philosophy, so in Divinity, sturdy doubts, and boysterous objections, wherewith the unhappinesse of our knowledge too neerely acquainteth us. [. . .] Thus the Devill playd at Chesse with mee, and yeelding a pawne, thought to gaine a Queen of me, taking advantage of my honest endeavours; and whilst I labour'd to raise the structure of my reason, hee striv'd to undermine the edifice of my faith. (24, 1.19)

Browne's solution to fend off what he calls "the Rhetorick of Satan" (25, 1.20) is a compromise between the three faculties that fight each other for control of the soul. As is evident in the preface, Browne abhors disorder and dissent in the commonwealth. Similarly, he imagines the ideal government of the soul as a political union of three factions – "affection, faith, and reason" – that resolve their "fewds and angry dissentions" into agreement by "a moderate and peaceable discretion":

> For there is in our soule a kind of Triumvirate, or Triple government of three competitors, which distract the peace of this our Common-wealth, not lesse than did that other the State of Rome.
> As Reason is a rebell unto Faith, so passion unto Reason: As the propositions of Faith seeme absurd unto Reason, so the Theorems of Reason unto passion, and both unto Faith; yet a moderate and peaceable discretion may so state and order the matter, that they may bee all Kings, and yet make but one Monarchy, every one exercising his Soveraignty and Prerogative in a due time and place, according to the restraint and limit of circumstance. (23–24, 1.19)

Faith must not be too literal, reason not too rigid, and the affections not too immoderate, for this system of mental checks and balances to work. Language and interpretation must be adapted accordingly, which is where Browne distinguishes good from bad rhetoric, his own non-coercive use of language from both that persuasive argumentation of Satan (who here represents unmitigated Baconian reason) and the "severe Schools" (15, 1.12), those "Churches and Sects" that "usurpe the gates of heaven,

---

[40] In this respect, Browne's argument resembles Milton's in the *Areopagitica*.

and turne the key against each other" (62, 1.56). Browne's good rhetoric is a rhetoric of *description* instead of *definition*, "soft and flexible" instead of "rigid" and "severe" (2012, 4, 15). The rhetoric of persuasion, on the other hand, is for the masses, the "vulgar, whose eares are opener to Rhetorick then Logick" and on whom the "invectives of the Pulpit may perchance produce a good effect" (8–9, 1.5). Such rhetoric, like the beggars in 2.2, is said to appeal "more to passion than reason" (67, 2.2) – and is clearly, for Browne, an inferior and disreputable use of language: to "thinke to recall men to reason, by a fit of passion" is a "compleate [. . .] piece of madnesse", he avers (71, 2.4). Indeed, he observes that "the Rhetoricke wherewith I perswade another cannot perswade my selfe" (61, 1.55). Browne's 'good' rhetoric is not a rhetoric of persuasion, but one of imagination, not aimed at persuading another but at understanding one's changing self.

In order to get a better understanding of Browne's thinking and its associated rhetorical manoeuvres, we need to look more closely at his idea of religion. In early modernity, religion is a crucial intersection between personal beliefs and communal duties, a place where individual subjects are decidedly not their own masters. Browne's *Religio Medici* attempts to find a position that remedies this irremediable paradox of freedom and subjection. Already in its title, the book is original and unusual for the insinuation that religion can be reduced to subjective experience and belief: the religion of a physician is a subjective business, or at least provocatively the business of a professional group, not the subject of a dogmatic treatise that purports to be applicable to *every* Christian, or at least to those on the right side of one doctrinal divide. It would be wrong to assume that Browne's concept of religion is a modern one that reduces it solely to a matter of individual discretion. Although he sometimes appears to come close to the Luhmannian notion that, in modernity, there are only religious reasons for being religious (Luhmann 2000), Browne's concept of individuality is not one of self-motivation and self-reliance, but is fraught with contradictions and paradoxes that make it impossible for him to draw any clear dividing line between individual experience and social communication. For Browne, religion is an intersection between the private and public domains, a place where one side of the distinction merges with the other. The private itself is not a unified whole but a complex organisation, a "Common-wealth" (2012, 23) with possibly disagreeing factions (reason, passion, and faith) that are in need of a mental balancing act. The precarious order of human inwardness mirrors that of the state; the physically embodied self and the body politic become metaphors for one another. Browne's political metaphors of selfhood derive from the medical and physiological discourse of his time. In Burton's *Anatomy*, brain, heart and belly form a political triumvirate, with the brain as "privy Councellour" and "the heart as king" (1: 144–46); in Thomas Wright's *The Passions of the Minde in Generall* (2nd ed. 1604), the soul is described as a "Common-weale" disturbed by "inordinate Passions." Wright's political language so closely resembles Browne's as to suggest a direct influence: "Passions either rebell against Reason their Lord and King, or oppose themselues one against another; [. . .]. This internall Combat and spirituall

Contradiction euery spirituall man daily perceiueth, for inordinate Passions, will he, nill he, cease not almost hourely to rise vp against Reason, and so molest him, troubling the rest and quietnesse of his Soule" (Wright 1971, 68–69). For Browne, mental flexibility and benevolence rather than rigid self-control are the basis of such order and stability of selfhood, and flexible, non-persuasive and nonviolent language is the means to promote it. More than any other kind of language, such discourse depends upon – and Browne therefore invokes – the tolerance of the "ingenuous Reader" (2012, 4). In this respect, Browne's writing and religion correspond.

We can now see how important and necessary the preface is for the *Religio*. Although its excuse of the "Rhetorical" and "Tropicall" latitude of the writing (Browne 2012, 4) appears so bland and conventional, it actually anticipates and underlines Browne's main argument. The preface demands the reader not to put the book to "the rigid test of reason" (ibid.), but this turns out to be a central message of the text that follows, which includes a plea for reason to be "more pliable to the will of faith" (13, 1.10). It is a demand for a not-too-literal interpretation of the Bible, a political image of the soul as a "Common-wealth" best governed by a flexible system of checks and balances (23, 1.19), and a concept of rhetoric that promotes flexible and imaginative self-exploration instead of polemic and polemogenic persuasion.

Victoria Silver's description of *Religio Medici* as an "inverse polemic" (1990, 96) is therefore particularly apt because the text proposes contingency instead of certainty and figures instead of definitions. Pitting a literal mode of thought, which confers a reality status upon artificial distinctions and thereby leads to the formation of sects and creeds, against a tropological mode in which words and concepts are shown as mental figments, Browne's "loose nominalism" (99) transforms his text into "a theater where linguistic usage symbolically enacts the religious and political conflict of his age" (105). The elements of this 'drama', however, are not characters speaking words and performing actions on a stage "but the tropisms of human intellection and discourse" (105). Yet not only in Browne's language is the conflict, religious as well as political, "symbolically enact[ed]" but also in the individual soul or mind. Browne performs his style of thought in a theatre of language. But even this metaphor should not be taken either too literally or too metaphorically. The traditional metaphor of the world as as stage is of little interest to him; he uses it in the *Religio*, with the usual trappings ("the world to mee is but a dreame, or mockshow, and wee all therein but Pantalones and Antickes to my severer contemplations", Browne 2012, 47, 1.41), but only to pass on to other, weightier matters. His writing is 'dramatic' by default; there is no other way of 'speaking the self' or of letting the self speak itself. Periphrasis, allegory, metaphorical language, and the "soft and flexible sense" (4) only enter into his considerations at those points (which, admittedly, are quickly reached in religious debate) when reason and experience – "the argument of our proper senses" (14, 1.10) – no longer suffice: "where I cannot satisfie my reason, I love to humour my fancy", he notes (13, 1.10).

Where concepts cannot reach, images act as supplements to rational contemplation. Browne calls the ability to generate such images "fancy" and "imagination" (sometimes in the plural as "imaginations"). This mental faculty establishes an inner sanctum protected from the intrusion of persuasive rhetoric, be it the devil's insinuations or even one's own doubts. He also uses 'fancy' as a verb to mean 'imagine' or even 'visualise', as in: "I [. . .] have fancyed to my selfe the presence of my deare and worthiest friends" (2012, 53, 1.47). 'Fancy' also extends to the activity of dreaming, which provides "surely a neerer apprehension of any thing that delights us [. . .] than [. . .] our waked senses" (82, 2.11). When the body and the senses are at rest, "the slumber of the body" (83) allows the soul to wake and dreams allow reason to be more "fruitfull" (ibid.) than in its waking hours. "[Sleep] is the ligation of sense, but the liberty of reason, and our awaking conceptions doe not match the fancies of our sleepes" (ibid.). Reason is thus, for Browne, not opposed to fancy and imagination, not confined to rationality, but it encompasses a wider and more general creative mental faculty, the proper activity of what Browne calls 'the soul'. This inner space of 'reasoning' is the proper sphere of individual religious experience for Browne, although it does not appear to be a space of immediate communication with the divine but of self-reflection and intellectual contemplation that attempts to appease the scientific thirst for knowledge and reconcile it with certain tenets of faith. This space is an individual, *private* sphere, removed from worldly pressures: Browne refers to it as "solitary recreation" (12, 1.9) and as "my solitary and retired imaginations" (14, 1.11) – the phrase recurs as "my retired and solitary imaginations" (53, 1.47), "my retired imaginations" (81, 2.10), and "our sequestred imaginations" (ibid.); other near-synonyms for this kind of inward experience are "my devotion" (15, 1.13) and "my humble speculations" (16, 1.13). The personal pronoun, indicating subjectivity, is never discarded.

Of course Browne, unlike Freud, does not sketch a more precise topology of this inner space, but it cannot be doubted that he conceives of it as a kind of contact zone with the external world and the divine: consider, for example, his assurance that "there is a common Spirit that playes within us, yet makes no part of us, and that is the Spirit of God" (36, 1.32). If Freud is credited with having disbanded the traditional notion of the psyche as a unified essence, Browne's ideas of the soul as a triple-governed commonwealth and as a meeting place or even a playing space for the divine spirit seem to anticipate this. Like the human body, whose "wals of flesh" (42, 1.37) cannot offer permanence because the body is "nothing but an elementall composition, and a fabricke that must fall to ashes" (ibid.), the soul for Browne is in danger of "corruption" (81, 2.10). Although it is an inner space unto itself, "sequestred" and "retired" from society, inner space mirrors social life and problems of interaction because "there is no such thing as solitude, nor any thing that can be said to be [. . .] truely alone, and by its self, which is not truely one, and such is onely God: All others doe transcend an unity, and so by consequence are many" (ibid.). The activity of self-reflection transcends the unity of a self by doubling or even further multiplying it; the self is also, apart from being a playground for the Holy Spirit, disturbed by the infiltrations of the devil, "that unruly rebel that musters up those disordered motions, which accompany our sequestred imaginations" (ibid.). Browne's concept of unstable selfhood displays a striking reliance on the political language of his time: corruption, rebellion, disorder, commerce, and the commonwealth.

In the second part of the *Religio*, which deals less with questions of theological dogma than with ethical questions of charity and love, the political theory of the soul is taken up again and even radicalised to some extent. Even more than theoretical questions of faith and hope, the necessity of making moral decisions leads Browne to an image of the self not as a unity but as a multiplicity of both internal and external forces in motion and in conflict:

> I were unjust unto mine owne conscience, if I should say I am at variance with any thing like my selfe, I finde there are many pieces in this one fabricke of man; this frame is raised upon a masse of Antipathies: I am one mee thinkes, but as the world; wherein notwithstanding there are a swarme of distinct essences, and in them another world of contrarieties; wee carry private and domesticke enemies within, publike and more hostile adversaries without. [. . .] Let mee be nothing if within the compasse of my selfe, I doe not find the battell of *Lepanto*, passion against reason, reason against faith, faith against the Devill, and my conscience against all. (2012, 75, 2.7)

"Conscience" is a new player in the game, introduced by Browne as "another man within mee that's angry with mee, rebukes, commands, and dastards mee" (ibid.). In the Battle of Lepanto, the Venetians defeated the Ottoman Turks in 1570; although Browne probably intends it as a metaphor of a victory of Christian faith against unbelief or false beliefs, it does not really seem appropriate to the battle that he describes, which is a battle among five distinct parties: passion, reason, faith, the devil, and Browne's conscience. It remains quite unclear who will emerge victorious from the fray. As in the earlier commonwealth analogy (1.19), the solution is a homeostatic system of checks and balances, although the terms with which balance is achieved are now much more difficult.

Browne had previously argued that the concept of the microcosm "or little world" was not "onely a pleasant trope of Rhetorick" but that "there was a reall truth therein" (39, 1.34). Now he gives it a moral significance: "It is no breach of charity to our selves to be at variance with our vices, nor to abhorre that part of us, which is an enemy to the ground of charity, our God; wherein wee doe but imitate our great selves the world, whose divided Antipathies and contrary faces doe yet carry a charitable regard unto the whole, by their particular discords preserving the common harmony, and keeping in fetters those powers, whose rebellions once Masters, might bee the ruine of all" (76, 2.7). If Browne is interesting as a writer on religion, he is at least as interesting as a political theorist. Both occupations are inextricably intertwined, as his thoughts on religion segue into meditations on the nature of man and the nature of state and government (see also Guibbory 1998, 119). His greatest difficulty as a political thinker is that he tries to define human thought and social organisation at the same time. As we have briefly glimpsed above, in reading the first paragraph of Dryden's *Essay*, this difficulty derives from the ontological problem of understanding the relation of a whole and its parts: society is composed of individuals, but at some point their individualities become indistinguishable in a "multitude, that numerous piece of monstrosity" and, at that point, dangerous to other individuals and to society as a whole (66, 2.1). As William Davenant puts it in his *Preface to Gondibert*: "Wolves are commonly harmlesse when they are met alone, but very uncivill in Herds" (1971, 12–13). Browne, however, proposes no practical or political solution to this Hobbesian problem, apart from the two instances (*Religio* 1.19 and 2.7) when he vaguely outlines a checks-and-balances system based on the proto–Mandevillean paradoxes that "particular discords preserv[e] the common harmony" (76, 2.7) and that "contraries [like virtue and vice], though they destroy one another, are yet the life of one another" (71, 2.4). It is tempting to read passages like these in the light of contemporaneous political theory. Their potential acceptance of the notion of a mixed government of king and parliament, which had only been introduced into official English political thought in 1642, combines, as these passages do, an older, authoritarian concept of hierarchical order (the 'great chain of being') with a republican concept of a kinetic order of mutually balanced elements (see Pocock 1975, 349, 358, 361–71). The consequences to be drawn from this discursive blend remain unclear because they are never systematically developed.

Browne radicalises the problem of parts and wholes when he takes a closer look at individuals and finds the same structure: a whole made up of discordant parts. The human microcosm is a fractal image of the macrocosm, which consists of numerous individuals who are themselves divided into smaller f(r)actions: a Leviathan consisting of Leviathans. Only if these warring forces are maintained in a 'reasonable' balance between reason, faith, and passion, with the devil kept at bay and the voice of conscience not completely excluded, can this precarious system achieve the homeostasis of good government, a balance that he sees embodied in religious tolerance and that his concept of 'good' rhetoric attempts to enact linguistically.

Browne's view of religious tolerance and human experience in the *Religio* owes much to classical stoic and skeptic philosophy (Shifflett 1998; Popkin 1964; Allen 1964; Kahn 1985; Lobsien 1999). In a section devoted to the sin of pride, it is "the uncertainty of knowledge" that leads the intellectual toward humility and skepticism: "I perceive the wisest heads prove at last, almost all Scepticks, and stand like *Janus* in the field of knowledge" (2012, 78; *Religio* 2.8). Browne goes on to recommend, in a humanist vein, that "it is better to sit downe in a modest ignorance, & rest contented with the naturall blessing of our owne reasons, then buy the uncertaine knowledge of this life, with sweat and vexation, which death gives every foole gratis" (ibid.). Nevertheless, he devotes much of his time and more than six hundred printed pages to a book dedicated to the improvement of just this "uncertaine knowledge" – a book that, like Burton, he kept revising and re-editing over a period of twenty-six years between 1646 (first edition) and 1672 (sixth edition): *Pseudodoxia Epidemica: or,*

Enquiries into Very many received Tenents, And commonly presumed Truths (Robbins 1981, liii; see Hack-Molitor 2001, 107–60).

In the *Religio,* Browne had come upon the epistemological principle for this book: "wee doe but learne to day, what our better advanced judgements will unteach us to morrow" (2012, 77, 2.8). He reiterates it in the preface to *Pseudodoxia*: "knowledge is made by oblivion; and to purchase a clear and warrantable body of Truth, we must forget and part with much wee know" (1981, 1). This Baconian programme separates *Pseudodoxia* from Burton's *Anatomy* and other encyclopedic projects of the age. Browne's purpose is not to collect and pass on knowledge gleaned from authorities but to weed out false knowledge. In collecting "vulgar errors" – an alternative title by which the book has also become known – *Pseudodoxia* succumbs to a paradox: false knowledge is not eliminated but preserved in yet another cabinet of wonder in book form. Moreover, its errors are far from "vulgar"; on the contrary, they derive from learned and revered authorities, mostly from antiquity and the Middle Ages. They range from the mundane and superstitious ("That bitter Almonds are preservatives against Ebriety") to the esoteric ("Of the Vnicornes horne") and from questions of history ("That the Army of Xerxes drank whole Rivers dry") to questions of biblical interpretation ("That there was no Rainebow before the floud").[41] Browne avoids more intricate speculation and focuses on issues that are irrelevant with regard to doctrinal debate: "indifferent truths", as he calls them in the preface (4): "We cannot expect the frowne of *Theologie* herein; nor can they which behold the present state of things, and controversie of points so long received in Divinity, condemne our sober enquiries in the doubtfull appertinancies of Arts, and Receptaries of Philosophy" (3–4). Unlike the literary bravura performance of the *Religio,* the style of *Pseudodoxia* is more restrained, matter-of-fact, defensive, intent on avoiding conflict. Instead of the 'recreative' private isolation of the *Religio,* the later book is of a decidedly public nature, even considering the – unrealised – possibility of coauthorship: it would have been "more advantageous [. . .] unto Truth, to have fallen into the endeavours of some cooperating advancers" (1).

Indeed, Browne's "single and unsupported endeavours" (1981, 1) have much in common with the scientific project of the Royal Society. The title page of the first edition bears an inscription from Scaliger, who contrasts knowledge gleaned from books and authorities with first-hand knowledge gained by observation of 'things themselves'. Accordingly, Browne's goal consists not only in "proposing [. . .] a large and copious List [of errors], but from experience and reason, attempting their decisions" (1). In a 1658 addition, he refers to "experience and solid reason" as "the two great pillars of truth" (288). The book is influenced by Francis Bacon's *Advancement of Learning* (1605/23) and his idea of progress in knowledge and science; Bacon had recommended the institution of a "*Calendar of Dubitations,* or *Problemes* in Nature" and a

---

41 Bk. 2, ch. 6; bk. 3, ch. 23; bk. 7, ch. 18; bk. 7, ch. 4.

"*Calendar of Falshoods*, and of *popular Errors* [. . .] that Sciences be no longer distemper'd and embased by them" (qtd. in Robbins 1981, xxx). Like Bacon, Browne begins with a general enquiry into the reasons and grounds of error, and his book roughly follows the structure of Bacon's *Advancement*. Browne used the 1640 English translation by Gilbert Wats, and the very words of Bacon's title appear in Browne's preface: "[. . .] those honoured Worthies, who endeavour the advancement of Learning" (4). Yet Bacon himself is mentioned but once, in a later passage where Browne refutes a minor experiment of "the learned Lord Verulam" (316).

Browne's interests are too deeply rooted in humanist learning to fit the new experimental science promoted by Bacon and, later, the Royal Society. His presentation of new knowledge is cast in the traditional mould of scholastic disputations, even though he shows an awareness that this mould is cracked. At the points where these cracks become particularly obvious, Browne most often resorts to wit, double entendre, and wordplay in order to communicate uncertainty. He adopts a rhetoric of contingency to overcome traditional patterns of thought more easily (see Nardo 1991, 174–75). Moreover, he retains a religious perspective on natural philosophy: the prime goal of expanding knowledge is wonder and admiration for God's creation. Thus 'knowledge' in *Pseudodoxia* can mean both *scientia*, knowledge of the nature of things, but also *sapientia*, knowledge in spiritual and religious matters – wisdom as well as learning. Truth is an attribute of God that man can only approximate imperfectly by the careful elimination of "untruths" (4).

Doubt and curiosity structure *Pseudodoxia* in ways reminiscent of early modern travel writing. When Browne presents himself as a traveller in an undiscovered country, "in the America and untravelled parts of truth" (3), such expressions may seem commonplace – they are echoed in Burton or Glanvill, for example – but the mode of travel structures *Pseudodoxia* inasmuch as it presents a blend of empirical observation and material taken from other sources; it contains detailed speculations about cultural and natural phenomena, including myths and folk tales. The traveller discovers not only new "parts of truth" (3) but also the relativity and uncertainty of one's own position (Campbell 1988). *Pseudodoxia*, then, is yet another stepping stone towards a literary culture understood as a culture of contingency.

The purpose of a travel narrative is both to inform and to entertain the reader. The Stationers' licence commends *Pseudodoxia* as "adorned with great variety of matter, and multiplicity of reading" (Robbins 1981, n. p. [lxiv]). Browne received congratulatory letters from correspondents like Henry Bate, who called his book "the greatest entertainement the kingdome could affoord mee" (qtd. in Robbins 1981, xxxix). Perhaps it is best understood as an early example of popular science writing. As such, it combines a range of compendious learning "to put [Browne's] contemporaries in touch with advanced, authoritative thought and discovery in mineralogy, botany, zoology, physiology, iconography, geography, history, theology, and classical scholarship" (Robbins 1981, xlix). Here we see the library and the cabinet of wonder combined; to write this book, Browne must have consulted "[a]bout 210 volumes in folio, 120 in quarto, and 120 in smaller formats" (Robbins xxi n.1). He is often so fascinated by the curiosities he presents that his interest in them outweighs his interest in the correction of errors. For example, when he cannot reach a satisfactory scientific explanation for "the Blacknesse of Negroes", he sees himself and his readers recompensed for the "capitall indiscovery" by the "many things of truth disclosed by the way": "And the collaterall verity, may unto reasonable speculations, some what requite the capitall indiscovery" (Browne 1981, 529–30).

Instead of presenting an unambiguous truth, Browne gives his readers a kaleidoscopic perspective on contingent truths. Moreover, he does not, like Burton, resign himself to the contingency of knowledge as an inevitable loss of certainty, but on the contrary regards the knowledge of contingency as a gain. This informs his entire thinking and writing. It is a style of thought that plays with contradictions, aporias and paradoxes, either resolved by referring them to a superior ontological unity (the union of contraries) or to a more radical admittance of undecidability. Browne's writing is characterised by an "enjoyment" of thought (Wiley 1952, 138) that is not "rigorous and logical" but "subjectively pleasing and imaginatively coherent" (Grant 1985, 109).

Browne's imaginative and unsystematic use of metaphysical concepts does not mean that he no longer takes metaphysical questions seriously. The risk he incurs lies in "confirming [. . .] the fictional status" of metaphysical language (Grant 1985, 104). But he never appears to see this as a problem, because this risk is controlled by a firm metaphysical belief in God as the only non-contingent element in Browne's thought. When he has demonstrated, in *Hydriotaphia,* that no human cultural and historical concept of an afterlife and of commemoration after death can ensure the "diuturnity" (2012, 131) of personal identity, he concludes that this can only be achieved by the Christian belief in resurrection: "But the most magnanimous resolution rests in the Christian Religion, which trampleth upon pride, and sets on the neck of ambition, humbly pursuing that infallible perpetuity, unto which all others must diminish their diameters, and be poorly seen in Angles of contingency" (138). In fact, though "God is the true and infallible cause of all" (23, *Religio* 1.18) and can do anything with his "little finger" alone (26, 1.21), Browne's theology depends on God's unknowability:

> God hath not made a creature that can comprehend him, 'tis the priviledge of his owne nature; *I am that I am,* was his owne definition unto *Moses*; and 'twas a short one, to confound mortalitie, that durst question God, or ask him what hee was; indeed he only is, all other things have beene or shall be, but in eternitie there is no distinction of Tenses; [. . .] what to us is to come, to his Eternitie is present, his whole duration being but one permanent point without succession, parts, flux, or division. (14, 1.11)

In contrast to God and the Angels, humans are confined to living and knowing according to 'distinction' and 'division' ("in divided and distinguished worlds", 40), and if they want to express what they know, they must obey the rules of grammar. Whereas the spiritual realm is one of absolute certainty, of "demonstrations", this side of the great divide – the domain of the contingent – has only "probabilities" to offer (38,

1.33). God, for Browne, is the supreme instance that gives the discourse of probability and contingency a firm metaphysical hold and an objective justification. God is the circle that contains all smaller circles: this image, derived from hermeticism, is Browne's favorite "allegoricall description" of God: "Sphæra cuius centrum ubique, circumferentia nullibi" (13, 1.10) – a sphere whose centre is everywhere and whose circumference is nowhere. Circular and cyclical imagery pervades Browne's writings and has been referred to as his master trope. In this figure, tensions and oppositions are "tempered by elaborate circular arguments" (Grant 1985, 112; cf. Huntley 1953, Griebel 1979; Breiner 1977; Poulet 1966). The circle, as a wheel in motion, becomes a self-reflexive image of Browne's own literary technique of constructing a flexible epistemology based on contingency and probability, its instability protected by the circle that contains it. This literary method then is not merely circular but follows the dynamic trajectory of a loop, projective and recursive, opening and closing, expanding and contracting, differentiating and uniting. As he explains in the preface to *Pseudodoxia* (1981, 1): "in this Encyclopædie and round of knowledge, like the great and exemplary wheeles of heaven, wee must observe two Circles: that while we are daily carried about, and whirled on by the swindge and rapt of the one, wee may maintaine a naturall and proper course, in the slow and sober wheele of the other."

Browne's epistemology and rhetoric of contingency thus have a theological foundation. Because God's unity with creation cannot be directly observed, any discourse about reality can only bear "a contingent, figural correspondence to" reality (Silver 1990, 101). This is the blind spot or virtual fixed point of all observation that allows Browne to be "content in uncertainties" (Bennett 1962, 192). As Achsah Guibbory explains, his "movement towards uncertainty [. . .] culminates in a transcendent reliance on God" (1976, 494). This is most clearly noticed in *Hydriotaphia*. Here, as Guibbory observes, the expectation of a progress in knowledge is finally thwarted: the urns dug up in a field near Walsingham promise a knowledge about the past, but these mute but eloquent, "silently expressing" objects (Browne 2012, 93) are not merely containers of information that can be easily deciphered. On the contrary, the process of interpretation transforms them into symbols "of man's [sic] ignorance and vanity" (Guibbory 1976, 494). The urns become figures of human ignorance, demanding a response of intellectual humility.

The abstract images that Browne constructs, whether his topic is self-observation (*Religio*), funeral rites (*Hydriotaphia*), or the mathematical harmony of nature (*Garden of Cyrus*), are not simply 'irrational' but offer the reader a possibility to recognise the contingent relations of comparison between the image and its referent, but also their distance from one another. They are neither mere metaphors nor logical concepts but something in between: image-concepts. Browne's imagery is always object-related, often concrete in its visuality. Unlike those Romantics who particularly admired him, he has no interest in a 'realist' fusion of subject and object; instead of creating involvement, his imagery creates and maintains a 'nominalist' distance between words and things. This is most acute in his later writings. It also explains why Browne does not really 'have' a unique 'style'. His style is operational, a flexible arrangement of various features selected to match the object, while acknowledging that such a match can only be approximate, probabilistic, and contingent. Browne's images come with their own frames.

Even in the least promising of topics, as in his *Brief Discourse of the Sepulchrall Urnes lately found in NORFOLK,* Browne finds ample opportunity for concrete visualisations of abstract ideas and near-abstractions of concrete images, mostly achieved by either the literalisation of a metaphor or the metaphorisation of a literal expression. Coining a new portmanteau, one might speak of *litaphorisation* as the rhetorical principle of blurring the boundaries of literal and metaphorical meanings:

> Though if *Adam* were made out of an extract of the Earth, all parts might challenge a restitution, yet few have returned their bones farre lower then they might receive them; not affecting the graves of Giants, under hilly and heavy coverings, but content with lesse then their owne depth, have wished their bones might lie soft, and the earth be light upon them; Even such as hope to rise again, would not be content with centrall interrment, or so desperately to place their reliques as to lie beyond discovery, and in no way to be seen again; which happy contrivance hath made communication with our forefathers, and left unto our view some parts, which they never beheld themselves. (2012, 97)

Consider the wordplay on "parts", for instance, in the first and especially the last line, where the more abstract early modern meaning of this word (parts = accomplishments, talent) collides with the very concrete meaning of body parts; the pun on "depth"; or the litaphorisation of the abstract idea of resurrection with the concrete visualisation of this event: "to rise again" – "to be seen again." Other passages confirm this as a crucial Brownean technique. For example, he first rehearses the metaphorical analogy of life and fire ("Life is a pure flame, and we live by an invisible Sun within us") and then immediately switches to the literal fire of a funeral pyre: "A small fire sufficeth for life, great flames seemed too little after death" (137).

Quick transitions are typical of *Hydriotaphia*: observations on the relation between body weight and the weight of the ashes of a burned corpse are followed by a comparison to the burning of different kinds of wood, a critique of business practices ("the common fraud of selling Ashes by measure, and not by ponderation"), a quick succession of historic and biblical examples to show "how little Fuell sufficeth", culminating in the observation that a man could, like Isaac, "carry his owne pyre" (119–20). Visual imaginations of "the deformity of death" (124) abound, sometimes with a humorous slant ("the body compleated proves a combustible lump", 120), sometimes with a macabre sequence of morbid details on the topic of decomposition that betray the influence of Shakespeare's *Hamlet* and the cultural context of European baroque:

> To be [knav'd]⁴² out of our graves, to have our sculs made drinking-bowls, and our bones turned into Pipes, to delight and sport our Enemies, are Tragicall abominations, escaped in burning Burials.
>
> [. . .] In carnall sepulture, corruptions seem peculiar unto parts, and some speak of snakes out of the spinall marrow. [. . .] Teeth, bones, and hair, give the most lasting defiance to corruption. In an Hydropicall body ten years buried in a Church-yard, we met with a fat concretion, where the nitre of the Earth, and the salt and lixivious liquor of the body, had coagulated large lumps of fat, into the consistence of the hardest castle-soap; whereof part remaineth with us. (121–22)

Here, too, the distance between words and reality is clearly marked. The words call attention to themselves as rhetorically and rhythmically arranged. Witness the rhythmic flow and the alliterations and assonances in this passage. The text calls attention to itself as an artefact – a 'well-wrought urn', as it were. Like the urns that trigger the discourse, the words are cut loose from their literal meanings. They lose their referential function but gain rhetorical power. The text becomes emblematic, extolling its own dysfunctionality as a conveyor of information and, in doing so, turning into a symbolic vessel not unlike the urns themselves.

The Garden of Cyrus, the companion piece to *Hydriotaphia* (the two were first printed in one volume), explores the problem of referential and metaphorical language from a different but related angle. In *Hydriotaphia*, concrete objects – the urns – are found to be unreliable witnesses of the past, attaining a symbolic or metaphorical meaning instead. In *The Garden of Cyrus*, it is the abstract notion of Paradise or the Garden of Eden that is first concretised and compared with a great number of historical and legendary gardens, turning the earthly garden into a metaphor of the divine. Browne seeks to establish a universal pattern in nature: the rhomboid or quincunx. This pattern is found in plants, animals and humans, demonstrating the "wisedome" (1964a, 142) of the divine order: "All things began in order, so shall they end, and so shall they begin again; according to the ordainer of order and mystical Mathematicks of the City of Heaven" (174). The text's physical ending is staged as being written at night: "But the Quincunx of Heaven runs low, and 'tis time to close the five ports of knowledge" (174); the themes of sleep and of death as the "everlasting sleep" (175) connects *Garden* to the theme of mortality and resurrection in *Hydriotaphia*: "when sleep it self must end, and as some conjecture all shall awake again" (175).

Browne explains this correlation in the prefatory epistle: "the delightfull World comes after death, and Paradise succeeds the Grave. Since the verdant state of things is the Symbole of the Resurrection, and to flourish in the state of Glory, we must first be sown in corruption" (1964a, 87). The purpose of the lengthy disquisition on

---

42 As Greenblatt and Targoff assert, there is good reason to reject the emendation 'gnaw'd', introduced by Geoffrey Keynes, since 'knav'd' associates *Hamlet* 5.1.70–71, "How the knave jowls it to the ground" ('it' being Yorick's skull). See Greenblatt and Targoff 2012, xli.

universal harmony is, again, not to produce certainty on theological questions but "delightful Truths" (174) collateral to the main theme. It ends on a rather uncelebratory note of uncertainty and "conjecture" (175). If its function were the resolution of those problems that had arisen in *Hydriotaphia,* one could hardly say that this function had been achieved; rather, *Garden* serves to illustrate, from an opposite angle, the same epistemological and rhetorical predicament that had characterised *Hydriotaphia.* The correlation of the two texts is strategic. As Browne describes it, *Garden* is like a flower garland wrapped around *Hydriotaphia* (87). This comment points to the ornamental nature of this text – which, as a text about a pattern, is itself meticulously patterned, designed, and constructed around the number five. In both texts, concreteness and visuality are not transported from the referential world into the text, but are the effects of verbal art. These are not fictional texts in a modern sense but texts that clearly mark the distance between language and reality. Words conceal as much as they reveal, just as "[l]ight that makes things seen, makes some things invisible" (167). Even in passages where the effect of concreteness is strongest, a self-referential distance between linguistic signs and material referents is inscribed into the text, commenting on the merely contingent connection between objects and representations. Browne calls this technique "periphrasis, or adumbration" (2012, 13; *Religio* 1.10; see also *Garden,* 1964a, 167). In its inversion of the epistemological metaphor of light (*umbra* meaning 'shadow' in Latin), adumbration as a 'shadowing' technique entails a switching of perspectives from a direct to an indirect, reflected observation and from an immediate recognition of reality to a way of knowing that is relative and relational. Words cast a shadow that allows the reader to glimpse the source of light behind them, the true reality or the "greatest mystery of Religion" (1964a, 167).

When Samuel Johnson refers to *The Garden of Cyrus* as "a sport of fancy" (qtd. in Post 1987, 145), he ignores the epistemological purpose of Browne's writing. Though Browne himself repeatedly uses the word "delight" to describe his intended effect, he understands writing and reading primarily as ways of exploring new, previously unknown self-images and perspectives of the world. They are modes of 're-creation' that might be entertaining, but their principal objective is to re-orient the self towards the world: towards God, towards other people and other cultures, towards natural phenomena, towards the past and its history. It is for this purpose that Browne cultivates unusual vantage points and stretches language to the limits of intelligibility. His poses, flexible as they are, do not primarily serve an aesthetic programme of verbal art but "provide a model for multilevel thinking" (Nardo 1991, 174). This is why conventional accounts of literary style fail to capture the particularities of his writing. Browne's variable style is part and parcel of a rhetoric of contingency, perfectly suited to the different occasions and topics of his texts but also expressive of a higher purpose: a language that could strike a balance between reason and faith and encompass the many faces and facets of contingent reality: "Some Truths seem almost Falshoods, and some Falshoods almost Truths" (1964a, *Christian Morals* 2.3). Indeed, "[i]f things were seen as they truly are, the beauty of bodies would be much abridged" (2.9).

Browne's late writings continue his concern with flexible perspectives, emphasising how even seemingly 'natural' observations are constrained by limits of human perception, by "the natural Edge of our Eyes" (*Christian Morals* 2.9). The self-conscious verbal artistry of these writings depends on this epistemological premise; it allows readers enough freedom for their own playful engagement with the text's game of constraining and enabling multiple dimensions of meaning. This playful engagement opens up further ways of 'recreation', from tracing the thought processes in the text to the re-creation and reformation of readers' lives.

The writings of Burton and Browne are important instances of the key features that determine seventeenth-century literary culture. They register a set of problems for which many contemporary texts seek their own solutions. While their responses to the problems of modern (print) communication are still shaped by the theoretical and practical assumptions of late humanism, their proposed solutions soon appear exhausted and are then superseded, as we shall see, by more pragmatic neoclassical answers. The fundamental problem of late humanist literary communication is the discrepancy between universalism and contingency. What follows from this, in terms of literary form, is a more hybrid array of genres – because traditional forms of literary communication have become less convincing – and an increase in direct appeals to the reader by means of rhetoric – because authors attempt to compensate for the loss of a more immediate connection with their audience. These changes are related to institutional and technological changes in early modern intellectual life: the "knowledge technologies" (Rhodes and Sawday) of print, the library, and the cabinet of wonder. With the extension and increasing differentiation of print culture, and the increasing realisation of modernity as an "open context" (Blumenberg 1979), it becomes increasingly possible to observe reality in multiple, alternative, and comparative ways. In other words, 'culture' becomes possible in its modern sense of observational relativism and the questioning of a status quo in terms of alternative possibilities (Luhmann 1995, 1998).

An increasing awareness of contingency, however, exerts a double pressure on the textual presentation of knowledge. On the one hand, the sheer extension of what can be known leads to a crisis of universalism; on the other hand, communication itself becomes contingent and problematic. The relationship between authors and readers becomes less and less predictable in such a setting. The writings of Burton and Browne respond to this by *staging* knowledge and thought in order to activate the reader – similar to earlier texts by Thomas More, Erasmus or Luther – but they inflate this staging and thereby shrink its communicative potential. They show marked tendencies to fictionalise their texts, emphasising their playful and artful nature while eclipsing the mode of personal, oral interaction as a model for written communication. Authorial strategies of presentation become more complex and more noticeable – evidence for the waning persuasiveness of humanistic discourse. Burton devises a complicated arrangement of (partly fictionalised) thematisations of the highly unstable relation between author, book, and reader, in a blend of lament and celebration of the contingency of modern knowledge. In staging a theatre of writing and reading, the unstoppable play of authorial negativity has as its goal the transformation of the reader into a humbled observer of global melancholy and of his own folly – a transformation that may in effect be a religious conversion. Melancholy becomes the universal aspect from which the entire world, including author and reader, can be known and understood. But this is merely one possible aspect of many – imagine, for example, a Burtonian *Anatomy of Phlegm* or any other instance of humoral pathology as the general framework of human knowledge. The worldmaking of Burton's *Anatomy* is strictly limited by its singular 'angle of contingency', the perspective of melancholy, and thus at least indirectly acknowledges the possibility of seeing the world through radically different eyes, influenced by a radically different complexion of humours. Thus the universalism of the *Anatomy* is undercut and limited by contingency.

For Browne, in contrast, contingency is not a limiting factor but an enabling condition. It is the starting point for a programme of self-observation and self-cultivation to which authors and readers contribute equally. Communication in this case is less hierarchical and more open to the reader's interpretations. For Burton, the text is like a net in which to catch and hold the reader; for Browne, it is the holes of this net that enable the reader to see through to alternative ways of knowing the world. Whereas the net of language is an instrument of restraint for the former, it is a tool of vision and exploration for the latter. For Burton, it serves to reduce complexity; for Browne, it serves to generate alternatives: a knowledge of contingency rather than a contingency of knowledge.

Whereas Burton organises a complex discourse of intertextual derivation and citational pastiche on the stabilising groundwork of totalised melancholy, Browne opens literary communication towards a wide range of meanings. Yet for him the knowledge of contingency does not imply an exaggerated sense of possibility, because it is limited and stabilised, epistemologically as well as rhetorically, by a concept of God that minimises the risks of contingency. Since everything is contingent except God, God alone can observe totality; all other observers are limited by a particular (contingent) perspective. God, for Browne, is truth, whereas contingent observations, in their operations and effects, can only ever be more or less *probable*. Under the index of the probable, literary communication can no longer claim an immediate access to truth, while its qualities as a mediating instance, and its media qualities, take centre stage.

Throughout the seventeenth century and beyond, the question remains relevant how literary communication functions in a society that is increasingly (functionally) differentiated. As the following chapters will show, other solutions than the ones proposed by Burton and Browne will become necessary in this context. Neither the conferral of a reality status to sense perceptions dominated by a particular humour (Burton) nor the taming of contingency in a theological framework (Browne) appear convincing in a society characterised by epistemic, religious, and political upheavals.

Along the fault line between late humanism and neoclassicism, there is more at stake than merely literature – there is a larger debate about why and how literature, in its combination of usefulness and pleasure, can be useful in society. The following chapters explore this debate and the functional conditions of English neoclassicism. Next, I examine the relation between visual and textual rhetoric in authors like Davenant and Milton. Here, the contingency that Browne so playfully celebrates as a wealth of alternative possibilities turns into a moral, social, and political problem. As is to be expected, the solutions proposed become more radical and aggressive as the Civil War rages. A problem of description grows into a conflict of norms that can no longer be solved merely by invoking God (as in Hobbes). Literature is drawn more and more into this debate about values, a debate that is now about secular rather than religious order: nature and/or the state, rather than God, are its ultimate points of reference. Nostalgic notions of social unity are increasingly replaced by a rationalist "analytico-referential discourse" (Reiss 1982a). This can not only be seen in Hobbes's *Leviathan* but also in Milton's *Paradise Lost,* which in this regard is a profoundly 'realistic' poem that historicises the lost unity as a thing of the past and thus makes it usable for the present, in the form of reflection, diagnosis and polemic: the loss of paradise becomes the precondition for human history.

Only towards the end of the seventeenth century can we then see a "cultivated semantics" (Luhmann 1980, 18, 19–20, 46) becoming institutionalised and politically implemented in the code of politeness and civility as a norm of communication. We can see the rise of a non-determinist attitude towards language, literary communication, and political differences, an attitude that is based – as it implicitly is in Browne – on probability and verisimilitude. The literary culture of neoclassicism is established on these foundations not as a radical break with the past (with humanism) but as an evolutionary process, as a development of certain discursive potentials and strategic solutions to certain problems, adapted to new situations. This order of discourse will remain in place throughout much of the (long) eighteenth century, and it will establish the foundations of a modern understanding of literature. Its epistemological, ethical, and political origins are the subject of the following chapters.

3 Writing, Reading, Seeing: Visuality and Contingency in the Literary Epistemology of Neoclassicism

> Strange it is that in the most perfect sense [*sc.* vision] there should be so many fallacies [. . .].
>
> Sir Thomas Browne, *Christian Morals* 3.15

> . . . . but to nobler sights
> Michael from Adam's eyes the film removed
> Which that false fruit that promised clearer sight
> Had bred: then purged with euphrasy and rue
> The visual nerve, for he had much to see[.]
>
> *Paradise Lost* 11.411–15

> Such as were blinde, and now can see,
> Let 'em use this Receipt with me,
> 'Twill cleare the Eye, preserve the Sight,
> And give the understanding Light.
>
> *The Eye Cleared* (1644), title page

Literary Epistemology

Histories of literature sometimes present their object as if it were the hero of a nineteenth-century *bildungsroman*. According to this narrative, literature has become increasingly autonomous in modernity, expanding its degrees of freedom and operating according to its own rules. Aesthetic autonomy is then seen to be fully implemented in romantic and post-romantic literature in the nineteenth century. It is doubtful whether any such teleological construct can ever be an accurate description of historical processes, particularly considering the instability of 'literature' as an object. In many respects, one might argue that complete autonomy in the arts – such as the power of literature "to say everything, in every way" (Derrida 1992, 36) – has never been achieved and remains a utopia, another "unfinished project" of modernity (Habermas 1997).

Are early modern developments merely the prehistory of an 'autonomous' literature? How are we to understand this? Traditionally, many literary histories locate decisive developments in the eighteenth century: together, these constitute the emergence of a modern framework in which literature works. There is no doubt that a number of important, or even essential, cultural achievements of the eighteenth century indeed depend on earlier developments; but I think it would be wrong simply to regard the seventeenth century as a mere way station towards something else or as the imperfect precursor of something less imperfect. I think the more rewarding task is to focus on seventeenth-century events in their own light, to present these processes in relation to their own 'contexture' – to view them not against the horizon of a 'no longer' or a 'not yet', but to come to understand them on their own terms.

This problem of literary historiography becomes particularly intense with regard to two major movements: empiricism and neoclassicism. These intellectual and artistic formations tend to be interpreted, retrospectively, as precursors of later developments: Enlightenment rationalism on the one hand, the aesthetic autonomy of the literary on the other. Indeed, if you look at it as a literary theory, and perhaps the first explicitly *literary* theory in modern Europe, neoclassicism can be read as a response to an increasing differentiation of discourses, media, and forms of communication. Such differentiation constitutes a core element of its critical reflections on the arts. Neoclassicism is not merely the result of a rediscovery or reappraisal of classical literary traditions. The 're' as 'neo': the name implies this of course, and like the term 'Renaissance', meaning 'rebirth', neoclassicism is a return to classicism, to classical traditions (Berensmeyer 2019). Among other important aspects, neoclassicism embodies a tendency to look at works of literature in isolation and to relate them to an abstract matrix of normative foundations. In other words, it seeks to read, to decipher the code of any literary work and to establish a critical discourse of value on the basis of this code: is this tragedy a good tragedy according to the norm that Aristotle has established in classical Greece? Relating the individual work to an abstract norm on the basis of a code, a kind of normative *decorum*, neoclassicism seeks to turn individual objects into cases that can be subsumed under general principles. In England, in distinction to French neoclassicism and in analogy to English law, distinctions between abstract norms and individual cases are handled a bit more flexibly and are seen in relation to one another as parts of an evolving continuum (see Norton 1999, 17–20).

Yet to argue for a differentiation among discourses is not at all the same as to argue for a becoming autonomous of the literary as distinct from other forms of culture, other performative dimensions of human activity and social behaviour. Normative generalisations about literature and the other arts, described by Timothy Reiss (1997) as "aesthetic rationalism", and the empirical functioning of literary and other types of communication may well overlap but they are not *prima facie* identical. They belong to different levels of cultural activity. To arrive at a theoretical coupling between these levels can be regarded as a particular achievement of neoclassicism under the pressure of discourses, media, and forms of communication. As we have seen in the cases of Burton and Browne, the centrifugal dynamic of knowledge and its textual organisation increasingly turns into a problem of contingency in literary communication. Neoclassicism can then be understood as a set of self-organising problem-solving strategies brought to bear on this problem.

The following chapters will circumvent the teleology of differentiation and instead trace the complex interweaving of continuities and discontinuities, focusing on phenomena of inertia and overlap with the aim to gain, by way of close readings and detailed analyses, a historically more saturated purchase on the literary epistemology of English neoclassicism. They will present the trajectory of neoclassicism between 1650 and 1700 in the performative contexts of English culture, i.e. in the media configurations in which texts and their reception are historically embedded. My enquiries are motivated by the following questions: what comes after the complexification, disintegration, and self-deconstruction of literary humanism that we have observed in Burton and Browne? How is contingency revalued in connection with textual communication, and how is it related to changing ideas of community, viewed alternatively as 'commonwealth' or as 'state'? Finally, where is the place of the 'individual', that celebrated Renaissance phantom, in the neoclassical order of things, and how is the relation between individualities and textualities (con-)figured in the later seventeenth century? How does modern communication emerge from premodern situations of writing and reading?

From what we know about the constitutive make-up of the 'republic of letters' in seventeenth-century England, any notion of autonomy in relation to other discourses is simply not on the map. Instead, we observe a turbulence of discourses driven by the unstable system of patronage and the underdeveloped economic resources of a literary market (Schoenfeldt 1999b). Rather than producing a homogeneous (national) literature, neoclassical criticism and creativity are marked by the co-presence of various mixed forms and, in the words of Lawrence Manley (1999, 347), "by an interorientation of urbane *decora* and a levelling confluence between polite and popular urban modes."

Yet, in theory at least – and, after 1688, increasingly in economic and practical terms – there is no denying that the English seventeenth century begins to conceive of a certain type of writing as distinct from other types, as separable, collectible, anthologisable (Zwicker 2003, 297–99; Benedict 1996). This kind of writing is increasingly connected to the individuality of an author, who writes for the sake of public recognition and fame (Miller 1986, Loewenstein 2002). Yet this is still not identical with the postulated autonomy of literature but rather the result of a 'conditioned co-production' (G. Spencer Brown) of literary and (other) cultural and social developments, for which the term 'neoclassicism' is a useful shorthand.

It is not only philosophical skepticism like Montaigne's or religious introspection like More's that leads to a more intense self-questioning and/as self-fashioning in the early modern period (Greenblatt 1980) but also a tendency towards individual gratification in a society of public spectacle and private capital accumulation, conspicuous consumption, and the circulating flow of commodities. Empiricism, materialism, and neoclassicism reflect the *intensification* of discourses. As a concrete image of this intensification, Stephen Greenblatt's famous metaphor of the "circulation of social energy" (1988) becomes a reality only from about 1630 onwards; it is more useful for Harvey (Rogers 1996, 16–27), Hobbes, and Milton than it is for Elizabethan theatre (Kroll 2002, 27–29; 2000, 104–11). Circulation, as a "new master image of the body" (Sennett 1994,

255) after the Harveian discovery of 1628, emphasises the analytic separation of a diffuse felt totality into its individual parts, which operate mechanically and separately, connected only by the flow of motion itself. In the flow of circulation, the individual becomes a mobile and flexible observer of self and others. When motion ceases, life ends. Apart from its political ramifications – articulated in Hobbes's *Leviathan,* where life is defined as "but Motion" (1.6) – the metaphor of circulation replaces a medieval configuration of fundamental sympathetic connection with one of separation, isolation, and individualisation (Sennett 1994, 255–81).

The developing book trade is merely one instance of this larger epistemic change. The marketable book, cut off from the intimate coterie setting of scribal publication, becomes a circulating mobile commodity, which gains meaning only from its circulation and its real or potential contact with individual readers or reading communities. Its value can now be measured in its saleability and expressed in the medium of money. A good example is Jacob Tonson's subscription system for Dryden's translation of Virgil, in which Dryden's work was financed by readers paying for it *before* it was completed. The author's name becomes a sign, a signature, a promise, a synecdoche for the work. As reputation accrues to the author from his or her work (in the sense of labour), his or her name confers coherence and authority upon the texts, gradually transforming a collection of writings into 'a work' – a work that, in the relative fixity of print, achieves an ideal unity of type removed from the contingency of any individual paper token or copy.

The functional change of literary communication in seventeenth-century England thus moves from a 'natural' or vitalistic concept of communication to a mechanistic one: from humanist metaphors of digestion, assimilation, and alchemical transformation (still evident in Burton and in Milton's *Areopagitica*) to a rather more technical vocabulary of machine interaction, which invokes procedures of distinction, coupling/uncoupling, and the metaphor of 'imprinting' as the fundamental mode of 'literate experience' (Barnaby and Schnell 2002). Prior to this epistemic change, whose origins probably lie in the second half of the fifteenth century, it is difficult to form an abstract concept of communication or a semiotic concept of signification.

In this context, it becomes compelling to argue that, in the words of Barnaby and Schnell (2002, 197), the "novel conceptualization of experimental discourse" in the seventeenth century "as an unending cooperative and communal exchange of ideas" – in other words, as a form of social circulation – ought to be regarded as the paradigmatic epistemic underpinning of neoclassical literary culture; not because it supposedly provides access to some objective reality but because it acknowledges the difficulty of attaining any certain knowledge about its objects of enquiry and develops discursive structures and procedures of coping with uncertainty. Knowledge must be mediated in language, but language is seen to be an opaque medium. For this reason, the contingent fit of language and truth must be made amenable to public negotiation and accountability, establishing a non-deterministic rhetoric of contingency that would come to dominate the discourse of neoclassicism (Kroll 1991, 52, 77, 85).

Contingency and difference, not autonomy and homogeneity, define the field of discourse. Nevertheless, there is in some areas a tendency to homogenise *specific* differences, for instance in the concept of the nation and its association with literary phenomena like the English 'mixed mode' (Docherty 1999); but even this should not be confused with an increasing autonomy of literature.

This discourse, then, involves much more than only literary theory. It dominates political thought and natural philosophy as well as debates about religion in the later seventeenth century and beyond. Hence, to regard it merely as a first step towards a modern and autonomous literary system would be to neglect, wilfully and prematurely, the actual cultural achievement and impact of English neoclassicism. Rather than arguing for their isolation, neoclassicism aims to observe the *circulation* among different levels and elements of the social, which it figures as mobile, dynamic and heterogeneous. Its modernity, in this view, resides precisely in its focus on the *connectivity* between individual elements and larger configurations, between parts and wholes, between bodies natural and the body politic. Such connections can no longer be taken for granted in the later seventeenth century: the old analogy between micro- and macrocosm has lost its binding force. It is replaced by the semantics of mechanical circulation in physiology as well as in political and economic thought (Bylebyl 1979; Rogers 1996, 16–27; Kroll 2000, 104–5).

The distinction between literary texts and other forms of discourse, the relation of the individual literary work to the general rules of art, all this is vividly discussed by Dryden in the *Essay of Dramatick Poesie*, a text that is often metonymically equated with English neoclassicism in a narrow, literary-critical sense. In writing about literature, seventeenth-century poets and critics are as far away from romantic assertions of genius or modernist assertions of impersonality as it is possible to imagine. Their concern is with the pragmatic embedding of literary objects in the real world instead of an ahistorical universality. For Davenant, writing in 1650, the connection between heroic poetry and its social setting is a case in point. Poetry, for Davenant, is a repertoire of cultural values towards which specific elements of the commonwealth (the army, the law, the church) stand in contingent relations. Poetry can then serve as a common unifying bond among these elements, which are in dire need of such a bond because of perpetual conflicts between them – a lesson of the Civil War. But this repertoire of values is not eternal and unchanging; rather, it consists of a selection of moral precepts, deemed useful for maintaining public order, which have to be changed and adapted if poetry is to remain useful in this way. Poetry – or fiction more generally – around 1650 thus does not exist in a space beyond society but is inextricably connected to it. Its function is ultimately understood as rhetorical, hortatory, performative – not as aesthetic, merely entertaining, or expressive of a 'higher' truth. Even though writers and critics begin to observe the literary in isolation from other discourses, it remains firmly connected to social and political concerns. In most cases, then, even theoretical arguments about literature in the seventeenth century have political implications.

Both empiricism and neoclassicism enjoin a certain perspective towards literary communication, a perspective that, without being simply utilitarian or ideological, situates literary activities in a network of mobile relations, in a framework of pragmatic exchanges that does not exclude what we would call ideological determinations. As a scientific attitude or, more precisely, a historical style of thought and representation, the "analytico-referential discourse" (Reiss 1982a) of empiricism and neoclassicism systematically introduces the contingency of experiences and observations into a generalised, normative order of communication. In his study on the connection between science and gentlemanly conduct in seventeenth-century England, Steven Shapin elucidates the moral bond of trust and belief that determines assent or denial of claims to factual knowledge; he describes the epistemological change that occurs in the seventeenth century as an "inversion of authority relations between word and world" (1994, 198). Whereas, in the Renaissance, personal testimony and authority were primary factors in determining the legitimacy of a new observation, which had to fit into "existing plausibility schemes", it is now a matter of adapting or even rejecting those schemes "because they conflicted with legitimate new experience" (198). The probable thus comes to be defined no longer as that whose truth is "warranted by authoritative and respected sources (as in 'probity')" but as a gauge for the remaining uncertainty of a hypothesis in relation to empirical evidence: "a quality of uncertain knowledge apportioned to the evidence available" (198) – which is the modern definition of probability (Hacking 1975, Shapin and Schaffer 1985).

It seems paradoxical that the modern concepts of science and the growth of knowledge should contain a greater degree of uncertainty than during earlier periods, which relied to a greater extent on derived authority to distinguish between true and false knowledge. In the seventeenth century, this uncertainty can still be cushioned in the social conventions of gentlemanly conduct. The semantics of the gentleman-scientist functions as a link between the older form of authority and the new ideals of scientific objectivity. Yet the evolution of science towards more and more complex and compartmentalised disciplines requires equally more complex modes of sorting true and false knowledge than mere appeals to morality are capable of supplying. Trust is no longer invested in individual authorities but in generalised structures or institutions: particular places of research like the laboratory or the dissecting room, associations of scientists like the Royal Society, certain organs of publication, etc. The stylistic norms of scientific communication are adapted to this shift. In the process, experiential and cognitive styles of abstraction and concreteness drift further apart (Claessens 1993).

The linked notions of 'experiential style' and 'cognitive style' (Schütz and Luckmann 1973) provide an important connection between a social history of knowledge and the history of ideas or mentalities – a connection that becomes more substantial if we relate the modern idea of science to the modern concept of reality as described by Blumenberg in terms of an 'open context' (1979). The discourse of empiricism is *one* instance in which this modern concept can be exemplified, in analogy to my understanding of neoclassicism and the epistemological foundations of seventeenth-century literary culture. Its horizon is open inasmuch as it is constantly modified by new observations and discoveries, so that its participants have to learn to expect the unexpected and to resist premature conclusions. For individuals, the farther-reaching consequences of this openness need not have immediate consequences for either their experiential or cognitive styles and will probably be eclipsed in the pursuit of everyday routines. But a reflection on the increasing production of knowledge and what it entails – the continual modification of reality *as it is experienced* – will not only result in greater individual uncertainty but will also increase demand for institutional consequences to absorb and ritualise this uncertainty. Now one becomes aware of the fact that the increase of knowledge is inevitably connected to an increase of ignorance, of blank spaces and uncertainty. As knowledge expands, so does the horizon of the unknown. We have already seen this dialectic at work in Burton and Browne. In the early modern age, the horizon of possible knowledge – including the number of potential follow-up questions – expands *ad infinitum*. "All sciences", writes Pascal, "are infinite in the expansion of their problems" (Pascal 1963, 526, my translation; cf. Berensmeyer 2003).

Neoclassicism is concerned with developing strategies to cope with the epistemic, social and political contingency that arises from this radical expansion of the horizon in modernity. It is thus closely linked to changes in the *episteme* of seventeenth- and eighteenth-century European culture, particularly the rise of "analytico-referential discourse" (Reiss 1999 and Reiss 1997, 135–200). These changes face the problem of contingency by developing techniques and procedures of safeguarding legitimate knowledge by means of method, rule-governed observation, and probable inference. They further involve a new understanding of language and rhetoric as a medium of communication for the public exchange of ideas and opinions. In this epistemic change, traditional ideals of stability, coherence, and certainty give way to a dynamic system of values expressed in a conceptual rhetoric of mobility, circulation, contingency, and probability.

If neoclassicism is identified as a strategy for dealing with contingency, also in the field of literature, one has to specify the epistemological preconditions of this strategy, the foundations on which it operates, and finally to answer the question how it establishes the functional boundaries of literary communication to other media, other performative levels of culture. With this guiding perspective in mind, the following readings focus on the embattled, polemic, and polemogenic relation between literary and visual forms of communication, between modes of visual immediacy and forms of rhetoric mediated through language. As can be seen in the writings of Milton, Hobbes, Davenant, and Cavendish, this relation is usually fraught with epistemological and political implications as well as problems of aesthetics and poetics; these problems and implications cannot easily be kept apart. The readings that follow in this chapter are all concerned with the potential *impact* of literary in comparison with other, predominantly visual, modes of communication. They also involve the question how seventeenth-century writers imagine the act of reading and how they adapt their literary strategies and tactics accordingly.

Against the background of the correlation between empiricist theories of sense perception and media performance, I shall try to demonstrate how literature and its neoclassical reflection compete with other media. For this purpose, I am first going to analyse functions of image and text in Milton and Hobbes, before turning to Hobbes's theoretical grasp of literary communication, especially the epic poem. The focus here will be on Hobbes's collaboration with Davenant, which should enjoy pride of place in any history of neoclassical, materialist poetics. Beside Davenant's *Preface to Gondibert*, the political dimensions included in neoclassical media and genre theory are finally illustrated by a reading of Margaret Cavendish's *The Blazing World* and its explicit convergence of discursive and political hierarchy.

"Not Truth, But Image, Maketh Passion": Optics and the Force of Reading in Milton and Hobbes

Their vast differences notwithstanding, Milton and Hobbes share a sharp awareness of the epistemic and political impact of images. They serve as ideal case studies for the correlation between seventeenth-century theories of (predominantly visual) sense perception and literary or media practices; in both writers, the convergence of empiricism and literary culture is also eminently political.

In 1649, a book is published to coincide with the trial and execution of Charles I, purporting to present an authentic and true image, even a religious 'icon' of this king. The frontispiece to *Eikon Basilike*, by William Marshall (Fig. 2), emphasises this idealising gesture in its presentation of Charles as a saintly martyr who has put off his wordly crown, holding a crown of thorns in his right hand and looking upwards to behold a luminous crown in heaven. A beam of light connects this heavenly crown with the eyes of the kneeling monarch.

As Jim Daems and Holly Faith Nelson remind us, *Eikon Basilike* – purportedly written by Charles I himself – becomes an instant bestseller in England and across Europe, with a total of sixty editions in 1649 alone (2006, 14). As a piece of PR intended to restore the king's reputation, the book was immensely successful. The impact of Milton's *Eikonoklastes* (1649), his printed rebuttal to *Eikon Basilike*'s royalist propaganda, was negligible in comparison. Milton's goal in this text is to deconstruct the king's iconic image, to be a 'breaker of images' or iconoclast, to destroy the "superstitious" idol by the power of rational argument, and to replace the king's image of a martyr with the image of a tyrant (Loewenstein 1990, 51–73). Milton engages a republican rhetoric of words (which he equates with rationality and analysis, as he does in *Areopagitica*) against the royalist rhetoric of images, which he denounces as "quaint Emblems and devices" (Milton 1957a, 343). He emphasises the theatricality, the illusory and stagey quality of these images, i.e. their

Fig. 2: Frontispiece by William Marshall and title page of *Eikon Basilike*. Beinecke Rare Book & Manuscript Library, Yale University. Wikimedia Commons.

lack of truthfulness, writing that they are "begg'd from the old Pageantry of some Twelf-nights entertainment at *Whitehall*" (343). This comparison also underlines the aristocratic distance of the royal image from the common people who are the target readers of *Eikon Basilike*, the book and its frontispiece. Against the visually mediated, (crypto-)Catholic ideology and eidology of tyranny, the republican Milton pits "the old English fortitude and love of Freedom" (344). For Milton, "the People" are not naturally inclined to barbarism and do not need a strong arm to control them; instead, their "low dejection and debasement of mind" is a product of the ideology and propaganda of "the Prelats" and "the factious inclination of most men divided from the public by several ends and humors of thir own" (344).

Milton, like Hobbes, has to face the problem of the multitude, of social unity. The staging of the royal image simply takes this unity for granted, or ignores its absence; Milton's words, however, have to develop a theoretical construct and a rhetorical strategy for its communication. Images are suggestive rather than analytic, and even though the Marshall 'icon' also requires interpretation, its effect is more immediate in addressing an audience, including the illiterate. Hobbes will later find a visual analogue to his theory of the state in the frontispiece to *Leviathan*. Milton the iconoclast has to expend quite a bit of rhetorical labour on constructing an implied audience, a public that can sustain the division between those "who adhere to wisdom and to truth" and "the vulgar sort", who are irredeemably lost to the anti-republican forces of superstitious zealotry and the magic of images (348). His syntax aches under the burden of semantic strain, having to keep these disparate forces together and to avoid the impression that even his own side, the rational and righteous republicans who wish to stem the "rage and torrent" of unreason, could only be "a sect or faction":

> Certainly, if ignorance and perversness will needs be national and universal, then they who adhere to wisdom and to truth, are not therfore to be blam'd, for beeing so few as to seem a sect or faction. But in my opinion it goes not ill with that people where these vertues grow so numerous and well joyn'd together as to resist and make head against the rage and torrent of that boistrous folly and superstition that possesses and hurries on the vulgar sort. (348)

The passage remains somewhat nebulous concerning the question who is pushing and who is pulling whom, and to what end precisely. Milton's language betrays an anxiety about the persuasive influence of images on "the vulgar sort" when he writes that image-based royalist propaganda may not convince "any wise Man" or "any knowing Christian" but may well

> catch the worthles approbation of an inconstant, irrational, and Image-doting rabble; that like a credulous and hapless herd, begott'n to servility, and inchanted with these popular institutes of Tyranny, subscrib'd with a new device of the Kings Picture at his praiers, hold out both thir eares with such delight and ravishment to be stigmatiz'd and board through in witness of thir own voluntary and beloved baseness. The rest, whom *perhaps* ignorance without malice, or some error, less then fatal, hath for the time misledd, on this side Sorcery or obduration, *may* find the grace and good guidance to bethink themselves, and recover. (601, my italics)

The hope expressed in the last sentence also betrays some degree of uncertainty about the possibility of converting, by rational argument and the power of words, those who have been "misledd" by images. But if the approval of the "rabble" is "worthles", why bother? The difficulty Milton has with the irrational power of images in relation to rational language can also be presented in terms of a problem with the political status of the London crowds, the largely illiterate lower classes or "vulgar sort", whose attention is more easily reached by visual than verbal means (Harris 1987). How can rational communication address these inferior parts of society which, even though they are intellectually "worthles" and – a striking phrase for a republican – "begott'n to servility", are yet of crucial importance to public stability and peace? Are images a stronger means to "catch the [. . .] approbation of [the] rabble" than spoken or printed words? The 'Catholic' image of the king on the frontispiece of *Eikon Basilike* seems to know better than Milton's Protestant faith in words: although the open book on the king's altar proclaims "In verbo tuo spes mea" – "in your word I place my hope" – the king's eyes are looking away from the book; they are turned up towards the heavens for a more immediate visual contact with the beyond than reading can provide. Even this image itself does not seem to believe in the word as much as in seeing the light visually, in a direct way.

The conflict between image and word becomes more complex as soon as words are printed rather than heard, having to enter a reader's mind by the same channel, as it were, as do images, through the sense of vision. The widespread distrust regarding the deceptive character of writing is only partially alleviated by making written language as much as possible resemble spoken language, though this effect can be highly artificial, as in the case of Milton's *Areopagitica*, written as a simulated speech for the medium of print.[43] With increasing intensity, Milton's texts turn towards oral and aural effects that circumvent, perhaps even contravene the visual impression of a page. The syntax and prosody of *Paradise Lost* are a case in point: Milton frequently uses enjambment, continuing sentences and phrases across the line breaks, thus breaking up the visual neatness of verse with the aural counterpoint of different rhythmic sequences. He relies on the reader's (as well as his own) ability to listen rather than visualise, to intuit and understand rather than to imagine and admire. The aim is to leave behind a passive, identificatory, and "image-doting" (if you like, satanic) mode of reading for a critical, confrontational, and self-transformative attitude. *Paradise Lost* and *Paradise Regained* are a 'training programme' teaching its readers how to approach visuality and how to interpret images and signs. This becomes particularly clear in the last two books of *Paradise Lost*, in which the Archangel Michael provides Adam – as a stand-in for the (male) reader – not only with privileged insight into salvation history but also with a crash course in techniques of reading and interpretation. If the intention of *Paradise Lost* is less to picture the Christian myth in an imaginative way than to achieve an intellectual, reflexive distance from myth (as well as from Milton's epic precursors), this may well be aided by Milton's preference of orality/aurality over visual 'effects'. *Paradise Lost* teaches its readers to question, to suspend, even to deny their power to visualise what is presented, in order to arrive at a 'better', more rational understanding of the unbridgeable abyss between deity and humanity. When Raphael describes the "war in heaven" using Homeric language but including modern artillery (for which Milton was ridiculed by Voltaire), this happens in full awareness of the unpresentable nature of heavenly events and according to the Pauline principle of accommodation. Working by means of verbal sound (Leonard 2001), the poem leads the reader into a confrontation with the paradoxes of vision, blindness, and non-visual insight as well as with the difficulties of language, meaning, and poetic form encountered by its epic speaker in his project of "justify[ing] the ways of God to men" (Milton 1998, 1.26). The difficulties are heaped up, above all, in the successive proems that, after a very strong start, turn more and more hesitant and doubtful.

Milton's own blindness may have been an important factor in foregrounding these paradoxes of vision and insight, but it is not essential to his argument. Rather, his literary enterprise takes part in an epistemological denigration of the visual that is characteristic of much of early modern philosophy and science, including techniques of

---

[43] On early modern reading, more generally, as both aural and visual, see Brayman Hackel 2005, 43–52.

religious meditation. As in arithmetic and geometry, which function as early modern paradigms for the scientific ethos of abstraction, universal validity and compelling persuasiveness, real objects that appear to the eye with all their uncertainties, warts and all, are reduced to and replaced by ideal, rational, and certain constructions. In this process, the blind man, who cannot be deceived by the visual illusions of the phenomenal world, becomes the guarantor of "solid and true" knowledge, of what Descartes calls "distinct and clear intuition" (1953, 37, 67). In the *Second Defense of the English People* of 1654, it is this very argument that Milton uses against his detractors, who interpret his blindness as divine retribution. Addressing his opponent Alexander More, he writes:

> as to my blindness, I would rather have mine, if it be necessary, than either theirs, More, or yours. Your blindness, deeply implanted in the inmost faculties, obscures the mind, so that you may see nothing whole or real. Mine, which you make a reproach, merely deprives things of color and superficial appearance. What is true and essential in them is not lost to my intellectual vision. (Trans. Helen North, Milton 1966, 589)

In the phrases that follow, "darkness" and "light" are transvaluated, as they are in some instances in *Paradise Lost*, to transform blindness from an "infirmity" to a perfection that makes possible the "keen [. . .] vision" of "an inner and far more enduring light" (590). But Milton's proems in *Paradise Lost*, those passages where he introduces the topic of his speaker's blindness, are much more complex than his counter-polemic in the *Defensio Secunda*. At first, they appear to emphasise the privileged reality of a 'higher' intellectual and theological vision in contrast to the unreliability of mere physical sight in the same way as Milton's earlier prose text had done. Interpreted in this manner, the reader would be invited to share or to imitate the speaker's privileged inner (blind) vision, whereas Satan (and, to a certain extent, both Adam and Eve) would be exposed as bad readers who are duped by the deceptive glamour of external appearances, either wilfully ignoring (in the case of Satan) or sadly misunderstanding (in the case of humankind) the more profound levels of divine reality.

Yet, in contrast to a rationalist or Cartesian belief in "distinct and clear intuition" or a mystical assertion of noetic superiority, the invocatory passages in *Paradise Lost* turn the trope of blindness into a dramatic assertion of trial, suffering, and radical uncertainty. Read superficially, they might appear as merely conventional elements of epic poetry, or – worse – poetic restatements of Milton's earlier polemic, asserting the epistemic and prophetic advantages of blindness:

> . . . . what in me is dark
> Illumine, what is low raise and support;
> That to the height of this great argument
> I may assert the eternal providence
> And justify the ways of God to men.
> (Milton 1998, 1.22–26)

> So much the rather thou celestial light
> Shine inward, and the mind through all her powers
> Irradiate, there plant eyes, all mist from thence
> Purge and disperse, that I may see and tell
> Of things invisible to mortal sight.
> (3.51–55)

Yet, in the context of the poem, these statements, injunctive as they are, never meet with any confirmation from the instance they invoke. The speaker even seems to invite a sceptical response at the beginning of Book 9, where he voices his doubts about the appropriateness of heroic epic as a form for his work. These doubts may be doubly ironic, evoking a disparity between Milton and his speaker:

> . . . . unless an age too late, or cold
> Climate, or years damp my intended wing
> Depressed, and much they may, if all be mine,
> Not hers who brings it nightly to my ear.
> (9.44–47)

Thus the speaker's blindness, rather than betokening either a condign punishment of sin or a privileged mystical contact with the divine, accentuates the contingency of human affliction and the inscrutable hiddenness of God – a cornerstone of Protestant theology, including Milton's (Silver 2001, 153–207). In Victoria Silver's analysis, Milton's speaker's project of justification is "revisionary" rather than merely visionary (2001, 207). As Silver argues, the epic invocation of the heavenly Muse is transformed, in *Paradise Lost*, into a dramatic enactment of lost assurance, a request rather than a ratification of prophetic vision (196, 199). Indeed, for the Protestant Milton "to presume the efficacy of invocation" would be "to commit idolatry of the same order as the Catholic mass" (202). Satanic and Adamic idolatry or "visualism" in *Paradise Lost* implies a negation of contingency and a relinquishing of "subjectivity – mind, volition, individuality – to the delusion of absolute and self-evident meaning" (338). Note that the nightly visitations experienced by the speaker are aural, not visual in nature ("to my ear").

Milton's project of justification is developed in the poem as a narrative of spiritual exertion, as an unceasing process of learning and searching that is experienced as painful because it can never arrive at the certainty of consummation. As Silver explains, "[t]he speaker too has only the ordinary consolation of his own perseverance in telling the story, with the result that speech here is the locus of revelation in a transfigured but not a supernatural sense" (2001, 195). The poem does not resolve the speaker's dilemma; his blindness may not be divinely ordained, but neither is it the certain sign of a privileged knowledge of the divine. Faith and hope can thus only be based on the word of revelation, as the frontispiece to *Eikon Basilike* also argues, but never in the self-assured and complacent way in which the royal martyr is depicted to be in contact with the deity, his line of sight directly corresponding to God's and thereby suggesting a continuity between the worldly and the divine. Rather, the text of *Paradise Lost* reproduces a Lutheran understanding of Scripture as an opponent to the reader; it resists assimilation by a reader who comes to it looking for mere information rather than self-transformation. The poem implicates the reader in the speaker's (and Milton's) labour of understanding, of justifying. It argues, as Milton's prose had done before, for the painful but ultimately salvific labour of deciphering and perfecting the always incomplete text of truth against the idolatrous gratification of curiosity in "distinct and clear" images.

But this complexity of unfinished and heterogeneous truth, which necessitates the exacting labours of interpretation as 'right reading', is extremely difficult to transform into a new political order, as Milton also had to realise and as we can see in the complexity of his late works, including *Paradise Lost*. In England, one of the greatest problems of the new republican state turns out to be its inability to find convincing images for its public representation. After the statue of the king at the Royal Exchange has been beheaded and removed, it is replaced by an empty, imageless space with the inscription "Exit Tyrannus regum Ultimus, anno primo restitutae libertatis Angliae 1648".[44] No image but a text, and in Latin too – this iconoclastic extreme probably did little to attract the masses and secure their "approbation". The absence of the royal body (Kantorowicz 1957) opens up an imageless vacuum that is abhorred by many as unnatural and deeply disconcerting. The new state's obvious problems with political iconography grows more severe during the Protectorate, as its attitude towards public display grows more ambiguous. An uncanny effect is produced, for example, by an engraving showing Cromwell on horseback, which, apart from the face, is virtually identical to an engraving of Charles I (both by Peter Lombart after Anthony van Dyck; reproduced in Schama 2001, n. p.). Cromwell, who keeps refusing all offers of a crown, is yet given an elaborate regal funeral after his death in 1658, including a traditional waxen effigy with royal insignia (Norbrook 1999, 379–82).

It is likely that pamphlets and chapbooks, which largely rely on visual cues for their propagandistic purposes, are more successful in convincing the "vulgar" than Milton's complex rhetoric. If, for Sir Thomas Browne, even the Scriptures have to use a technique of accommodation to aid readers in understanding otherwise "unspeakable mysteries" (2012, 51, *Religio* 1.45), then secular authorities like the English Republic can hardly be expected to trust their "vulgar" subjects with greater intellectual powers. In fact, texts and images, reading and visuality are connected in early modernity on a yet deeper level, independent of social distinctions like that between the 'vulgar' and the 'person of quality'. This concerns the physiological process of reading itself. Here, there is no strict distinction between the processing of images and that of texts – both

---

44 "Exit the tyrant, the last of kings, in the first year of England's restored liberty, 1648[/9]." The date is given in old style, according to current practice. Cit. in Norbrook 1999, 199. On the visual poverty of Commonwealth and Protectorate, see also Sharpe 2000b, 223–65.

converge in visual perception and then work on human passions. The widespread "discredit surrounding printed books" (Johns 1998, 423) is not only due to the usual concerns about eloquence and rhetoric but is reinforced by the visual nature of reading. The conflict between sight and hearing in Milton also stems from the cultural predominance of the visual sense, above all in materialist philosophy. For Hobbes, vision is "the noblest of [th]e senses" (1646, fol. 2^v), and his theory of sense perception is based on detailed studies and experiments in the field of optics. Hobbes's and Descartes's work on optics advance the scientific exploration of light and vision in mechanistic and mediumistic terms. What Hobbes and Descartes share, in the words of Jan Prins (1996, 138), is an understanding of "vision [as] an acquired capacity based on complicated, unconscious inferences, presumably based on comparing experiences through trial and error. In a sense, both Hobbes and Descartes consider the relation between vision and the visible as the product of an illusion" – as, we might add, does Milton. Because Hobbes believes all natural phenomena to be reducible to local motion of material bodies, he thinks of light as action at a distance, propagated to the eye through a medium. Visual perception is produced by the pressure (motion) of the agent, passed on by the medium to the eye, which passively receives the motion and communicates it via the optic nerve into "the brain, or spirits, or some internal substance in the head" (Hobbes 1994, 25; *EL* 1.2.7). Vision is a mechanical response to a stimulus. As Hobbes explains in the *Elements of Law* (1.2.8), "the interior coat of the eye is nothing else but a piece of the optic nerve, and therefore the motion is still continued thereby into the brain, and by resistance or reaction of the brain, is also a rebound in the optic nerve again, which we not conceiving as motion or rebound from within, think it is without, and call it light" (1994, 25).

According to Hobbes's *Tractatus Opticus I* (c. 1640), "all action is local motion in the agent, as all passion is local motion in the patient",[45] so that vision is a "passion" (*passio*) in the sensing subject. Agents have a power to move, while patients have an inherent power to be moved. These ideas underpin Hobbes's psychology and, ultimately, his social theory as well. In the mechanistic understanding, psychological powers, like sense, understanding, and appetite, operate as properties of the 'animal spirits', which are conceptualised as imperceptible but nonetheless material substances that circulate through the body, connect its several parts, and direct all operations of the organism by propagating motion from one part of the body to another. These spirits are passive; they can function as agents only when they have been set in motion by something else, when they have received a mechanical stimulus.

---

45 "Omnis actio est motus localis in agente, sicut et omnis passio est motus localis in patiente: *Agentis* nomine intelligo corpus, cujus motu producitur effectus in alio corpore; *patientis*, in quo motus aliquis ab alio corpore generatur" (Hobbes 1839–1845a, 5: 217).

In Hobbes's epistemology, what we perceive as reality is comprised by the internal appearances of the objects beyond us, caused by motion, so that "we compute nothing but our own phantasms" (1839–1845b, 1: 92).[46] The ontological status of the outside world can only be inferred from the fact that, because "there is nothing whereof there is not some cause" (*EL* 1.6.9; 1994, 42), there must be something 'out there' that acts on the senses and the mind: "The things that really are in the world without us, are those motions by which these seemings are caused" (1.2.10; 1994, 26). The motions of the visual lines or optical axes are a controlled movement determined by attention and interest, "based on the motions around the heart" (Prins 1996, 143). On this level, seeing and reading are analogous processes. Silent reading is a special case of visual sense perception (Elsky 1989, 128; Saenger 1997, Olson 1994). Widespread and influential as mechanist epistemology is in seventeenth-century learned circles, it can help us understand the political distrust of the spread of printed texts and the increase of literacy. With Hobbes (and, below, Davenant) we also approach a contemporary conception of how literature works and how the split between word and image might be overcome.

Adrian Johns has succinctly summed up "what early modern men and women thought actually happened when they read" as follows (1998, 442; cf. Johns 1996): "They saw letters on a page through eyes that resembled the device known as the camera obscura, which conveyed images, through the body's animal spirits, onto the brain's *sensus communis*. There imaginative and perceptual images combined, and animal spirits mingled and departed to drive the body's responses to both." Reading thus has an effect on mind and body alike, affecting the interface between them (for Hobbes, there is no Cartesian separation here, because the heart and the brain are sense organs). In weaker minds, reading can trigger potentially dangerous mental and physical responses through its impact on the passions. This term 'passion' is somewhat equivocal in Hobbes, and its meanings can sometimes overlap in an interesting way. In some instances, where the word is used in a more abstract sense, it denotes the passive quality of a patient as opposed to an agent. More frequently, it is used in close proximity to the term "affections", both being concrete acts of "that power of the mind which we call motive" in contrast to "power cognitive" or "conceptive" (*EL* 1.6.9; Hobbes 1994, 43). According to the expectation of pleasure or pain, the motion produced by the "power conceptive" is communicated, via the mind's "power motive" ("that by which the mind giveth animal motion to that body wherein it existeth") to the "heart," stimulating or inhibiting ('helping' or 'hindering') "the vital motion" of the body (1.7.1; 43). Thus reason and passion – "the principal parts of our nature" (1994, 19) – are not opposing forces (head vs. heart or mind vs. body) but belong to a continuum of motions in different physical locations of the body,

---

46 *De corpore* 1: 2.7.1: "ne [. . .] quidem [. . .] aliud computamus, quam phantasmata nostra" (Hobbes 1839–1845a, 1: 82).

"within the head" and "about the heart" (1.7.1; 43).⁴⁷ The lack of precision in this physiological description is probably intentional, as it emphasises the ubiquity and continuity of "internal [. . .] animal motion" (1.7.2; 43–44) in Hobbes's anthropology, which is not based on a clean Cartesian separation between *res cogitans* and *res extensa*. Pleasure and pain are interpreted as internal motions of attraction and repulsion, which are "the first unperceived beginnings of our actions" (1.12.1; 70). In the transition from internal and unperceived to external and perceptible motion, the passions play the role of a catalyst, intensifying or inhibiting: "appetite" and "aversion" or (prospectively, as the expectation of future displeasure) "fear".

In the rather broad and terminologically imprecise concept of passion, Hobbes appears to have found a way of preserving a porous boundary between emotional and rational desires (such as the long-term desire for self-preservation). The lengthy enumerations of individual passions in the *Elements of Law* (1.9) and *Leviathan* (1.6) list what modern psychologists would probably describe as emotionally coloured mental states, from love and hatred to curiosity and admiration. For Hobbes, the rational and the emotional are not mutually exclusive human dimensions but form a continuum on a scale ranging from 'reason' to 'madness', from control of the passions to their uncontrolled excess (*Leviathan* 1.8). Thus emotional desires are not in themselves irrational, but they can become irrational when they conflict with what is perceived as rational.

In their influence on men's actions, the passions are of decisive importance, as the title to chapter 1.12 of the *Elements* makes unmistakably clear: "HOW BY DELIBERATION FROM PASSIONS PROCEED MEN'S ACTIONS". Here is the crucial link between anthropology, epistemology, and political theory. In the *Leviathan*, Hobbes confirms the optical foundations of his theory of perception by comparing the passions to magnifying lenses or telescopes (*L* 2.18; 1996, 129): "For all men are by nature provided of notable multiplying glasses, (that is their Passions and Selfe-love,) through which, every little payment appeareth a great grievance." Looked at through the lens of the passions, the individual's public duties appear exaggerated out of all proportion in relation to self-interest. For Hobbes, what people lack but need are the corrective "prospective glasses, (namely Morall and Civill Science,)" which will lead them towards a recognition of the superior value of the common interest (ibid.).⁴⁸

---

47 From 1643 onwards, Hobbes explicitly locates the central organ of sensory perception, where 'phantasms' are processed, in the heart rather than the brain. Prins (1996, 141) cites a passage from Hobbes's critique of *De Mundo* by Thomas White (1643) as the turning point. The act of vision is then "defined as an outwardly directed reaction evoked in the heart by the action of a luminous or illuminated body" (142).
48 On the optical qualities of prospective glasses, which combined fragments of images into one new image, as a metaphor of higher-level cognition in Hobbes (and an analogy to the functioning of the Leviathan), see Bredekamp 1999, 83–94; cf. Gilman 1978.

The passions are perceptual filters that determine the interpretation of the 'phantasms' of perception. The term that is sometimes used for these filters is again an optical one: 'colour', a term from classical rhetoric that denotes a manipulative twist or spin (Bacon 1996, Hobbes 1986; Skinner 1996, 195–98). By influencing these filters, through language or by other (e.g. visual) means, it is possible to influence men's actions. Passions not only colour but distort people's view of reality, including their political situation. This anthropological predicament can be exploited for political (ideological) purposes. Another chapter heading in the *Elements of Law* is "HOW BY LANGUAGE MEN WORK UPON EACH OTHER'S MINDS". Hobbes develops an early form of speech act theory, in which language is not merely a tool to describe the world but in which it also has pragmatic and performative functions (cf. *Leviathan* 1.14 on promises; see Brekle 1975, 295; Sorell 1996, 163).[49] Language can excite or calm the passions; it can be used to communicate a speaker's opinions and attitudes, or to influence the opinions and actions of others. In this respect, it carries the "tincture of our different passions" (*L* 1.4; Hobbes 1996, 31).

> And therefore in reasoning, a man must take heed of words; which [. . .] have a signification also of the nature, disposition, and interest of the speaker; such as are the names of Vertues, and Vices; For one man calleth *Wisdome*, what another calleth *feare*; and one *cruelty*, what another *justice* [. . .]. And therefore such names can never be true grounds of any ratiocination. (Ibid.)

Language, in this view, is what makes science possible, but it can also generate misunderstanding and confusion. Hobbes describes its negative consequences for social life in more detail in *De homine* 10.3 (1658). In distinction to animals, only human beings "can devise errors and pass them on for the use of others" (Hobbes 1991, 183).

> Man if it please him (and it will please him as often as it seems to advance his plans) can teach what he knows to be false from works that he hath inherited; that is, he can lie and render the minds of men hostile to the conditions of society and peace; something that cannot happen in the societies of other animals, since they judge what things are good and bad for them by their senses, not on the basis of the complaints of others, the causes whereof, unless they be seen, they cannot understand. Moreover, it sometimes happens to those that listen to philosophers and Schoolmen that listening becomes a habit, and the words that they hear they accept rashly, even though no sense can be had from them (for such are the kind of words invented by teachers to hide their own ignorance), and they use them, believing that they are saying something when they say nothing. Finally, on account of the ease of speech, the man who truly doth not think, speaks; and what he says, he believes to be true, and he can deceive himself; a beast cannot deceive himself. Therefore by *oratio* man is not made better, but only given greater possibilities. (Ibid.)

In this context, the two meanings of 'passion' overlap: speech is an agent that "works upon" the mind as a *passive* recipient; more precisely, speech acts upon the

---

[49] Hobbes is not the only author to develop a performative understanding of language in early modernity; he summarises skeptic, Baconian, and Grotian attitudes towards language. See, e.g., Grotius 1977, 1: 292–93 on promises.

passions as catalysts of the internal motions ("endeavours") by which conceptions are translated into actions. We can infer that the spread of printed pamphlets, communication at a distance, only aggravates the potential abuse of speech by providing even "greater possibilities" than verbal interaction.

In a public sphere swayed by rhetoric, the passions of pity and indignation "are most easily raised and increased by eloquence", which can for instance "magnify" a person's "success" (*EL* 1.9.10–11; Hobbes 1994, 53–54).[50] Weak or uneducated minds, who have difficulties controlling their passions – because, to stay with the optical metaphor propounded in *Leviathan*, they can see only fragments of reality magnified through the distorting lenses of passion, unable to assemble the complete picture out of its dispersed elements – are a sitting target for the lures of rhetoric and therefore need special attention, education and control. In a Miltonic gesture at the interpretative and educational authority of a minor segment of the polity, Hobbes notes in the *Elements of Law* (1.13.3) that "commonly truth is on the side of the few, rather than of the multitude" (1994, 74).

If it is the disagreement of private judgements that creates moral and social conflict, Hobbes suggests politics as its solution, understood as the decision-making of a minority for the whole of society:

> But this is certain, seeing right reason is not existent, the reason of some man, or men, must supply the place thereof; and that man, or men, is he or they, that have the sovereign power [. . .]; and consequently the civil laws are to all subjects the measures of their actions, whereby to determine, whether they be right or wrong, profitable or unprofitable, virtuous or vicious; and by them the use and definition of all names not agreed upon, and tending to controversy, shall be established. As for example, upon the occasion of some strange and deformed birth, it shall not be decided by Aristotle, or the philosophers, whether the same be a man or no, but by the laws. (*EL* 2.10.8; Hobbes 1994, 181)

Hobbes's political theory is an absolutism based on epistemological relativism. Its foundational assumption is that multitudes of people are incapable of acting according to a rational consensus. The lack of objective rational criteria for human action requires the coordination of individual moral judgements by the sovereign (*L* 1.6; Hobbes 1996, 39).

In his reflections on pedagogy, Hobbes is particularly suspicious of books and book knowledge. The contemporary epistemology of reading, as we have seen, confirms this suspicion. As we have seen, the meaning of words for Hobbes is always dependent on their use in a defined or definable context; theoretically, the only solution to the problem of contingency is to have the meaning of disputed terms

---

50 The word "magnifying" might be read as an early instance of the optical metaphor elaborated in *Leviathan* 2.17: "that art of words, by which some men can represent to others, that which is Good, in the likenesse of Evill; and Evill, in the likenesse of Good; and augment, or diminish the apparent greatnesse of Good and Evill; discontenting men, and troubling their Peace at their pleasure" (Hobbes 1996, 119–20).

assigned by the sovereign. This makes Hobbes very sceptical of the success of learning from books, because books lack a clear indication of the "contexture" of their utterances (*EL* 1.13.8; Hobbes 1994, 76). This accounts for the difficulty of discovering the author's true "opinions and intentions". In contrast, this problem is not nearly so severe in "the presence of him that speaketh", because in situations of interaction we can infer, from "sight" and perhaps from other means of guessing the speaker's present intentions, what he means to say (76–77). But for printed texts, it is easier to persuade than to teach.

It is therefore quite understandable that control over what was being printed and published should be a major political and governmental concern. If, because of its physiological, especially visual foundations, the act of reading, like rhetoric, appeals to the passions more than to the intellect, this influential ideological weapon has to be controlled and used for the 'right' purpose – which can only be defined by the sovereign. This is even more important because, by means of print, rhetorically skilful demagogues can enormously expand the pernicious influence of their inflaming words and endanger the stability of the political order. In the absence of firm moral criteria for individual decision-making, the prince has to govern by manipulating his subjects' beliefs in order to ensure public peace:

> [I]t is annexed to the Soveraignty, to be Judge of what Opinions and Doctrines are averse, and what conducing to Peace; and consequently, on what occasions, how farre, and what, men are to be trusted withall, in speaking to Multitudes of people; and who shall examine the Doctrines of all bookes *before they be published*. For the Actions of men proceed from their Opinions; and in the wel [sic] governing of Opinions, consisteth the well governing of mens Actions, in order to their Peace, and Concord. (Hobbes 1996, 2.18, my italics)

We have now come close to discerning the specific function of *literary* communication, which Hobbes elaborates in close connection to his political, anthropological, and epistemological considerations. In Hobbes's diagram of the "SUBJECTS OF KNOWLEDGE" in *Leviathan* 1.19, poetry is classified as a branch of natural philosophy, on a par with rhetoric, logic, and jurisprudence. Poetry is not an autonomous realm of study but one of the disciplines concerned with language. The distinction between poetry and eloquence appears to be rather fluid, as Hobbes derives the very definition of poetry from rhetorical epideixis: "*Magnifying, Vilifying*, &c." (1996, 61). Poetry communicates opinions that influence the passions, similar to the 'colours' of rhetoric. It makes isolated fragments of reality appear greater than they really are by means of an optical trick. Poetry uses "Metaphors, and Tropes of speech" (*L* 1.4; 1996, 31) that work on the fancy rather than judgement: in poetry, these 'inconstant' forms of signification have a decorative rather than persuasive function; they are "less dangerous, because they profess their inconstancy" (31).

Poetry for Hobbes is legitimate as innocent play with words, its purpose "to please and delight our selves, and others, by playing with our words, for pleasure or ornament, innocently" (*L* 1.4). The 'danger' arises when poetic use of speech is confused with the literal, when the line that separates poetry from persuasive rhetoric is crossed and "reasoning" is based on metaphors instead of definitions – which can only lead to "contention, and sedition" (1.5; 36). Judgement is therefore needed to keep this line of demarcation between poetry and rhetoric stable. In Hobbes's thought, the boundary between fictional and factual modes of representation is not systematic and clear-cut; like the meaning of words, these modes are dependent on context and use. This is quite clearly stated in *The Elements of Law* (1.13.7):

> Another use of speech is INSTIGATION and APPEASING, by which we increase or diminish one another's passions; it is the same thing with persuasion: the difference not being real. [. . .] And as in raising an opinion from passion, any premises are good enough to infer the desired conclusion; so, in raising passion from opinion, it is no matter whether the opinion be true or false, or the narration historical or fabulous. For not truth, but image, maketh passion; and a tragedy affecteth no less than a murder if well acted. (Hobbes 1994, 76)

Imaginative literature, independent of genre – "whether it be *Epique,* or *Dramatique*" (*L* 1.8; 1996, 51) – has an effect on its readers or audiences because it works upon the passions. It is this performative character of producing opinions from passions that counts in Hobbes's theory, rather than formal definitions of genre. The end here justifies the means: "any premises are good enough to infer the desired conclusion" (1994, 76). The psychological effect (arousal or appeasement) depends on the context in which it occurs, on the intention of those who wish to produce it, and on the degree of perfection in the performance ("if well acted"). Apparently, Hobbes is here thinking in terms of larger audiences, crowds in a Greek amphitheatre or an English playhouse. When he does consider individual readers, he emphasises the production of fictitious images in the mind: "when a man compoundeth the image of his own person, with the image of the actions of an other man; as when a man imagins himselfe a *Hercules,* or an *Alexander*, (which happeneth often to them that are much taken with reading of Romants) it is a compound imagination, and properly but a Fiction of the mind" (*L* 1.2; 1996, 16). Here he actually talks about reading novels, describing a *Don Quijote* situation of identifying with a fictional character. The meaning of the word "image" in this passage is complex; if it is related to the phrase "image maketh passion" cited above, it becomes clear that "image" cannot only be understood here as a visual representation in the mind but needs to be read as a representation that is 'coloured' by opinion: to imagine oneself a Hercules is to have an enlarged opinion of one's own abilities or one's heroic character. An image, in this sense, can never be true but must always have a certain falsifying or beautifying spin to it.

Evidently, Hobbes for the most part does not think about literature in aesthetic terms. This is not because such terminology would not have been available to him (Neoplatonism as well as French neoclassicism would have offered him ample precedents); rather, he deliberately avoids it for strategic reasons. Instead, he writes about poetry in terms of a psychology of perception – a decisive step for English neoclassicism. Not for Hobbes the Neoplatonic talk of "everlasting beauty" or "inward light" promoted by Sidney (Sidney 1973, 77, 91). For the materialist, after all, "[l]ight is a fancy in the minde, caused by motion in the braine, which motion againe is caused by the motion of [th]e parts of such bodies, as we call lucid" (Hobbes 1646, fol. 3^r).

Poetry, like rhetoric, has an ideological and ultimately political function for Hobbes and many of his contemporaries: its purpose is to modify the ways in which people perceive their conditions of living and those who govern them. Hobbes explicates and radicalises what is already inherent in Renaissance literary theory: the connection between poetic language and human action. For Sidney, for example, poetry is not defined by formal criteria but by its intentions and effects: what makes a poet "is not rhyming and versing" but "that feigning notable *images* of virtues, vices, or what else, with that delightful teaching" that leads to "virtuous action" (1973, 81, 83, my italics). Hobbes, who typically thinks in terms of populations rather than individuals, transforms Sidney's celebration of poetry as "of all sciences [. . .] the monarch" (1973, 91) into a pragmatic admonition to the sovereign concerning the dangers and uses of poetic language. The study of poetry, for Hobbes, is the science of controlling these dangers and converting them into useful instruments of politics.

This conception is elaborated in Hobbes's collaboration with Davenant. Although Hobbes is busy writing *Leviathan*, he obliges Davenant, who like him has been an exile in Paris since 1646, with a written reply to his preface to *Gondibert*, in which Davenant praises Hobbes as the philosophical mastermind behind his ambitious epic poem. Both the preface and Hobbes's "Answer" are printed together in Paris in 1650, a year before the incomplete poem itself – and Hobbes's *Leviathan* – are published.[51] Hobbes's "Answer to the Preface" contains "the clearest exposition of [Hobbes's] theory of the fancy" (Skinner 1996, 333) and of his ideas of the function of poetry. Taken together, the two texts form a sort of manifesto for a materialist understanding of literature at mid-century, one year after the execution of Charles I and the proclamation of the English Republic. Surprisingly, it is Davenant, not Hobbes, who explicitly lingers on the political and ideological uses of poetry. Hobbes begins more conventionally, by repeating the commonplace Renaissance definition of the role of poets as laid down in Sidney's *Defence*: "by imitating humane life, in delightfull and measur'd lines, to avert men from vice, and encline them to vertuous and honorable actions" (Hobbes 1971a, 45). The matrix of poetic genres he devises to describe "the Nature and differences of Poesy" (45) is a system of correspondences between three major "sorts of Poesy" (heroic, scommatic, pastoral), "regions of the universe"

---

[51] Davenant 1650a (Wing D334A), Davenant 1650b (Wing D322). Wing D322 has the alternative title *A Discourse upon Gondibert* and contains two dedicatory poems by Waller and Cowley on Davenant's "two first Books of Gondibert, finished before his voyage to America" – a short-lived enterprise, since Davenant's ship was intercepted by the republican navy and Davenant was taken back to London. Critical attention to the Hobbes-Davenant connection has been scanty. Notable exceptions are Dowlin 1934, Reiss 1982b; Sharpe 1987, 101–8; Young 1986, Jacob and Raylor 1991; Springborg 1997.

(heaven, air, earth) and "regions of mankind" (court, city, country) (Reik 1977, 139). These "sorts of Poesy" are further distinguished "in the manner of *Representation*, which sometimes is *Narrative* [. . .] and sometimes *Dramatique*" (Hobbes 1971a, 45–46), resulting in six different genres, of which the epic poem – the genre of Davenant's *Gondibert* – is the highest and noblest, associated with the heroic, with heaven and the court. This matrix typifies the normative, prescriptive style of thought that dominates early modern neoclassical poetics (Reik 1977, 151, 220; Simon 1971, 15).

As in his other writings, Hobbes derives his idea of style from the rhetorical tradition: good style is what is appropriate in a given communicative situation, determined by conventional and rational principles. The ability to know what is appropriate in different situations and to act accordingly – which I take to be Hobbes's definition of "wit" (*L* 1.8) – depends on "judgement" (also called "Discretion", the rational ability to distinguish differences and resemblances) rather than "fancy" (associative imagination).[52] Judgement is also needed to control the fancy by means of necessary restrictions: perspicuity, property, decency. "Judgement begets the strength and structure; and Fancy begets the ornaments of a Poeme" (1971a, 49). Again, Hobbes anticipates what will become a commonplace in English neoclassical literary theory: the need to exert rational control over the "Wild and Lawless" imagination.[53] Yet in the context of Hobbes's thought, this competition between fancy and judgement can be explained as a reflex of his philosophical work on the relation between images and truth, rhetoric and science, which ultimately stems from a concern about the correct and virtuous handling of (performative) language. Judging from Hobbes's use of the term "image", the "copious Imagery discreetly ordered, and perfectly registred in the memory", which

---

[52] In the "Answer", the distinction between judgement and fancy is slightly different than in *Leviathan*: judgement, memory's "severer Sister," "busieth her selfe in grave and rigide examination of all the parts of Nature, and in registring by Letters, their order, causes, uses, differences and resemblances"; fancy, on the other hand, is "swift motion over" the "materials at hand and prepared for use [sc., by judgement]," the high-speed mental processing of "copious Imagery" (1971a, 49). In *Leviathan*, Hobbes applies these terms outside of a literary context, in a wider psychological and moral significance; there, he identifies fancy (or "imagination") as the processing of resemblances and judgement as the processing of distinctions (cf. 1.8), places them in a hierarchical order of value, and adds the third term 'wit': "Fancy, without the help of Judgement, is not commended as a Vertue: but the later which is Judgement, and Discretion, is commended for it selfe, without the help of Fancy. [. . .] So that where Wit is wanting, it is not Fancy that is wanting, but Discretion. Judgement therefore without Fancy is Wit, but Fancy without Judgement not" (1996, 1.8).
[53] Cf. Dryden's epistle dedicatory to *The Rival Ladies* (1664): "Imagination in a Poet is a faculty so Wild and Lawless, that, like an High-ranging Spaniel it must have cloggs tied to it, least it out-run the judgement" (1962, 101); epistle dedicatory to *Annus Mirabilis* (1666): "the faculty of imagination in the writer [. . .], like a nimble Spaniel, beats over and ranges through the field of Memory, till it springs the Quarry it hunted after" (1956, 53). Even the spaniel seems derived from Hobbes who, in *The Elements of Law*, compares the "quick ranging" of the mind with the "ranging of spaniels" searching for a scent (1994, 1.4.3); cf. Watson 1962, 1: 8 n. 2. On the presence of Hobbes in Dryden's writings, see Dryden 1995a, 328–29 n. 56; Winn 1987, 133–34, 216–18.

forms the "materials" of fancy (1971a, 49), is not exclusively visual but includes rhetorical 'colours' and figures of speech. According to Quentin Skinner (1996, 365), "Hobbes's thesis is [. . .] that the use of *ornatus* represents the natural way of expressing the imagery of the mind, a commitment that makes him one of the earliest writers in English to employ the general term 'imagery' to refer to the figures and tropes of speech." Fancy is verbal as well as visual creativity, and its products are potentially deceptive unless they are supplemented and controlled by rational principles of selection, contrasting and ordering (judgement), which are the methodic foundations of science. In this respect, because he insists on a neat separation and opposition between fancy and judgement, the Hobbes of 1640 appears more 'neoclassical' than the Hobbes of 1651, who argues (and *Leviathan* is a rhetorical turning point in this respect, in part prepared for by the "Answer") that a case could be made not for maintaining a clear separation between the two opposed faculties or forms of wit but for establishing an alliance between them. 'Science' can then legitimately resort to rhetorical techniques of adornment and make deliberate use of imagery ("similes, metaphors, and other tropes", *EL* 1.10.4; 1994, 61) in order to persuade others of the truth of what judgement has distinguished, thereby to produce "very marvellous effects to the benefit of mankind" (1971a, 49). "For wheresoever there is place for adorning and preferring of Errour, there is much more place for adorning and preferring of Truth, if they have it to adorn" (1996, 484; see Skinner 1996, 364–66).

In the "Answer", the argument for a necessary alliance between judgement and fancy is applied to works of literature ("Poesy," "fiction": 1971a, 46, 51). This leads to a normative understanding of literary creation and literary theory, which parallels the normative definitions and demonstrations of Hobbes's moral science. In politics as well as literary theory, Hobbes is concerned with the limits of liberty, as can be seen in his proposition that "the Resemblance of truth is the utmost limit of Poeticall Liberty" (1971a, 51). This normative understanding involves establishing criteria of probability, of decorum (i.e. the observation of discursive and generic boundaries, normative distinctions between poetry and history, for example, or between the various literary 'sorts', and the emphasis on an intramundane, empirical, and rational foundation of subject matter ("the subject of a Poeme is the manners of men, not naturall causes", 46) and poetics. In close alignment to his political arguments against enthusiasm, Hobbes mocks those versifiers who "would be thought to speak by a divine spirit" (48) or who profess "to speak by inspiration, like a Bagpipe" (49). Making the same connection to enthusiasm, Davenant, in his Preface, calls 'inspiration' "a dangerous word" (22).

Hobbes applies to the theory of literature a literal and pragmatic (action-oriented) version of Renaissance poetics and practices of reading. As in his political writings (Tuck 1996, 193), he transposes reading and interpretation from the level of the individual reader to the level of a larger group, a multitude or an entire population, so that imaginative literature is viewed in the light of its social functions and political utility. In Renaissance theory, the conventional view of the purpose of 'true reading' had been to follow the advice of Plutarch: "to search for Philosophie in the writings of Poets: or rather therein to practise Philosophie, by using to seek profit in pleasure, and to love the same" (Plutarch 1603, 19–20). Readers were encouraged to extract, or to import from outside, "the moral philosophy that good authors mixed with their fictions" (Wallace 1974–75, 278) and to deduce applicable precepts from literary examples. The individual reader enjoyed a comparatively "wide latitude of response" (Wallace 1974–75, 275), but it was an early modern commonplace to assume that one read literary or historical texts for the purposes of (mostly moral) applicability, and that literary texts contained arguments about moral or philosophical truth that could be explicated in *sententiae* (Jardine and Grafton 1990).

Hobbes, in the "Answer", effectively turns this idea on its head, transforming a programme of aesthetic reception into a norm of aesthetic production. His question is not how an utterance could be extracted from a text by the reader, but how the author must construct a text so that it will impart a certain message and produce the intended effect upon its readers. In other words, Hobbes suggests solving the problem of contingency in early modern textual communication by means of a theory of effect. This effect is achieved by a method similar to the optical principle of the prospective glass:

> I beleeve (Sir) you have seene a curious kind of perspective, where, he that lookes through a short hollow pipe, upon a picture conteyning diverse figures, sees none of those that are there paynted, but some one person made up of their partes, conveighed to the eye by the artificiall cutting of a glasse. I find in my imagination an effect not unlike it from your Poeme. The vertues you distribute there amongst so many noble Persons, represent (in the reading) the image but of one mans vertue to my fancy, which is your owne; and that so deeply imprinted, as to stay for ever there, and governe all the rest of my thoughts, and affections [. . .]. (1971a, 55)

While reading, the reader's fancy is "deeply imprinted" with an "image" of "vertue", an image that the text does not contain on the surface, explicitly, but which it communicates to the mind by an optical trick: uniting fragments of an image into an unexpected new image. The image that appears is "some one person made up of their partes", which exactly corresponds to the Hobbesian principle by which political sovereignty is constructed and which the artist of the *Leviathan* frontispiece presents as a visual composite image: "the Multitude so united in one Person" (L 2.17; 1996, 120). This 'imprint' is "to stay for ever" in the reader's mind "and governe all the rest of [his or her] thoughts" (1971a, 55). The poem has reached its intended goal when it has fulfilled its function of moral teaching by permanently imprinting the master image of the composite sovereign.

Hobbes commends Davenant's heroic poem for achieving this ideal goal, but also because the content of its teaching corresponds to Hobbes's own political philosophy: "when I considered that also the actions of men, which singly are inconsiderable, after many conjunctures, grow at last either into one great protecting power, or into two destroying factions, I could not but approve the structure of your Poeme, which ought to be no other then such an imitation of humane life requireth" (1971a, 50). For "such an imitation of humane life", the aid of metaphysical concepts is no longer required, but such notions can still be reinscribed as a metaphoric illustration of a rational theory; as is the case when Hobbes gives a hermeticist description of the "wonderfull celerity" of the imagination that can "fly from one *Indies* to the other, and from Heaven to Earth [. . .], into the future, and into her selfe, and all this in a point of time" (49), or when he compares the influence of the stars on human behaviour with the influence of the sovereign: "For there is in Princes, and men of conspicuous power (anciently called *Heroes*) a lustre and influence upon the rest of men, resembling that of the Heavens" (45).[54] Hobbes reads Davenant's poem as a device in which this "influence upon the rest of men" is literally operative: its "motive" is "to adorne vertue, and procure her Lovers" (48), i.e. to persuade readers of the sovereign's "vertue" and to convince the individuals that make up the commonwealth that they have to be lovers of virtue: to form a composite image of their unity, in obedient submission to a sovereign, for the sake of peace and security. In the "Answer", Hobbes himself applies the principles of his theory to this brief text: the image that the reader is supposed to see has to be composed from disparate fragments and "diverse figures" in the text. Shortly after this, the technique of this "curious [. . .] perspective" (55) is graphically applied to the title page of *Leviathan*. In the literary and then visual production of this composite image, the conflict between visual and literary rhetoric is finally reconciled.

A greater contrast than between Milton on the one hand and Hobbes and Davenant on the other can hardly be imagined. And yet they sometimes employ similar metaphors and conceits that document what they have in common despite extreme differences in class, religion, and political conviction. After all, they have all imbibed a typical Renaissance education and rhetorical training. Moreover, they share a common problem, perhaps the most fundamental political problem of the seventeenth century: how to resolve or at least to reconcile the tricky relation between the 'state' and 'the people', the interests of power and the interests of liberty. Although their proposed solutions are as different as they can be, their means of finding possible answers are the same, stemming from the same traditions of literary culture and education. None of them are blessed with success: Davenant's major poem turns out to be a busted flush; Hobbes's *Leviathan* fails to find favour with the exiled court and is banned after the Restoration; Milton already writes *Paradise Lost* in the political underground, vaguely hoping for a "fit audience [. . .], though few" (Milton 1998, 7.31). And yet some of Hobbes's ideas and even some of his expressions show up again in the liberal political theory of John Locke in the 1680s, and Davenant's rationalist poetics at least enjoyed something of an afterlife during the Restoration and beyond (Gladish 1971, xxiii). In order to see how a poet

---

54 Both comparisons also occur in Davenant's Preface: "*Witte* is [. . .] dexterity of thought; rounding the world, like the Sun, with unimaginable motion; and bringing swiftly home to the memory universall survays" (1971, 18); on astrological influence, cf. 13, 38.

intends to apply Hobbes's theories of optics, of politics and of the physiology of reading in a programmatic manner, we must now turn to Davenant's *Preface to Gondibert*.

"The Conquests of Vertue": Mimesis and Strategic Visuality in Davenant's *Preface to Gondibert* (1650)

In contrast to Hobbes's "Answer", Davenant's own preface is anything but soft-spoken. He straighforwardly recommends his *Gondibert* as an ideological tool for inculcating obedience to the sovereign, offering it as a form of political advice to the monarch. Its political message is a justification of absolute sovereignty in Machiavellian terms, which is legitimised not by divine decree but by the presence of inner-worldly problems and demands (Davenant 1971, 30, 36). Consequently, like Hobbes, he excludes the supernatural from his concept of epic poetry (6). In its historical and social context, Davenant's preface can be read as a store-house of political and literary clichés, but like Hobbes's "Answer", it has been influential for the development of English neoclassical criticism.

Written and published at mid-century, the *Preface to Gondibert* sums up moral, aesthetic, and political discussions of its time, not in the manner of an academic analysis but from a certain perspective and with a clear political intention: it is an action- and goal-oriented utterance directed at a royalist courtly audience. Its context is the Civil War and the abolition of the monarchy in England: at the time of writing, the execution of Charles I in 1649 is still a recent event; Charles II has made his famous escape from England and is now a twenty-year-old exile without political power. Even absolutist France is shaken by violent outbreaks of civil unrest: in 1649, the Fronde revolt temporarily forces the French royal family to withdraw to Saint Germain (Knachel 1967). The text's immediate audience is the royalist community in Paris, not least Charles II himself, but its background (like that of *Leviathan*) is a more fundamental political conflict between sovereign and parliament that has a continental dimension as well. The text is confidently located by Davenant at the centre of power where the French sovereign has been reinstated: "*From the Louvre in Paris / January 2. 1650*" (i.e. 1651). But it is not surprising then that many of the metaphors and similes used by Davenant are derived from warfare – ambush (1971, 18, 24), scout (18, 23, 26), forces (25), enemy (17, 23, 26, 33) conquest (39), etc. – since he had himself seen military action during the war.

The preface addresses Hobbes in the style of a letter, using him as a philosophical authority, a representative of the 'new science' and a "Guide" across the battlefield of learning (24). Like Hobbes, Davenant is concerned with the very same question that led Burton and Browne to devise complex literary strategies: how to cope with the precarious relation between authors and readers in print culture, if communicative intentions are difficult to find out (by the reader) and equally difficult to achieve (by the author)? Davenant's answer is radically simpler than all those we have encountered until now. For him, critics and readers are all "Enemyes" (17) of writers. The author has to conquer or overpower the reader in military fashion. He does not complain about this predicament; he merely explains it by the "imperfect Stomacks" of readers who "either devour Bookes with over hasty Digestion, or grow to loath them from a Surfet" (25). The cause of readerly indigestion is literary overproduction, which leads to a loss of interest or understanding: "so shy men grow of Bookes" (24). This explains why "commonly Readers are justly Enemyes to Writers" (17). The author must become inventive: he must "court, draw in, and keep [the reader] with artifice" (24), he must "have [. . .] successe over the Reader (whom the Writer should surprize, and as it were keep prisoner for a time) as he hath on his Enemy's" (17). Aesthetic strategies are deployed as stratagems. For Davenant, as for Milton and Hobbes, the arts of rhetoric are weapons to persuade and win an audience, turning enemies into allies and "incredulity" (11) into belief. In terms that echo Sidney, but also Milton (cf. Milton 1953a, 816–18), Davenant describes heroic poetry as the most pleasing and therefore "easy" means to "the Conquests of Vertue" (39). He even develops an early functionalist understanding of literary illusion, what Coleridge would much later call the "willing suspension of disbelief" (1965, 169): "For wee may descend to compare the deceptions in Poesy to those of them that professe dexterity of Hand, which resembles Conjuring, and to such wee come not with the intention of *Lawyers* to examine the evidence of facts, but are content [. . .] to pay for being well deceiv'd" (11).

In Davenant's programmatic statements, this act of deception has a didactic purpose: "to governe the Reader (who though he be noble, may perhaps judge of supreme power like a very Commoner, and rather approve authority, when it is in many, then in one)" (24). Here poetic communication is conceived as pragmatic, goal-oriented, and strategic; he avoids to tackle the contingencies of communication between authors and their audience, but opts for a solution by means of communicative strategies, namely the effective, manipulative use of literary techniques of suspense and illusion ("being well deceiv'd"). Its influence on Restoration literary theory is notable in Dryden, for example, who cites Davenant's Machiavellian understanding of the author as an absolute sovereign and the audience as his subjects who must be persuaded and conquered. These are precisely the terms in which Dryden, in "Of Heroique Playes" (1672), argues for the use of realistic theatrical effects:

> these warlike Instruments, and, even the representations of fighting on the Stage, are no more than necessary to produce the effects of an Heroick Play; that is, to raise the imagination of the Audience, and to perswade them, for the time, that what they behold on the Theater is really perform'd. The Poet is, then, to endeavour an absolute dominion over the minds of the Spectators: for, though our fancy will contribute to its own deceipt, yet a Writer ought to help its operation. (Dryden 1978, 13–14)

Davenant distinguishes the performative character of poetry from the imitative character of history, whose task is "to record the truth of [past] actions" (Davenant

1971, 5). History is concerned with "Truth narrative, and past", poetry with "truth operative, and by effects continually alive" (11). Literature communicates a "truth in the passions" (5), but it does so "in reason" (11). Davenant's poetics is a rational one based on probability and verisimilitude (cf. 3, 16), on "explicable vertue" and "plaine demonstrative justice" (9). Poetry is judged from the perspective of utility ("how usefull it is", 28) rather than its aesthetic qualities. Poetry "charm's the People, with harmonious precepts" (30). It presents versified lessons in morality in a highly stylised rhetorical language, ultimately teaching "a willing and peaceful obedience" (30) to the sovereign monarch and towards "Superiors" in general (30).

But Davenant's poetics also has a social dimension, which strictly limits his target audience for poetry. From the noble title of the author's "Enemyes", the lower ranks of society are excluded. This saves Davenant the labour of performing complicated rhetorical manoeuvres around the problem of social cohesion and the possibility of teaching obedience to commoners by rational and linguistic means (a problem that also haunts Milton's *Areopagitica*). Davenant has no illusions about the usefulness of measured language in 'conquering' "the People", whom he also derogates as "the Rabble", "the meanest of the multitude" (15), and "this wilde Monster" (30). The positive influence of poetry does not reach that far down the social ladder. For Davenant, "the People" have a status no higher than animals: "They looke upon the outward glory or blaze of Courts, as Wilde beasts in darke nights stare on their Hunters Torches" (12). "The common Crowd (of whom we are hopelesse) we desert; being rather to be corrected by lawes (where precept is accompany'd with punishment) then to be taught by Poesy; for few have arriv'd at the skill of Orpheus [. . .] whom wee may suppose to have met with extraordinary Grecian Beasts, when so successfully he reclaim'd them with his Harpe" (13). The antagonism legible in these comparisons betrays an insecurity about the stability of the relation between the governors and the governed, understandable perhaps if we consider that a republic has just been established in England: the "Wilde beasts" might turn around to attack their hunters at any moment, and no Orpheus would be capable of appeasing them. Indeed, Davenant's argument sounds more Machiavellian than Hobbesian: "who can imagine lesse then a necessity of oppressing the people, since they are never willing either to buy their peace or to pay for Warre?" (12).

Davenant takes up Hobbes's optics of the passions when he explains that everyone imagines himself a sovereign, so that this egoism accounts for the people's tendency to disobey and resist (cf. 12). In analogy, divisions within the commonwealth are compared to internal divisions within individuals in a way that is theoretically diffuse and undeveloped (and which Hobbes prefers to ignore in his Answer). The problem arises from the difficulty of reconciling "publique Interest" with the rights of "Private men" (36). Unlike Hobbes, Davenant sees "the State" and "the People" as antagonists analogous to the opposition between reason and passion. His passing reference to "the Law of Nature" as a rational instead of a divine basis of legitimation (according to Davenant, the law of nature makes it our duty to act rationally and to "side with

Reason" against passion) is a mere shadow compared to the complexities of current natural law theory:

> the State and the People are divided, as wee may say a man is divided within him selfe, when reason and passion dispute about consequent actions; and if wee were calld to assist at such intestine warre, wee must side with Reason, according to our duty, by the Law of Nature; and Natures Law, though not written in Stone (as was the Law of Religion) hath taken deep impression in the Heart of Man, which is harder then marble of *Mount-Sinai*. (36)

What remains unclear in this exposition is the precise relation between "Man" as an abstraction, in whose "Heart" is inscribed the law of nature, and "a man", who is internally divided between reason and passion. The abstraction remains curiously unrelated to the concrete individual who, if he could read the law of nature, would not have to "dispute about consequent actions" but would not hesitate to act with certainty according to rational principles. Hobbes's *Leviathan* offers a theoretical answer to this tricky question by thinking sovereignty and the multitude together, as a unity rather than in opposition; but Davenant's muddled pronouncements on this subject allow us to see how fervently such an answer was desired and sought after at midcentury.

Davenant is unable to bridge the gap between the 'usefulness' of heroic poetry for inculcating obedience to the sovereign in the upper echelons of society and its uselessness for the vulgar multitude; but he attempts to compensate for this by including a social component in his otherwise Aristotelian theory of mimesis. It is enough, he claims, to educate those who can be educated; the others will follow suit because they always imitate their "Superiors": "to Imitation, Nature [. . .] perhaps doth needfully encline us, to keepe us from excesses" (8). Imitation is a human constant ("constant humor", 9) that checks social excesses "for the safety of mankinde [. . .] by dulling and stopping our progresse", setting "limits to courage and to learning, to wickedness and to erour" (9). Davenant here describes a social mechanism of self-control that is central to an early modern understanding of individuality: imitation is a technique of observing the self as if this observation came from the outside, from the "Opinion" of others (8). This technique enforces a moderation of the passions and promotes behaviour conforming to social norms. The heroic poem presents "patternes of human life, that are (perhaps) fit to be follow'd" (12). This view of a social 'governmentality' would also prove influential in Restoration aesthetics, in courtesy books, and education; in this respect, the seventeenth century is also the first inventor of 'pattern drill' (Salmon 1979, 26–27). The didactic ideal of imitation and repetition is still fully present at the end of the century. In the epistle dedicatory to his translation of the *Aeneid*, Dryden states that "[t]he shining Quality of an Epick Heroe, his Magnanimity, his Constancy, his Patience, his Piety, or whatever Characteristical Virtue his Poet gives him, raises first our Admiration: We are naturally prone to imitate what we admire: And frequent Acts produce a habit" (1987, 271). Earlier, in his dedication of *The Conquest of Granada* to the Duke of York, Dryden defended the loftiness of heroic drama in terms similar to Davenant's arguments: "The feign'd Heroe inflames the true: and the dead vertue animates the living. Since, therefore, the World is govern'd by precept and Example; and both these can onely have influence from those persons who are above us, that kind of Poesy which excites to vertue the greatest men, is of greatest use to humane kind" (1978, 3).

If techniques of social observation and imitation can transcend differences of social rank, no levelling of poetry is necessary to achieve its intended trickle-down effect, which will – by a top-down process of osmotic social mimesis beginning "from those persons who are above us" – will eventually reach even 'commoners': "Nor is it needfull", writes Davenant, "that Heroique Poesy should be levell'd to the reach of Common men; for if the examples it presents prevaile upon their Chiefs, the delight of Imitation [. . .] will rectify by the rules, which those Chiefs establish of their owne lives, the lives of all that behold them" (1971, 13). Having imbibed heroic poetry and having been 'conquered' by virtue, the "Chiefs" become copies of epic heroes, and their bravery and loyalty to the sovereign will in turn be imitated by their social inferiors.

This social mimesis as a functional principle of poetry is only one part of Davenant's literary theory, though. Another important aspect is the question of how the "Vertue" that poetry is supposed to teach is to be specified more concretely. Here again Davenant runs into a problem of contingency, because even the "Chiefs" are unable to agree among themselves which norms and patterns for action are politically desirable. In a striking image alluding to the contingency of Machiavellian *fortuna*, the state is compared to a ship driven by "uncertaine" winds while various pilots cannot agree on the right course to "the Land of Peace and Plenty" (34). The passage is a variation on the medieval topos of the 'ship of fools' but also a reminiscence of classical political theory, particularly Plato (*Politikos* 297e–298e, 302a): "me thinks Goverment [sic] resembles a Ship, where though *Divines, Leaders* of *Armys, Statesmen,* and *Judges* are the trusted Pilots; yet it moves by the means of Windes, as uncertaine as the breath of Opinion; and is laden with the People; a Freight much loosser, and more dangerous then any other living stowage; being as troublesome in faire weather, as Horses in a Storme" (1971, 34).

After presenting the different viewpoints and mutual observations of the four pilots, Davenant concludes that every party's perspective determines its perception of reality, leading them to "an emulous warr among themselves" which weakens their power. To save them from such multiple contingencies, he proposes the "collaterall help" of poetry. This time, his earlier qualifications about social restriction have curiously disappeared, because now he does suggest that poetry might serve as an ideological weapon to constrain "the People" (37):

> wee shall not erre by supposing that this conjunction of Fourefold Power [Religion, Armes, Policy, Law] hath faild in the effects of authority, by a misapplication; for it hath rather endeavord to prevaile upon their bodys, then their mindes; forgetting that the martiall art of constraining is the best; which assaults the weaker part; and the weakest part of the People is their mindes; for want of that which is the Mindes only Strength, *Education*; but their Bodys

are strong by continuall labour; for Labour is the Education of the Body. Yet when I mention the misapplication of force, I should have said, they have not only faild by that, but by a maine error; Because the subject on which they should worke is the Minde; and the Minde can never be constrain'd, though it may be gain'd by Persuasion: And since Persuasion is the principall Instrument which can bring to fashion the brittle and misshapen mettall of the Minde, none are so fitt aides to this important worke as Poets: whose art is more then any enabled with a voluntary, and cheerfull assistance of Nature; and whose operations are as resistlesse, secret, easy, and subtle, as is the influence of Planetts. (37–38)

Uneducated minds are easy prey for rhetorical weapons of mass persuasion. For Davenant, heroic poetry is of "particular strength" in this respect because it "hath a force that overmatches the infancy of such mindes as are not enabled by degrees of Education" (38).[55] In terms recalling Francis Bacon's celebration of the new science as an attack on nature (imagined as a woman to be 'enjoyed'; cf. 17), Davenant presents the conquering of people's minds as a "ravishment of Reason" (38). Yet whereas Bacon's aggressive scientific exploration is meant to produce an increase of scientific knowledge, Davenant's "delightfull insinuations" (38) are to generate political obedience in a proto-behaviorist act of 'imprinting', which may also echo Descartes's argument for manipulating emotional responses to sensory stimuli in his *Passions de l'Ame* of 1649 (Jacob and Raylor 1991, 219).

Similarly, Davenant's definition of wit as "dexterity of thought; rounding the world, like the Sun, with unimaginable motion; and bringing swiftly home to the memory universall surveys" (18) not only presents an allusion to hermeticist traditions, probably mediated through Italian Neoplatonism.[56] Its construction of a (geocentric) equivalence between the 'motion picture' of imagination and the motion of the Sun also implies a panoptic, controlling, and hierarchical observer position (Foucault 1979). Flatteringly, Davenant's praise of Hobbes places the philosopher in this privileged solar position: he travels "like the Sun" to "enlighten the world" (24). As in Aristotelian optics, seeing and emitting light are the same process. Rather than a glimpse of transcendence, Davenant's poetry is to provide "universall surveys" of "the world". Wit, for Davenant, is the ability to survey the volatility and complexity of the world, like a solar sovereign (the image anticipates Louis XIV's description as *Roi Soleil*) and to influence this reality. "[A]ll that finde its strength [. . .] worship it for the *effects*" (18, my italics). These effects of wit could be specified according to different offices (Condren 2002), different duties or roles, as perceived qualities of successful

---

55 The contradiction between this passage and the earlier exclusion of the common people from the persuasive powers of poetry is only resolved in Davenant's later *Proposition for Advancement of Moralitie* (Jacob and Raylor 1991), where he argues for the utility of heroic multi-media spectacles in educating the 'vulgar', effectively democratising the court masque. Perhaps what he has in mind is a distinction between two kinds of poetry for two different audiences, an elevated style for the educated and a simple style for the uneducated.
56 Francesco Patrizi's *Nova de Universis Philosophia* (1593) was contained in Hobbes's 'ideal library' (Pacchi 1968).

social action: "It is in Divines Humility, Exemplarinesse, and Moderation; In Statesmen Gravity, Vigilance, Benigne Complaisancy, Secrecy, Patience, and Dispatch. In Leaders of Armys Valor, Painfulnesse, Temperance, Bounty, Dexterity in Punishing, and rewarding, and a sacred Certitude of promise. It is in Poets a full comprehension of all recited in all these; and an ability to bring those comprehensions into action" (Davenant 1971, 18–19). The function of poetry is to recall "the true measure of what is of greatest consequence to humanity, (which are things righteous, pleasant and usefull)" (19). This function is exclusively secular and rational: it is to negotiate the different perspectives of the proto-systemic 'official' divisions of the time (religious, political, military, legal) in a unified, higher-order perspective ("what is of greatest consequence to *humanity*"). Its goal is not to totalise any of these perspectives but to present a harmony in diversity. What these perspectives have in common is the classical notion of *humanitas* as a virtue that transcends the specifications of office, a residue that is nevertheless reserved "for potential respecification in terms of further official attributes" (Condren 2002, 116).

This perspectivism of a higher order can be linked to the comparison Davenant makes between poetry and painting, particularly the modern genre of landscape painting. Literary texts, like painting, use techniques of illusion to achieve their intended effects. Like the landscape painter who uses the technique of single-point perspective – and like the Sun, who inhabits God's birdseye view – poets, if they have wit, can aspire to be "considering" observers who visualise and control a prospect they can align along a grid (like the spider in its web, in Davenant's conceit [18]) and "represent" as "the Worlds true image" (4) to the view of other spectators. Understood in terms of perspective, wit is for poetry what the vanishing point is for painting: it ensures that the representation is configured in such a way that the spectator/reader is made to see "the Worlds true image" just as the painter/poet intended it to be seen. The truth of the image depends on the observer's perspective and can be ideologically determined *ad libitum*.

The *Preface to Gondibert* not only anticipates central points of neoclassical literary theory in England, especially from Dryden's famous essays, by a number of years – especially the rationalist understanding of poetry as "the best Expositor of Nature" (40). It is also a highly strategic text, not only reflecting on literature as a tactical instrument of power but also employing such tactics directly. Davenant uses what he perceives as the authority and influence of Hobbes to address the monarch himself, certainly with the intention of gaining favour. In 1650, Hobbes, the former mathematics tutor of Charles II, was on his way to becoming an important political advisor to the king in exile; a future destroyed shortly afterwards, most probably at the hands of Edward Hyde, with the publication of *Leviathan*. The extreme density of rhetorical flourishes in the preface to *Gondibert*, together with obsequious declarations of service to the exiled king, are evidence enough that Davenant used the preface – and doubtless *Gondibert* itself – as a means of self-promotion in the eyes of the monarch and his court. His aim was to assert not only the king's (and Hobbes's), but also his own position as chief of court poets and as a literary advisor to Charles II.

This reading can be corroborated by Davenant's own comments. In the preface, he not only reveals his bluntly utilitarian, no-nonsense attitude towards poetry but also towards his own motivations for writing. He frankly confesses "that the desire of Fame made me a Writer" (26). He is very conscious of the observation of others and thus of the presence or absence of royal favour. After the first books of *Gondibert* prove a critical failure, Davenant sees no point in continuing the poem and returns to a form that is more compatible with his talents – theatre. He becomes a successful theatrical entrepreneur. His gifts would make him not only the father of English neoclassicism but also of English opera (with *The Siege of Rhodes*, still during Cromwell's reign; Clare 2019) and of Restoration drama as well. Theatre and opera turn out to be Davenant's second and more successful solution to the problem of integrating verbal, visual, and auditory media for the sake of uniting literature and politics. In 1660, when Charles II returns to England, he authorises Thomas Killigrew and Sir William Davenant to run the duopoly of the King's and the Duke's Company. The royal warrant is drafted in Davenant's own hand (Public Record Office ms. SP 29/8/1).

If Hobbes's claim that Davenant contributed ideas to the writing of *Leviathan* is true, some possible points of inspiration can be found in the preface to *Gondibert*. They concern Hobbes's specialty: optical metaphors and perspectives. In Davenant's text, the leaders of armies observe politicians "with the Eye of Envy (which inlarges objects like a multiplying-glasse [. . .] and think them immense as *Whales*" (35).[57] In *Leviathan*, this image is applied to "all men" and generalised to a definition of egoism: "For all men are by nature provided of notable multiplying glasses, (that is their Passions and Selfe-love,) through which, every little payment appeareth a great grievance" (Hobbes 1996, 2.18). Davenant also makes a comment on "the generality of men" using the image of an inverted telescope: "who think the best objects of theire owne country so little to the size of those abroad, as if they were shew'd them by the wrong end of a Prospective" (1971, 11). Other optical figures of speech in Davenant include the topical mirror of mimesis: "in a perfect glasse of Nature [the Heroick Poem] gives us a familiar and easy view of our selves" (3), and "Poets [. . .] should represent the Worlds true image often to our view" (4). Hobbes appears to agree with both: "Poets are Paynters: I would faine see another Painter draw so true perfect and natural a Love to the Life, and make use of nothing but pure lines" (1971a, 50), and yet he inserts a characteristic qualification that distances himself from Davenant's

---

[57] The whale also appears in a previous passage in Davenant's text, where it is said that "the Mindes of Men are more monstrous [. . .] then the Bodies of Whales" (31). It should not be forgotten that Leviathan is the name of a biblical sea-monster, often identified with a whale (Job 40–41). Hobbes's theory uses this monstrosity as a motivation (fear) for resolving it, by transposing it to the higher order of the 'body politic', which appears monstrous only on the outside, not to those who inhabit it and are protected by it.

self-congratulatory statements and conventional allusions: "For *in him that professes the imitation of Nature*, (as all Poets do) what greater fault can there be, then to bewray an ignorance of nature in his Poeme" (51–52, my italics). Hobbes appears less interested in Davenant's "perfect glasse" than in glasses that are 'artificially cut' (cf. 55) and that do not simply reproduce an image but generate a new and different image by technical means. Whether this disagreement, slight though it may appear, can be attributed to a more deep-seated divergence between Hobbes and Davenant is a question that can only be answered very tentatively (Berensmeyer 2012).

The two texts are meant to be read side by side. They were most probably conceived by Davenant as a strategic intervention in the literary and political culture of 1651, more particularly in the local court culture of the Paris exiles. In his "Answer", by commending the poem, Hobbes goes to some lengths to avoid direct comments on the preface; his text is less an answer to Davenant's *preface* than a response to his *poem*. Whether this amounts to a veiled critique on Hobbes's part can only be a matter of speculation. Nevertheless, it is tempting to consider that the birth document of English neoclassicism could have been the outcome of a misunderstanding, with Hobbes evading any too firm commitment to Davenant's project and his (and many of his fellow royalist exiles') more absolutist ideas. In this – admittedly rather murky – light, one might detect a few ruptures in what would otherwise appear to be a strategic alignment between literature, politics, and representation at midcentury. After the Restoration, this project is continued, with slightly different emphases, by Margaret Cavendish, whose efforts to unite 'science' and 'fiction' are the topic of the next section in this chapter.

Visuality and Imagination between Science and Fiction: Margaret Cavendish's *Observations upon Experimental Philosophy* and *The Blazing World* (1666)

In Burton's *Anatomy*, fictionalised peritexts form part of a strategy of mobilising readers, teasing them to acknowledge the limits of their understanding. In Browne, these elements seamlessly enter the main text in order to make readers realise the plurality and contingency of perceived reality. As we found above, in the discourse of neoclassicism, the concept of fiction assumes at once a more precise and a more limited definition, as fictions are harnessed to achieve specific rhetorical effects. This is the case in Davenant and Hobbes, also to some extent in Milton. In marked distinction to humanist practices, these effects are more often allegorical and/or ironic than metaphorical. Fiction is employed as a marker of intellectual distance rather than as a medium of emotional closeness – intended to keep readers out rather than to invite them in. It is not so much geared towards fostering than controlling the reader's imagination and his/her physiognomic, identificatory or impassioned responses to a text. Writers resort to fiction not in order to enhance but to reduce or at least to control experiential complexity. This is one reason why the romance, for example (such as Sales's *Theophania* or Herbert's *The Princess Cloria*), uses the schematic forms of pastoral literature as a means to ignore the harsh realities of social and political 'modernisation' in the Interregnum and the Restoration; why imitations and continuations of Spenser's *Faerie Queene* are written; or why Davenant's ambition, during his exile in France, should be to produce a heroic epic set in medieval Lombardy.

Fictionalising as distancing is accompanied by a tendency towards an increasingly normative distinction of genres. This is promoted not only by near-formulaic theatrical productions that cling to the rules of their respective genres, but also by the increasing frequency of theoretical writings like Dryden's essays and later critical articulations by the likes of John Dennis or Charles Gildon – texts that transform reflections on literary genres into a genre of its own. In Restoration literary culture, this separation has consequences for the relation between *oral/aural*, *visual*, and *verbal* forms of cognition and rhetoric, which keep drifting further apart and become increasingly compartmentalised according to different functions. The tensions between visuality, oral rhetoric, and textuality that we could find in Milton, Hobbes, and Davenant become more pronounced, culminating in the normative distinction between (cognitive and abstract) reason and (visual, poetic, and concrete) fancy that will dominate the eighteenth century until it is softened again by Burke and Coleridge, among others.

This trend towards an increasingly strict separation between philosophical-scientific discourse and literary fiction is also borne out by one of the many publications by the long-neglected Margaret Cavendish, Duchess of Newcastle: *Observations upon Experimental Philosophy. To which is added, The Description of a New Blazing World* (London, 1666; 2nd ed. 1668). This volume is literally split down the middle between a 'scientific' and a 'literary' part, symptomatic even in its faithful reproduction of the cultural priority of natural philosophy over literary fiction. The books are bound together, though they were printed separately, with different signatures and page numbers.[58] The fiction is a supplement, merely "added" to its more serious counterpart. This split has been carried even further in modern editions that treat the *Observations* and *The Blazing World* as completely separate works: one, a long neglected "serious treatise" (Lilley 1994, xxiv) of "natural philosophy in the age of scientific revolution" (O'Neill 2001, xxxv), the other its improbable and somewhat

---

[58] In the following, I quote from the 1666 edition (as available on EEBO) but, for ease of reference, I distinguish between the *Observations* (Cavendish 1666a) and *The Blazing World* parts 1 and 2 (1666b and c) in order to keep track of the various page numbers. I am, however, always referring to the same document (Wing N857) as available on EEBO in a facsimile of a copy in the University of Illinois.

frivolous "fictional companion piece" (Lilley 1994, xii). Some of these editions do not even mention the fact that the two were originally published in the same volume. A recent collection of critical essays on Cavendish also distinguishes – rather anachronistically – between her "non-fictional" and her "imaginative writings" (Cottegnies and Weitz 2003, 5).

What is irrecoverably lost in such a separation is the relation of contiguity between science and fiction that is staged by the very form of Cavendish's book: it combines two forms of writing even as it distinguishes between them. Yet the resulting tension can hardly be called ironic, dialectic or dialogic in a Bakhtinian sense. The fictional addendum does not establish a superior, critical, ironic or distancing perspective on its scientific companion, but is on the contrary most affirmative in that it serves to enhance, embellish, and support a number of philosophical points that have been made in the *Observations*. Thus *The Blazing World,* from within a deliberately fictionalised setting, fulfils a rhetorical purpose in the Hobbesian sense: as the intensifier of a theoretical argument. More explicitly than in other cases, the literary aspect of the work is separated from the rest; yet it is not declared autonomous but subordinated to the main body of the book, which is of considerably greater length (their proportion is roughly three to one). The space between science and fiction is not bridged but remains an open and visible gap.

How does Cavendish address the relationship between science and fiction in her writings, and how does she justify her management of their difference to her prospective readers? To answer this question, we first need to consider her particular status and communicative situation in the literary landscape of seventeenth-century England. Cavendish writes natural philosophy from the position of an outsider: a woman with no formal education in philosophy and no official context, apart from her private circle, in which to profess and publish her ideas. Her books can be described as vanity publications: beautiful editions that she relentlessly sends to universities and with which she hopes to reach a largely unresponsive audience of male philosophers who either find her obnoxious or even pronounce her mad. Cavendish is motivated by an irrepressible urge to write and an unconcealed desire for fame (not unlike Davenant in this respect); her books are crowded with peritextual matter that appeals to the reader's recognition of Cavendish as an "Authoresse" and original genius (Douglas 2000; Rees 2003).

In her extravagant staging and celebration of authorship and originality, Cavendish even surpasses Robert Burton, who had remained much more sceptical about the possibility of authors communicating with readers in such a way as to be fully and correctly understood. One of three frontispieces commissioned by Cavendish from Abraham van Diepenbeeck in the 1650s depicts her in an empty study, above an inscription that includes the lines "Her Library on which She look's / It is her Head her Thoughts her Books" (Cavendish 1671). The empty space around her may have been intended to signify her independence from other sources, but it also illustrates her isolation.[59] She tries to compensate for the lack of serious responses to her work by creating a dialogue with her own ideas: by publishing her own "Commentaries" (Cavendish 1666a, sig. e2^r) on her system of organicist materialism,[60] by employing the device of fictional letters in which she compares the systems of other thinkers to her own (*Philosophical Letters*, 1664), and by inserting an abundance of prefaces and peritextual matter – her fifth book, *Nature's Pictures drawn by Fancy's Pencil to the Life* (1656), begins with no less than six prefaces to the reader.

Some would describe this phenomenon in pathological terms, and Cavendish would even have agreed with them to some extent.[61] Yet one of her main objectives in celebrating her authorship and originality is to fill the empty space of public response with fictionalised elements of discourse and with a blatant and over-the-top apotheosis of her author position. Fictionalisation does not serve a purpose of concealment or mere ornament, nor is it used in a sceptical manner to question the relations between author, text, and reader (as it certainly is in Burton and Browne). It is rather used to suggest a firmly established hierarchy between these, even in soliciting the acceptance and collaboration of the "Curteous Reader" (1666a, sig. d2^r). The *Philosophical Letters* unfold a monologue in the form of an epistolary dialogue; in the *Observations*, there is a prefatory "Argumental Discourse" (h1^r) that stages "a Dispute [. . .] between the rational Parts of [Cavendish's] Mind concerning some chief Points and Principles in Natural Philosophy" (h1^r), even "a war" (h1^r) between Cavendish's earlier and her more recent thoughts. In compliance with the neoclassical rhetoric of contingency, this dispute is referred "to the Arbitration of the impartial Reader, desiring the assistance of his judgement to reconcile their Controversies, and, if possible, to reduce them to a setled peace and agreement" (h1^{r-v}).

In the *Observations,* the reader is directly engaged in a hierarchical dialogue in the preface "To the Reader" (Cavendish 1666a, sig. d2^r), which Cavendish uses to explain, clarify, and comment on some twenty particular points, preempting criticism in syntactically repetitive phrases that follow the schema: 'When I say X I do not mean Y but my meaning is Z.' After these clarifications, the reader is asked to

---

[59] On the critical reception, see O'Neill 2001, xvii–xxi. The unwillingness of her contemporaries to respond to Cavendish is best illustrated by a letter of Henry More to Anne Conway on the occasion of Cavendish's *Philosophical Letters*, in which More states that Cavendish "may be secure from anyone giving her the trouble of a reply" (Conway 1992, 237).

[60] For a concise outline of Cavendish's system of natural philosophy see O'Neill 2001, xxi–xxv.

[61] Cf. her remarks at the beginning of "The Preface to the Ensuing Treatise" in the *Observations*: "Tis probable, some will say, that my much writing is a disease; but what disease they will judg it to be, I cannot tell; I do verily believe they will take it to be a disease of the Brain, but surely they cannot call it an Apoplexical or Lethargical disease: Perhaps they will say, it is an extravagant, or at least a Fantastical disease; but I hope they will rather call it a disease of wit" (1666a, sig. c1^r). Cavendish gives no cause for "the disease of writing" (c1^v), such as Burtonian melancholy, but calls writing "the onely Pastime which imploys my idle hours" (c1^v). In the preface to *The Blazing World*, she refers to her "melancholly Life" (1666b, sig. b*2^r).

suspend judgement until (s)he has "read all" (sig. g2.2ʳ). The reading process is thus anticipated and built into the text: a complete reading is allocated a place in the work's perfection, but it is not conceived as a creative or independent enterprise because the work is thought to contain all the answers in itself:

> These are *(Courteous Reader)* the scruples which I thought might puzle your understanding in this present Work, which I have cleared in the best manner I could; and if you should meet with any other of the like nature, my request is, You would be pleased to consider well the Grounds of my Philosophy; and as I desired of you before, read all before you pass your Judgement and Censures; for then, I hope, you'l find but few obstructions, since one place will give you an explanation of the other. In doing thus, you'l neither wrong your self, nor injure the Authoress, who should be much satisfied, if she could benefit your knowledg in the least; if not, she has done her endeavour, and takes as much pleasure and delight in writing and divulging the Conceptions of her mind, as perhaps some malicious persons will do in censuring them to the worst.   (sig. g2.2ʳ, italics reversed)

While her presentation of the hierarchical relationship between author and reader is based on an implicit fictionalisation of either position, her explicit concept of fiction is much more conventional and rhetorical. According to Cavendish, fiction – like the rhetorical 'images' in Hobbes – serves to make 'the conceptions of mind' more palatable and to ease the reader into accepting them as true or correct. Fiction is used to provide "pleasure and delight" (g2.2ʳ). But although Cavendish herself uses fictionalising strategies in establishing (or, at times, simulating) communication with her unwilling – mostly male – readers, her concept of fiction is explicitly subordinated to that of philosophy. She distinguishes very clearly between "serious Philosophy" and "Poetical fancy" (sig. Oo1ʳ, p. 141). To fiction, the medium of fancy, is relegated a specific communicative genre and function. In her first publication, *Poems, and Fancies* (1653), which includes a number of poems on atoms, Cavendish excuses herself for choosing to write natural philosophy in verse: "the Reason why I write it in *Verse*, is, because I thought *Errours* might better passe there, then in *Prose*; since *Poets* write most *Fiction*, and *Fiction* is not given for *Truth*, but *Pastime*" ("To Natural Philosophers", Cavendish 1653, sig. A6ʳ). As she puts it in the preface to *The Blazing World*: "The end of Reason, is Truth; the end of Fancy, is Fiction" (1666b, sig. b*1ᵛ).[62] Here, then, as in Hobbes and Davenant, fiction is rhetorical adornment: a secret purveyor of truth or a beautiful lure for the unwary reader who is open to suggestion and willing to suspend judgement when reading certain generically marked texts in certain situations. Fiction here is in the service of aesthetic rationalism as a ruse of reason.

---

[62] On the relation between philosophical and poetic discourse in *The Blazing World*, cf. Nate 2001, 210–14, who traces its Baconian and skeptical ramifications and asserts that the split between different discourses does not entail their mutual incommunicability; on p. 228, Nate also provides a useful diagram of the fictional 'worlds' of *The Blazing World*. Cf. Lobsien 1999, 263–87 for a reading that situates Cavendish in the contexts of early modern empiricism, skepticism, Neoplatonism, and cabbalism.

Cavendish's subsequent works banish such explicit intrusions of fiction into the discourse of science; the desire to be taken seriously is too great to permit such trifling exercises of 'fancy'. Her later books no longer reveal the strategic game of text and genre as radically as the passage just quoted. The relationship between fiction and philosophy in her later texts is as hierarchical as her model of communication, which reflects the strictly hierarchical order of society that she supports and that she reproduces in *The Blazing World* in the mode of fiction.

This hierarchy is also the reason of the split between science and fiction that goes right through the volume that contains both the *Observations* and *The Blazing World*. Her justification for adding a fictional text to a scientific work of natural philosophy is a very concise argument for the distinctions between 'truth' and 'fiction', 'reason' and 'fancy', while at the same time explaining the unity of what is being distinguished:

> If you wonder, that I join a work of Fancy to my serious Philosophical Contemplations; think not that it is out of a disparagement to Philosophy; or out of an opinion, as if this noble study were but a Fiction of the Mind; for though Philosophers may err in searching and enquiring after the Causes of Natural Effects, and many times embrace falshoods for Truths; yet this does not prove, that the Ground of Philosophy is meerly Fiction, but the error proceeds from the different motions of Reason [. . .]; and since there is but one Truth in Nature, all those that hit not this Truth, do err, some more, some less; for though some may come nearer the mark then others, which makes their Opinions seem more probable and rational then others; yet as long as they swerve from this onely Truth, they are in the wrong: Nevertheless, all do ground their Opinions upon Reason; that is, upon rational probabilities, at least, they think they do[.]
>
> (1666b, sig. b*1^{r-v})

Reason and truth are firmly aligned in an epistemology that is proto-Lockean in its emphasis on "rational probabilities" and neoclassical in its acknowledgment of epistemic contingency ("some may come nearer the mark then others"). This is one side of Cavendish's distinction; the other side is described in the following sentences:

> But *Fictions* are an issue of mans Fancy, framed in his own Mind, according as he pleases, without regard, whether the thing, he fancies, be really existent without his mind or not; so that Reason searches the depth of Nature, and enquires after the true Causes of Natural Effects; but Fancy creates of its own accord whatsoever it pleases, and delights in its own work. The end of Reason, is Truth; the end of Fancy, is Fiction[.]   (b*1^v, emphasis original)

Fancy, whose product is fiction, thus appears disconnected from any concern with what Cavendish calls "Truth", which she defines as correspondence to an existing reality exterior to the mind, in "Nature". But it is not wholly separate or disconnected from reason, as she explains in the following:

> But mistake me not, when I distinguish *Fancy* from *Reason*; I mean not as if Fancy were not made by the Rational parts of Matter; but by *Reason* I understand a rational search and enquiry into the causes of natural effects; and by *Fancy* a voluntary creation or production of the Mind, both being effects, or rather actions of the rational parts of Matter; of which, as that is a more profitable and useful study then this, so it is also more laborious and difficult, and

> requires sometimes the help of Fancy, to recreate the Mind, and withdraw it from its more serious Contemplations. (b*1ᵛ, emphasis original)

In accordance with her continuum theory of matter, all "parts of Matter" (b*1ᵛ) are unified by "a single, rational force" (O'Neill 2001, xxviii), and therefore fancy and reason, though distinct, are yet united in that both are "actions of the rational parts of Matter" (b*1ᵛ). They are, as it were, different genres and of different value – reason is "more profitable and useful", "more serious", while fancy serves "to recreate the Mind", "to divert" the author "and to delight the *Reader* with variety, which is always pleasing" (b*1ᵛ) – stock elements of neoclassical literary criticism.

Despite their opposition, reason and fancy are "joined" in Cavendish's book, she explains, "as two Worlds at the ends of their Poles" (1666b, sig. b*1ᵛ) – a phrase that echoes a description of the world in the fictional text itself, in which the other world into which the heroine is transported is described as "joined close to" the North pole (1666b, 3). The image of two worlds mirrors the bipolar arrangement of the book that contains the *Observations* (reason, truth) and *The Blazing World* (fancy, fiction) in a single volume. Read alongside each other, the two texts reveal a number of obvious connections or points of contact, which are also legible as connections between scientific empiricism and literary neoclassicism. Fancy provides an alternative, less rigorous purchase on the observations of reason. As "a voluntary creation or production of the Mind" (b*1ᵛ), it triggers an unconstrained process of imaginary worldmaking that can at the same time function as unlimited (and hence unexpectedly democratic) wish-fulfilment, as documented by Cavendish's concluding remarks in the preface:

> though I cannot be *Henry* the Fifth, or *Charles* the Second, yet I endeavour to be *Margaret* the *First*; and although I have neither power, time nor occasion to conquer the world as *Alexander* and *Cæsar* did; yet rather then not to be Mistress of one, since Fortune and the Fates would give me none, I have made a world of my own: for which no body, I hope, will blame me, since it is in every ones power to do the like. (b*2ʳ, emphasis original)

Cavendish here transforms Hobbes's cautionary statement about the potential dangers of excessive imaginative reading into a celebratory argument for the powers of fiction. Hobbes had commented on the 'compounding' of images in the fancy in a passage worth quoting again: "So when a man compoundeth the image of his own person, with the image of the actions of an other man; as when a man imagins himselfe a *Hercules,* or an *Alexander,* (which happeneth often to them that are much taken with reading of Romants) it is a compound imagination, and properly but a Fiction of the mind" (*L* 1.2; Hobbes 1996, 16).

As we have seen, the word 'image' for Hobbes not only denotes a visual impression in the mind, but also involves an emotional or opinion-based colouring that can be used for rhetorical effects of intensification. This explains the usefulness of 'images' for poetry. If, for Hobbes, Cavendish's compensatory self-magnification must have had a Quixotic aspect of the delusional about it, for Cavendish herself this pathological dimension of the fancy is cushioned by the liberty of imaginative fiction as a distinctive *genre*, a type of communication where the ordinary rules of truth and decorum do not apply. Fiction is here already a mode of mere play, distinct and disconnected from reality or seriousness. This is why Cavendish can dare to hope that "no body [. . .] will blame" her for it (b*2^r). This distinction is enabled by a clear, rationalist separation between different domains of discourse, a distinction which in turn enables the observation of connections between these separate domains.

One such connection between the *Observations* and *The Blazing World* is the epistemological problem of modern optics, telescopy, and microscopy. The book is at least in part a response to Robert Hooke's *Micrographia* of 1665 and an attempt at a "devaluation of optical science" (Linden 2001, 614; cf. Battigelli 1996). In the *Observations*, Cavendish is extremely critical of optical instruments. In the "Preface to the Ensuing Treatise", she maintains that "the Art of Augury was far more beneficial then the lately invented Art of Micrography; for I cannot perceive any great advantage this Art doth bring us" (1666a, sig. c2^v). She regards "most of these Arts" as "Fallacies, rather then discoveries of Truth" and as a deception of the human senses that "cannot be relied upon" (sig. d1^r). Major sections of the text are concerned with an elaboration of this argument in direct response to Hooke and to Henry Power's *Experimental Philosophy* of 1664: cf. chapter titles such as "Of Micrography, and of Magnifying and Multiplying Glasses", "Of Pores", "Of the Eyes of Flies", "Of the Seeds of Vegetables", "Of Telescopes" etc. In a satirical vein, this topic of telescopy and microscopy returns in *The Blazing World*, where the Empress institutes academic "societies of the Vertuoso's" (1666b, 19) with whose members she engages in intellectual disputes, asking them questions about the substance of the air, about "how Snow was made" (23) or about "the nature of Thunder and Lightning" (25). In a fit of passionate anger at the epistemic insufficiency of telescopes, the Empress commands her "Bird-men" to destroy them because they "are false Informers, and instead of discovering the Truth, delude your senses" (27). After some dispute, she agrees to allow them to keep their glasses, but only "upon condition, that their disputes and quarrels should remain within their Schools, and cause no factions or disturbances in State, or Government" (28).

In the framework of her fictional world, Cavendish makes a statement about art and science that is profoundly Hobbesian. Like the potentially delusive impact of fiction, the potentially seditious effects of scientific disputes need to be kept firmly in check – by means of a careful differentiation of discursive levels. Her hierarchical concept of society allows for a contingent plurality of competing and differing voices, but only if they "confine [their] disputations to [their] Schools, lest besides the Commonwealth of Learning, they disturb also Divinity and Policy, Religion and Laws, and by that means draw an utter ruin and destruction both upon Church and State" (1666b, 59–60). The need to control transgression, including excessive curiosity, is almost paradoxically foregrounded in this text: "Natural desire of knowledg [. . .] is not blameable, so you do not go beyond what your natural reason can comprehend" (86). While the Empress acknowledges that "no particular knowledg can be perfect" (59), she does not transfer this insight to her understanding of politics and religion. In these respects, *The Blazing World* contains an unmistakable plea for religious uniformity and unquestioning obedience to the sovereign. In the utopian counter-world of the Blazing-world, monarchy is presented as "a divine form of government", for the simple reason that "as there is but one God, whom we all unanimously worship and adore with one Faith, so we are resolved to have but one Emperor, to whom we all submit with one obedience" (16). Monotheism, unity of religious worship, and political obedience are combined into one overarching unity. When the Empress converts the religiously underdeveloped Blazing-world to her own religion, she wisely pursues a course of non-violent persuasion, echoing Davenant's arguments about public education:

> And thus the Emperess, by Art, and her own ingenuity, did not onely convert the Blazing-world to her own Religion, but kept them in a constant belief, without inforcement or blood-shed; for she knew well, that belief was a thing not to be forced or pressed upon the people, but to be instilled into their minds by gentle perswasions; and after this manner she encouraged them also in all other duties and employments, for Fear, though it makes people obey, yet does it not last so long, nor is it so sure a means to keep them to their duties, as Love. (63)

These lines about the "gentle perswasions" of "Love" are in stark contrast to a later statement, made in the text by the Duchess of Newcastle herself, whose soul enters the Blazing-world to act as a scribe to the Empress. Here the Duchess declares that "the chief and onely ground in Government, was but Reward and Punishment" (92). Whereas the Empress appears to follow the teachings of Hobbes and Davenant, the Duchess has apparently internalised the Machiavellian precepts of her husband, William Cavendish, whose *Advice* to Charles II on the eve of the Restoration is of a similar bluntness (Cavendish 1984; Condren 1993). When the Duchess tries to invent a world according to Hobbesian principles of pressure and counterpressure, she ends up with a headache (Cavendish 1666b, 100). The Duchess advises the Empress to maintain the principles of uniformity she has established:

> to have but one Soveraign, one Religion, one Law, and one Language, so that all the World might be as one united Family, without divisions; nay, like God, and his Blessed Saints and Angels: Otherwise, said she, it may in time prove as unhappy, nay, as miserable a World as that is from which I came, wherein are more Soveraigns then Worlds, and more pretended Governours then Governments, more Religions then Gods, and more Opinions in those Religions then Truths; more Laws then Rights, and more Bribes then Justices, more Policies then Necessities, and more Fears then Dangers, more Covetousness then Riches, more Ambitions then Merits, more Services then Rewards, more Languages then Wit, more Controversie then Knowledg, more Reports then noble Actions, and more Gifts by partiality, then according to merit[.] (121–22)

Cavendish here uses the topos of the inverted world, familiar from utopian narratives since More's *Utopia,* only she inverts the narrative situation to let a character from the familiar world give an account of it in the imaginary counter-world. The polemical intent of *The Blazing World* – as a celebration of absolutist values in Restoration England – is evident. It is only apparently paradoxical that her panegyric to monarchy as the most natural and rational form of government should be couched in an epistemology of contingency that evokes imperfection, the plurality of worlds, and an ethical imperative of moderation.[63]

Earlier, the Empress had conceded academic freedom to her scientists on condition that their pursuits be "beneficial to the publick" (48); now the Duchess enjoins her "to dissolve all their societies; for 'tis better to be without their intelligences, then to have an unquiet and disorderly Government" (122). It is this inner strength of her reformed state, we are invited to assume in the course of the narrative, that allows the Empress to win the sea-battle in the second part, reigning as she now does "most happily and blessedly" (1666c, 1). From the point of view of the Hobbesian sovereign, the phrase from La Fontaine's fable of the wolf and the lamb is affirmed: "la raison du plus fort est toujours la meilleure" (La Fontaine 1991, 44).

It is this political dimension of literary culture that Cavendish's text envisages in terms of absolutism even as it operates according to the rules of an imaginary liberalism. Literary communication, for Cavendish, is a means to realise phantasies of absolute sovereignty in a literary setting – transforming the harmful delusion of every subject (according to Davenant and Hobbes) into a politically harmless fictional game. Everyone can be an absolute monarch in a fictional world of their own making, as the spirits of the Blazing-world explain to the Duchess and the Empress:

> But we wonder, proceeded the Spirits, that you desire to be Emperess of a Terrestrial World, when as you can create your self a Celestial World if you please. What, said the Emperess, can any Mortal be a Creator? Yes, answered the Spirits; for every humane Creature can create an Immaterial World fully inhabited by immaterial Creatures, and populous of immaterial subjects, such as we are, and all this within the compass of the head or scull; nay, not onely so, but he may create a World of what fashion and Government he will, and give the Creatures thereof such motions, figures, forms, colours, perceptions, &c. as he pleases, and make Whirlpools, Lights, Pressures and Reactions, &c. as he thinks best[.] (1666b, 96–97)

For Cavendish's own authorship, as she presents it in "The Epilogue to the Reader", this means that she esteems literary sovereignty more highly than political power: "By this Poetical Description, you may perceive, that my ambition is not onely to be Emperess, but Authoress of a whole World[.] [. . .] And in the formation of those Worlds, I take more delight and glory, then ever *Alexander* or *Cæsar* did in conquering this terrestrial world" (1666c, sig. Ii1ʳ). She counters the heroic imagination as described by Hobbes ("as when a man imagins himself a *Hercules*, or an *Alexander*" (*L* 1.2; 1996, 16) with her own self-glorification in the mode of fiction:

---

[63] "I perceive that the greatest happiness in all Worlds consist in Moderation" (Cavendish 1666b, 105). On the plurality of worlds, see Cavendish 1666b, 105. Cavendish here anticipates Fontenelle's *Entretiens sur la pluralité des mondes* of 1686 (Lobsien 2003).

> I [. . .] instead of the figures of *Alexander, Cæsar, Hector, Achilles, Nestor, Ulysses, Helen*, &c. chose rather the figure of Honest *Margaret Newcastle*, which now I would not change for all this terrestrivl [sic] World; and if any should like the World I have made, and be willing to be my Subjects, they may imagine themselves such, and they are such; I mean, in their Minds, Fancies or Imaginations; but if they cannot endure to be subjects, they may create Worlds of their own, and Govern themselves as they please[.] (1666c, sig. Ii1ᵛ)

Only in fiction, in a world of the imagination, can subjects become sovereigns or subject themselves to others at their own free will. By means of her literary creativity, Cavendish not only gains freedom from her temporal, worldly troubles for the time being; she is also able, at least for a while, to harmonise private fancy with public reason and to defuse the conflicts between visuality and rhetoric, philosophy and imaginative literature, knowledge and power that otherwise continue to torment English literary culture in the seventeenth century.

Literary Worldmaking

In the early modern period, the relations between authors and their addressees become asymmetrical and contingent. What follows from this are numerous attempts to restructure these relations: in a hierarchical, absolutist manner (as in Davenant and Cavendish) or in a republican, prophetic fashion (as in Milton), but in each case involving a pedagogic and at times polemic component. Political models of textuality arise from the necessity to bridge the gap between author and audience. Milton's *Areopagitica* (see below) unfolds one such model, Davenant's *Preface to Gondibert* another; Hobbes, Cavendish, and Dryden also each reflect, more or less explicitly and in their different ways, political preconditions and strategies of literary communication. Neoclassicism develops its global strategy of rational method and hierarchical communication partly in response to political experiences of contingency.

Contingency and uncertainty are addressed in the writings of Thomas Browne, but they are ultimately presented as unproblematic against a theological background that is non-negotiable: secular contingency is itself viewed as contingent in relation to the eternal stability provided by the grace of God. At the end of days, the Last Judgement will resolve any secular differences once and for all. What follows from this belief, however, is that it would be an act of hubris for mere mortals to attempt to solve the knotty problems of religion and philosophy in *this* world. Political and social differences may be experienced as problematic but it is safer, in this view, to ignore their pressures on reality. What Browne lacks is a language beyond the humanist and classical heritage to connect his intellectual concerns with the political questions of his time. To do so, he would have to develop a concept of *social* contingency in close alignment to his philosophical concept of contingency; but this seems out of his reach. For Browne, a particular order of society, a particular distribution of rights and property, even a particular religious orientation of some flexibility and tolerance are indisputable social norms that should be immediately obvious to any well-intentioned citizen or 'person of quality'. This may help explain the very real shock, the horror that Browne feels and that he registers in 1643 when faced with the unthinkable – the destruction of the political order as he knows it. The fate of his text and the imminent toppling of the monarchy are parallelled in the preface to *Religio Medici* and the letter to Digby. The "liberty of these times" (Browne 1964a, 76) is a perversion of the natural order manifested in the breakdown of censorship and the changing world of literature. Here textuality and politics converge for Browne. In the textual noise of the Civil War, his draft of a flexible, non-persuasive rhetoric is a damp squib. It is time for more aggressive rhetoricians on both sides of the political and religious spectrum.

Browne's humanist analogy between exterior and interior, secular and spiritual nature (in *The Garden of Cyrus*) is secularised in Izaak Walton's *Compleat Angler*. Against the backdrop of the political events of the English Civil War, Walton creates a pastoral counter-world that is obviously fictional. The garden is now an artificial paradise, placed in opposition to civilisation, and its loss is merely registered with some wistfulness but, in contrast to Milton, without any eschatological or even political vision. In Margaret Cavendish, we have found a similar fictional counter-world that is playful and, even though it contemplates a distinctly feminine counter-world, remains a fantasy. *The Blazing World* uncovers and constructs a region of individual political fantasy by rehearsing and radicalising a neoclassical materialist perspective on the psycho-social function of poetry. The imaginary sovereign who is synthesised in Hobbes's *Leviathan* and from the fragments of Davenant's *Gondibert* finds his female counterpart in Cavendish's Empress governing "most happily and blessedly" (Cavendish 1666c, 1) – in part because she is able to preserve her dominion from the irruption of epistemological contingencies in the shape of deceitful telescopes. Thus the topic of visuality leads us, almost inevitably, from epistemological to political questions. In neoclassical discourse (poetic, scientific, political), definitions of what is to count as rational and natural are inflected by political and historical contingencies. It is these contingencies that the following chapter will set out to analyze in greater depth, focussing on ideas of the 'state of nature' in the political imaginary and in literary culture between Civil War and Restoration. As we shall see, debates about nature and natural law are an important part of literary theory, rhetoric, and literary practice in seventeenth-century England. In these debates, the conflicts between visual, verbal, and aural forms of communication are not so much resolved as transposed to a different stage, a stage prepared by the increased awareness that the division between natural and political norms, exacerbated by the Civil War and its reflections on social theory, can no longer be healed.

To "chuse to create another World" (Cavendish 1666c, sig. Ii1^v), then, is a tempting possibility, especially for writers, but not as easy as the epilogue to *The Blazing World* makes it sound. Even purely imaginary fictional worlds tend to bear the traces of the reality in and for which they were created. During the Interregnum, when

Royalists turned to the genre of heroic romance, they created fictional counter-worlds opposed to the political reality of their time. For Davenant's *Gondibert* as well as for Walton, these fictional worlds still carry political meaning, but only as distinct from 'real' politics, which takes place on entirely different battlefields. Even Davenant's preface, with its brutal assertion of the political function of epic poetry, cannot change this; the *humanitas* it professes to sponsor as 'virtue' remains a formulaic void. The chivalry of *Gondibert*'s Lombard knights turns into an allegory that runs at a standstill, out of touch with the political reality around 1650 but still under the "form and pressure" (*Hamlet* 3.2) of its time.

Although this political reality is about to change yet again with the Restoration, the rupture between nature and *civitas* that is reflected in these texts can no longer be completely healed despite all efforts in this direction. This is certainly due in part to far-reaching discursive and economic changes (Schweikart 1986; Sennett 1994, 255–81). The court of Charles II, attached to an idealised and nostalgic view of the Elizabethan age, distances and isolates itself further from its more flexible, heterogeneous, and dynamic urban and parliamentary environment. This contrary development almost inevitably leads to an overt political conflict between court and parliament. The court's isolation reaches its most profound literary expression in the hermetically sealed pornographic fantasy of *The Farce of Sodom* (1684, attributed to the Earl of Rochester), whereas the acceptance of provisional solutions that characterises the urban and parliamentary mindset culminates in the worldmaking of Milton's *Paradise Lost* and Locke's *Two Treatises of Government*. The writings of mid- to late-period Dryden are particularly interesting in this respect because they attempt to mediate between these extremes. Dryden wants to preserve the old order in a new time, which is why he also attempts to overcome or at least conceal the divide between nature and politics.

In this way, nature and natural law are not only decisive foundations for seventeenth-century political thought but also a conceptual contexture of literary communication, in which ancient, especially stoic, patterns of thinking correlate with modern experiences, and new forms of a literary public sphere are created. Literary configurations of social life have to take up ever new positions in the conceptual space between nature and *civitas*. In doing so, writers need to develop appropriate media strategies for dealing with contingency between rhetoric, politics, and theatre, and between remembering and forgetting.

4 Literature as Civil War

> Nature; a thing so almost Infinite, and Boundless, as can never fully be Comprehended, but where the Images of all things are always present.
> Dryden, epistle dedicatory to *The Rival Ladies* (1664)

> Rome is but a wilderness of tigers.
> Shakespeare/Peele, *Titus Andronicus* 3.1.53

> Had you dissembled better, Things might have continued in the state of Nature.
> Congreve, *The Way of the World*

Ciceronian Moments: State of Nature and Natural Law in the Cultural Imaginary

"There was a time when men wandered at large in the fields like animals and lived on wild fare; they did nothing by the guidance of reason, but relied chiefly on physical strength; there was as yet no ordered system of religious worship nor of social duties; no one had seen legitimate marriage nor had anyone looked upon children whom he knew to be his own nor had they learned the advantages of an equitable code of law." In these words, Cicero presents a 'state of nature' before the foundation of society or civilisation (*De inventione* 1.2; trans. in Tuck 1979, 33).[64] Cicero's origin story becomes very relevant in early modern political thought. Could the divine covenant between the sovereign and his subjects be broken? If so, what would be he consequences of such a rupture? Would society revert to the state of nature, a state of disorder and amorality where, as some thought, nothing was forbidden? Only a minority of theorists held that this permission only extended to whatever served the purpose of self-preservation. Would people again "wander at large in the fields like animals" before the powers of rhetoric and of rational thought convinced them that they could do better? According to Cicero, civilisation was the result of a transformation of beast-like human beings into rational creatures, effected by the "reason and eloquence" of an orator (ibid.; cf. *De oratore* 1.33). Whatever the answers to these questions looked like, the seventeenth century had no other language in which to formulate them except that of natural law and natural rights theories. The language of natural law provides the framework for historical, anthropological, and political speculations. It gives a local habitation and a name to the

---

[64] Other passages from classical works are quoted from the Loeb editions, modifying their translations where appropriate.

vague hopes and fears circulating in the cultural imaginary. In this sense, the state of nature is a necessary fiction that is employed in response to pressing cultural and political questions of the time; a fiction that makes the articulation and rational debate of those very real questions possible (Castoriadis 1998). As such, images of the state of nature are frequently invoked in literary fictions, from *The Compleat Angler* via *Paradise Lost* to *Absalom and Achitophel*.

When violence erupts in the English Civil War, the spectres of anarchy and civic dissolution begin to wander at large in the fields of political thought, embodied in the idea of a possible reversion to the brutality of the state of nature. Bestiality and terror are combined in this figure of thought, which becomes a central plot element in political and literary fiction. There is some justification to speak of a 'Ciceronian moment' in English thought at this time, which decidedly turns against Aristotle's concept of man as a "political animal" born fit for society (*Politics* 1.2, 1253a3) and instead adopts the stoic idea of the natural savagery of pre-political human beings. Society and civilisation, according to this theory, originate in a radical break with and in opposition to what precedes them ('nature'). All kinds of texts, from Leveller pamphlets to royalist treatises, from satirical poetry to heroic drama, explore and exploit the conceptual idiom and imagery provided by Cicero's ur-scene of political institutionalisation.

The stoic idea of the state of nature is rediscovered in the sixteenth and early seventeenth century by the Thomist philosophers of the counter-reformation (Vitoria, Molina, Suárez, Bellarmine). These thinkers require a concept of *status naturae* in order to argue the political necessity (rather than mere possibility) of creating political institutions, and to present these institutions as *human* inventions rather than as a gift from God, as the Lutherans claimed. Suárez's *Tractatus de Legibus ac Deo Legislatore* (*Treatise on the Laws and God the Lawgiver*, 1612) presents a sophisticated and detailed constitutionalist theory of politics that anticipates Locke and Rousseau in its explanation how a naturally free individual can become the subject of a legitimate polity. The idea is also present in Huguenot political thought of the 1570s and in Calvinist resistance theory, most notably in George Buchanan's *De Iure Regni apud Scotos* (1579), a text which is said to have provided Cromwell with sufficient reassurance about the lawfulness of executing Charles I as a tyrant (Skinner 1978, 2: 135–84 and 338–48).

Given its wide appeal, the 'state of nature' becomes a kind of *passepartout* formula used to present the origin of political rationality as a defining event in human history. What speaks for this argument is the observation that it is employed by virtually all colours of the political spectrum. Alll camps and factions can use it to speak about the essence of what it means to be human in a political sense, and it enables them to do so in a graphic, intuitive manner that virtually everyone can understand. The numerous animal metaphors in Hobbes and others continuously alert readers to the danger of reverting to a bestial condition of "meer Nature" (*L* 1.13; 1996, 90) where men, presumably, are little better than "bruit Beasts" (1.14; 97) and live like "Lyons, Bears, and Wolves" (1.4; 24).[65]

In this respect, the figure of the state of nature can be read as a functional equivalent for the lacking universal signifier in the writings of Burton and Browne. It compensates for this lack by opening up an overarching, unifying conversation about general norms of thought and action against the backdrop of 'nature'. The state of nature and its dependent theoretical constructions of natural rights and natural laws suspend the contingencies of the modern political order by giving them a historical origin (which is only later, with Locke, located outside history). They legitimise the institutions of society in the present, but they also make it possible to discuss them as potentially provisional man-made institutions (rather than timeless conditions of human existence). The state of nature also contains a narrative nucleus that is flexible enough to lend support to various theoretical versions (liberal, oligarchist, absolutist, Puritan) of the origins and ends of political arrangements.

In Cicero's version of this narrative, the power of eloquence is of foremost importance in transforming brute barbarians into civilised citizens: it makes them listen more attentively and thus makes them more susceptible to the arguments of reason. Eloquence is now used by some theorists to expound, in ever more garish fashion, the horrors of the 'other' of civilisation – a Project Fear intended to make readers prefer to accept the political status quo rather than risk everything they hold dear, including their well-being in the afterlife, for the sake of some ill-defined 'liberty' promised by misguided radicals. The concept of liberty becomes particularly problematic from the perspective of natural law. For the conservative thinkers gathered in the Tew Circle around Lucius Cary, Viscount Falkland (among them the politicians Edward Hyde and Dudley Digges, the theologian William Chillingworth, and the poet Edmund Waller), "native liberty" – liberty in the state of nature – means the "unlimited power to use our abilities, according as will did prompt" (Digges qtd. in Tuck 1979, 103).[66] The consequence of this absence of moral limits in the state of nature is "feares and jealousies, wherein every single person look't upon the world as his enemy" (ibid.). For Henry Hammond, the state of nature is therefore "a state of common hostility", "a wilderness of Bears or Tygers, not a society of men" (qtd. in Tuck 1979, 103). The most famous exponent of this way of thinking is of course Thomas Hobbes, who returns to this point again and again in his writings: "the estate of men in this natural liberty is the estate of war" (*EL* 14.11; 1994, 80); "men's natural state, before they came together into society, was War; and not simply war, but a war of every man against every man" (Hobbes 1998, 29, 1.12); "In such condition, there is no place for Industry; because the fruit thereof is

---

[65] Reiss 1992, 10–41 reads such animal metaphors as part of a poetics of disgust with a world that is 'out of joint', and as a counterpart to the pastoral idyll; cf. also Yates 1977, 74–76.
[66] Tuck quotes from Digges's posthumously published *The Unlawfulnesse of Subjects, Taking up Armes against their Soveraigne* (n.p., 1644).

uncertain: and consequently no Culture of the Earth; [. . .] no account of Time; no Arts; no Letters; no Society; and which is worst of all, continuall feare, and danger of violent death; And the life of man, solitary, poore, nasty, brutish, and short" (*L* 1.13; 1996, 89). Hobbes also famously uses animal metaphors derived from the classical tradition, most notably the *homo homini lupus* ("Man is a wolf to Man") from Plautus's *Asinaria* (Hobbes 1998, 3).

All of these writers follow in the footsteps of the English humanist and legal scholar John Selden (1584–1654), whose major contribution to natural rights theory is the introduction, in the words of Richard Tuck, of "a strongly individualistic psychology and ethical theory" (Tuck 1979, 82). Selden uses a concept of egotistical motivation to explain the binding force of moral obligations. He postulates an original condition of absolute liberty, which he presents in terms taken almost verbatim from Cicero: "There was once a time when men wandered through the countryside like animals, sustaining a bestial existence and managing their lives by brute force rather than reason" (trans. qtd. in Tuck 1979, 93). But Selden postulates a state of nature that is irretrievably transformed not merely – as in Cicero – by 'right reason', the intuitive insight into what is beneficial for the common good, but by the introduction of law. It is a contract that obliges everyone to submit their interests to a higher authority: "For pure, unaided reason merely persuades or demonstrates; it does not order, nor bind anyone to their duty, unless it is accompanied by the authority of someone who is superior to the man in question" (94). To break this contract would inevitably incur punishment – either from the magistrate or, ultimately, from God. Fear of divine punishment is the main motivation for turning absolute freedom into restricted and specified liberty and transforming potentially deviant people into law-abiding subjects. In Selden's general theory of obligation, subjects are forced to keep their contracts absolutely (which they may have entered into simply by the fact of having been born) without any right of resistance even in extreme cases of a magistrate's injustice against them – a right that is included, for example, in the more liberal view propounded by Grotius. In his *Table Talk*, Selden tersely states that "[e]very law is a contract between the king and the people, and therefore to be kept" (qtd. in Tuck 1979, 96). Yet although he may sound like an apologist for absolutism, Selden in fact supports the parliamentary side in the Civil War. The idea of the contract introduces a bilateralism into politics that makes it impossible to revert to old beliefs about the divine right of kings; instead, it calls for new kinds of rational calculation. For Selden, the contract is legally binding for both sides, which ensures the correct balance between prerogative and liberty: "To know what obedience is due to the prince, you must look into the contract between him and his people; as if you would know what rent is due from the tenant to the landlord, you must look into the lease" (99).

In his classic study of English historical thought in the seventeenth century, J.G.A. Pocock has analyzed how, for Selden and his followers, including Hobbes, the state of nature (as absolute liberty, equality, and fear) and the construction of civilisation through the introduction of legal obligations "ceased to be a convenient fiction and was heatedly asserted as literal historical truth" (Pocock 1987, 37) – at least until Locke replaces such historical literalism with a normative idealism.[67] Hobbes is notoriously vague about the historical reality of his state of nature: "It may peradventure be thought", he writes in *Leviathan*, "there was never such a time, nor condition of warre as this; and I believe it was never generally so, over all the world: but there are many places, where they live so now. [. . .] Howsoever, it may be perceived what manner of life there would be, where there were no common Power to feare" (*L* 1.13; 1996, 89–90). The state of nature is, for Hobbes at least, not merely a convenient but a necessary and highly probable fiction.

In a "polemical situation" (Pocock 1987, 53) it is not surprising that the state of nature, as a figure of thought that postulates a *historical* origin of society, can also become ammunition for violent conflict. We find such a situation in the English Civil War, in which traditional institutions experience a crisis of meaning that becomes particularly evident in legal debates. In the seventeenth century, the medieval concept of "universal unmade law" (Pocock 1987, 234), embodied in the idea of a common law based on immemorial custom, has collapsed. It is replaced by a theory based on a concept of sovereignty and institution. Selden and his disciples are among those who argue that "every law originated in some man's will and that such a man must have possessed sovereignty and transmitted it to his heirs" (234–35). As a markedly *historical* fiction of origin, the narrative of how the 'state of nature' came to be replaced by the introduction of civilised society supervenes upon the myth of immemorial custom: thus a figure of the constant preservation of the same comes to be replaced by a figure of radical, voluntarist, authoritarian transformation. In Hobbes, the formation of political order is further radicalised into a creation out of nothing. The political can only become thinkable in contrast to a condition in which it is completely absent (Bredekamp 1999, 117–19).

If this appears only appropriate for a polemical period of radical social and political change, in which differences between social groups are more easily diagnosed than resemblances, it is still striking what enormous success the notion of the 'state of nature' and its transformation has, even – and especially – outside of arguments in favour of absolute monarchy, which still tend to prefer legitimation by divine right. The different stories told about the state of nature fundamentally agree about its historical existence, or at least its probability. The point where they differ is the essential question how and under which conditions people had come to

---

[67] In Locke's conception of the state of nature in the *Two Treatises*, the state of nature is no longer relegated to the human past, but is "the condition in which God himself places all men in the world, prior to the lives which they live and the societies which are fashioned by the living of these lives" (Dunn 2003, 53). Locke's speculations on the state of nature are thus less anthropological and naturalistic (as in Hobbes) than theological and legalistic; see also the more detailed account in Dunn 1969, 96–119.

leave it behind. Was it an orator or a jurist who convinced them to form a *civitas*? Did they decide to do so through the "rational apprehension of what is right", as the young Locke (in contrast to the older Locke) maintained (trans. and qtd. in Tuck 1979, 168)?[68] Or, as Selden and Hobbes claim, because the sovereign's will and his authority made them do it? "It is not Wisdom, but Authority that makes a Law" (Hobbes 1971b, 55), Hobbes asserts, arguing against the existence of "right reason": "seeing right reason is not existent, the reason of some man, or men, must supply the place thereof" (*EL* 2.10.8; 1994, 181). Or did they rather leave the state of nature, as Calvinist resistance theorists such as John Ponet and George Buchanan argued, because God had told them to do so? According to them, the divine command had come after the Flood, through the ban on homicide in *Genesis* 8, and so political life was not a creation of fallen man. Religious opposition groups at the beginning of the Civil War were keen to emphasise the divine character of political association to support their opposition to the king (Tuck 1979, 42–44, 144). The question of the anthropological and historical foundations of political order – a question that would not have made much sense to the humanists – is now put forward with ever increasing urgency.[69]

In later developments of political theory, above all in the Netherlands in the 1660s, a much more secular combination of Machiavellian, Hobbesian, and Cartesian ideas leads to a decidedly republican picture of the origin of politics. Velthuysen, de la Court, and also Spinoza expand Hobbes's ideas about the state of nature with Cartesian psychology and Machiavellian politics. In de la Court's state of nature, people "were deemed to be capable of making Machiavellian calculations about what constitutions and social arrangements were likely to utilise and control their passions in such a way that the community benefited" (Tuck 1979, 141). Later developments will take up again the contractarian ideas of John Selden, though giving them a decidedly more liberal Grotian twist. During the 1640s, the Levellers had already presented a political theory that explained the relation between the people and their sovereign as based on the notion of trust rather than authority: "I conceive it is now sufficiently cleared, that all rule is but fiduciary, and that this and that Prince is more or lesse absolute, as he is more or lesse trusted," Henry Parker writes in 1642 (qtd. in Tuck 1979, 146), and in 1647 Richard Overton claims that authority "as all things else in dissolution" will return "from whence it came", namely to the people, who are "the *Trustees*" of power (149). These theorists argue against the Seldenian idea that

---

68 Tuck quotes from Locke's Oxford lectures from the 1660s: "omnis enim obligatio conscientiam alligat et animo ipsi vinculum injicit, adeo ut non poenae metus sed recti ratio nos obligat" ("all obligation binds conscience and lays a bond on the mind itself, so that not fear of punishment, but a rational apprehension of what is right, puts us under an obligation"); Locke 1958, 184–85.
69 For the humanists, consider Lipsius, who has humanity leave the state of nature almost automatically when "a certaine communion necessarily began among them, and a social participation of divers things" (Lipsius 1594, 26).

natural freedom had, at some point in human history, been abandoned. In embryonic form, they already harbour the Enlightenment idea of human rights as natural and inalienable. As in Grotius's *De iure praedae*, the civic state in their eyes possesses no rights (above all, it has no right to punish offenders) which the individuals did not formerly possess even in the state of nature (Tuck 1979, 62–63). Furthermore, they interpret the contract between sovereign and people as revocable in cases of severe crises or breaches of trust. Most famously, Locke argues in this manner in the *Two Treatises of Government* that sovereignty is created by agreement and therefore no sovereign has the right to abuse his power and to act in unjust ways towards his subjects.

Some political theorists and polemicists simply posit the state of nature as a historical reality; some (Hobbes among them) argue its high probability, and some (including Grotius) even use the calculation of probabilities as a crucial element not only in their arguments but in their description of how people decide to leave the state of nature: through a rational decision based on the "probability [that] we shall be in lesse danger, living amongst men who have agreed to be governed by certaine Lawes, then if every one followed his owne inclination."[70] Cherished beliefs of the past turn into uncertainties that can only be controlled by means of calculating probabilities – and thus, ultimately, by means of fiction.[71]

For all sides in the political and religious conflicts of the seventeenth century, such calculations and fictions play an important role. What unifies their different positions is the stoic idea that human beings are not born fit for society, but that they have to learn civilisation; in their postlapsarian and postdiluvian world, they have to argue, fight for, and work towards "the meanes of peaceable, sociable, and comfortable living" (*L* 1.15; Hobbes 1996, 111). For republicans as well as royalists, for the godly as well as the ungodly, education is a central factor in recruiting and training personnel for this fight and in providing them with ideological ammunition for the political struggle that is about conquering not only bodies but minds. For this purpose, texts (written and printed) and cultural communication generally play a key role as ways of negotiating between the political exigencies of the present, expectations for the future, and the legitimising functions of the past. As we shall see, there is an almost seamless continuity between argumentative, theoretical

---

70 *An answer to a Printed Book, intituled, Observations upon Some of His Majesties late Answers and Expresses* (Oxford, 1642), sig. C3ᵛ, qtd. in Tuck 1979, 104. A product of the Tew circle, *An answer* was composed by Falkland, Chillingworth, Digges, and others in a collaborative effort in reaction to Parker's *Observations*.

71 Chillingworth had already given a rationalist, Pascalian account of probability in his *The Religion of Protestants a Safe Way to Salvation* (1638). Though Hobbes was capable of entertaining such a modern notion of probability (*EL* 1.4.10), he did not apply it to his political theory – he was apparently unwilling to present men as gambling in the state of nature, because he wanted them to be *certain* that they would be better off in a civilised society, and because he wanted to present his theory in the form of 'geometric' deductive conclusions (for a discussion of this, see Tuck 1979, 128).

writings and narrative literary productions, on stage as well as in printed books. In different guises, the fiction of the state of nature pervades the "wars of Truth" (Milton 1953b, 562) in seventeenth-century England, in whatever form these are being fought, from political theory to lyric poetry and from drama to pastoral allegory.

In this respect, rhetoric provides a crucial link not only between past and present, but also between political goals and the way to their realisation, which means control of public opinion. Rhetoric also links theoretical and narrative fictions. Texts circulating in the 'republic of letters' have an eminently political function in a politicised and almost infinitely divided society. To speak of a 'republic' of letters underlines the political understanding of literary culture in early modernity. The term also emphasises the lack of central control and the potentially egalitarian character of public communication in the age of print. By those in power, texts are regarded as potentially dangerous to public order and obedience because of their uncanny powers of persuasion by means of rhetoric; on the other hand, these powers could be extremely useful if wielded by the right people in 'appropriate' situations. The theme and practice of state licensing (or censorship) is pervasive in seventeenth-century discussions of writing and rhetoric (Patterson 1984). Furthermore, political arguments from all sides of the spectrum are embedded and embodied in literary texts in all sorts of genres that employ rhetorical techniques for political purposes, as well as in texts that we would classify as straightforward political propaganda. Visual elements such as frontispieces, illustrations, paintings, medals also play an important role in transporting rhetorically charged arguments, and sometimes texts are used to respond to powerful visual images with the heavy guns of rhetoric, irony, and wit (as in Milton's *Eikonoklastes* or Dryden's *The Medal*).

The line between these forms of communication is sometimes difficult, sometimes impossible to draw in any clear-cut, objective, genre-oriented fashion. The question to ask instead is a question of media use: how did people read, how did they respond to texts and images against the background of debates about nature, politics, and rhetoric? Considering the integrating as well as potentially destructive potential of rhetoric for the *polis,* and also considering how fictions articulate this ambivalence of rhetoric, the task is to describe the inner structure of the 'republic of letters'. As a configuration of media and media use, it provides a platform for the inevitable clash of convictions, discourses, and techniques of persuasion. It is the specific, and very heterogeneous, form of an early modern public sphere in which literary culture finds its place in society.

Words as Weapons: Rhetoric and Politics in Hobbes and Milton

There is an awareness of words as weapons already in the classical tradition. The orator who could sway a multitude by the power of rhetoric alone could be extremely useful to the *polis* but also highly dangerous for the very same reason. That is why another important consequence following from the Ciceronian origin myth of society is to be wary of eloquence. Once the foundations of the commonwealth have been established by persuasive rhetoric, who can guarantee that another powerful orator will not be able to shake them and plunge society into another civil war? If words are weapons, they are double-edged swords. Quentin Skinner has pointed out that the term *ornatus* in classical theories of rhetoric "is the word ordinarily used to describe the weapons and accoutrements of war" (1996, 49). *Ornatus* designates the orator's equipment for battle; his *vis verborum* or force of words is a form of violence, a sword wielded against the opponent (according to Quintilian, *Institutio oratoria* 8.3.5; Skinner 1996, 49–50). This military derivation was probably still understood by Renaissance rhetoricians and others who were well-versed in Latin; but whereas classical theorists held that orators should, if possible, seek to promote the truth, Hobbes underscores the aggressive, violent, and manipulative dimension of rhetoric (Hobbes 1986; Tuck 1996, 195–97). The orator's language is *ornatus* because it has to fulfil a particular function: its purpose is to win the fight for public assent, to sway opposing opinions for the benefit of a cause.

In the classical tradition, it is speech that creates the public realm, and the talented communicator has an eminent responsibility for maintaining public order. For Cicero, the positive aspects of eloquence prevail, since the capacity to "reproduce our thought in word" is what makes human beings "superior to animals". "What other power", he asks, "could have been strong enough either to gather scattered humanity into one place, or to lead it out of its brutish existence in the wilderness up to our present condition of civilization as men and citizens [*humanum cultum civilemque*], or, after the establishment of social communities [*constitutis civitatibus*], to give shape to laws, tribunals, and civic rights?" For Cicero, in short, it is "the wise control of the complete orator" that "chiefly upholds [. . .] the entire state" (*De oratore* 1.8.33–34).[72] According to Cicero, efficacious speech must be used in a careful and considered, wise and moderate way, in a way that supports the civic virtues and preserves the *humanum cultum civilemque*. But such use depends entirely on the orator's good intentions, and for this reason even those early modern thinkers who stand in a Ciceronian tradition have severe doubts about the uncanny powers of political oratory. After all, rhetoric can be used with the intent "to reconcile meanings and audiences" but also "to divide and confuse" them by means of metaphor or equivocation that "fragment understanding by exploiting the desires and prejudices of each individual" (Silver 1996, 338; cf. Kahn 1985, 152–81).

Rhetoric, as a public form of communication, provides the crucial link between individual subject, the population (as a mass of individual subjects), and the sovereign. It is powerful in its political effects and implications, and its danger to public safety

---

[72] On Cicero's ideal of the perfect orator as the perfect statesman, and particularly on its afterlife in humanist education, see Grafton and Jardine 1986, 210–20; cf. Kahn 1985.

and stability is observed by Hobbes to be greatest in those forms of society where sovereign control is weakest, particularly in democracies: "where there is *popular control* [*dominatio*], there may be as many *Neros* as there are *Orators* who fawn on the *people*. For every Orator wields as much power as the *people* itself [. . .]. Besides, private power has a certain limit beyond which it will ruin the commonwealth; because of it monarchs must sometimes take steps to see that no harm comes to the Country [*Respublica*] from that direction" (1998, 120, 10.7, italics original). For Thomas Sprat, historian of the Royal Society, language is a "Weapon [. . .] as easily procur'd by bad men as good", and therefore "*eloquence* ought to be banish'd out of *civil societies* as a thing fatal to Peace and good Manners" (Sprat 1958, 111, italics original). Hobbes, as usual, approaches the same subject with more skill for conceptual differentiation. There are two sorts of eloquence for Hobbes: one he calls logic, the other rhetoric. The first is "a lucid and elegant exponent of thought and conceptions, which arises partly from observation of things and partly from an understanding of words taken in their proper meanings as defined" (Hobbes 1998, 139, 12.12). This is the sort of eloquence he claims for the language of 'science' in his own works; introducing *The Elements of Law*, for example, Hobbes says "whilst I was writing I consulted more with logic, than with rhetoric" (1994, 19). In *Leviathan*, logic is defined as knowledge of the consequences of language "In *Reasoning*", rhetoric "In *Perswading*" (*L* 1.9; 1996, 61). The ideal of this first kind of eloquence is the "compulsively intelligible speech" (Silver 1996, 341) that he admires in the demonstrative clarity and cogency of Euclidean geometry and in the "coherent, perspicuous and persuasive [. . .] narration" (Hobbes 1975, 17) of Thucydides, the kind of eloquence that "doth secretly instruct the reader, and more effectually than can possibly be done by precept" (1975, 18) – a kind of logical 'imprinting' of the truth, without which truth would be no less true but less effective.

The second kind of eloquence is the dangerous sort, transforming "man's tongue" into "a trumpet to war and sedition" (Hobbes 1998, 71, 5.5):

> The other *eloquence* is an agitator of the passions (e.g. *hope, fear, anger, pity*), and arises out of a metaphorical use of words, adapted to the passions. The former fashions speech from true principles, the latter from received opinions of whatever kind. The art of the one is Logic, of the other Rhetoric. The end of one is truth, of the other victory. [. . .] From the actual work which they have to do it is easy to see that a *powerful eloquence* of this kind, divorced from a knowledge of things, i.e. from wisdom, is the true feature of those who agitate and incite the people to revolution. [. . .] But their ability to render their hearers insane (who were merely stupid before); to make men believe that a bad situation is worse than it is, and that a good situation is bad; to exaggerate hopes and to minimize risks beyond reason, is due to eloquence; not the eloquence which expounds things as they are, but the other eloquence, which by communicating the excitement of the speaker to the minds of others makes everything appear as he had seen it in his own excited mind. [. . .] Thus *stupidity* and *eloquence* unite to subvert the commonwealth [. . .].
> (Hobbes 1998, 139–40, 12.12–13)

In *Leviathan* (1.4), Hobbes lists among the "*Abuses of Speech*" the possibility of using language as a weapon, wielded by men "to grieve one another: for seeing nature hath armed living creatures, some with teeth, some with horns, and some with hands, to grieve an enemy, it is but an abuse of Speech, to grieve him with the tongue" (1996, 26). But he makes an important distinction about this (ab)use of language insofar as the sovereign has the right, and the duty, to wield the weapon of rhetoric: if the enemy is "one whom wee are obliged to govern [. . .] then it is not to grieve, but to correct and amend" (ibid.). In the hands of rebels, rhetorical power is dangerous and unlawful; in the hands of the sovereign, propaganda based on rhetoric is a tool of correction and education.

For Hobbes, the study of history teaches the sovereign about the connections between speech and political action; by providing historical examples, history offers an intellectual method for understanding a present situation with the aid of vicariously gained experience. Hobbes's dedication of his translation of Thucydides's *Eight Bookes of the Peloponnesian Warre* (1629) to the Earl of Devonshire is quite clear on this point. He recommends the writings of Thucydides "as having in them profitable instructions for noblemen, and such as may come to have the managing of great and weighty actions" (Hobbes 1975, 4; cf. Silver 1996, 334–37). Hobbes, who had himself been teaching the art of rhetoric to the young William Cavendish (later Duke of Newcastle and husband of Margaret Cavendish) and would continue to act as his advisor, is well aware of the political significance of rhetoric. His translation of Thucydides can be read as "a model for the citizen" (Norbrook 1999, 60). Already the title page presents an explicit political argument in its visual layout: a comparison between Sparta and Athens, monarchy and democracy. On the left, the Spartan side, we see a kind of privy council (described as *"hoi aristoi"*, 'the best') presided over by a crowned and sceptred king, engaged in reasonable and unhurried debate, a scene of so little excitement that one of the councillors even finds time to look up something in a large book – perhaps he is reading some history. On this side, people rely on reason and education. On the right-hand, Athenian side, by contrast, we see a crowd (*"hoi polloi"*, 'the masses') being agitated by an orator in a pulpit above them.

The message of this image-rhetoric is unmistakable: the opposition between logic (wisdom, good government) and rhetoric (insanity, tumult, revolt) is a political contrast. As Hobbes explains it in his introductory essay (1975, 13):

> For his [Thucydides's] opinion touching the government of the state, it is manifest that he least of all liked the democracy. And upon divers occasions he noteth the emulation and contention of the demagogues for reputation and glory of wit; with the crossing of each other's counsels, to the damage of the public; the inconsistency of resolutions, caused by the diversity of ends and power of rhetoric in the orators; and the desperate actions undertaken upon the flattering advice of such as desired to attain, or to hold what they had attained, of authority and sway amongst the common people.

In his autobiographical *Verse Life* of 1672, Hobbes compresses this position into a single couplet: according to him, Thucydides "says Democracy's a Foolish Thing, / Than a Republick Wiser is one King" (Hobbes 1994, 256). His translation of Thucydides was intended, he states in this autobiographical text, as "a Guide to Rhetoricians" (ibid.), i.e. a topical warning against the supporters of parliamentary rule.[73] Hobbes's teaching of rhetoric and logic, then, has a necessary and inevitable political slant. Its purpose is to make sure that the rhetorical weapons of mass persuasion are in the hands of the 'right' people at the 'right' moment.

∽

Despite their radically different political beliefs, this view of rhetoric as a powerful and potentially dangerous political instrument is shared by Milton. A fervent republican who is appointed Secretary for Foreign Tongues to the Council of State in 1649, a position in which he remains for ten years before embarking on his major poetic work, Milton conceives of knowledge not as the result of an 'imprinting' of the truth but as a kind of continuous armed struggle between differing ideas. Truth for Milton is a warlike figure, embodied in tropes of militancy, emerging from the battle of discourse (Barker 1990). Whereas for Hobbes, truth and obedience to the sovereign are as necessarily aligned as the geometric certainties of scientific reason and the legitimation of secular power, Milton's truth is at once more dynamic and less stable than Hobbes's (Rosendale 2004).

This becomes particularly evident in Milton's wartime pamphlets *Of Education* and *Areopagitica*, both of which were issued in 1644. In *Of Education*, Milton famously links education to republican military discipline. In these connections, he invokes quite explicitly the military metaphors of classical rhetorical terminology (Norbrook 1999, 119). His groups of students are compared in size to "a foot company, or interchangeably two troops of cavalry" (Milton 1953b, 381); the process of learning is likened to the battle lines of an army ("middle ward", 406; "rear", 407), and the confirmation and solidification of learning is "like the last embattelling of a Romane legion" (407). The object of education is the propagation of civic virtue or "civility" (381): "I call therefore a compleate and generous Education that which fits a man to perform justly, skilfully and magnanimously all the offices both private and publike of peace and war" (378–79). The study of law and politics is to turn students into bulwarks against tyranny, "stedfast pillars of the State" (389). Their daily schedule includes not only theoretical contemplation but practical exercises in state-building and maintenance: sword practice, wrestling (409) and military manoeuvres. After this intense training, including visits to the Navy, Milton's ideal students "may as it were out of a long warre come forth renowned and perfect

---

[73] The *Verse Life* is an anonymous translation, published in 1680, of Hobbes's Latin poem written in 1672 and published in 1679 as *Thomae Hobbes Malmesburiensis Vita Carmine Expressa*. In the original, the cautionary character of the 'guide' is much clearer (Hobbes 1839–1845a, 1: lxxxviii): "Is democratia ostendit mihi quam sit inepta / Et quantum coetu plus sapit unus homo. / Hunc ego scriptorem verti, qui diceret Anglis, / Consultaturi rhetoras ut fugerent." Cf. Skinner 1996, 229–30.

Commanders in the service of their country" (412). Education is, literally, a warlike discipline for Milton. His ideal student is a kind of republican samurai.

But *Of Education* has little to say about the actual use of rhetoric or the ways of limiting its risks for the state. This is the topic of *Areopagitica,* a text that has been the subject of much debate since its publication. *Areopagitica* links London with Athens and the English Parliament with the Areopagus, the ancient Athenian court traditionally located on the hill of Ares (the god of war). This court was held in high esteem by early modern republican theorists, including James Harrington and Algernon Sidney, as a just and venerable institution. The republican orientation is clear in Milton's preference for the Athenian model of democracy (in contrast to Hobbes's preference for Sparta). However, the Areopagus also serves as an aristocratic counterweight to the democratic assembly, the *ekklesia*. Milton's reference to it may be somewhat ironic but could also signal his confidence in the stability of established institutions (such as the House of Lords) and their ability to prevent an ochlocracy. Unlike the Levellers, Milton did not demand the abolition of the House of Lords, and he addresses both "Lords and Commons" throughout his 'speech' (Norbrook 1999, 130, 132).

Areopagitica presents a highly rhetorical argument "For the Liberty of Unlicenc'd Printing" (Milton 1953b, 486) addressed to Parliament. Its topic is the new republican state's attitude towards the dissemination and control of printed texts and, more generally, freedom of speech and freedom of opinion. It is thus an attempt to align politics and literary culture in a framework of liberty; in this context, it is also a reassessment of rhetoric, which can be seen in the very form of Milton's text. *Areopagitica* is an oration that was never verbally delivered (Milton would have had no right to speak in Parliament) – like its model, the speech of the ancient Athenian rhetorician Isocrates. Though far from unique in this regard, since many contemporary pamphlets were printed as addresses to Parliament (Norbrook 1999, 129), *Areopagitica* is writing that simulates speech, imitating and exploiting the pseudo-oral character of many contemporary pamphlets.

To illustrate his argument against pre-publication censorship by the state, Milton uses the myth of Cadmus, founder and first king of Thebes, who is also traditionally credited with importing the invention of writing from Phoenicia to Greece (cf. Hobbes 1996, 1.4; Hobbes 1971a, 47). Milton, in what is surely the most famous passage of this text, associates this myth with the "potencie of life" (Milton 1953b, 492) that writing contains, using the language of alchemy to describe how a printed book may contain, and immortalise, the "living intellect" of its author but also spread ideas far beyond the originator's intention:

> Books are not absolutely dead things, but doe contain a potencie of life in them to be as active as that soule was whose progeny they are; nay they do preserve as in a violl the purest efficacie and extraction of that living intellect that bred them. I know they are as lively, and as vigorously productive, as those fabulous Dragons teeth; and being sown up and down, may chance to spring up armed men. (492)

After slaying the serpent of Mars that guards a sacred grove near his newly founded city, Cadmus is told by Pallas Athena to sow the dragon's teeth into the ground; instantly, the dragon's three-tiered dentures are transformed into fully armed warriors that fight one another. After their battle, which Cadmus watches like an interested bystander, only five warriors are left alive who now help him build his city (Ovid, *Metamorphoses* 3.95–126). Milton's message in using this myth is not only that texts are potentially lethal weapons in an armed conflict – which could be used as an argument *for* pre-publication licensing and control of the press "to prevent Discord and Civill Warre", as Hobbes would propose it a few years later (*L* 2.18; 1996, 125). Milton also uses this myth to impress on his audience that these warriors would fight among themselves and eliminate one another. Dissident opinions cancel each other out; those that remained would help secure the stability of the community. Furthermore, liveliness and vigorous productivity are not the epithets normally used to characterise public enemies. For Milton, the struggle for truth is powered by the energy of warfaring opinions. The outcome of victory over tyranny and civil war is not a return to the state of nature but a more energetic and vigorous republican polity. In this light, the loss of a potentially valuable truth outweighs the short-term gain of public security:

> We should be wary [. . .] what persecution we raise against the living labours of publick men [. . .] since we see a kinde of homicide may be thus committed, sometimes a martyrdome, and if it extend to the whole impression, a kinde of massacre, whereof the execution ends not in the slaying of an elementall life, but strikes at that ethereall and fift essence, the breath of reason it selfe, slaies an immortality rather then a life. (Milton 1953b, 493)

Milton is clearly, unlike Hobbes, not afraid of rhetoric as a destructive political force, but he presents himself as an advocate of open conflict between different opinions for the sake of (republican) truth, which will emerge victorious from the fray: "all opinions, yea errors, known, read, and collated, are of main service & assistance toward the speedy attainment of what is truest" (513). He is unafraid of Hobbes's *bête noire*, opinion, "for opinion in good men is but knowledge in the making" (554). For Hobbes, on the contrary, "if every man were allowed this liberty of following his conscience" (*EL* 2.24; 1994, 137) – which he defines as a mere "opinion of evidence" (1.6; 42) in contrast to scientific certainty – "in such difference of consciences, they would not live together in peace an hour" (2.24; 137).[74] Apparently, Milton fears the decay of learning, the "dull ease and cessation of our knowledge" (1953b, 545) incident upon censorship more than the potential danger to the state that arises from dissent. Both Milton and Hobbes invoke reason to support their arguments. But whereas for Hobbes reason and conflict are mutually exclusive, Milton regards reason as plurivocal

---

[74] Cf. Hobbes 1998, 6.11 and 12.1–7 on seditious opinion as a cause that tends to dissolve the commonwealth, repeated in *L* 2.29.

("all manner of reason", 517; truth "may have more shapes then one", 563) and the commonwealth as a dynamic structure that emerges from conflict and is protected by those pure "pillars of the State" (389) who are so well trained that their integrity cannot be contaminated by reading a bad book now and then:

> For books are as meats and viands are; some of good, some of evil substance [. . .]. Wholesome meats to a vitiated stomack differ little or nothing from unwholesome; and best books to a naughty mind are not unappliable to occasions of evil. Bad meats will scarce breed good nourishment in the healthiest concoction; but herein the difference is of bad books, that they to a discreet and judicious Reader serve in many respects to discover, to confute, to forewarn, and to illustrate. (512–13)

The digestive imagery echoes the topical connection between reading and eating that we have encountered in Burton's *Anatomy*, above – as well as in Davenant, who complains about the "imperfect Stomacks" of readers (1971, 25). It is also found in Bacon's essay "Of Studies" (1597): "Some books are to be tasted, others to be swallowed, and some few to be chewed and digested" (Bacon 1996, 81). Milton enlarges on this and gives the imagery a political and ideological significance. The passage also echoes his recommendation, in *Of Education*, to teach students "how to manage a crudity" (i.e. a fit of indigestion, 1953b, 392–93) and to preserve their "healthy and stout bodies" (393) by careful nourishment and exercise in order to be able to fend off sickness. The means to this end, in matters physical as well as spiritual, is a well-kept balance between internal conditions and external influences ("those actions which enter into a man, rather then issue out of him", 513). In the case of reading as well as eating, what Milton proposes is a kind of immunisation to detrimental influences by controlled exposure: "He that can apprehend and consider vice with all her baits and seeming pleasures, and yet abstain, and yet distinguish, and yet prefer that which is truly better, he is the true warfaring Christian. [. . .] [T]hat which purifies us is triall, and triall is by what is contrary" (514–15).

Milton's metaphors are physiological and epidemiological[75] but also mercantilist and military. They emphasise the public character of print communication and the civic value of truth as a public good, even as a kind of export commodity ("our richest Marchandize", 548). *Areopagitica* maintains an intermediate position between a humanist and a neoclassical or rationalist outlook – a position that fits with most of Milton's other writings including his poetry. He is here quite skilfully using the traditional analogy between the body politic and the body natural, but this analogy is now mechanised in the image of circulation.

The urgency of the rhetoric that supports Milton's plea for unlicensed printing is liable to make readers forget that he is not at all opposed to *post*-publication

---

[75] "infection" 517, 519; "contagion" 518; "to instill the poison" 518; to "infuse" 518, "drugs," "med'-cins" 521, "to take nothing down but through the pipe" 536–37, etc.; cf. the extended conceit linking popular morale and physical constitution, 557.

censorship by the state. His argument should not be confused with a modern notion of liberal publishing or freedom of speech (Shawcross 1989, 9; Kolbrener 1997, ch. 1; Norbrook 1994). Milton does not object to the suppression of reactionary royalists or Catholic propagandists; rather, his goal is to protect radical Protestant groups from a centralised state monopoly on religious debate (Norbrook 1999, 120–21). In *Areopagitica,* he celebrates the utopian ideal of a republic based on Greek and Roman models: "a Nation not slow and dull, but of a quick, ingenious, and piercing spirit, acute to invent, suttle and sinewy to discours, not beneath the reach of any point the highest that human capacity can soar to" (1953b, 551). This ideal is a polity that unites necessary control with a flexible, dynamic, and martial concept of truth which is to emerge from a war of discourses waged by means of rhetoric. The speech culminates in the pathos-laden patriotic image of London as "this vast City; a City of refuge, the mansion house of liberty" (553–54), protected by God and engaged in forging "the plates and instruments of armed Justice in defence of beleaguer'd Truth" both literally and literarily: "others as fast reading, trying all things, assenting to the force of reason and convincement" (554).

The logic of conviction here functions similarly to Hobbes's notion of 'imprinting'. But Milton's religious rationalism describes a process of civilisation that is sharply distinct from Hobbes's thought in that it is not conceived as a unique one-off event but as a permanently ongoing "reformation" (Milton 1953b, 550–51, 555). If Hobbes ever read Milton's *Areopagitica,* he must have abhorred this as a permanent civil war. In stark contrast to Hobbes, Milton valorises dissent as a formative element in the architectural structure of his ideal polity, the "house of God":

> when every stone is laid artfully together, it [the house of God] cannot be united into a continuity, it can but be contiguous in this world; neither can every peece of the building be of one form; nay rather the perfection consists in this, that out of many moderat varieties and brotherly dissimilitudes that are not vastly disproportionall arises the goodly and the gracefull symmetry that commends the whole pile and structure. (555)

The balance that Milton argues for in his ideal republic is a *concordia discors*, a "symmetry" constructed from the discord between integrating and (to some extent) disintegrating social and intellectual forces. It is an order that emerges from the interplay between information and noise, order and disorder. This order is made "manifest" in the very language of the text, in the self-consciously rhetorical style of *Areopagitica,* made "manifest by the very sound of this which I shall utter" (487). Order and the emergence of order are dramatised in the "precarious symmetry" of Milton's style, his "dazzling, almost surreal clusters of images and his asymmetrical periods" (Norbrook 1999, 138) that make the difficult process of constructing *one* edifice out of several different opinions audible and legible.[76]

---

[76] Locke may have had precisely such rhetoric in mind when he remarked in 1660 "that there hath been no design so wicked which hath not worn the vizor of religion, nor rebellion which hath not

Characteristically, Milton's *Areopagitica* does not make use of the stoic tradition of a 'state of nature'. It remains unclear then what would happen if the political system and public order were to disintegrate. The possibility of failure is not taken into account when Milton describes the process of reformation. Instead, he uses Ciceronian or even Hobbesian adjectives to describe the condition of the people under the old regime, as compared to the new republic: "We can grow ignorant again, brutish, formall, and slavish, as ye found us; but you then must first become that which ye cannot be, oppressive, arbitrary, and tyrannous, as they were from whom ye have free'd us" (Milton 1953b, 559). The bestial state here is not the state of nature but the product of false government. The same legitimising structure (comparison of a civilised present with a barbaric past) is at work in *Areopagitica* as it is in other political treatises of its time. Its anomaly is that *Areopagitica* does not identify the barbaric past with a postulated state of nature governed by natural law, but more polemically identifies it with an older and, for Milton and the republicans in 1644, now superseded form of government. For the religious poet and monist thinker Milton, nature cannot serve as a counter-image of divine and human forms of order, since it is itself part of the one indivisible divine substance: "one almighty is, from whom / All things proceed" (Milton 1998, 5.469–70); "one first matter all, / Indued with various forms, various degrees / Of substance" (5.472–74; cf. Lewalski 2003, 419, 427–28, 475–76; Fallon 2001, 334–39). What follows from this, however, is that for Milton, as for Hobbes, politics as an earthly and human state of affairs is anything but 'natural' and that rationalism keeps the upper hand inasmuch as human beings are themselves responsible for their political order. As the Father puts it in *Paradise Lost*, human beings are "authors to themselves in all / Both what they judge and what they choose: for so / I formed them free, and free they must remain" (Milton 1998, 3.122–24). At least this view is common to both *Leviathan* and *Paradise Lost* despite their many other differences.

There is evidence to suggest that Milton's rather optimistic views of eloquence changed after the failure of the English Republic. The extent to which Satan in *Paradise Lost* relies on the persuasive force of rhetoric in order to corrupt the free will of Adam and Eve is a case in point. His is a rhetoric of acoustic traps and verbal entanglements. Milton would have associated such Satanic "abuse of Speech" (Hobbes 1996, 26) with royalist rhetorical tricks and artful manipulations of language in texts like the Declaration of Breda or Dryden's *Astræa Redux*. In *Paradise Regained*, Milton's Jesus rejects Satan's invitation to study the techniques of "the famous Orators" of ancient Athens "whose resistless eloquence / Wielded at will that fierce Democraty" (Milton 1957b, 4.268–69; cf. Quint 1993, 269).

---

been so kind to itself as to assume the specious name of reformation [. . .], that none ever went about to ruin the *state* but with pretence to build the *temple*" (Locke 1993, 144).

As a normative foundation for political thought, nature is a spent force for Hobbes and also for Milton (at least after 1660). Rhetoric and/as politics is a technique to manipulate whatever nature may have given for the sake of governing and controlling, even creating social reality. As such, rhetoric is cultivated by the royalists and employed in the later 'wars of truth' after the Restoration, particularly during the crises of the later Stuart era (Popish Plot, Exclusion), on both sides of the aisle. During these years, attempts (including literary ones) to create order increasingly lose touch with a more and more heterogeneous and complex social reality that is shot through with contingency. Rhetoric loses its power to persuade and preserve its value when it is confronted with audiences that are already split according to party lines: Whig and Tory, with little or no common ground between them. This can be seen already in royalist pastoral discourse of the 1650s, as the example of Izaak Walton will show. Walton's nostalgic vision harks back to Sidney and Spenser and to an idealised image of the Elizabethan age. *The Compleat Angler* attempts to establish a temporary counter-movement to the rationalist de-naturing and rhetoricisation of politics. Nature, in Walton and in the royalist romance, is transformed into the utopian, 'romantic' counter-image to an unwelcome political reality; it turns into a transient sanctuary whose temporary bliss partly anticipates the positive revaluation that the state of nature will be given by Rousseau much later – but whose realisation depends on conditions that are already social.

Pastoral Politics: Crypto-Royalism in Izaak Walton's *The Compleat Angler* (1653–1676)

> Of all recreations, Fishing is the most agreeable to contemplative Spirits, as being a sedate quiet sport; free from those clamours, and disturbances of the senses, which usually accompany other pleasures of the field; and not so ingrossing the mind, but that withal it is at a freedom to intertain it self with good thoughts.
>
> William Waller, *Divine Meditations Upon Several Occasions* (1680)

In the writings of Sir Thomas Browne, above all in *Religio Medici*, the flexible switching of 'reason' among different kinds of knowledge and different observer positions (science, faith, fancy, conscience) serves the purpose of an *art de vivre* that is called 'recreation'. This recreation has a clear pragmatic function: through a consonance of mental faculties, its purpose is to reorient the individual towards the world in its manifold aspects. In 1653, ten years after the first authorised edition of *Religio Medici*, the draper Izaak Walton (1593–1683) publishes a book that will prove no less popular than Browne's: *The Compleat Angler or the Contemplative Man's Recreation* can be considered a bestseller of the seventeenth century, and it remained a favourite with readers well into the Victorian period. Only the Bible appears to have been reprinted more often (Horne 1970).[77]

The Compleat Angler invites comparison with Browne's *Religio* not only because of their temporal proximity, their shared royalist sympathies, or because Walton's text carries Browne's keyword "recreation" on its title page, but above all because Walton appears to take a significant step away from Browne's urgent meditations ('urgent' because of the uneasy equilibrium between different levels of reason and passion) towards a "contemplative" life that appears to be free of content, defined only by its freedom from pragmatic, everyday concerns. Walton's "recreation" is thus much closer to the modern sense of relaxation than Browne's. In the political context of republican England, it provides an invitation for royalists to engage in passive resistance rather than explicit opposition to the powers that be, by retreating into the countryside. In its celebration of idyllic nature, *The Compleat Angler* allegorises a pastoral state of nature that is less reminiscent of Cicero and the political theories of neoclassicism than it appears to anticipate Romantic and Rousseauvian ideas of nature. Abstaining from public political rhetoric, it stages a retreat into the private world as a negation of politics. Its pastoral quality is overtly anti-political even though it harbours a political allegory.

The aim of Walton's book, as stated in the preface, addressed "To THE *Reader of this Discourse*: But especially, *To the* honest ANGLER", is to provide the reader with a fishing manual that is not only informative but entertaining – as entertaining as the pastime of fishing it describes and extols:

> I wish the Reader [. . .] to take notice, that in writing of it, I have made a recreation, of a recreation; and that it might prove so to thee in the reading, and not to read *dull*, and *tediously*, I have in severall places mixt some innocent Mirth; of which, if thou be a severe, sowr complexioned man, then I here disallow thee to be a competent Judg. For Divines say, *there are offences given*; and *offences taken, but not given*. (Walton 1983, 59)

Like Browne, Walton uses the preface to justify his project and to fish for the reader's benevolence; unlike the doctor from Norwich, he is not concerned at all with a discourse of truth, so he does not have to justify "meerely Tropicall" (Browne 2012, 4) expressions that might also have been given in plain language. The purpose of his "innocent Mirth" (Walton 1983, 59) is not to facilitate discussions about questions of religious doctrine but to leaven his subject matter with a light touch. The phrase "innocent Mirth" is not quite as innocent as it may sound, though, because it targets those who find any sort of mirth uncalled-for, even noxious: the Puritans. Thus Puritan interventions are excluded from his concerns at the very outset, in a way that is

---

[77] There are five editions during Walton's lifetime, each with substantial alterations, the last one in 1676. I have used the edition prepared by Jonquil Bevan (Oxford: Clarendon Press, 1983), which gives both the text of the 1653 and the 1676 edition. Unless stated otherwise, I refer to the 1653 text.

much more polemical than anything in Browne: "if thou be a severe, sowr complexioned man, then I here disallow thee to be a competent Judg" (59). Their counterpart is the "honest Angler", which in contrast to the "severe, sowr complexioned man" probably refers to the Cavalier or *honnête homme*. Walton's book, then, is ostensibly designed to provide its (non-Puritan, "honest") readers not with a new view of reality or truth in religion but with practical and technical information on "*fish* and *fishing*" (59), made more entertaining by "innocent Mirth". It celebrates a culture of conviviality and sociability closely connected to the old social order and the royalist party, as they are also frequently addressed in royalist drinking poems at the time – most famously in Lovelace's "The Grasse-hopper" (Scodel 2002, 226–30; McDowell 2008, 130–32). "Mirth", then, because Walton emphasises its innocence, might be seen as a defence of the book as harmless and politically innocuous, but it is also a token of allegiance, a badge of loyalty to the old regime (Marcus 1986; Zwicker 1993, 60–89).

After ten years of civil war, Walton's 1653 audience are just witnessing the dissolution of the Rump Parliament and Cromwell's rise to power as Lord Protector. In the name of 'godly rule', the "Divines" (Walton 1983, 59) now judge not only in matters of religion but also in matters of entertainment. Walton therefore makes shrewd use of their own jargon to defend his book against possible "sowr complexioned" (59) objections. What is more, he avoids stating which particular side of the doctrinal divide his "Divines" are affiliated with. They are an authority without local habitation or name, a mere allusion to the 'climate of opinions' (Glanvill 1661) and the contemporary language of religious and political debate ("offenses given" vs. "offenses taken, but not given", Walton 1983, 59). This calculated vagueness is a part of Walton's strategy in relation to the religious and political questions of his time: like Browne, he seeks for an escape from doctrinal warfare, but his escape route no longer leads *through* religious questions but is a retreat from them as "compleat" as the angler of his title. His book can be read as part of a more general royalist strategy of literary communication that includes gestures of allegory and classicism (e.g. Roman history as a code for modern politics) and/or pastoral elements of rural retreat.[78]

In its retreat from religious questions, Walton's book can to some extent be read as a secularised rewriting of Browne's *Religio*. Their similarities and differences point towards an epochal change from the erosion of late humanist conventions towards a new order of discourse. Walton's focus, like Browne's, is on the individual, the "contemplative man" and his "recreation." Also, both texts mirror their author's "disposition" (Walton 1983, 59) and proceed from the assumption that people

---

[78] See Zwicker 1993, 223 n. 4 for a list of royalist pastoral publications including *Il Pastor Fido* (1647), Mildmay Fane's *Otia Sacra* (1648), Clement Barksdale's *Nympha libethris, or The Cotswold Muse* (1651), *The Bucolicks of Baptist Mantuan* (1656), Evelyn's *Essay on . . . Lucretius* (1656), and others; cf. Patterson 1986, Loxley 1997.

adapt their behaviour patterns flexibly to different situations. In Walton, however, this is no longer a question of difficult cognitive distinctions as that between rationality and faith; these are simply ignored. The pastime of fishing creates a behaviour pattern of leisure that overrides (and, for a while, erases) such distinctions. Its aesthetic attitude to life can be interpreted as a democratisation of certain elements of court culture and ritual. Walton's "contemplative man" no longer contemplates God, the devil and the state of his own soul but rather the best bait for carp or the best way to cook trout. Browne's "soft and flexible sense" (2012, 4) here no longer involves a complex mental balancing act but is a result of the temporality of leisure – based on sociability and time-management. What is essential for this is the assignment of certain "daies and times" exclusively to innocent pleasure: "I am the willinger to justifie this *innocent Mirth,* because the whole discourse is a kind of picture of my owne disposition, at least of my disposition in such daies and times as I allow my self, when honest *Nat.* and *R.R.* and I go a fishing together" (59).

In this spirit, Walton makes clear that he writes "for pleasure", not for "money" (60) or fame. He wishes to share this pleasure with like-minded readers. This is also why the text emphasises the aspect of entertainment above that of giving practical information; here, *delectare* is more important than *prodesse. The Compleat Angler* is more than a fishing manual, and this surplus may well be responsible for its huge success. The connection between pleasure and money is a constant, though hardly acknowledged, theme of the text. Walton's strategy throughout is to deny the importance of money for his gentle anglers, knowing full well that there would be no fun in fishing without sufficient funds – it is a pastime, not a means to put food on the table. To address this dependency on financial security (like those on class and gender) would violate the conventions of the pastoral idyll as a genre.

The implication of the preface is that readers, in order to be able to enjoy the book, need not have any concrete interest in learning how to fish. Even if they dislike the text, they should, Walton facetiously adds, "like the pictures of the *Trout and other fish*" (58). Whereas Browne, at least in the preface to *Religio Medici,* is anxious to preserve a wary sense of distance between the authorial persona and his readers, Walton directly addresses the reader with the familiar pronoun 'thou'. He imagines the reader as a kind of (male) companion and pictures the ideal setting for reading his book: "[I] wish thee a *rainy evening* to read this book in" (60). Much more consciously than Browne's texts, Walton's *Angler* is written with a particular readership and reading situation in mind. Its ideal readers share certain values, norms and beliefs, which can therefore be treated as self-evident. Although justificatory formulae and some genuflection to theological authorities are still obligatory, Walton caters to an entirely different literary market; he provides light entertainment in book form while hiding his serious argument in the subtext.

The Compleat Angler is in the form of a dialogue, a form cut out for the communication of new (scientific) knowledge and much employed by Renaissance humanist writers (Erasmus, Castiglione, Galileo, More), though not quite as common in English literature. In adherence to the humanist tradition, the characters Walton chooses for this dialogue are given Latin names: "Piscator" (the fisherman) and "Viator" (the traveller). Their roles of master and pupil are established early in the text: Piscator and Viator address each other as "Master" and "Scholer" (84). A few other characters appear briefly and then vanish again: the huntsman, the hostess, the "handsome Milk-maid" (89) and her mother (ch. 2), Piscator's brother Peter and his friend Coridon (ch. 3) – the text has a striking mix of realistic and fantasy names. Yet these characters never disrupt the basic binarism of the master-pupil dialogue or Piscator's lengthy monologues; they usually disappear after having contributed some extra information (in the case of the hunter) or some "innocent Mirth" by means of a poem or song. As John R. Cooper has pointed out, this structure is influenced by William Samuel's *The Arte of Angling* (1577), also a dialogue between a "Piscator" and a "Viator" but different from Walton's in its "sense of earthy realism" as opposed to Walton's "more formal, more aristocratic, and, above all, more literary world" (Cooper 1968, 83). Later editions of *The Compleat Angler* complicate this structure by introducing three main characters: Piscator, Venator (the hunter) and Auceps (the falconer), "each commending his Recreation" (Walton 1983, 173).

The text's fictional setting is not very elaborate; there is no attempt at a realistic description of landscape, of the character's physical appearance, of their inner lives or their history; there is no narration outside of dialogue; transitions are often abrupt. Later editions do nothing to change this. Yet the combination of dialogue and sketchy descriptions achieves something very important: an integration of the humanist discursive model with a pastoral setting, with a celebration of country life and the value system of the "honest Country man" (92). The 'reality effect' (Barthes 1994) provided by the dialogue itself is bare and skeletal. The location, at least, is clearly identifiable, as the first lines of the text indicate: the 'events', such as they are, take place in the early summer in rural Hertfordshire, in the Lea Valley. A few place names are given in the very first lines of the text: "*Totnam Hil*", "*Ware*", "*Hodsden*" (i.e. Hoddesdon). The pastoral world of *The Compleat Angler* is not Arcadia or continental Europe but rural England; its theme is not the amorous play and the sexual innuendo of self-concealment and self-discovery of gentlefolk who play at being shepherds, but the strictly homosocial hobby-horses of ale-quaffing, bed-sharing gentlemen. Their inner lives are not particularly interesting, apparently, at least they are far less of a problem than they are in Sidney's *Arcadia*. The hostess is there to do the cooking; she never comes into view as an erotic object nor, for that matter, as a fully realised person. The aim of Walton's pastoral discourse is not to present the codified play of self-transformation but what one could describe as the (equally codified) relaxation of weekend tourists. As Anna K. Nardo puts it, reading this text in the light of the psychology of 'flow' (Csikszentmihalyi 1990): "Fishing and writing about fishing are a temporary retreat from conflict, not a way to live within it. [. . .] Leaving all controversy, whether theological or legal, behind, the angler delimits his field of action to exclude the unpredictable world of humans and to include only the predictable habits of fish" (Nardo 1991, 187). And yet, underneath the "innocent Mirth", something like an agenda becomes visible. The exclusion of conflict is the temporary pastoral utopia of the gentleman who engages in a play-world that he controls.

The "most honest, ingenious, harmless Art of Angling" (Walton 1983, 69) that Walton commends by citing biblical and classical authorities as an ideal combination of *vita contemplativa* and *vita activa* (68–70), serves as a gentleman's recreation in politically difficult times. There are numerous allusions to religion: e.g. to Christ's parable of the sower ("Trust me, good Master, you shall not sow your seed in barren ground", 93), to the early Christians (112), to the "*Fishers of men*" (97) and the Sermon on the Mount ("what my Saviour said, that *the meek possess the earth*", 150). The anglers recite verses by Marlowe and Ralegh but also by George Herbert ("Vertue", 111–112) and John Donne ("Come live with me, and be my love", 138). In this way the *Compleat Angler* also develops into a literary anthology (Benedict 1996). The second edition of 1655 also includes the poem "Common-Prayer" from Christopher Harvey's *The Synagogue* (2nd ed. 1647, 260–61). Ten years after the abolition of the *Book of Common Prayer*, the inclusion of this poem is "perhaps Walton's most explicit statement of his unswerving Anglicanism" (Cooper 1968, 171). But all religious conflict, like any other, is avoided, and all religious differences are suspended or marked as contingent: thus Walton's Piscator quotes a poem by an unnamed "Poet" (his modern editor speculates on Walton himself as its author) which repeats an argument familiar from continental skeptics like Charron and Montaigne but also from Lipsius (Walton 1983, 82):

> – Many a one
> Owes to his Country his Religion:
> And in another would as strongly grow,
> Had but his Nurse or Mother taught him so.

Piscator praises this poem as "reason put into Verse, and worthy the consideration of a wise man" (82). One could see this geographical relativisation of religious differences (according to the saying *cuius regio, eius religio*) as an – albeit somewhat trivialised – consequence of Browne's "indifferency" in matters of doctrine and of his English cosmopolitanism ("All places, all ayres make unto me one Countrey; I am in *England*, every where, and under any meridian", 2012, 65, *Religio* 2.1). It can also be seen as an anticipation of the growing "concern for the environment of learning" (Novak 2001, 48) and the nature vs. nurture debate that was started by Locke's blank slate view of the mind. Charles Morton, for example, Defoe's teacher, held that "Men are much what the Custom and usual practice of the place is, where they live. He that is bred, or much conversant, in the country; gets there a simple plain heartedness; or perhaps a Rough Rusticity: He that is much in the City, has more of Civility, Sagacity, and Cunning" (Morton 1692, 24; cf. Novak 2001, 48). In the context of mid-seventeenth-century royalism, Walton's poem can be associated with rationalist attempts to mediate between religion and reason. In Davenant's *Gondibert* 2.6, for example, the Court of Astragon is praised for its handling of religion as follows: "Religion's Rites, seem here, in Reasons sway; / Though Reason must Religion's Laws obay" (Davenant 1971, 159).

In *The Compleat Angler,* the distinction between substantial faith and accidental custom is downplayed so far as to vanish almost entirely. "But of this no more", Piscator continues, immediately deflecting the conversation from this contentious topic, "for though I love civility, yet I hate severe censures: I'll to my own Art, and I doubt not but at yonder tree I shall catch a *Chub,* and then we'll turn to an honest cleanly Ale house" (82–83). In effect, what we have here is an early example of what would later become "a new social rule" among the elite under the banners of civility, common sense, and politeness: the rule "that civilized, civil people keep politics and religion out of the conversation" (Spurr 1998, 27). In the more immediate context of 1653, *The Compleat Angler* shares the preference of royalist political thought for secrecy, privacy, covertness, and indirectness over publicity and public communication (Potter 1989).[79]

Walton's book is a recipe for 'the good life', a life of leisure, as lacking in religious contention as it is without economic problems or desires: "No life, my honest Scholer, no life so happy and so pleasant as the Anglers, unless it be the Beggers life in Summer; for then only they take no care, but are as happy as we Anglers" (Walton 1983, 112). Later editions omit the beggars and instead foreground the difference between leisure and professional work: "No life, my honest Scholar, no life so happy and so pleasant, as the life of a well governed *Angler*; for when the *Lawyer* is swallowed up with business, and the *States-man* is preventing or contriving plots, then we sit on *Cowslip-banks,* hear the birds sing, and possess our selves in as much quietness as these silent silver streams, which we now see glide so quietly by us" (261). Slowly but surely, the language of religion that structures seventeenth-century discourses about the self and its (re-)creation is superseded by the idiom of politics, finance, and labour. The focus is then less on self-knowledge and self-fashioning than on self-possession. In a similar manner, the language of love is invaded by the metaphorics of mercantilism in Restoration comedy.[80] The practice of leaving a fishing-rod in the water overnight is compared to the increase of interest on capital: "let me tell you, this kind of fishing, and laying Night-hooks, are like putting money to use, for they both work for the Owners, when they do nothing but

---

[79] Sharon Achinstein argues that the royalist "philosophy of secrecy" is not merely a result of censorship and oppression but inherent to a royalist outlook that regarded politics as "a private matter" and preferred the coterie and the patriarchal system of "personal rule" over public debate (1994, 132–33). On the historical context, see also Sharpe 1987 and 1992.
[80] Numerous examples of this new language could be cited from Aphra Behn's *The Rover* alone, e.g. the exchanges between Willmore, Angellica, and Moretta in 2.2 on "selling" love "by retail", "at a cheap rate", "at higher rates", "the whole cargo or nothing" and so on; see Behn 1995, 28.

sleep, or eat, or rejoice, as you know we have done this last hour" (112). Later editions of *The Compleat Angler* display a greater awareness of social distinctions and their financial grounding, reducing the pastoral illusion to a more realistic depiction of leisure as opposed to labour. The beggars are then no longer envied for their pleasant life, and in one of the numerous poems and songs the phrase "*Hail blest estate of poverty!*" (150) is replaced, from the third edition onwards, by the less specific "*Hail blest estate of lowliness!*" (334). The classical allusion, in both cases, is to Horace's second Epode, which praises a quiet country life in explicit contrast to business, warfare and political power games; there 'poverty' (*paupertas*) means the lack of luxury rather than destitution. In Dryden's translation (1995b, 2: 378):

> How happy in his low degree,
> How rich in humble poverty is he
> Who leads a quiet country life!
> Discharged of business, void of strife,
> And from the griping scrivener free.

The pastoral society, represented by way of synecdoche in the homosocial bonding between Piscator and Viator (or in later editions Venator), is based on "simple courtesy and affection" (Cooper 1968, 66). These, however, are less "simple" than they may at first appear. Society in the pastoral state of nature works (for a limited amount of time) because parts of social reality are strategically and systematically excluded. It works because both participants in the dialogue agree on the hierarchical distribution of their roles. Similarly, the peasants and the hostess never question their social inferiority; they 'know their places' (cf. Empson 1974, 11) in the order of things. Even in the song contests, Walton emphasises the absence of any real contention among the participants. In accordance with the conventions of pastoral and in keeping with the common royalist nostalgia for the Elizabethan period, the rural qualities of simplicity and moral purity are contrasted with the joyless drudgery of busy city life and its complexities. This moralising tendency is intensified in the 1676 edition by the introduction of a lengthy sermon, delivered by Piscator towards the end of the text, in which he compares a rich man to a silkworm "that when she seems to play, is at the very same time spinning her own bowels, and consuming herself. And this many rich men do; loading themselves with corroding cares, to keep what they have (probably) unconscionably got. Let us therefore be thankful for health and a competence; and above all, for a quiet Conscience" (363).

This pastoral ideal of quietness, including political quietism, is part of Walton's gentlemanly honour code, which is already fully present in the 1653 version and remains unchanged later: "I would rather prove my self to be a Gentleman, by being *learned* and *humble*, *valiant* and *inoffensive*, *vertuous* and *communicable*, then by a fond ostentation of *riches*; or (wanting these Vertues my self) boast that these were in my Ancestors; (And yet I confesse, that where a noble and ancient Descent and such Merits meet in any man, it is a double dignification of that person)"

(68; cf. 191). Walton's concept of the ideal gentleman resembles the concept of gentility based on virtue and self-control as developed by Richard Brathwait in *The English Gentleman* (1630). It combines a remnant of the older concept of social distinction by birth with a moral concept that 'proves' the gentleman by his behaviour and his actions. The conflict between patriarchal privilege and political virtue is a key concern in mid-seventeenth-century social and political conflicts.

While subscribing to an idea of gentleness by virtue rather than privilege, Walton also rejects the emerging form of social distinction by money – what C. B. Macpherson (1962) has called "the political theory of possessive individualism". Walton's pastoral vision is pervaded by a critique of material wealth used as a status symbol. The world he presents is one in which money has no real function and in which possession of material goods or the lack thereof never poses any problems, so that the gentlemen can simply "possess [their] selves" (261) rather than having to support their status by wealth. Money can neither add to nor subtract from the gentleman's 'self-possession'; it is a mere contingency. So, it seems, is religion. The difference between *The Compleat Angler* and traditional pastoral literature is the fact that Walton's text addresses the topic of money or "riches" at all, and that the awareness of its reality goes so far as to excise the celebration of idyllic "poverty" from later editions. Although money is not allowed to play a role in their interactions, it is clear that the characters have sufficient funds at their disposal – otherwise they could not afford to "go a-fishing" for mere pleasure.

Compared to the heated religious and political conflicts of the Commonwealth and Protectorate and to a society increasingly aware of the political relevance of economic conditions, the virtual world of *The Compleat Angler* is less a 'natural' counter-world to seventeenth-century English society than a very limited selection of reality segments. This selection results in a "reduction of complexity to a manageable scale" (Nardo 1991, 198). It is based on three major factors: a temporal demarcation of leisure from work; a system of social value (the gentleman ideal); and the premise that only men are allowed the privilege to "go a fishing" while women exist to provide basic services and "innocent" entertainment. To the 'real world', this virtual world bears only a tenuous relation. It is conceptualised as a temporary and yet 'compleat' retreat from everyday life – "innocent" also in that it has no impact on life outside of the idyll itself.

The lack of connection between Walton's pastoral fiction and its immediate historical context is even more blatant in later versions of the text. In subsequent editions until 1676, *The Compleat Angler* takes on increasingly nostalgic and anachronistic aspects. In the new context of Restoration splendour and its ruthlessly cultivated immorality, Walton's encomium of the "quiet" and "vertuous" life (1983, 371) must have appeared out of step with its time, harking back to the 'good old days' – perhaps even comparable to Milton's evocation of a lost paradise. A darker, more nostalgic tone also creeps into the repeatedly altered preface until the passage quoted above, which in 1653 justifies the "innocent Mirth" of the text, finally reads as follows in 1676:

> And I am the willinger to justifie the pleasant part of it, because though it is known I can be serious at seasonable times, yet the whole discourse is, or rather was, a picture of my own disposition, especially in such days and times as I have laid aside business, and gone a fishing with honest *Nat.* and *R. Roe;* but they are gone, and with them most of my pleasant hours, even as a shadow, that passeth away, and returns not. (170)

The distance from 'real life' thus grows in later editions: from the distance provided by a selected leisure-time activity towards a greater temporal and socio-historical distance. This is exacerbated for later generations of readers who are likely to skip the information and read only the entertaining parts of the book, which in one edition from 1750 were even typographically set apart from the rest (Cooper 1968, 5–6). Increasingly, Walton's recreation is thinned out to result in a reading experience that is no longer interested in the book's instructive aspects: "All the scientific part you may omit in reading", Charles Lamb advised Coleridge (Lamb 1935, 1:21). The state of nature presented in *The Compleat Angler*, coded in 1653 as a counter-image to its contemporary republican setting, is transformed into an epitome of romantic retreat from the world. In the eighteenth and nineteenth centuries, it is read as a fictional text into which Romanticism can inscribe itself. Wordsworth's sonnet "Written upon a Blank Leaf in 'The Compleat Angler'" (1819) is paradigmatic of this tendency; Wordsworth gives a symptomatic appraisal of the text's changed function when he notes that Walton's depiction of nature is highly unnatural: "Fairer than life itself, in this sweet Book, / The cowslip-bank and shady willow-tree; /And the fresh meads [. . .]" (Wordsworth 1977, 398, ll. 11–13). Wordsworth has forgotten about the political context of this idealisation and 'beautification' of nature in the seventeenth century. As we have seen, however, Walton's *Compleat Angler* of 1653 with its idyllic presentation of a peaceful natural world in 'merry old England' is nothing less than a strategic intervention in royalist political discourse. In this, it is similar to other pastoral writing and the epic romance of its time, as for instance Sir William Sales's *Theophania* or Sir Percy Herbert's *The Princess Cloria* (Salzman 1985, 155–76) – although Walton appears to be at pains to exclude politics rather than reflect it explicitly. Nature, for Walton, is a counterweight to the reality of public life; only in nature, he appears to say, is it possible to communicate among equals without being constrained by political power. In Walton's state of nature, political differences are contained in recreational activity, absorbed by natural beauty.

Conceptually, *The Compleat Angler* pushes the state of nature from a historical foundation in political thought towards a proto-romantic ideal that is located both outside history and outside the complexities of human society (without as yet using nature, as Locke and Rousseau will do later, as a normative basis for civility and legitimacy). Walton's book seems to have been intended at first to provide its readers, especially the landed gentry, with a survival guide for the Cromwellian Interregnum. After the Restoration, its political message of royalist secrecy and privacy becomes increasingly a thing of the past. Utopia turns into nostalgia. The last edition seen through the press by Walton appears in 1676, two years before the Popish Plot. In the political crises of the late 1670s and 1680s, the message of *The Compleat Angler* is no longer relevant to an audience increasingly divided along party lines. As we shall see, politics and literature will then once again be part of a public debate about the foundations of the commonwealth, but one from which it no longer seems possible to escape into (exterior or interior) 'nature'.

Between *Astræa Redux* and *Paradise Lost*: Cultural Memory and Countermemory in the Restoration

> The Devil take him that remembers first, I say.
> Congreve, *The Way of the World*

Walton's *Compleat Angler* is a political manifesto of creative ignorance, deploying the formal conventions of Sidneian pastoralism and Arcadian fiction that Davenant, in 1650, had come to deride in unmistakably Hobbesian terms as unrealistic given the wolvish and "uncivill" nature of mankind: "If any man can yet doubt of the necessary use of Armys, let him study that which was anciently call'd a Monster, the Multitude (for Wolves are commonly harmlesse when they are met alone, but very uncivill in Heards) and he will not finde that all his kindred by *Adam* are so tame, and gentle, as those Lovers that were bred in *Arcadia*" (Davenant 1971, 12–13). In its celebration of rural values, Walton's book functions as a royalist palliative that works largely by excluding any potential area of social conflict, while depending on quite specific social and economic conditions. Its celebration of 'merry England' is equally nostalgic and (in its Cromwellian context) polemic because it can be read as a call to arms for a return to the pre-republican past. After all, 'merry England' was a powerful projection of royalist ideology (Cavendish 1984, 64). The book's success demonstrates that, in a period as uprooted, divided, and trembling at its very core as mid-seventeenth century England, strategies of forgetting, amnesia, and amnesty could become realistic options in politics; the more so in a literary culture that was increasingly hard pressed to find convincing aesthetic and rhetorical ways of mediating between political ideals and social realities.

As Steven Zwicker has argued, irony and generic blending, masquerade and satire function as techniques of dealing with the instability and opportunism rampant in Restoration England. If, in this view, the restoration of the monarchy in 1660 is itself at least partly an ironic and anachronistic event ("the fixing of old forms atop new facts"), irony is its most appropriate cultural expression, evoking "the necessity of familiar political and spiritual and cultural formations while compromising their authority and denaturing their integrity" (Zwicker 1997, 182). Irony embodies and celebrates a stability of the 'as if' (Vaihinger 1922), promoting faith in consciously contrived "fictions of state" (Love 1993, 164) that are endlessly suspended and confirmed in turn. Only arbitrary belief in "the necessary fiction of a commonwealth" (Kahn 1985, 181) is thought capable of fending off an imminent reversion of society into the state of nature, i.e. chaos.

In the memory culture of the later Stuart period, and in the play of memory and countermemory – a term inspired by the concept of "counterhistory" as "the systematic exploitation of the adversary's most trusted sources against their grain" (Funkenstein 1992) –, irony and satire fulfil a key function of distancing and reflecting political contingencies. They become more important in understanding the Restoration not as a monolithic political and cultural event but as "a multiple discursive reorientation" that brings into play the very "terms by which a society must revise the pressures of the immediate past" (Kroll 1991, 38–39). These terms include rhetorically charged representations of what counts as 'natural' in relation to the contingencies of culture, history, and politics. As a cultural moment or series of moments, the Restoration is characterised by the urgency of finding acceptable representations of history and memory to stabilise the present.

In this and the following section, I will enquire into the cultural uses of forgetting and remembering between 1660 and 1688, as well as into the interplay and exchange between officially produced or officially sanctioned fictions and dissenting literary-political representations or counter-fictions. For obvious reasons, the 'heroes' of these two sections will be Dryden and Milton, but I shall also take into account less canonical works: the poems of Abraham Cowley and the tragicomedy *The Adventures of Five Hours* by Sir Samuel Tuke (1662).

Studies of cultural memory tend to focus on remembrance rather than forgetting, although many of them have also shown an awareness of the necessary interplay of remembering and forgetting in memory processes (Assmann and Harth 1991; Assmann 1999; Bal, Crewe and Spitzer 1999; Erll and Nünning 2008). Without forgetting, there can be no remembering. The complete retention or 'total recall' of sense impressions, experiences, and thoughts is hard to imagine and would most probably result in psychosis. Nevertheless, as Freud knew, what is superficially forgotten or repressed into what he called the 'unconscious' may resurface or be re-remembered at a later date. The pendulum swings between forgetting and remembering that structure the latencies of cultural memory also characterise the political and social world of the Restoration. We have already encountered the first examples of this in the quarrel for politically powerful and representative images of the state after the revolution. The surprisingly non-violent regime change of 1660 is initially pervaded by an atmosphere of Arcadian innocence, at the same time artificially contrived and depicted as 'natural', as if it had sprung immediately from the pages of a royalist romance, from *Gondibert, The Compleat Angler* or a revival of Elizabethan pageants. This 'fiction of state' cannot remain stable for very long under the pressures that pull court and city ever further apart. It is undermined by the return of more realistic and more crudely 'natural' catastrophic events: plague, fire, wars, soon aggravated by plots, factions, and rebellion. The 'innocence' of the Restoration, like *The Compleat Angler,* depends on the exclusions of certain differences and divisions, but these cannot be made to disappear simply by forgetting them. In the longer term, the Waltonesque way of dealing with these disturbing cracks in the foundation of the new state is doomed to fail. Rhetorical appeals as to what or whom to forget and what or whom to remember sound more and more frantic as these divisions move away from religious, philosophical, and constitutional debates and begin to congeal into political party lines between Whig and Tory. During this time, literary productions and publications are not only a seismographic register of and a running commentary on these events; they are part and parcel of the cultural process of managing the difference between remembering and forgetting in strategic ways, both in support of and in opposition to government policies. Cultural memory in the English seventeenth century thus becomes a site of political contest and conflict. Irony and satire are rhetorical weapons in this, but they are wielded most frequently (unless in the hands of the Earl of Rochester) for the sake of a particular side in the struggle and not to shine an ironic light on the struggle itself.

Like many other epochal moments of historical change, the restoration of the monarchy in 1660 entailed a number of strategic acts of remembering and forgetting. For example, on 23 May, Samuel Pepys accompanies the king and his royal entourage on their crossing from Scheveningen to Dover. In his diary, he registers the ease with which the flagship of the Commonwealth, the *Naseby* – its name commemorates a decisive victory of parliamentary forces over royalist troops in 1645 – is renamed and repainted as the *Royal Charles*. He writes: "After dinner, the King and Duke [. . .] altered the name of some of the Shipps, *viz.* the *Nazeby* into *Charles* – the *Richard*, *James*; the *Speaker*, *Mary* – The *Dunbar* (which was not in company with us) the *Henery* – *Winsby*, *Happy returne* – *Wakefield*, *Richmond* – *Lamport*, the *Henretta* – *Cheriton*, the *Speedwell* – *Bradford*, the *Successe*" (Pepys 1970–1983, 1: 154).

Already in the republican and Cromwellian 1650s, however, forgetting, though not necessarily forgiving "the late troubles" and "the differences that caused them" (Cowley 1656, sig. (a)4ʳ) were a necessary condition for engagement in constructing a new kind of state. After the Civil War, forgetting the past becomes, in the words of Andrew Shifflett (2003, 101), "a positive value, the theme for a new intellectual *ethos*". It was also a practical necessity because there was no possibility to claim legal damages for injuries incurred during the revolution. The destruction of royal monuments after the execution of Charles I in 1649 is accompanied by complex acts of reinscription, which in turn have to be 'forgotten' and replaced after the Restoration. The euphemism 'Interregnum', a term still used by historians, often without questioning its problematic nature, itself speaks volumes about these reconstructive and recuperative efforts (Norbrook 1999). The new state has to construct its own political present, history, and iconography on its own terms.

Abraham Cowley, after having written an epic poem on *The Civil War* from a royalist point of view, realised what was required of him by the new republic in 1656 at the latest when, in the preface to his *Poems* of that year, he wrote of the obligation to give up the fight after its outcome has been decided by the will of God:

> Now though in all *Civil Dissentions*, when they break into open hostilities, the *War* of the *Pen* is allowed to accompany that of the *Sword*, and every one is in a maner obliged with his *Tongue*, as well as *Hand*, to serve and assist the side which he engages in; yet when the event of battel, and the unaccountable *Will* of God has determined the controversie, and that we have submitted to the conditions of the *Conqueror*, we must lay down our *Pens* as well as *Arms*, we must *march* out of our *Cause* it self, and *dismantle* that, as well as our *Towns* and *Castles*, of all the *Works* and *Fortifications* of *Wit* and *Reason* by which we defended it.
> (Cowley 1656, sig. (a)4r)

A few years later, after the Restoration, Cowley must have been more than a little embarrassed by these lines and by his premature submission to the republican regime. Yet he received a royal pardon, and in a second act of palimpsestic erasure, he deleted these lines from a new edition of his *Poems* in 1667. In 1656, however, he had gone even further than merely submitting to the new regime, pleading for memory to be silent:

> The truth is, neither *We*, nor *They* [i.e. neither the defeated royalists nor the victorious republicans], ought by the *Representation* of *Places* and *Images* to make a kind of *Artificial Memory* of those things wherein we are all bound to desire like *Themistocles*, the *Art* of *Oblivion*. The enmities of *Fellow-Citizens* should be, like that of *Lovers*, the *Redintegration* of their *Amity*. The Names of *Party*, and *Titles* of *Division*, which are sometimes in effect the whole quarrel, should be extinguished and forbidden in peace under the notion of *Acts* of *Hostility*. And I would have it accounted no less unlawful to *rip up old wounds*, then to *give new ones* [. . .].
> (Cowley 1656, sig. (a)4^{r–v})

It is not without irony that Cowley's nominalist "*Art* of *Oblivion*", suggested in 1656 and intended for Cromwell, was to become official government policy after the restoration of the monarchy in 1660. Cowley's sin, in the eyes of his fellow royalists, was not that he decided to let bygones be bygones or that he chose to represent the atrocities of the Civil War in terms of a lovers' tiff but, as Andrew Shifflett explains, that he offered "poetry as the vehicle, agency, or court for such things [. . .] at a time when kings claimed original and ultimate authority over the agencies of forgiving and forgetfulness" (2003, 109). To maintain oblivion as a political fiction of clemency was difficult and precarious enough for the restored court; to see it explicitly extolled as a *poetic* fiction, and by a lapsed royalist to boot, was intolerable. After 1660, it is again the court that claims authority over the fictions it deems wise to sponsor and propagate, and the poets once again oblige. Court policy echoes Cowley's lines in his version of "The Second Olympique Ode of Pindar" in the *Poems* of 1656 (sig. Bbb1^v):

> For the past sufferings of this noble Race
> (Since things once *past*, and fled out of thine hand,
> Hearken no more to thy command)
> Let *present joys* fill up their place,
> And with *oblivions silent stroke* deface
> Of foregone Ills the very *trace*.

In the Declaration of Breda (4 April 1660), later transformed into law in the *Act of Oblivion,* Charles II offers his subjects "a free and general pardon" on the occasion of his triumphal return to England (qtd. in Kenyon 1986, 331). In the text of this declaration, which anticipates key elements of Restoration policy, the word "restoration" resonates with the *"silent stroke"* of oblivion that Cowley had celebrated in 1656. Now it signals the complete erasure from national memory of England's republican decade: "restoration both of king, peers and people to their just, ancient and fundamental rights" (331). In contrast to this fairly precise constitutional outline of a return to the past, recent political events are veiled in generalities: "the general distraction and confusion", "so long misery and sufferings" (331), "the passion and uncharitableness of the times", "the continued distractions of so many years and so many and great revolutions" (332) At the close of the document, the year 1660 is referred to as "the twelfth year of our reign" (332). The dynastic gap between father and son is thus closed in a stroke of the pen that resembles the king's magic healing powers: "that those wounds which have so many years together been kept bleeding may be bound up" (331). "[H]enceforward", Charles proclaims, calling upon his subjects to forget the past, "all notes of discord, separation, and difference of parties [are to] be utterly abolished among all our subjects, whom we invite and conjure to a perfect union among themselves [. . .]" (331–2).

The return to the idealised past – frequently viewed in nostalgic terms as a return to the 'merry England' of Elizabeth, 'Astraea redux' (Yates 1977) – is presented, in the Declaration of Breda, as a step forward into a more peaceful and tolerant future, a step made possible by a deliberate act of oblivion, presented in terms of curative treatment. It becomes law in the *Act of Free and General Pardon, Indemnity and Oblivion* of 1660 (Kenyon 1986, 339–44). The exceptions from this act were so few that they could be listed by name. In the regicide trials, twenty-seven men were convicted of treason, and ten of these were executed (Nenner 1997). The way the new authorities dealt with the regicides gives the impression of a surgical operation rather than a ritual of revenge, even though the executions were gruesome as usual. This appears to have been intended as an act of restoring the body politic to its natural state of health. Healing wounds by overcoming, or at least camouflaging, differences of opinion was the strategy of the hour. This is clearly reflected in official publications as well as theatrical productions of the early 1660s, which followed the ideological fault line to a fault, albeit with different degrees of skill and subtlety. Their highest priority, it seems, is to prevent a return to the Hobbesian state of nature that is civil war.

One of the less well-known writers employed in this literary 'restoration' effort is Sir Samuel Tuke (knighted in 1664). Before the Restoration, Tuke had "pass'd eighteen Years of his Time, in the Service and Court" of Charles II (Tuke 1660, 4); upon the king's return, he publishes *A Character of Charles the Second,* a pamphlet in praise of the king's "generous Qualities" (1660, 8) and virtues such as fortitude and clemency. In 1662, Charles II encourages this loyal servant to adapt a Spanish 'cape and sword' play, *Los empeños de seis horas,* for the English stage. The original, first performed in

Seville in 1642, is now assumed to be by Antonio Coello (1611–1652) but was attributed to Calderón at the time (Braga Riera 2009, 75; Loftis 1973; Vander Motten and Daemende Gelder 2006). *The Adventures of Five Hours* – one hour is lost in the adaptation, possibly to bring the duration of the action closer to the real time of performance (Braga Riera 2009, 111) – has its premiere at court in December 1662 and its first public performance in January 1663 (Womersley 2000, 2). Pepys praises it above Shakespeare's *Othello* (20 August 1666, Pepys 1970–1983, 7: 255), with which it shares the theme of jealousy. In hindsight at least, the choice of this play by Charles II himself appears a shrewd move at this juncture. In Tuke's translation, *The Adventures* turns into a deeply anti-Puritan play about overcoming differences – in very concrete terms: how to avoid bloodshed and vengeance. It stages the reconciliation of lovers, taking up again Cowley's metaphor of the Civil War as a lovers' quarrel.

The "Prologue at Court" dutifully stages the author's inspiration by the king. Its inclusion in the first printing also lends an official character to the play by associating it with the king's own wishes, who takes over the function of the Muse in inspiring the playwright. Tuke's invocation of the king is cast in provocatively religious terms: "Light" is emitted "by a Ray from th'upper Sphere" – resembling the iconographic cliché on the frontispiece to *Eikon Basilike* – to which the poet responds with "Zeal" (1663, sig. a1^v). Key elements of the Protestant or Puritan idiom are ironically appropriated according to an ideal of courtly wit – an unmistakable jibe at the godly. Tuke's prologue modestly presents the act of writing as an act of obedience and an attempt at reading the king's mind, possibly also in order not to allow the king to be blamed for the play's potential failure. It also recommends this approach as a political model of the relationship between subjects and their sovereign (sig. a1^v):

> So should Obsequious Subjects catch the Minds
> Of Princes, as your Sea-men do the Winds.
> If this Attempt then shews more Zeal, than Light,
> 'T may teach you to Obey, though not to Write.

As we know from the dramatic and poetic theory of Sir William Davenant, teaching to obey is the most important purpose of literary production (Jacob and Raylor 1991). Davenant is directly responsible for the production of *The Adventures of Five Hours*, one of his greatest successes (Visser 1975, 57). Tuke's play provides a form of entertainment that is perfectly suited to the official taste of early Restoration England. This connection to its original political context gives it a special resonance.

Pepys's comparison of *The Adventures* to *Othello* is quite appropriate since both are about the dangers of jealousy, although they deal with it in strikingly different ways. Like its original, *The Adventures* is set in Spain, in the city of Seville. Yet the play's historical context, the Spanish Wars of Religion in the Netherlands, remains in the background, merely serving as "the largely neutral backdrop to a series of romantic escapades" (Womersley 2000, 2). This loss of importance of religiously motivated warfare can be read as a calculated comment on the play's historical moment in England, which, as we have seen, is all about forgetting the cruelties of the Civil War and the "Names [. . .] and *Titles* of *Division*" (Cowley 1656, sig. (a)4ᵛ). Tuke's play thus paves the way for the dominant formal qualities of early Restoration drama not only in its scenic conventions and its Spanish setting but also in its "provocative shallowness" (Womersley 2000, 2).[81]

Tuke's way of dealing with the dangerous passions of jealousy and an exaggerated sense of honour is perfectly aligned to the play's function of teaching the civic virtues of obedience. As Davenant argues in his "exercise in practical Hobbism" (Jacob and Raylor 1991, 205), the *Proposition for Advancement of Moralitie* (1653), theatrical techniques ought to be used to engender positive or negative passions in the audience: appetite or aversion for those objects that the sovereign judges to be good or bad. Dangerous and destructive passions – like the "fears and jealousies" so often adduced by Parliament to justify its actions during the Civil War – could thus be overcome by replacing them with passions that were "politically correct" (Jacob and Raylor 1991, 225).

The prologue takes on an important task in this respect. It declares kingship sacred using the metaphors of light and blindness. The prologue addresses the king in person and involves him in the performance in a manner that harks back to the Jacobean and earlier Caroline court masque. Printed marginalia in the 1663 edition add stage directions for the prologue: "He looking up and seeing the *King* starts. He Kneels. He Rises" (Tuke 1663, sig. a1ᵛ). Suiting the action to the word, he delivers the following speech:

> Ha! he is there himself. Pardon my sight,
> My Eyes were dazled with Excess of Light;
> Even so the Sun, who all things else displays,
> Is hid from us i' th' Glory of his Rays;
> Will you vouchsafe your Presence? You, that were given
> To be our *Atlas*, and support our Heaven?
> Will You (Dread Sir) Your Pretious Moments lose
> To Grace the first Endeavours of our Muse,
> This with Your Character most aptly suits
> Even Heaven it self is pleas'd with the first Fruits.
>
> (sig. a1ᵛ)

---

[81] The vogue for 'Spanish' comedies triggered by Tuke can be gauged in Dryden's plays *The Rival Ladies* (1664), *An Evening's Love* (1668), and – to some extent – *The Assignation* (1672), even though that play is set in Rome. Visser (1975, 118) speculates that the first production of *The Assignation* at Lincoln's Inn Fields (1672) might even have used the original stage sets of *The Adventures of Five Hours*. Scenic conventions established by Tuke and Davenant include "the whole apparatus of houses, balconies, doors, night gardens, walks and arbours" (Visser 1975, 119) that forms the Restoration stage machinery as well as the formal properties of most Restoration plays, at least before the opening of the more elaborate Dorset Garden Theatre in 1671; on the latter, see Milhous 1984.

This obsequious prologue may not be much more than a virtuoso set-piece of royalist brown-nosing, but it too sets the scene for the 'innocent' carelessness, moral duplicity, wit, and ironic mixture of genres that is so characteristic of Restoration aesthetics in general as well as of its court life and the "Character" of Charles II himself. Not only in Tuke's prologue but also outside of a theatrical context, the king is almost consistently viewed as an actor who *performs* kingship – even in Dryden's most celebratory poems, *Astræa Redux* and *Annus Mirabilis* (Gordon 2002). "Sun", "Glory", "*Atlas*", "Heaven", "Muse", "first Fruits": Neoplatonism, Greek mythology, and Mosaic law are fused into a quasi-"perfect union" (Kenyon 1986, 332) of mutually communicating, if doctrinally and syntactically incoherent, metaphors. Only the king's persona or "Character" can hold them all together. In contrast to Milton's tentative mediation between pagan and Christian traditions in *Paradise Lost*, always careful to keep them separate and acknowledge their differences, here we have a very playful combination of heterogeneous elements fused into *one* ideology.

The play's rather too familiar love-plot is driven by a concern for elevated moral sentiments. Two pairs of young lovers, Porcia and Octavio and Camilla and Antonio, see their marriage plans thwarted by the girls' brothers, Carlos and Henrique. The brothers' objections are exposed as ill-founded in the course of the play, based as they are on a series of misunderstandings and false information. Parallel to the high plot, the play includes a bit of low comedy centered on Octavio's servant Diego, who at the end is forced to marry Porcia's waiting-woman Flora. More to the point, the play is concerned with circumventing a potentially tragic outcome by almost any means – another feature that this play shares with many plots of the early 1660s. Tuke's didactic intention is established early on. Don Henrique is depicted as a stern and hot-blooded Spaniard with a strict and severe code of honour: "The Blemish once received, no Wash is good / For stains of Honor, but th'Offenders blood", he exclaims already in the first scene of Act I, whereupon Don Carlos reminds him that he is "too severe a Judge of point of Honor" (1663, 2). The play then argues for the necessity of avoiding premature judgements; it urges the control and moderation of the passions of excessive honour and jealousy while seeking for a way of preventing future "Love-disasters" (4). While the entertainment it provides is markedly, deliberately light and conventionally comical, its cultural and political purpose of speaking out against radicalism and vengefulness is everywhere evident – an impulse it shares with other early Restoration comedies, e.g. Sir Robert Howard's *The Committee* (1662) (Hume 1976, 111–16; Corman 2000, 58). Later revisions adapted the play's language to the fashionable, highly polished speech patterns of heroic drama to make it even more palatable to Restoration court culture and its public representation in the city.

With characteristic nonchalance, the play develops into a plea for graceful and gracious acts of oblivion. It involves an exhortation to cool the passions of religion and ambition, which are interpreted as stimuli for civil unrest and rebellion.

Discussing the rebellion in the Netherlands, the Spaniards' servants in *The Adventures*, Geraldo, Ernesto, and Sylvio, demonstrate a strikingly modern understanding of international politics as motivated by the mercantilist forces of trade and finance:

> Ger. Pr'ythee, Friend, can these Dutch *Borraccios* Fight?
>
> Ern. They can do even as well, for they can Pay Those that can fight.
>
> Sylv. But where, I pr'ythee, do they get their Money?
>
> Ern. Oh, Friend, they have a Thriving Mystery;
> They Cheat their Neighbouring Princes of their Trade,
> And then they Buy their Subjects for their Soldiers.
>
> (Tuke 1663, 11)

In the same discussion, Tuke carefully mobilises existing anti-Dutch sentiments in his English audience in order to downplay *English* religious differences as a motivation for internecine conflict (11):

> Ger. What a Gods name could come into the Heads
> Of this People, to make them Rebell?
>
> Ern. Why Religion, that came into their Heads A Gods name
>
> Ger. But what a Devil made the Noble-men Rebel?
>
> Ern. Why that which made the Devil himself Rebel, Ambition.

This exchange denigrates religious experience as an obtrusive and external force ("Religion [. . .] came into their Heads"). The ironic tag "A Gods name" suggests a superior position of political prudence – the position from which the sovereign governs wisely and justly. By mentioning the devil, this dialogue also suggests a politicisation of Christian mythology, which is promptly reduced and rationalised in a Hobbesian fashion by describing rebellion as an effect of seditious passion ("Ambition"). It thus involves a denial of the relevance of religion for secular politics. All this is a familiar strategy of anti-Puritan polemic (cf. Walton's remarks on religion and nationality above, and Dryden's below). It is a strategy that Milton at this time was busy turning on its head (or feet, depending on your angle of vision) in writing *Paradise Lost*, when he invokes Satanic ambition as a sarcastic analogue to Stuart governmentality (Davies 1983, 3–8; Quint 1993, 269).[82]

---

[82] This level of political allusiveness is well concealed beneath the literary complexity and decorum of *Paradise Lost*, which elevates it above "the allegorical and tropical tendency of extremer sectaries", helping it pass the censor (von Maltzahn 1996, 486).

Yet while *Paradise Lost* is keen to keep the ruptures and dissonances of its time almost painfully visible, without pretending to resolve them, the plot of Tuke's play winds up in an unmistakably moral appeal to the honourable virtue of moderation, setting the constructive power of "Reason" (1663, 68) against the ravages of erroneous and agitating passion. Here, Don Carlos appeals to his cousin Don Henrique:

> Good Cozin, I conjure you to restrain
> Your Passion for a while, there does lie hid
> Some Mystery in this, which once unfolded,
> May possibly produce the means of making
> That Reconcilable, which now seems Desp'rate.
> (64)

This speech by Carlos, whose name (though taken from Tuke's Spanish source) associates Charles II, echoes the very terms of the restored king's declaration, two years previously ("*conjure* to a perfect union", qtd. in Kenyon 1986, 332). Carlos's intentions are in agreement with this declaration, which introduces as its prime goal the idea of healing the country by means of restraint and reconciliation. "Sweetly propos'd, Sir, an Accommodation?", asks Henrique (Tuke 1663, 64), indirectly confirming the 'sweetness' of the Carolean compromise that promises to "adjust this Competition" (67) between the rival impulses of honour, love, and revenge. The epilogue, spoken by the servant Diego, explicitly confirms the parallel to the declaration of Breda. The style of the play, Diego says, "is as easie as a Proclamation, / As if the play were Pen'd for th'whole Nation" (72). This statement also asserts the public and hortatory nature of Tuke's play: it *is* "Pen'd for th'whole Nation", not for any particular faction in the Civil War nor for a particular group or rank. The fact that it is the servant speaking this emphasises the play's being written for the higher and lower orders alike, thus conforming to Davenant's pedagogical ideals of teaching obedience to the common people by means of stage entertainments (Jacob and Raylor 1991). It also makes for a neat parallel with the prologue, in which the author explicitly introduces himself as the king's servant. Strikingly, the epilogue employs the very young concept of the "whole Nation" to signify the common bond that transcends social and political differences – a concept that is here already mobilised against an external enemy, the Dutch.

The ideological thrust of *The Adventures* is towards establishing justice and the rule of law, and towards forgiveness and non-violent solutions for personal and social problems. Yet the play also warns against the risks involved in forgetting and forgiving too quickly amid the general rejoicing of a happy ending. The passionate Don Henrique, who may stand for the Puritan anti-royalist in Tuke's version of this play, can still be a danger to the achieved compromise of "union" (Charles II, qtd. in Kenyon 1986, 332) and "*Redintegration* of [. . .] Amity" (Cowley 1656, sig. (a)4^v):

> *Carl.* But let's take heed, *Antonio*, lest whilst we
> Are Joying in our mutual Happiness,

> *Don Henrique's* scarcely yet compos'd Distemper
> Revive not, and Disorder us afresh:
> I like not his Grim Posture; you know well
> After a Tempest, though the Wind be laid,
> There often does remain for a good while
> A dangerous Agitation of the Waves;
> He must not yet be trusted with himself.
> (Tuke 1663, 70)

Don Henrique finally realises that he "must consent, [. . .] or worse will follow" (70) because "Our Strength, and Wisdom must submit to Fate. / Stript of my Love, I will put off my Hate" (71). He accepts the Cowleyan solution of forgetting as a necessary and curative step forward in the civilising process. Tragedy is averted, and the play closes with a scene of peaceful reconciliation, again expressed by an image of storm becalmed: "Thus end the Rare Adventures of Five Hours; / As sometimes Boisterous Storms in Gentle Shours" (71). This imagery is a topical echo of many panegyric verses upon the return of Charles II, including Dryden's *Astræa Redux*, which consistently works with this imagery because it traces the sea-voyage of Charles II from Scheveningen to Dover. Cowley's own *Ode, Upon the Blessed Restoration and Returne of His Sacred Majestie* calls upon the stars "To calm the stormy *World*, and still the rage of *Warrs*" (Cowley 1660, sig. A2).

The brief "Epilogue at Court" firmly places the play in the contemporary constitutional setting of a restored sacral kingship, only half-jokingly referring to Parliament in feudal terms as the king's "Vassals". This additional epilogue closes with a circular confirmation of the royal will, without which the play would never have been written. Once again, in 'passing' its audience like a law that is passed in Parliament, the play harmonises legislative, political, and aesthetic concerns of the Restoration:

> W'have pass'd the Lords, and Commons; and are come
> At length, Dread Sir, to hear Your Final Doom.
> 'Tis true, Your Vassals, Sir, may Vote the Laws,
> Their Sanction comes from Your Divine Applause.
> This Shining Circle then will all sit Mute,
> Till one pronounce from you, *Le Roy le Veut*.
> (Tuke 1663, 72)

In its final moments, *The Adventures of Five Hours* attests to the consolidation of royal policy and the way it will be presented and performed in the early sixties, alluding to French absolutism and the 'solar' mythology of kingship associated with Louis XIV. Dryden's panegyric on the return of Charles II, by contrast, reveals more of the insecurities and uncertainties of the moment, despite its declared purpose of unmitigated celebration. Written a mere month after the king's triumphal arrival in London in May 1660, *Astræa Redux. A Poem on the Happy Restoration and Return of His Sacred Majesty Charles the Second* is published at the end of June. Merely a year earlier, Dryden had published an elegy on the death of the Lord Protector and walked in Cromwell's funeral procession alongside Milton and Marvell. Now, the Restoration has inspired a change of heart in this twenty-eight-year-old poet – though, perhaps wisely, this sudden tergiversation goes uncommented.

Astræa Redux belongs to a series of writings connected to the topic of oblivion in the 1660s not only because of Dryden's personal change of allegiance but because it is a poem of negation, exorcism, and forgetting as well as celebration. Its Latin title carries a range of connotations: it evokes the Virgilian motif of the return of the goddess of justice (Astraea), a figure also associated with imperial secular power and the return of a golden age after the 'iron age', which began to be associated with the Cromwellian regime (on the title, see the editor's commentary in Dryden 1956, 213, 219). In the second half of the seventeenth century, justice, as a rational response to violence, is promoted to a key concept of neoclassical order and its representation in politics and aesthetics (Reiss 1992, 130–32, 160–91). The return of Astraea also marks a return to the Elizabethan age, viewed with nostalgia as 'merry England'. For Dryden's modern biographer, the exuberant (if traditional) imagery of the poem "indicates a loss of control" as well as simple "euphoria": "Dryden, like many of his countrymen, appears to have believed, at least for a moment, that the Restoration could miraculously negate or exorcise the events of the previous twenty years" (Winn 1987, 194). It is the combination of panegyric and repression that explains the poetic force of this poem, which indeed ushers in "a new and more muscular kind of political poetry" (112) because it assumes poetic authority over cultural memory. The poem is launched as a piece of mythmaking and magic, a conjuring trick to engender what the Declaration of Breda called a "perfect union" of nation and king (Kenyon 1986, 332). It successfully captures the common mood of the moment in a religious rhetoric of guilt, atonement, and forgiveness which effectively eases the transition to the new regime – for the benefit of Dryden's readers as well as his own – by emphasising the aspects of healing and unity.

A striking feature of *Astræa Redux* is its blend of classical allegory (mostly referring to Virgil's *Aeneid*, aligning Charles II with Aeneas) with rather daring allusions to Christian revelation. Mining both of these cultural traditions as a repertoire for political metaphor, subtle puns, and copious imagery, Dryden – similar to Tuke – offers a provocative secular transformation of religious experience (revelation) and religious habits of reading (typology) into poetic material, largely without distinguishing between Christian and pagan elements. With the same nonchalance, the poem compares Charles II to Jupiter and Aeneas as well as to Adam, Moses, David, and Christ. In his lack of concern for Christian pieties, Dryden seems to anticipate the Romantics; but one can also relate this more concretely to the poem's historical context and read it as a negation of religious, particularly Puritan claims to authority over the interpretation of contemporary political events. Typology, after all, "was the vehicle by which [Puritan] revolutionaries raised the events of their time above history; it provided a way to equate their struggle with that of Israel, and thereby served to rationalize their revolution as the work of God wrought through his agents on earth" (Berry 1976, 129; cf.

Cohn 1970, Miner 1977). Dryden denies this authority by turning the Puritans' typological weapons against them and devising a flexible typology of his own.

How does the poem stage the past and mobilise it for an interpretation of the present? Which past, which parts of tradition are selected or ignored? These aspects of selection and manipulation also point forward to Dryden's later strategic use of biblical material in *Absalom and Achitophel*. They also accentuate the stark contrast between Dryden and his poetic arch-rival, Milton. *Astræa Redux* and *Paradise Lost* can be read as competing acts of cultural memory and forgetting in the Restoration period. Their contrast and conflict is the more fascinating because they have equal poetic powers and use similar material to propound their opposing arguments: classical and Christian mythology, Virgil and the Bible.

Dryden's speaker in *Astræa Redux* seems confident but tense. He even admits to some anxiety ("doubtful thoughts") at one point, even if only about how to present the adventures of the young king in the appropriate aesthetic light, which turns out to be the religiously coloured light of the 'fortunate fall': "How shall I then my doubtful thoughts express / That must his suff'rings both regret and bless!" (1956, 24, ll. 71–2). Charles is then immediately compared to David (who, in typological readings of the Bible, prefigures the Messiah): "Thus banish'd *David* spent abroad his time, / When to be Gods Anointed was his Crime" (ll. 79–80). Dryden also rehearses the traditional Christian imagery of light and darkness, of (physical) blindness and (spiritual) insight – also used in a celebratory manner, as we have seen, by Tuke in the prologue to *The Adventures of Five Hours*, and adapted by Milton in a completely different way: "struck with rayes of prosp'rous fortune blind / We light alone in dark afflictions find" (ll. 95–6); fortunate fall, again.[83] Charles is "Made [. . .] at his own cost like *Adam* wise" (l. 114). Like Christ, he is said to be of "Heavn'ly Parentage and earthly too" (l. 257); Charles's birth, in 1630, like Christ's, was accompanied by the appearance of a star at midday: "The Star that at your Birth shone out so bright / It stain'd the duller Suns Meridian light" (ll. 288–89). Several eulogists were keen to exploit this astronomical fact at the time (see Dryden 1956, 232), but while lesser panegyrists were content with interpreting it as a portent of "future *Glories*" (Cowley 1660, sig. A2, l. 16) Dryden exceeds them by drawing an explicit parallel to the Star of Bethlehem. He even claims that this same star has returned, "Guiding our eyes to find and worship you" (Dryden 1956, 30, l. 291). Again, we find the divine ray of light giving directions to human eyes, as in the frontispiece to *Eikon Basilike* and the prologue at court to Tuke's *Adventures*. The Christmas allusion is in line with Dryden's strategy of integrating the restoration of the monarchy firmly into English folk customs. The royalists were keen to revive old customs that the Puritans had despised as sacrilegious and superstitious, including "May Games, Moris Dances, the Lord of the

---

[83] The trope of the fortunate fall is reinvoked at ll. 209–10: "But since reform'd by what we did amiss, / We by our suff'rings learn to prize our bliss".

may, & Lady of the May, the Foole & the Hoby Horse" (Cavendish 1984, 64). When Charles II, entering London, "renew[s] the expiring Pomp of *May*!" (Dryden 1956, 30, l. 285), he is as much a pagan prince of May as he is a reborn Christ entering London/Jerusalem.

The specious frivolity of Dryden's analogies and figures for Charles II is probably a well-calculated attempt at overcoming Puritan restraint – the references to springtime fertility, promising dynastic potency, are perfectly attuned to this tactic. Blending pagan (English as well as classical) and Christian allusions, the poem is busy wresting religious semantics away from Puritan culture and reinserting it into a royalist world picture that is profoundly anti-Puritan: at once festive and physical, neo-Elizabethan, neo-pagan, and deist.[84] . Heaven is invoked many times throughout the poem (l. 13, 38, 40, 59, 73, 137, 145, 147, 196, 238, and 318); other words with Christian connotations are "Pilgrimage" (54), "Miracles" (14, 241), "Fate" (13, 51, 321), "Destiny" (63), "blessings" (137, 141), "Martyrs" (186), "indulgence" (240), "th'Almighty" (262), "Vowes" (319), and verbs like "sinn'd" (207), "worship" (291), and "bless'd" (240). Particularly noteworthy are the recurring references to the Calvinist doctrine of predestination: "Providence" occurs twice in connection with political events (151, 238); a variant is "Heav'ns prefixed hour" (147). Without ostensible irony, the speaker invokes the power of prayer in bringing back the king:

> Yet as he knew his blessings worth, took care
> That we should know it by repeated pray'r;
> Which storm'd the skies and ravish'd *Charles* from thence
> As Heav'n itself is took by violence.
> (Dryden 1956, 26, ll. 141–44)

The poem is consistent in its efforts to discredit and invert the language of Puritanism and the old regime: "Jealousies" (l. 213), a keyword of Civil War parliamentarianism, springs up innocently in a simile likening the English people to "early Lovers whose unpractis'd hearts / Were long the May-game of malicious arts" (211–12). The lovers' "Jealousies" are then found to have been "vain" (213), which leads to reconciliation and increase of love. Dryden obviously pursues a similar strategy of oblivion as Cowley had proposed in his *Poems* of 1656: figuring citizens (in Dryden's case: subjects) as lovers whose conflicts lead to a "*Redintegration* of their *Amitie*" (Cowley 1656, sig. (a)4^v). In the preceding couplet, Dryden alludes to the Puritan discourse of religious reformation and political reform, inverting it to describe the return to monarchy as the outcome of a process of suffering, atonement, and regret ("vertuous shame", Dryden 1956, l. 206): "But since *reform'd* by what we did amiss, / We by our suff'rings learn to prize our bliss" (ll. 209–10, my italics). Less subtly, his anti-Puritan animus denounces the intentions of the

---

84 Cf. the mechanistic physiology of the famous lines comparing the body natural to the body politic, in which God is referred to as "Mans Architect" (l. 165).

republicans as mercenary, intemperate, and blasphemous (cf. l. 186 on their drinking "to excess on Martyrs tombs"): "Religions name against it self was made; / The shadow serv'd the substance to invade" (ll. 191–92).[85] Genuine theological argument is carefully avoided in these lines, but the distinction between appearance and reality (shadow and substance) insinuates that genuine religiosity is on the side of the royalists and the established Church. The republican experiment, Dryden argues, has led to ochlocracy, destructiveness, lawlessness, and the anarchy of a Hobbesian or Ciceronian state of nature (ll. 43–48):

> The Rabble now such Freedom did enjoy,
> As Winds at Sea that use it to destroy:
> Blind as the *Cyclops*, and as wild as he,
> They own'd a lawless salvage Libertie,
> Like that our painted Ancestours so priz'd
> Ere Empires Arts their Breasts had Civiliz'd.

The sacral May-King who comes, legitimised by God and by his subjects' obedience, to bring back the rule of law after the period of Cromwellian injustice, is called upon to rule with mercy: "Not ty'd to rules of Policy, you find / Revenge less sweet then a forgiving mind" (ll. 260–61). For the Dryden of *Astræa Redux*, the king is "above the Laws" only in his "Goodness" (267), submitting his "Cause" to "Justice" (266).

As we have seen in *The Compleat Angler*, the natural order of things (rather than the Hobbesian state of nature) for an orthodox, high-church royalist *is* the state of "perfect union" of subjects under a sacral, patriarchal kingship. A similar political vision can be found in Robert Filmer's *Patriarcha*. In this order of things, moreover, all subjects, by divine decree, are the property of the sovereign (Filmer 1991; Dunn 1969, 58–76). This understanding of sovereignty also underpins the appeals for mercy we find in Dryden's *Astræa Redux*; it will also be ratified once more, against all the other political theories discussed there, at the end of *Absalom and Achitophel* (see below).

In *Astræa Redux*, Dryden enacts an anti-republican countermemory. Its ideological content is mirrored in its form, the "perfect union" of subjects and sovereign and the hierarchical order of things poetically expressed in the well-ordered, harmonious form of the couplet. Against this backdrop, Milton's *Paradise Lost*, first printed in 1667 but probably completed two years earlier, takes on a perhaps "surprising topicality" (Zwicker 1997, 192) as a dissenting countermemory to the royalist politics of oblivion. If the restoration of the monarchy is generally idealised as a return to an imaginary origin and as a negation of the republican 'Interregnum', then *Paradise Lost* can be read as a repudiation of almost all of the cultural values of this restoration. There is a similar idealisation of the natural also, for example, in Milton's *Areopagitica*, where it is strategically related to the concept of reformation

---

[85] Paul Hammond glosses the word "made" in l. 191 as "pressed into military service, enlisted (*OED* 15a)"; see Dryden 1995b, 1: 47.

and its religious, civic and individual connotations. Yet *Paradise Lost* complicates such an idealisation because it distinguishes between a pre- and postlapsarian state of nature, with the consequence that 'reformation' is conceptualised not as given by nature but as a rational and political process. In response to the royalist transvaluation and repression of the concept of reformation, *Paradise Lost* does not simply consign irony, wit, and compromise to hell (cf. Zwicker 1997, 192) – if it did so, it would be a much less fascinating poem – but dares to tell a far greater story of innocence, temptation, and fall, and reflects on the possibilities of telling such a story in modernity. From its high-altitude perspective, the failures and shortcomings – but also the successes – of the early Restoration period dwindle in importance as merely contingent events that may be regrettable but that are irrelevant when it comes to salvation, the ultimate goal and end of human history.

Whereas *Astræa Redux* uses Christian imagery (on a par with imagery derived from pagan literary and folk traditions) to convey authority and legitimacy to a certain interpretation of the political events of 1660 – at times implying the self-conscious spuriousness and fictitiousness of such an act of authorisation –, *Paradise Lost* and *Paradise Regained* reverse this rhetorical structure, this relation between strategy and repertoire. In Milton's Christian epics of the fall and the temptation of Christ, there is merely the odd swipe at current political events, whereas the cultural authority of its narratives does not require legitimation. Milton does not need to resort to superficial irony in order to place his political opponents in perspective. From the point of view of his poems, the Restoration and Charles II are mere episodes – already forgotten. In *Astræa Redux*, Dryden celebrates Charles II as a revenant of Jupiter, Aeneas, Adam, David and Christ; Milton indirectly reproaches Dryden (and countless others) for their scattershot approach to allegory by writing a very serious epic poem about the first and last things, a poem that makes the royalist panegyrics of the 1660s – and indeed any other work of this period – look rather insipid and insignificant. He exposes the frivolousness of their biblical allusions. Where *Paradise Lost* is most directly conceived as a counterforce to royalist allegory and imagery is in its critique of the magical view of language: like Satan, the royalists treat their utterances as if they could bring about what they "conjure" (that crucial word from the Declaration of Breda), illegitimately aspiring to the power of the divine Word, whereas postlapsarian language is in fact characterised by conjecture and contingency, by instability and provisionality. It is a matter of individual or communal interpretation rather than national "Proclamation" (Tuke 1663, 72). One of the themes of *Paradise Lost* is precisely the liberty and accountability of human beings for their own actions and their use of language. As the Father makes clear in his speech in book 3:

> They trespass, authors to themselves in all
> Both what they judge and what they choose; for so
> I formed them free, and free they must remain,
> Till they enthrall themselves: . . . .
>   (Milton 1998, 3.122–25)

This freedom includes the responsibility to remember, and it implies the ability to make one's own reasonable choices: "reason also is choice" (3.108), or "reason is but choosing", as Milton argues in the *Areopagitica* (1953b, 527). Hence the task is to choose the right memory, responsibly and without repression, even though – or precisely because – the homology of "true liberty" and "right reason" has been lost after the Fall (Milton 1998, 12.83–84). Thus it is the political outcast, the radical Protestant "fallen on evil days" (7.25) who recognises and poetically shapes the possibility of a rescue by means of self-reliance. For Milton's Adam and Eve, at the end of the poem, the world has opened up, spatially as well as temporally and politically: "The world was all before them" (12.646), while such a proto-democratic opening would be the equivalent of plunging into chaos for Dryden. Compared to other texts of the period, Milton's epic poem feels more 'modern' in that it presents the *search* for order (in its constructible and precarious status) as an open process, whereas Dryden leaves the classical homologies of Virgilian epic poetry intact and presents its prefabricated order as natural and eternal, if in need of reassertion. He can treat it with some detachment, with irony and wit, but these ultimately support a vision of stability that is also expressed in the form of the heroic couplet. According to Dryden, rhyme is "more fit for the ends of government" (1967, 7); Milton, by contrast, regards rhyme as a "constraint" and offers his dramatic blank verse with its numerous run-on lines as a literary equivalent of "ancient liberty recovered" (1998, 54–55). In Lukács's terminology, *Astræa* and *Absalom* would qualify as (brief) epic poems, giving "form to a totality of life that is rounded from within", but *Paradise Lost* would already be a novel, which "seeks, by giving form, to uncover and construct the concealed totality of life" (Lukács 1971, 60).

Dryden himself is among the first to realise this drastic diagnostic and critical quality of Milton's epic poem, if we may believe that the remark attributed to him on the first printing of *Paradise Lost* is authentic: "that Poet has cutt us all out" (qtd. in Winn 1987, 81). Even though this phrase refers to playing cards, the act of cutting also reminds us of the seventeenth-century sense of rhetoric as a weapon. In Dryden's later "Discourse concerning the Original and Progress of Satire" (1693), he compares a successful satire to the sharp blade of the skilful executioner: "A witty Man is tickl'd while he is hurt in this manner; and a Fool feels it not. [. . .] Yet there is a vast difference betwixt the slovenly Butchering of a Man, and the fineness of a stroak that separates the Head from the Body, and leaves it standing in its place" (Dryden 1974, 71). We may conclude that Dryden felt the cut – he was, after all, no fool – but that he was tickled rather than hurt. He would come to feel the physically painful consequences of satire – his own – when he was brutally beaten by three thugs in Rose Alley on Dec. 18, 1679 (Winn 1987, 325–29). He also learned from Milton. When the crisis of the Stuart monarchy becomes much more severe in the late 1670s and early 1680s, Dryden pursues much the same strategy in *Absalom and Achitophel* as Milton had done in *Paradise Lost*. But this time Dryden uses a biblical narrative explicitly for the sake of supporting the Stuart regime, making a final attempt to resolve the contingencies of early modern politics by means of calculated acts of oblivion. He does so in a literary narrative that has the cheek to equate insincerity and irony, as instances of *virtù*, with decorum and urbanity and to present them as 'natural' cardinal virtues of modernity.

Contingency, Irony, Sexuality: Nature, Law, and Kingship in *Absalom and Achitophel* (1681)

> I never read nor heard that *lex* was *rex;* but it is common and most true that *rex* is *lex*, for he is *lex loquens*, a living, a speaking, an acting law.   Sir Robert Berkeley, 1638

Approaching Dryden's *Absalom and Achitophel* from an interest in Restoration memories and countermemories, the poem is quite an extraordinary text. It is motivated by the intention to wrest the specific idiom of Puritan political awareness and its traditional discourse of scriptural righteousness away from the crown's opponents and to use it to legitimise hte king's lawful right to rule.[86] As in *Astræa Redux*, typological readings of history are the context against which Dryden proposes an alternative normative vision, imagining a social consensus in order to contain the political threat of dissent (Achinstein 2003). As Steven N. Zwicker explains (1998b, 107), the stakes in such an attempt to undermine the biblical rhetoric of Whig anti-royalists at a critical historical moment are particularly high:

> to allegorize political crisis as sacred history in 1681 was hardly to present an original template; it was rather to insist on an idiom that not only excited the memory of familiar ways but indeed risked, and perhaps willingly courted, platitude rather than novelty. Politics allegorized as Scripture could only have recalled the days of "dreaming saints," of insurrection and enthusiasm. That was of course the point: to suggest to the whole of the poem's readership that the ill-affected were once again stirring civil war and that the history of the Jews applied to English politics allowed more than one party to claim narratives of exile and election as their own.

Indeed, *Absalom* may be seen as a culmination point in a poetic struggle over the legitimate uses of scriptural and pagan sources and idioms, a struggle that also characterises *Astræa Redux* and *Paradise Lost*. What can be read as an ideological and aesthetic conflict between Dryden and Milton in part prefigures the early modern Quarrel of the Ancients and Moderns (Levine 1991, Gelber 1999, 193–200). Both Milton and Dryden, equals and rivals on opposing political sides, fight for cultural authority over the adequate interpretation and adaptation of classical sources and traditions in a modern context. They contest established but no longer convincing solutions for the problem of contingency; they develop strategic answers to the question how a (modern) temporality of contingency can be related to an extra-

---

86 For a historical perspective on the cultural and literary development of this discourse between 1650 and 1700 – from Hebraic righteousness to Roman virtue –, see Zwicker 1988.

temporal, supra- or anti-historical dimension: the counter-temporality of the state of nature or of paradise as "an aboriginal condition which can be used to indict any objectionable portion of the historical story" (Dunn 1969, 101).

This is not to assume that Dryden, in planning and writing *Absalom* in the midst of the Exclusion Crisis,[87] still has Milton immediately in mind as a political opponent and poetic rival. Dryden's intellectual attitude towards Milton is characterised by a rather abstract theoretical acknowledgement, even admiration, but by moments of evasion and revision in his own poetic works – at leasts until the fall of James II, when Dryden begins to find himself in a similarly marginal cultural and religious position as Milton had occupied after the Restoration. In Dryden's operatic version and revision of *Paradise Lost*, *The State of Innocence and Fall of Man* (1674), the topical, polemic and political concerns of Milton's epic are defused and transformed (Gabel 2016). Long before Dennis, Addison, and Johnson, Dryden is one of the first critics who aestheticise, depoliticise, and universalise *Paradise Lost*.[88] Milton's presence in Dryden is for the most part as spectral as that of Hobbes is in Locke (Dunn 1969, 81; Williamson 1970; Ferry 1968). By the time of the Exclusion Crisis, other, more immediately political opponents – most notably the first Earl of Shaftesbury – have replaced those representatives of Milton's generation who still yearn for 'the good old cause'. Milton dies in 1674, six years before *Absalom*. Yet Dryden's technique of invoking a biblical text for the purpose of political allegory is so well-calculated that it must have reminded readers immediately of similar literary ventures, including *Paradise Lost*. *Absalom* is Dryden's most consistent demonstration that scriptural discourse is not the exclusive domain of republicans and Puritan sectaries.

In 1681, such a project has become extremely more difficult than it may have been in the early years of the Restoration. As we have seen above, the 1660s are not lacking in attempts at writing or rewriting English political history from a royalist perspective. Those who celebrated Charles II on his return to the throne now begin to find themselves on the defensive as the repressed problems of the Restoration compromise continue to resurface. By the time of the Popish Plot and the Exclusion Crisis, "a policy of damage-limitation" obtains even in literary politics, as Thomas N. Corns observes with regard to Dryden's *Absalom* (1992, 302): "Dryden, far from celebrating the monarch, demonstrates his superiority to rivals of decidedly limited or destructive character and he concedes that dissent, contradiction, and the

---

[87] On the historical context, see Jones 1978, 197–216. *Absalom and Achitophel* was published anonymously in November 1681, shortly before the trial against Shaftesbury – in which he was to be acquitted by a Whig jury – began (cf. Dryden 1972, 209).
[88] On the position of Milton in Dryden's critical canon, see Gelber 1999, 18, 20, 232. On Dryden's revisionist rewriting of Milton in *The State of Innocence*, see Frank 1993; Gabel 2016. On the competition between Milton and Dryden as dramatists, focusing on *Samson Agonistes* and *Aureng-Zebe*, see also Sauer 2002. For a political reading of *Paradise Regained* as a challenge to Restoration heroic drama, see Zwicker 1995.

construction of alternatives abide at the heart even of the royal court." Even though *Absalom* is designed to argue for a traditional legitimation of political power, its starting point is the assumption that the semantics and practices of such legitimations have become questionable. It can indeed be seen to mark a crucial turning point in seventeenth-century literary culture because its construction of the connection between poetry and society differs from any that we have encountered so far, not least its position on the relationship between the poet and the public (political readings of *Absalom and Achitophel* include Kinsley 1955, Schilling 1961, Maresca 1974, Conlon 1979, Zwicker 1993, 130–72).

This position is vividly argued in a brief authorial preface "To the Reader" comprising only some eighty lines of prose. Its wit and complexity arise from this compression as it engages several levels of meaning – commentary, allusion, irony, and insult – simultaneously. It thus prepares some key aspects of the poem, which is also a masterpiece of epic compression. Published anonymously, the text does not allow Dryden to rely on his celebrity, which would make his loyalty to the court immediately evident. Instead, he professes to trust in the *literary* (rather than political) quality of his writing: "if a *Poem* have a Genius, it will force its own reception in the World. For there's a sweetness in good Verse, which Tickles even while it Hurts: And, no man can be heartily angry with him, who pleases him against his will" (Dryden 1972, 3). The balance implied in the Horatian and neoclassical doctrine of *docere et delectare* is explicitly tilted to the side of *delectare* – somewhat unusual for the genre of satire, which Dryden acknowledges as *Absalom*'s literary mode: "I confess, I have laid in for [the more Moderate sort (of readers)], by rebating the Satyre, (where Justice would allow it) from carrying too sharp an Edge" (3). Here and throughout the preface, Dryden's authorial speaker can be seen as disingenuous in his acceptance of readerly contingency as a mere matter of fact. This is most visible in the final paragraph, which takes up again the metaphor of published writing as a form of medicine for the body politic, a metaphor that pervades this text as it does the language of restoration in the early 1660s, as we have seen in the Declaration of Breda. But Dryden's text mixes this discourse of healing with metaphors of cutting and surgery, conflating the bandaging of wounds with their infliction:

> The true end of Satyre, is the amendment of Vices by correction. And he who writes Honestly, is no more an Enemy to the Offendour, than the Physician to the Patient, when he prescribes harsh Remedies to an inveterate Disease: for those, are only in order to prevent the Chyrurgeon's work of an Ense rescindendum, which I wish not to my very Enemies. To conclude all, If the Body Politique have any Analogy to the Natural, in my weak judgment, an Act of Oblivion were as necessary in a Hot, Distemper'd State, as an Opiate would be in a Raging Fever. (5)

"Ense rescindendum" (= it must be cut away with the knife) is a quotation from Ovid's *Metamorphoses* (1.190–91), where it occurs in a passage on the Titans' revolt against Jupiter, the subalterns against the monarch. It refers to the surgical practice of amputating an infected limb when less "harsh Remedies" have failed. This amounts to an overt threat against potential traitors, promising them the same fate as the regicides in 1660. In Dryden's preface, the Ovid quotation forms a link to earlier knife metaphors: "too sharp an Edge" and "Tickles even while it Hurts". The latter phrase resonates with potential violence, with the force of the literary as a rhetorical weapon that we have already encountered in Milton and Hobbes. The resonance is intensified when we compare these phrases to a similar passage in Dryden's 1693 "Discourse concerning the Original and Progress of Satire" prefacing the translation of the satires of Juvenal "by Mr. *Dryden*, and Several other Eminent Hands" (Dryden 1974, 2). There, comparing Juvenal to Horace, Dryden notes that the former's writing "was, an *Ense rescindendum;* but that of *Horace* was a Pleasant Cure, with all the Limbs preserv'd entire" (1974, 71–72), and he asserts that "*Juvenal*'s Times requir'd" such "a more painful kind of Operation" (72). The aggressive stance behind Dryden's 'tickling' is revealed in 1693 – more than a decade later, at a time when, at least politically, Dryden had nothing left to lose – when he remarks on "the Mystery of that Noble Trade" (70) of satire:

> Neither is it true, that this fineness of Raillery is offensive. A witty Man is tickl'd while he is hurt in this manner; and a fool feels it not. The occasion of an Offence may possibly be given, but he cannot take it. If it be granted that in effect this way does more Mischief; that a Man is secretly wounded, and though he be not sensible himself, yet the malicious World will find it for him: Yet there is still a vast difference betwixt the slovenly Butchering of a Man, and the fineness of a stroak that separates the Head from the Body, and leaves it standing in its place. (71)

He adds that he considers his *Absalom* to have succeeded in this, at least in the character of Zimri (the Duke of Buckingham). In the preface to *Absalom,* this elaborate fantasy of the satirist as public executioner is strategically muted but nevertheless still visible. Dryden's poetry is still poetry in the service of the crown, just as Davenant's was before him. But the tasks to be fulfilled by this poetry have changed significantly – from positive moral teaching in the epic poem to the negative excision of "Follies" and "Vices" from the body politic by means of satire (1972, 3). The conventional analogy between satire and medicine is laced with sarcasm when Doctor Dryden seems to prescribe another Act of Oblivion, a second general amnesty as an opiate for the "Raging Fever" that has befallen the "Hot, Distemper'd State" (5). Yet as Zwicker and Bywaters remind us (in Dryden 2001, 542), "contemporary medical theory held that an opiate was no remedy for a raging fever" (cf. Poyet 1995, 114), so this prescription can only be ironic. On the contrary, as the poem itself knows: "Lenitives fomented the Disease" (Dryden 1972, 33, l. 926). Dryden's "amendment of Vices by correction" calls for stronger judicial measures against "the Offendour" (1972, 5).

Dryden knows, then, that the time for general amnesties, for a culture of forgetting religious and political differences, is over. The Exclusion Crisis has foregrounded the court's inability to rally the support of the political establishment. The stand-off between crown and parliament over a potential Catholic successor to the throne (Charles II's brother James, Duke of York, later James II) may well erupt in another rebellion and civil war. Dryden's predicament as a royalist apologist in this situation is entirely different from that of the young panegyrist of *Astræa Redux*. The change is pithily summed up at the beginning of his preface: "'Tis not my intention to make an Apology for my *Poem*. Some will think it needs no Excuse; and others will receive none. The Design, I am sure, is honest: but he who draws his Pen for one Party, must expect to make Enemies of the other. For, *Wit* and *Fool*, are Consequents of *Whig* and *Tory*. And every man is a Knave or an Ass to the contrary side" (3). Poetry no longer communicates eternal truths to its readers, nor can it simply be relied upon to educate 'the people' or 'the nobility' in the virtues of civility and obedience. The problem is no longer how to persuade a multitude of potentially recalcitrant readers; the problem now is that the author can be *sure* of being condemned by a particular segment of the public. The *de facto* contingency of literary impact is already taken for granted. Earlier (for Hobbes and Davenant, for example), any opinion was potentially seditious compared to the 'truth' of official proclamations. Now, conflicting opinions contest each other's claims to truth, and any utterance can be undermined by partisan distinctions and divisions. Author and audience are no longer a pair of opposites; the author himself is implicated in a network of mutually exclusive positions that observe each other with suspicion. Without expressly formulating it in theoretical terms, Dryden describes the effects of the emergence of a modern political system, even though the word "Party" refers to a loose cluster of people sharing certain interests rather than a formal organisation in the modern sense. But he clearly records the dependence of perception on prejudice, the replacement of a hierarchical truth with a decentralised, contingent set of observations that operate recursively: the terms "*Wit* and *Fool*, are Consequents of *Whig* and *Tory*. And every man is a Knave or an Ass to the contrary side" (2: 3).

The emergence of partisan opinion as a judge of intellectual and artistic merit has inevitable consequences for literature, which can no longer assume a stance of detachment from partisan politics. Nor can it presume to provide a non-contingent perspective above or beyond the individual and collective agencies of different 'sides' or factions. In the epic poems of Davenant and Milton, the purpose of poetry had been to elucidate a higher order of reality that should either idealise (Davenant) or "justify" (Milton) the political reality of their time. In *Gondibert*, this normative idealisation was laid down in the chivalric ethos of heroic poetry and romance; for Milton, justification could only be conceived in religious terms. It becomes apparent that these options are no longer open to the Dryden of *Absalom*. Politics breaks apart into opposing opinions with no possibility of a common ground or a superior vantage point (traditional, rational, or religious) from which to judge these opinions. The crisis of late seventeenth-century English politics is also a crisis of literary representation. The exclamation "What shall we think!" in *Absalom* (1972, 28, l. 759) is a symptom of the loss of cherished certainties and, at least in part, a plea for rational thinking in an age pervaded by scepticism. This age can no longer be subsumed under a single heading – it requires at least two: 'Whig' and 'Tory'. The ironies of this poem ultimately infect and corrode the function of poetry itself, at times threatening to drag it down to the level of merely topical contingency – to the level of polemical allegory, whose "Edge" (3) is thus blunted from the start because its intended readership is already divided into two political camps. Furthermore, it is not quite clear whether Dryden still hoped to persuade a part of the other half of his readership, even though he addressed his poem to "the more Moderate sort" (3).

The strengthening of the role of political opinion in public life entails a weakening of the role of poetry as political discourse, even as it turns a poem into an explicitly topical political statement. The hierarchy between poetry and politics has been reversed and displaced by a many-voiced choir of opinions, which the poem is required to join. This forces the text to be more consistent and coherent. Instead of the celebratory and playful scattering of allusions in *Astræa Redux*, we find *Absalom* relying on a single and controlled allegory: a unilinear reading of contemporary politics through the lens of the second Book of Samuel. Creative energies are harnessed rather than disseminated in *Absalom*, even though the poem begins with images of sexual promiscuity. Charles is no longer Moses or Christ, as he was in *Astræa Redux*; but now he has to be David in much greater detail, "a comedic or even a picaresque figure" (Carroll and Prickett 1997, 342). This does not make Dryden's task of supporting royal prerogative any easier. The narrowing of focus goes together with a hardening of the frontlines between aesthetic and moral judgements in the preface: "If you like not my *Poem*, the fault may, possibly, be in my Writing: [. . .] But, more probably, 'tis in your Morals, which cannot bear the truth of it" (Dryden 1972, 4).

Dryden presents himself as "the Historian" rather than "the Inventour" of his "Piece" (1972, 4), perhaps in allusion to his dual role as poet laureate and historiographer royal; but in doing so he elides Davenant's distinction between "Truth narrative" and "truth operative" (Davenant 1971, 11) in favour of *a single* truth that is literal and (supposedly) factual. Yet again, this remark may be doubly ironic in referring to Puritan understandings of the Bible as history and as a ground on which to base fundamental political truth claims. By this Miltonic move, which Dryden denies even as he makes it, he seeks to subvert – or to pretend to subvert – the newly contingent relation between observation and truth in a modern political setting. As we will see, at the poem's conclusion, it is difficult to take Dryden's invocation of the theological trope of divine right entirely seriously.

On this level of anti-Whig, anti-Puritan polemic, the preface contains another even more explicit allusion to *Paradise Lost*. Of course, *Absalom* as a whole can be read as a satirical counter-text to Milton's epic; one of the things it is 'about' is "Dryden's absorption and compression of *Paradise Lost* into its own poetic intentions" (Kroll 1991,

305).⁸⁹ Yet there is at least one remark in the preface that may help to show how carefully Dryden models his biblical allegory on Milton's use of Genesis. Commenting on the character of Absalom (Charles II's illegitimate son, the Duke of Monmouth), Dryden writes that "'tis no more a wonder that he withstood not the temptations of *Achitophel*, than it was for *Adam*, not to have resisted the two Devils; the Serpent, and the Woman" (Dryden 1972, 4).⁹⁰ By placing Achitophel/Shaftesbury in the position of Milton's Satan, consigning him to eternal punishment with no hope of salvation, Dryden parodically narrows Milton's more abstract theological narrative (which is, among other things, about the problem of free will) into a character assassination worthy of a satirical political pamphlet. Adam's error, on the other hand, is downplayed to the level of a sexual joke, while Absalom/Monmouth – perhaps "Made [. . .] at his own cost like *Adam* wise" (*Astræa Redux* l. 114, Dryden 1956, 25) – can at the end still hope for a reconciliation with his father.

Absalom is not a brief epic like *Paradise Regained*, but rather an abbreviated epic because of its lack of closure in telling its biblical story. In some respects, it might even be read as a mock epic: instead of performing heroic deeds, Dryden's protagonists are parliamentarians waging a war of words (Canfield 1989, 202). In abbreviating epic form, Dryden can rely on his readers' knowledge of Scripture to complete the story of Absalom and Achitophel by themselves – including Achitophel's suicide. He exploits epic conventions and epic significance for the sake of political satire, emphasising the modern meaning of the allegory and not, as Milton had done, its biblical and theological foundations. In doing so, he takes the risk of reducing the force of the religious dimension, as the famous first line of the poem clearly demonstrates: "In pious times, e'r Priest-craft did begin" (1972, 5). Dryden's use of Scripture is first and foremost polemic, but it allows him to develop an argument that conflates political with religious rebellion and declares both kinds of rebellion unnatural and blasphemous (cf. Canfield 1989, 205).

Dryden's response to the political crisis of the moment is not to transcend politics for the sake of a higher (e.g. religious) order of reality but to subordinate a biblical level of reference to a contemporary political narrative: "The system is designed to bring the past to bear on the present in all its polemical particularity, particularity heightened by the poem's ability to hold the details at a very slight distance"

---

89 Philip Harth (1993, 119–21) reads all of the Miltonic allusions in *Absalom* as referring to *Paradise Regained* rather than *Paradise Lost*. The parallels to *Paradise Regained* are also pointed out by Canfield 1989, 199–209; cf. Gelineau 1994, 41–32; Walker 2001.

90 Two more passages in the preface allude more generally to theological concepts rather than to *Paradise Lost* in particular: one to Origen's "hope [. . .] that the Devil himself may, at last, be sav'd" (Dryden 1972, 4–5, directed at Achitophel/Shaftesbury), and one to God's infite mercy compared to the limited mercy of God's "Vicegerent" the king (5). In the poem itself, there are several instances that could be construed as referring to *Paradise Lost* (e.g. l. 30 "And *Paradise* was open'd in his face," ll. 51–52 "These *Adam*-wits, too fortunately free, / Began to dream they wanted libertie").

(Zwicker 1993, 153). The poem has considerable work to do to refine the very terms it operates with and to manage the "system" or frame of allusions and correspondences it depends on – and which it nonetheless presents in an ironic light. Through the "slight distance" (Zwicker 1993, 153) at which it presents the objects of its satire, the poem exposes the artificiality and contingency of its own construction. Yet it maintains a delicate balance between the stability and instability of allegorical signification, a balance that, in the poem, is also recommended as politically virtuous as well as expedient. 'Balance' is a keyword for Dryden not only in his figural and poetic economy but also in his political one (Poyet 1995, 109). It allows him to preserve the homologies of politics and aesthetics, if only in an elaborate "fiction of state" (Love 1993, 164). It is, first and foremost, in the character of King David that this balance between fixity and flux, constancy and mobility is epitomised:

> In pious times, e'r Priest-craft did begin,
> Before *Polygamy* was made a sin;
> When man, on many, multiply'd his kind,
> E'r one to one was, cursedly, confin'd:
> When Nature prompted, and no law deny'd
> Promiscuous use of Concubine and Bride;
> Then, *Israel*'s Monarch, after Heaven's own heart,
> His vigorous warmth did, variously, impart
> To Wives and Slaves: And, wide as his Command,
> Scatter'd his Maker's Image through the land.
> *Michal*, of Royal blood, the Crown did wear,
> A Soyl ungratefull to the Tiller's care:
> Not so the rest; for several Mothers bore
> To Godlike *David*, several Sons before.
> But since like slaves his bed they did ascend,
> No True Succession could their seed attend.
> (Dryden 1972, 5–6, ll. 1–16)

The rhetorical strategy pursued in these lines aims at sexualising keywords of contemporary political theory. We have already seen this strategy in the way Adam's temptation is sexualised in the preface. 'Nature' in these lines becomes a synonym for sexual desire; monarchy here means first and foremost a hierarchical sexual relationship between the monarch and his women. The focus is on the personal and familiar, centred on David/Charles, whose kingship, as in *Astræa Redux,* is vaguely aligned with divine right theory ("after Heaven's own heart", l. 7, "his Maker's Image", l. 10). Readers might ask whether this descent to the level of Charles II's well-known and often (by Rochester, for example) satirised promiscuity is not damaging Dryden's intentions to support the king. If it is not subversive, what could be its intent? I think these lines and their flirting with scandal are part of a well-calculated plan. In contrast to the bluntness of a Rochester, Dryden's intention is to align David/Charles *as a person* with the concept of "Nature" (l. 5) – a concept that, like many others from the field of political theory, is kept quite vague and ambiguous in

Absalom. "When Nature prompted, and no law deny'd" (l. 5): out of the many possible meanings of the word 'nature', Dryden selects one that foregrounds a human (more narrowly: sexual) dimension of desire as opposed to – unnatural – "law" that controls and curbs ('denies') natural desire. The king's sexuality thus appears as a blessing of nature. In the rhetorical economy of *Absalom*, the terms 'nature' and 'law' perform a complex dance of initial opposition and subsequent convergence in the person of David/Charles. Their initial separation works towards a negation, or at least a devaluation, of the concept of 'natural law', invoked by Whig theorists as a juridical and political possibility *anterior to* the establishment of political order and sovereignty (Tuck 1979). The same devaluation of political language by dint of eroticisation befalls the word "slaves", which assumes an almost exclusively sexual connotation ("like slaves his bed they did ascend", l. 15). By making the king's indiscriminate desires stand for the 'natural', the poem carefully extends this epithet to the king's "Godlike" benevolence and magnanimity ("Godlike *David*", l. 14). The king 'naturally', i.e. in his physical body as an expression of the body politic (Kantorowicz 1957), combines the apparent opposites of nature and law; even his "Lust" can then be associated with the adjective "divine": "Whether, inspir'd by some diviner Lust, / His Father got him [sc. Absalom] with a greater Gust" (ll. 19–20).

Incited to rebellion by the evil counsellor Achitophel/Shaftesbury, the king's illegitimate son Absalom/Monmouth has to acknowledge this royal quality:

> My Father Governs with unquestion'd Right;
> The Faiths Defender, and Mankinds Delight:
> Good, Gracious, Just, observant of the Laws;
> And Heav'n by Wonders has Espous'd his Cause.
> . . . .
> Mild, Easy, Humble, Studious of our Good;
> Enclin'd to Mercy, and averse from Blood.
> If Mildness Ill with Stubborn *Israel* Suite,
> His Crime is God's beloved Attribute.
> (1972, 15, ll. 317–28)

Next to mercy and mildness, 'ease' is a significant quality of a king who behaves naturally and is naturally "observant of the Laws" (l. 319) even in fornication. The just king unites the attributes of nature with those of political order; he reconciles, even heals the rift between nature and the state. Furthermore, the ease with which he accomplishes this is a quality that he has passed on to his "Scatter'd" illegitimate offspring. In the first description of Absalom's character, we read that "[w]hat e'r he did was done with so much ease, / In him alone, 'twas Natural to please" (6, ll. 27–28). 'Easy', 'natural', and 'pleasing' thus become near-synonyms that stand for the positive qualities of divinely ordained kingship, qualities under which the more salacious aspects of Charles's character are easily and naturally subsumed. His fertility is then only one more sign to prove his election "after Heaven's own heart", even though it is only manifest outside of the matrimonial bond and bed.

This stability of order, justice, and goodness – *semper eadem* being the motto at the base of the monarch's coat of arms (Gelineau 1994, 30) – is guaranteed by the union of nature and law embodied in the "Godlike" king. By contrast, Dryden's speaker presents the king's opponents as slippery, insecure, and unstable. In the process, terms like 'liberty' and 'fortune' are played off against terms like 'loyalty' and 'virtue' in such a way that the former – key terms of the Whig vocabulary – are rhetorically connected to images of instability, uncertainty, and flux, even illegitimacy or lawlessness. In the "natural Instinct" that leads the people to "change" their sovereign "once in twenty Years" (Dryden 1972, 12, ll. 218–19), the term 'nature' is again brought into proximity to lawlessness, to the Hobbesian state of nature that is Dryden's *bête noire*: "Nature's state: where all have Right to all" (29, l. 794), the state of anarchy to which "Government it self at length must fall" (l. 793) if hereditary monarchy were to be abolished.

Whereas the king's desires are merely of an erotic nature and ultimately harmless, the contempt of law shown by his opponents results in "wild desires" (7, l. 55), in a savage (or what one might call Hobbes-natural) urge to rebel:

> These *Adam*-wits, too fortunately free,
> Began to dream they wanted libertie;
> And when no rule, no president was found
> Of men, by Laws less circumscrib'd and bound,
> They led their wild desires to Woods and Caves,
> And thought that all but Savages were Slaves.
> (ll. 51–56)

These lines can be read as parodying the closing lines of *Paradise Lost* in their emphasis on the aspect of freedom and the 'fortunate fall'. Here, freedom is equated with lawlessness and anarchy, which lead directly out of civilisation and back into "Woods and Caves". The worst accusation Dryden's speaker can find against Achitophel is that he is "unfixt in Principles and Place" (10, l. 154), a social climber and opportunist whose ambition is as wild as the desires of the people and who stands for the instability of passion (here: ambition) in contrast to the fixity of royal virtue: "But wilde Ambition loves to slide, not stand; / And Fortunes Ice prefers to Vertues Land" (11, ll. 198–99). In the figural economy of the poem, "Ice" offers no firm ground to stand on; it also provides a further contrast to the "vigorous warmth" (l. 8) of the king which, apart from its possible allusion to ancient Greek physiology (see Sennett 1994, 34, 42), associates the temperature of the royal semen with the personal quality of 'warm-heartedness' and generosity. Intrigue, on the other hand, is best served cold as ice. The cold mobility of Machiavelli's *fortuna* is contrasted with the warm "Vertue" of a traditional ideal of the ruler – which does not (yet) reveal itself as *virtù* (Pocock 1975, 1985; Skinner 1981).

Small wonder then that, in this world of classical analogies and correspondences, Achitophel's son is "born a shapeless Lump, like Anarchy" (Dryden 1972, 10, l. 172), whereas David's son Absalom has the grace and charm of his royal father, "[h]is motions all accompanied with grace; / And *Paradise* was open'd in his face" (6, ll. 29–32). For the speaker of *Absalom*, deformity, but above all personal disintegration and lack of character are sure signs of political extremism and untrustworthiness. This is most visible in the character of Zimri/Buckingham, who is depicted as

> A man so various, that he seem'd to be
> Not one, but all Mankinds Epitome.
> Stiff in Opinions, always in the wrong;
> Was every thing by starts, and nothing long:
> But, in the course of one revolving Moon
> Was Chymist, Fidler, States-Man, and Buffoon:
> Then all for Women, Painting, Rhiming, Drinking;
> Besides ten thousand freaks that dy'd in thinking.
> (21, ll. 545–52)

Zimri is incapable of integrating all his numerous interests and contradictions into one character. He squanders first his wealth and ultimately himself (ll. 559–68) in a variety of roles, activities and mental "freaks" (552). The motif of procreation that pervades *Absalom* is here taken up again in describing the stillbirth of crude ideas. Zimri's barrenness is contrasted with the fertility of David. In the myopic perspective of *Absalom*, such fragmentation of character is the central medium of presenting abstract political reflections about disorder, anarchy, and injustice in concrete terms. In contrast to these loose and lawless figures, the king is – again in phallic imagery – a 'pillar' that props up the edifice of lawful government and saves the nation from downfall: "Kings are the publick Pillars of the State, / Born to sustain and prop the Nations weight" (33–34, ll. 953–54).[91]

Dryden's metaphors evoke fears of falling and drowning, associating revolt or revolution with the deluge: "For as when raging Fevers boyl the Blood, [cf. the remark on fever and opiates in the preface] /The standing Lake soon floats into a Flood" (9, ll. 136–37). The faithful Barzillai is said to have "withstood" rebels "[i]n Regions Waste, beyond the *Jordans* Flood: / Unfortunately Brave to buoy the State; / But sinking underneath his Masters Fate" (30, ll. 819–21). Dryden's supplementary repertoire of images for modern politics is equally based on biblical material that associates the Flood, implying that only the righteous (Noah and, by implication, David/Charles) will be saved in order to establish a new covenant, a new political order sanctioned by God. This opens up a second allegorical layer underneath the story of David. These tropes achieve their rhetorical purpose when they recur in those parts of the poem that directly address political theory, supporting a conservative position against its threatened dissolution: "That Kingly power, thus ebbing out, might be / Drawn to the dregs

---

[91] Cf. Milton's description of his republican students in *Of Education* (1644) as "stedfast pillars of the state" (1953b, 389).

of a Democracy" (12, ll. 226–27). "What Standard is there in a fickle rout, / Which, flowing to the mark, runs faster out?" (29, ll. 785–6). In his central passage on government, the speaker finally calls on his readers to "fix the Mark" and draw a boundary, a limit beyond which the reform of a political system leads to its demise: "Thus far 'tis Duty; but here fix the Mark" (29, l. 803). This "Mark" can also be read as a tide-mark indicating the necessary height of a barrier to stave off the flood; the "Ark" with which it rhymes in the next line ("For all beyond it is to touch our Ark", 804) would then be ambiguous. Its more immediate reference is to the Ark of the Covenant, which houses the tables of divine law and which no one is allowed to touch; but in this context one might also associate Noah's Ark as the ship of state, kept afloat by the king.[92]

The figural terms in which Dryden presents political issues in *Absalom* are carefully prepared at the poem's beginning: first in the eroticisation and feminisation of the word 'slave' – which later recurs, presumably keeping its earlier connotation, in expressing the fear that kings might become "*slaves* to those whom they Command, / And Tenants to their Peoples *pleasure* stand" (28, ll. 775–76, my italics) – where the word 'pleasure' takes on an erotic meaning by contagion. The calculated use of such figures also shows itself in Achitophel's speech to Absalom (12–14, ll. 230–302), which reveals its satanic strategy of temptation in Miltonic allusions to "Fruit [. . .] upon the Tree" (ll. 250–51) and to the "Prince of Angels", who "from his height, / Comes tumbling downward with diminish'd light" (ll. 273–74). Achitophel, as the king's opponent, raises fortune above virtue, desire above law, and instinct above writing when he declares:

> And Nobler is a limited Command,
> Giv'n by the Love of all your Native Land,
> Than a Successive Title, Long and Dark,
> Drawn from the Mouldy Rolls of *Noah*'s Ark.
> (14, ll. 299–302)

This is the first time that the two meanings of "Ark" as ship and legal archive are conflated in the poem. The documents proving the king's legitimacy are here daringly disparaged as "Mouldy Rolls", identifying the law with the medium on which it is written. Achitophel's words also imply that the law loses its power with age, when the material surface on which it is inscribed rots away. Instead, he places his confidence in the love of the people, which has to be won by means of rhetoric. He sets up a contrast between writing (law) and speech (rhetoric), recalling the contrast – in Hobbes's translation of Thucydides – between Sparta (monarchy, writing, wisdom, stability) and Athens (democracy, rhetoric, demagoguery, instability). Achitophel, like Satan in *Paradise Lost*, opts for Athens, the populist choice. Yet in

---

92 To touch the Ark of the Covenant was met with instant divine retribution; see the punishment of Uzza in 1 Chronicles 13, or indeed *Raiders of the Lost Ark*. Cf. Winn 1987, 339–41 on Dryden's use of Noah's Ark.

doing so, he unmasks himself as an unreliable speaker by confusing one Ark with another, and – again like Milton's Satan – as a bad theologian.[93]

In Achitophel's second speech (ll. 376–476), his subversive understanding of kingship is formulated in terms of "Trust" rather than tradition or written law: "All Empire is no more than Pow'r in Trust, / Which when resum'd, can be no longer Just" (17, ll. 411–12). By implication, Dryden's speaker takes care to associate Achitophel's unstable concept of the basis of government with injustice. For Achitophel, justice is subject to popular consent, but the rhyme of "Trust" and "Just" in the couplet constructs a link *ex negativo* to the true connection between divinely ordained hereditary monarchy and the proper sense of justice that stems from divine law. Dryden takes risks in allowing Achitophel to voice an oppositional political theory – which indeed resembles Locke's ideas as set down in the *Two Treatises of Government*, which Dryden could not have known about, even if they had already been partly drafted in 1681 (Laslett 1988, Wootton 1993) – but he takes these risks only because he trusts in the efficacy of his rhetorical strategies. He trusts that his figural economy will serve to subvert and unmask Achitophel's statements, and perhaps he trusts that Shaftesbury is going to be convicted of treason in his upcoming trial. His willingness to engage in (mock) debate with the opposition about questions of political theory and the basis of legitimate government might be construed as a weakness and as a symptom of the constitutional and political difficulties of 1681 as against 1660, which are indeed severe. But in giving the arguments so much room, he also demonstrates his skill in arguing *in utramque partem*.

Achitophel's Machiavellian opportunism (he exhorts Absalom to "Prevail your self of what Occasion gives", l. 461) is brilliantly captured in the line "They who possess the Prince, possess the Laws" (476). Here as elsewhere, Dryden plays off a theological concept of law (in support of hereditary monarchy) against an entirely secular Hobbesian concept of man-made laws, which have to be obeyed not because they are inherently just but because they are enforced by the sovereign. "It is not Wisdom, but Authority that makes a Law", as Hobbes had written in the *Dialogue between a Philosopher and a Student of the Common Laws of England* (1971b, 55). Slippery like a serpent and inconsistent in his argument, Achitophel the snake-oil salesman speaks of "Self-defence" as being "Natures Eldest Law" (l. 458), invoking a natural law theory that squares badly, if at all, with his subsequent Machiavellian argument.

Dryden's speaker has few difficulties, then, taking apart Achitophel's specious arguments in the poem's central passage on government, which invokes the concept of the ancient constitution ("Native Sway", 28, l. 760; cf. Pocock 1987), confusing the power of law with the power of tradition (Poyet 1995, 109) and finding in

---

93 Satan exposes his bad theology in *Paradise Lost*, for instance, when he addresses Eve as "Fairest resemblance of thy maker fair" (1998, 12.538), although in Milton's view only Adam was created in the image of God.

Filmerian patriarchalism a protection against anarchy and "publick Lunacy" (Dryden 1972, 29, l. 788):

> What shall we think! can People give away
> Both for themselves and Sons, their Native sway?
> Then they are left Defensless, to the Sword
> Of each unbounded Arbitrary Lord:
> And Laws are vain, by which we Right enjoy,
> If Kings unquestiond can those laws destroy.
> (28, ll. 759–64)

The standards of "the Crowd" (l. 765) or "Crowds" (787) are no standards at all; they can provide no security of "private Right" (779) and "Property" (777). A popular consensus is not automatically a reasonable one: "The most may err as grosly as the few" (782). Dryden repeats some anti-democratic reservations against the monstrous 'multitude' that we have already encountered in Browne, Hobbes, Davenant, and – in a more complex articulation – Milton. For Dryden, legitimacy and authority reside in the few, not the many. His guarantee of political stability lies in the personal integrity of the monarch, sanctioned by divine decree and the binding force of tradition.

Only in the person of the king are nature and law reconciled, can the chaotic and contingent forces of arbitrary desires be harnessed and harmonised to the controlling forces of morality and order. This perspective on the personal, the contingent, and particular, which is the narrative focus of the poem, enhances the impression that its political discussions are largely disingenuous. A genuine debate about questions of political theory is not intended; rather, *Absalom* is a poem that *avoids* conceptual theorising by replacing it with strategies of personalisation, figurative language and irony. Even in alluding to political debate, political discourse is attenuated and ultimately abandoned for a metaphorical idiom of patching and mending (Zwicker 1993, 150–53). The Hobbesian state of nature is invoked as a threat to civil society, but neither the legitimation of monarchy nor the denial of a popular right to resist is presented in precise theoretical terms:

> All other Errors but disturb a State;
> But Innovation is the Blow of Fate.
> If ancient Fabricks nod, and threat to fall,
> To Patch the Flaws, and Buttress up the Wall,
> Thus far 'tis Duty; but here fix the Mark:
> For all beyond it is to touch our Ark.
> To change Foundations, cast the Frame anew,
> Is work for Rebels who base Ends pursue:
> At once Divine and Humane Laws controul;
> And mend the Parts by ruine of the Whole.
> The Tampering World is subject to this Curse,
> To Physick their Disease into a worse.
> (29, ll. 799–810)

Instead of engaging in political argument, Dryden reverts to the metaphor of governing as a form of medicine, of the body politic in analogy to the body natural, with which he had closed his preface. In the poem, his line of argument seems paradoxical, camouflaging his recommendation of harsh remedies – the surgical removal of "Rebels who base Ends pursue" (l. 806) from the body politic. It anticipates the execution of some of these rebels and plotters in 1683 (Jones 1978, 223–24). Moreover, this passage is logically inconsistent, since it propounds the patching of flaws as a correct way of government and in the same breath condemns the "Tampering World" (l. 809) as proceeding from bad to worse. And yet the rhetorical force of the poem owes much to its (Miltonic) urge to overcome the contingent by means of the absolute, the political (at the level of patching and tampering) by means of the divine, instinct and desire by means of law and method, the erosion of social meaning in oral "process of speech" (Milton 1998, 7.178) by means of permanent inscription: "here fix the Mark" (Dryden 1972, 29, l. 803; on the conflict between instinct and writing in *Absalom,* see Kroll 1991, 310, 317–18).

In his final speech, the king answers his opponents by confirming his "Lawfull Pow'r" (35, l. 1024) and threatening them with "the Sword of Justice" (l. 1002). Having finished his speech, the king is confirmed as at once natural and lawful (in the sense of: divinely ordained) by "Th'Almighty" himself (36, l. 1026), in a passage that could be read as an abbreviated parody on the third book of *Paradise Lost*:

> He said. Th'Almighty, nodding, gave Consent;
> And Peals of Thunder shook the Firmament.
> Henceforth a Series of new time began,
> The mighty Years in long Procession ran:
> Once more the Godlike *David* was Restor'd,
> And willing Nations knew their Lawfull Lord.
> (ll. 1026–31)

In God's direct response to the king's speech, this ending stages, quite literally, the contact between the contingent and the absolute – that recurring key problem in almost any literary negotiation of the relation between nature and politics in the seventeenth century. In a mere six verses, it presents a theological model of legitimising secular government. The radically compressed form suggests parody, perhaps self-parody, or even a double bluff: if it is a put-down of the Puritan ethos, it still claims divine support for the king. The fact that Dryden requires the stage device of a *deus ex machina* for the conclusion of *Absalom* shows again that, towards the end of the seventeenth century, there is no longer any obvious connection between concepts of nature, law, and kingship. In the terminological process of the poem, the "Consent" of God (l. 1026) "Once more" (1030), and finally, replaces the "Consent" of the people (978) in order to restore the king as a foundation of 'naturally' legitimate government. Dryden's *Absalom* is a last-ditch attempt at reconciling the disintegrating forces of political and personal contingency in a sacral image of kingship – yet again, as in *Eikon Basilike* and *The Adventures of Five Hours*, imagined as an immediate contact with the Godhead, here "nodding [. . .] Consent" (1026). Yet in important respects *Absalom* is already *merely* a poem, *merely* a satire and no longer or not yet political theory. The loss of old political and cultural certainties has made contact between literature and society increasingly fragile and tenuous. Only die-hard Tories will have found Dryden's presentation of the relation between nature, law, and kingship truly convincing. Dryden himself may have believed in it as a "necessary fiction" (cf. Kahn 1985, 181). As the chasm widens between public officialdom, different situations of writing, and private spaces of self-exploration in the long eighteenth century, new possibilities for realigning literature and society emerge.

Spaces of Distinction

The decline of classical models of political order and the demise of the modalities of their literary articulation call for a reassessment of the relations between individuals, crowds, and the structure of society. Hobbes, Milton, and Dryden already see the demand for such a reorientation when they engage, each in his own way, with the problem of the multitude. Their political failure may be symptomatic of the enormity of the problem and the strain of having to reconcile traditional literary forms with contemporary political pressures. How can public communication accommodate the heterogeneity of diverse audiences and the interests of individual subjects (as subjects or citizens, as part of the crowd or the nation) if each individual's 'fancy' is unpredictable?

The problem becomes even more urgent in the 1680s. During this period of successive political crises, before the systematic reboot of the political system post-1688, there is a revival of many fears and desires from the past. The very foundations of society are at risk during the Exclusion Crisis, when the fierce spectre of civil war raises its ugly head and, lurking at its back, the phantom of the state of nature once again threatens the social order. Yet literature can no longer offer any convincing solutions at this time; instead, it becomes a part of the problem. No longer able to unify a society split along political and denominational lines, literature positions itself on one side of the fault line between Whig and Tory. Despite its skilful manipulation of the imagery of the king's two bodies, Dryden's *Absalom* cannot conceal the fact that this figural language has lost its former binding force. How to re-establish the relation between individual subjects and society? How to overcome the divide between individual and communal interests?

For Browne and other humanist thinkers, the inner lives of people are a *polis*, a city or commonwealth that is disturbed and endangered by internal as well as external forces. These forces require the individual to engage in rigorous self-observation, self-control, and self-cultivation. For Burton, too, the individual is an interface between different streams of information "both private and publike"

(1989, 5). These two spheres of influence can become dangerously imbalanced in times of political crisis and social upheaval, as Browne argues in the preface to *Religio Medici*. Even where the self is conceived as a privileged inner place of private intellectual and spiritual activities like thinking, reading, writing or praying, it is not monadic but criss-crossed by dangerous influences and affects, passions, and desires, not least by rhetoric. Deliberately appealing to private sensitivities, rhetoric seeks to mobilise the passions and desires of each individual and thereby to unite individuals into a docile mass of political pawns.

In this context, the word 'private' should not be mistaken for a modern understanding of a positively defined subjectivity; rather, it denotes an area of human existence that is not filled by functions of public office – a classical and medieval concept of *privatus* that only has meaning in relation to its antonym, public life. This classical tradition still undergirds the duality of the mystical and material body of the king in early modern thought (Kantorowicz 1957, Reiss 2003, 441–45, Condren 2002). In the theory of the king's two bodies, the difference between public and private is imagined as an unbreakable unity. It still forms the basis, however contested, of Dryden's depiction of Charles II in *Absalom*. In such a model of society, there is no possibility of a contrast between 'private' will and 'public' weal, between sovereignty and law, and between politics and religion, because both terms are united in one and the same contexture. The state *is* the body of the king. For example, in Thomas Carew's poem "Upon the King's Sickness" of 1624, the final illness of James I is described as affecting not only the "royal limbs" of the king but also "his mystic limbs", the people:

> Ent'ring his Royal limbs that is our head:
> Through us (his mystic limbs) the pain is spread.
> That man that doth not feel his [share] hath none
> In any part of his dominion;
> (Carew 1893, 32–33, l. 19–22)[94]

In the seventeenth century, we find a residual presence of such mystical ideas next to an emerging sense of privacy as the spatial seclusion of an individual. Architects begin to build interior spaces (closets or private libraries) that allow their owners to retreat and spend some time alone, isolated from others. Montaigne, for example, enjoyed his own library as a "private space [. . .] completely cut off from the rest of his family" (Morse 1989, 258; cf. Jagodzinski 1999b, 13–17). At a time when 'family' still means 'household', such a privilege of temporary solitude is at first an element of *social* distinction. The private sphere thus comes into existence as a result of separating and spatially isolating an individual from others, from the family, and by extension

---

[94] Cf. Reiss 2003, 443. Reiss quotes from Seneca's *De clementia* 1.5.1, where the emperor is referred to as the rational soul (*animus*) of the state and the state as his body. Louis XIV abbreviates this to the famous dictum *L'état c'est moi*.

from the multitude. In seventeenth-century England, the production and reception of literature are still more public than private activities. The republic of letters is a widespread social network of relations in which the question of a contrast between private and public aspects of individuality hardly ever comes up. When it does, however, it is mostly in connection with classical traditions such as the debate concerning the pros and cons of an active or contemplative life (Mackenzie and Evelyn 1986). Yet as these classical and humanist semantic residues recede, the split between inner selves and public lives gains political urgency, and new suggestions for *specific* ways of bridging it are required. The pressure of this problem also affects the discourse of neoclassicism with consequences for the literary representation of human inwardness.

The seventeenth century witnesses the ultimate breakdown of ancient and medieval ideas of social and human unity. There is a demand for new questions and different answers than those provided by tradition. Bacon and Descartes establish new epistemologies, Hobbes and Locke craft new theories of politics, emancipating themselves to a large extent from older ways of thinking (see Reiss 2003, 469–518 on Descartes). In this process, the concept of the person also changes: "Person was no longer nexus of multiple communal circles, exemplary figure or divine instrument, nor fraught erratic mover. Person was becoming universal actor and knower in a rational universe, whose agency could intervene in and resolve the very sources of conflict" (Reiss 2003, 519). When, with William Harvey at the latest, one chooses to describe both the human body and the state in mechanist and materialist terms, one also rethinks the relations between private and public activities, person and society, individual and communication in ways that are no longer mystical and participatory but rational, atomistic, and dynamic. This is the moment when the metaphors of 'circulation' become defining for an understanding of modernity (Rogers 1996, 16–27; Kroll 2007; Kroll 2000, 104–11). These metaphors pave the way for a *mediation* (instead of unity) of distinct levels and elements of discourse. This new normative order, which I here refer to as neoclassicism, can be observed in the later seventeenth century; it will come to dominate the eighteenth century under the name of Enlightenment. Neoclassicism mediates between individual perceptions and social meanings: in epistemology with the rational tool of the concept, in politics with that of the contract, and in aesthetics with that of taste (Reiss 2003, 524–26).

What interests me is how such neoclassical 'angles of contingency' shape private selves and public lives between 1680 and 1700, as novels and plays rethink the relations among authors, characters, and readers. How this happens and in what contexts; which functions literature takes on as a means of practicing and reflecting on techniques of reading and communication; and how English neoclassicism is established as a normative discourse on the basis of contingency and probability – this is what the next chapter is going to explore in reading Aphra Behn's *Love-Letters Between a Nobleman and His Sister* (1684–87) and William Congreve's *The Way of the World* (1700).

5 Private Selves and Public Lives: Neoclassical Perspectives

Inwardness, Probability, and Wit

It is often claimed that modern concepts of individuality or the public sphere did not yet exist in the early modern period; or if they did, they looked and (probably) felt very different. There is a range of sociological and historical models and conceptual approaches to explain the emergence of a modern self-awareness of 'individuals' between 1300 and 1800 (see, for example, Greenblatt 1980; Taylor 1989; Mascuch 1996; Porter 1997). The problems begin with the word 'individual', which was not used in its modern meaning in the seventeenth century but may have "suggest[ed] a *relation*" rather than "a separate entity" (Stallybrass 1992, 606; see also Ferry 1983, 33–39). Similarly, the word 'self' was not used to denote the intrinsic, authentic, essential core of *one* human being (Ferry 1983, 39–45; Reiss 2003) and the word 'subject' did not mean an autonomous subject of decision and action but the subject as *subditus*, as subjected to the sovereign, sometimes contrasted to the 'citizen'. Did the early moderns, then, not have a coherent and stable concept of selfhood or subjectivity?

In contrast to this view, others emphasise "the conceptual importance of personal inwardness" (Maus 1995, 27; cf. Schoenfeldt 1999a, 11–13, 16–18). They focus on the textual traces of historically specific connections between concepts of privacy, inwardness, and personhood; they opt for a more pragmatic and limited analysis of the ways in which something like individuality becomes discernible in distinctions between inside and outside or between public and private spaces. From this vantage point, 'subjectivity' no longer appears as a (fairly) precise philosophical concept but as "a loose and varied collection of assumptions, intuitions, and practices that do not all logically entail one another and need not appear together at the same cultural moment" (Maus 1995, 29). That is to say that the imposition of a radical difference between modern and premodern forms of subjectivity (Barker 1984, Belsey 1985) can be as misguided as the assumption of continuity between them (Jagodzinski 1999b, 1–22). Continuities are almost inevitably evoked in conceptual histories that trace the semantic changes in words like 'self' and 'individual', too hastily assuming the existence of some entity to which the words are thought to refer. Conversely, the absence of a word in a certain period does not necessarily prove the non-existence of the concept in question.

Inwardness, then, is less a concept than a cluster of "assumptions, intuitions, and practices" (Maus 1995, 29) which can be observed in different historical configurations. In this chapter, I present two case studies to explore how and why the distinction between personal interiority and exteriority gains relevance and urgency, and how this is addressed by the discourse of neoclassicism towards the end of the seventeenth century. How are 'individualities' and 'textualities' realigned? How is inwardness, understood as concealed and opaque, related to the neoclassical ideal of wit, understood as transparent intersubjective communication? I use the terms 'individualities' and 'textualities' in the plural and with preliminary scare quotes as ciphers for two oppositional complexes, without intending these complexes to be homogeneous or a clearly specified duality. They are interpretative constructs – similar to Lacan's domains of the imaginary and the symbolic – that serve here to mark an point of intersection in early modern culture where modes of private experience and belief, however articulate or inarticulate in themselves, meet, converge, or conflict with modes of social behaviour and action. The latter are encoded in language, collective forms of expression that do not belong to the individual, who becomes a social being by using language, producing texts and being interpellated as a social subject by language.

The history of English Renaissance literature is full of examples of the growing complexity and urgency of the inside-outside distinction, from the sonnets of Wyatt and Surrey to those of Shakespeare, and from Spenser's Redcrosse to Shakespeare's Hamlet, Beatrice, or Olivia, or Jonson's *Every Man In/Every Man Out*, to name but a few. Donne's famous lament about the loss of "cohaerence" in *The First Anniversary* – "'Tis all in peeces, all cohaerence gone" (Donne 2001, 199, l. 213) – may also refer to the demise of an (ideal) harmonious unity of public and private aspects of life. Something similar happens in *Hamlet* when the protagonist registers the decline of the mystical doctrine of the king's two bodies and suffers the unreliability of previously stable relations in and on his own body: "The body is with the King, but the King is not with the body" (4.2.25–26); "I could be bounded in a nutshell and count myself a king of infinite space, were it not that I have bad dreams" (2.2.248–50; see Kaufman 1996, 103–49; Hillman 1997).

Given the complexity of the historical material, it would be reductive to explain it only by reference to two causes: the social pressures of urbanisation and religious persecution (of Catholics as well as radical Protestants) (cf. Maus 1995, 15–26). Relevant as these certainly are, I also think it is necessary to examine the changing conceptual landscape, the terminology and the generic patterns used by historical actors to describe human inwardness: for example, when Spenser depicts the struggle for a virtuous life as a psychomachia in *The Faerie Queene*, as a series of quests within the *paysage moralisée* of epic romance, or when Sir Thomas Browne depicts the inner life in terms of a *polis*, disturbed by frightening forces that require rigorous self-control and temperance, in language derived from the stoics, or when Robert Burton envisages the individual as a point of intersection between "both private and publike" streams of information (Burton 1989–2000, 1: 5). What belongs to the most private "secrecie" (Browne 2012, 4) of a person can only be made accessible by means of figurative language, a language that has to draw its image repertoire from publicly available sources. Even in the form of the diary, as in the case of Samuel Pepys, self-observation is practiced as if it were coming from outside the self (Turner 1995, 97). During prayer or private reading, the individual person becomes the site where conflicts of belief and difficulties of interpreting Scripture are located. Solitary reading, for Protestants, also gains an even more personal significance as they attempt to discern for themselves, individually, whether they have attained the divine gift of grace and salvation (Jagodzinski 1999b, 23–48; Lebrun 1989).

The opacity of inwardness is a problem and a stimulus for communication. Yet it also leads to a problem of power and control, as we have seen in Davenant and Hobbes. This problem hinges on the precarious distinction between mind and body, a distinction that becomes politically significant because it separates opinions from actions, distinguishing between "an arena of opinions – figured as conscience, mind or spirit, and ascribed to an interior realm" from "an 'external' [. . .] arena of actions in which the body is involved" (Maus 1995, 81). Hobbes and Davenant are much more interested in the mental side of this distinction: minds are susceptible to the influence of communication (rhetoric), whereas bodies can simply be coerced by force. Mental rather than physical inwardness is therefore the proper object of the political philosopher and the poet. Yet both physical or physiological and mental forms of inwardness depend on external signs to become readable. Signs, however, only admit a *probable* interpretation. This is why the theory of signs and visual expressions assumes such a central position in Hobbes's theory of politics. Inwardness can only be inferred, never made transparent or directly represented. Because it is concealed, it can only be read in its external symptoms – but these might be faked to deceive the observer. Conversely, hypocrisy, the concealment, equivocation, simulation, and dissimulation of inward states of mind can be recommended as a necessary practice for those who are victims of religious persecution or (in the classic Machiavellian argument) those who wield political power and therefore need to hide their true intentions (Zagorin 1990, Kahn 1994, Hadfield 2017).

The problem of mediating between inward selves and public personas, between concealment and communication, authenticity and "show" has consequences for early modern culture, in the fields of politics, religion, forms of knowledge and the arts. Theatre in this context is a key medium for exploring this predicament. When Hamlet says "I have that within which passeth show" (*Hamlet* 1.2.85), he distinguishes between outward expressions of grief that can be simulated and his own genuine feelings of mourning; he "demands that we see his own performance of mourning as a counter-performance against empty histrionics" (Döring 2006, 13). Paradoxically, however, dressing up in "trappings" and "suits" (*Hamlet* 1.2.86) is precisely what actors do to create dramatic illusions – and *Hamlet* is largely about the protagonist's inability to express his inward feelings and to translate them into appropriate actions (Berensmeyer 2007, 56, 84–86). Human inwardness is a site where conflicts between intention and action, internal deliberation and external expression are played out; it is also an arena of conflicts between competing discourses (religious, political, social). Literature is a sounding board for such conflicts, particularly when traditional forms of knowledge are in decline and new answers need to be found. How can the precarious distinction between external and internal dimensions of human reality be managed without breakdown or failure (as in *Hamlet*)? Which solutions can English neoclassicism propose for a successful negotiation between 'individualities' and 'textualities'?

The neoclassical keyword 'wit' comes closest to defining a personal quality that is seen to be decisive for both individual, social, and aesthetic success. Wit is a quality that transcends the dimension of individuality by emphasising the network of social and sociable relations among different persons, usually belonging to the 'higher sort'. Wit can only be observed in communication, in discourse. It depends on the functioning of these relations and their apparently effortless management by the individual ("ease" in *Absalom and Achitophel*, similar to *sprezzatura* in Castiglione's *Book of the Courtier*). Its purpose is not geared towards honesty or sincerity but towards propriety, civility, politeness. In this respect, wit necessarily remains an elusive, floating, and unstable signifier whose circulation can best be observed in Restoration comedy – in Etherege, Wycherley, Behn, Congreve, and others.

Those who, on stage, attribute wit to themselves as a personal quality or a stable character trait inevitably end up as fops and 'Witwouds' (a character in Congreve's *Way of the World* but also in Southerne's 1692 play *The Wives Excuse*), i.e. would-be wits who are exposed to the laughter of their peers and the audience. To their own detriment, these characters – and their real-life models – neglect the communicative and social dimension of wit that is essential to its functioning. The free circulation of wit as an element of discourse is described by Shaftesbury in 1709 in analogy to commerce: "[. . .] wit is its own remedy. Liberty and commerce bring it to its true standard. The only danger is the laying an embargo. The same thing happens here as in the case of trade. Impositions and restrictions reduce it to a low ebb. Nothing is so advantageous to it as a free port" (Shaftesbury 1999, 31).

On the level of social discourse, wit presupposes a stable, balanced configuration of relations among epistemology, morality, and language: a belief in the possibility of a correspondence between words, actions, and beliefs. Its linguistic ideals are clarity, transparency, and elegance. One of the contemporary definitions of wit is "a propriety of Thoughts and Words" (Dryden 1995a, 97).[95] This correspondence no longer rests on hidden patterns of analogy (e.g. between human inwardness and external behaviour) but on a new understanding of representation and signification. The relation between signs and things is now seen to be arbitrary, and meaning is not generated by reference to objects but rather to ideas, which only in rare cases (geometry) admit of certainty (Aarsleff 1982, 24–31, 42–83).[96]

---

[95] The quotation is from Dryden's preface to *The State of Innocence*, 1674 ("The Authors Apology for Heroique Poetry; and Poetique Licence").
[96] On the medieval discourse of patterning and its replacement by the "analytico-referential discourse" of experimentalism since the sixteenth century, see Reiss 1982a, 9, 55–107, 351–85; Olson 1994; Kroll 1991.

One of the qualities of wit is that it can handle this arbitrary relation correctly and appropriately; it can convincingly decide between different probabilities. The ability to manipulate language – and with it social reality – according to the ideal of wit depends on "the ability to perceive proper distinctions between and among objects and ideas" (Kroll 1986, 728). Under the pressure of this intellectual, cultural, and social ideal, a distinction between nature and culture (or nature and society) becomes increasingly less relevant. In some Restoration comedies, as in the philosophy of Locke, "true speech is at once socialized and naturalized", and the function of wit is to expound and exploit "the flexible social and political implications of ordinary language" (Kroll 1986, 752), language that has become conventional and "entirely functional" (Aarsleff 1982, 28).

These social and political implications amount to a dominant normative cultural discourse of probability and contingency – dominant in the sense that "a critique of discourse is no longer able to affect the premises or the functioning of that discourse" (Reiss 1982a, 351). Avoiding excess and extremes, this discourse is soon aligned with concepts of common sense and taste. Probability is an epistemic criterion of evaluating signs, a criterion for the correct application of procedures of inference and conjecture ('reading'), while the concept of contingency serves as a dual index: an index of the constraints imposed on intellectual and political fictions of autonomy, as well as an index of the relative liberty contingent upon the flexible but homogeneous alignment of language, society, and knowledge. Rather than drawing a sharp distinction between religion and science, seventeenth-century neoclassicism institutes the same hermeneutic principles in a wide range of intellectual pursuits from natural philosophy to theology. It prefigures the formal procedures of Enlightenment reasoning (see Kroll 1986, 729–31 on Isaac Barrow). Those who neglect the probabilistic implications of rational discourse, those who perhaps refuse all social instances of mediation and seek to assert a counter-public sphere of their own, are accused of being 'enthusiasts' who base their arguments on neither verifiable nor falsifiable claims to a privileged inwardness. Those, on the other hand, who are capable of handling these implications to their advantage are esteemed as 'polite' and 'sociable' members of gentlemanly society (Knox 1950, Heyd 1995, Pocock 1998, Klein 1998). The degree to which a successful balance can be struck between these conflicting modes of experience (consciousness vs. communication, articulate vs. inarticulate, internalised vs. externalised) determines the degree of contingent freedom available to a person. Yet rather than resulting in an empirical observation of a difference between individual and society in the modern sociological sense, neoclassicism develops into a distinct cultural mode of *negotiating* between the domains of the individual and the textual.

Literary forms of writing can be seen to embody this mode of dealing with contingency and probability in a circular, self-legitimising fashion. They present characters who themselves have to write and read texts. The contest between different modes of experience is projected directly onto scenes of writing and reading, so that reading is turned into a synecdoche of experiencing the self and the world. By being made to observe characters engaged in acts of encoding and deciphering, readers and spectators are encouraged to improve their own practice in such acts of "literate experience" (Barnaby and Schnell 2002, 1–12, 197–200). They are encouraged to attempt to negotiate more successfully between the terms of their individualities and the textual networks in which these need to be communicated. Literary discourse, never completely aestheticised, thus assumes important functions of orientation in the world. Even though it is sometimes employed for the rather callous purposes of political propaganda, as in the cases of Dryden and Behn, literature towards the end of the seventeenth century is neither completely purposeful nor completely aesthetic. Usefulness and pleasure, *prodesse et delectare* are combined in such a way that readers do not merely receive didactic messages about cultural norms and values but that they are encouraged, 'moved' to engage with these values and norms actively and deliberately. What is new is not this triad of *prodesse, delectare,* and *movere* but the anticipation of dissent and the openness for dissenting opinions, which in contrast to earlier forms of authorial communication no longer presuppose the reader's agreement, perhaps not even a fully shared experiential world. Instead of despairing about the contingency of different world views, contingency is built into texts from the outset – the norm rather than the exception. A plethora of literary genres – panegyric, satire, didactic poetry as well as philosophical writing (Locke, Shaftesbury) – now begin to rely not on the assent of readers, implied as well as real, but on their collaborative effort. Literary culture in the late seventeenth century develops flexible ways of bringing the contingent views of authors and readers into alignment without necessarily harmonising them and trying to elide their differences. In narrative fiction, we see this trend in the rise of more dynamic forms of focalisation and changing points of view, challenging readers to fill the gaps in these stories; in the essay, we see it in a more flexible and fragmentary presentation of individual or idiosyncratic perspectives on the world; in drama, in performative enactments of the contingencies of different modes of experience; in philosophy, among other aspects, in the "degrees of assent" that Locke (1979, 4.16) sketches as a condition for successful communication. If literature towards the end of the seventeenth century engages with the 'rise of the invididual', it does so in careful alignment with social and institutional forms and shared spaces of living together.

The 'Rhetoric of Love': Inwardness, Reading, and the Novel in Aphra Behn's *Love-Letters Between a Nobleman and His Sister* (1684–87)

Bakhtin's famous essay on the chronotope emphasises the public form that individuality took in antiquity: "There was as yet no internal man [. . .] nor any individualized approach to one's own self. An individual's unity and his [sic] self-consciousness were exclusively public. Man was completely *on the surface*" (Bakhtin 1981, 132, italics original). Completely on the surface: as Bakhtin points out, pre-modern subjectivity knows no distinction between the exterior and interior dimensions of a self. To some extent, such 'surface individualities' continue to be imagined and presented in early modern drama, poetry, and prose fiction. Yet this is less a question of representational realism (as expressed, for example, in E. M. Forster's well-worn distinction between 'flat' and 'round' characters) than a moral question: one that hinges, in the early modern period, on the distinction between stable and unstable, constant and inconstant characters – consider the case of David vs. Zimri and Achitophel in Dryden's *Absalom*. In this point, representational and moral 'realism' (for want of a less anachronistic term) converge. Thus, by definition, a shapeshifter like Milton's Satan, unwilling to remain in his place, or someone "determined to prove a villain" (*Richard III* 1.1.30) in preferring "Fortunes Ice [. . .]to Vertues Land" (*Absalom* l. 199), can never be a trustworthy character. Early English prose fiction puts this semantics of (in)stability to work, but it also activates the reader's moral judgement more directly than Dryden is prepared to do in *Absalom*. The novel, and – as we will see – the epistolary novel in particular, reflects on representational modes and plays with forms of characterisation while abstaining from overt authorial value judgements. As the example of Aphra Behn will show, this does not exclude moments of political propaganda. Yet novels and plays, well aware of the essential superficiality of fictional characters, bring their characters' interiority into view mostly indirectly, by means of *perspective* or *point of view*. While thus guiding their readers or audiences in certain directions, novels and plays can also make us aware of the blind spots and indeterminacies that relate to our knowledge of literary or dramatic characters, as well as to our own cognitive limitations in guessing at the mental states of other people.

Aphra Behn's *Love-Letters Between a Nobleman and His Sister*, published in three volumes between 1684 and 1687, provides one of the best examples of a strategic literary game with the superficiality of fictional characters, whose inwardness can only be inferred from information contained in the text. The novel reflects this on the diegetic level in the form of epistolary communication. The characters who reveal or conceal their inward selves in letters do so for the benefit of the letters' addressees, who in turn decode the information they receive in these letters and project their own assumptions and conjectures onto the 'black box' that is the other person. This process within the fiction is repeated in the act of reading the novel: the reader observes the characters as both writers and readers of letters to each other. Behn exploits this structure of characterisation and reflexivity to make a philosophical, moral, and political point. The novel's mode of representation is closely connected to actual social practices and political events of its time, events that Behn (or her paymasters) hope to influence by means of the novel. Behn uses the form of love letters to caricature the over-emphasis on inwardness and emotional authenticity that is a staple of the romance genre. It is this hyped-up emotionality that her novel depicts, in sum, as morally reprehensible and politically damaging. But Behn is not simply making a nihilistic or cynical point about human nature, about the unreliability of lovers or the essential emptiness of the person. While it would not be wrong to say that, for Behn, at least in this text, the person is a blank, and the characters in the novel exploit this predicament in various ways (some more successfully than others), the novel's predominant concern is a more general one: it is the question to what extent inwardness can be communicated and what happens when inwardness is translated into writing, into the intimate form of the love letter, which more often than not defines itself as a private space in marked contrast to (indeed shut off from) public uses of language. What the novel shows, I argue, is that such an isolation is impossible to maintain – there is no private language, not even one that might be shared by two lovers. In doing so, the novel plays some variations on old philosophical oppositions such as sense vs. sensibility, mind vs. body, and reason vs. passion – this at a time immediately after the Exclusion Crisis and on the eve of the 'Glorious Revolution' in the late 1680s. In this context, Behn's advocacy of certain strategies of reading and writing also invites political consequences.

Like Milton in *Paradise Lost*, Behn is interested in practising 'right' reading based on criteria of probability. Her novel thematises reading on several levels: (1) as a technique of deciphering the inwardness of other people (who are physically *present*) by interpreting external signs (words, sounds, gestures, physical reactions); (2) as an inferential conjecture of the innermost feelings and thoughts of other people who are *absent* by reading their letters; and (3) as a general technique of interpretation or a 'way of worldmaking' (Goodman 1978), which is recommended to the reader of the novel as a general procedure of assessing and comparing probabilities. Finally, I argue that *Love-Letters* is also about a literary conflict between different attitudes to reading and different modes of reading, not least a conflict between different ways of reading novels: is the emerging genre of the novel primarily a medium of entertainment or is it rather a didactic tool that teaches its readers something worth knowing?

In the history of the novel,[97] Aphra Behn (c. 1640?–1689) is an important transitional figure. Her prose fiction was rejected by later critics used to the conventions established and refined in the novels of Defoe, Richardson, Smollett, and Fielding, among others, as either indecent (for their explicit erotic content) or imperfect (because they lack consistency in character depiction or authorial intentions) or both (cf. Novak 1973 and Warner 1998, 66 n. 9). Yet *Love-Letters Between a Nobleman*

---

97 On the much debated topic of the 'rise' or 'emergence' of the novel, see Watt 1962; McKeon 1987a; Doody 1996; Hunter 1990; Brown 1997; Warner 1998; Ballaster 1992; Richetti 1992; for the early epistolary novel, see Day 1966; Perry 1980.

and His Sister allows a fascinating insight into the development of the type of writing that would come to dominate the literary market in the eighteenth and nineteenth centuries: narrative, fictional or fictionalised, often formulaic, plot-driven, and intent on gratifying the novel-reader's primary interest: pleasure. In this respect, *Love-Letters* has much in common with Restoration comedy. Published anonymously and first attributed to Behn in 1691 (Todd 1993), the novel is an adaptation of a French genre, the novel of amorous intrigue (Beasley 1982, 2), for an English audience; it is also a work of political propaganda, written – like Dryden's *Absalom* – for the Tories during the crisis of the 1680s and probably also paid for by members of this faction (Todd 1993, viii).

Behn wrote the three instalments while the political events following the Popish Plot (1678–79) – a feigned Catholic conspiracy to assassinate Charles II in order to enthrone his Catholic brother James – and the Rye House Plot – an actual conspiracy in 1683 aiming to murder both King Charles *and* his brother – were still ongoing. The novel is set during the unfortunate Monmouth rebellion; it follows the Whig rebels, led by the Duke of Monmouth (Charles's natural son, who is Dryden's 'Absalom' and Behn's 'Cesario'), into exile on the Continent (on the novel's representation of the Duke of Monmouth, see Bowers 2009). The final pages of the third part report on their defeat by the forces of James II. In the manner of a *roman à clef*, real places, events, and persons are thinly disguised in the fiction, and contemporary readers would have had little difficulty identifying them: 'France' is England, 'Paris' is London, 'the Louvre' is 'Whitehall', 'the Bastille' is 'the Tower', and so on. The names of the main characters are taken from the stock of court masques and pastoral romance: Silvia, Philander, Octavio, Sebastian, Cesario. Others are French or meant to sound French, like 'Briljard' and 'Antonett'. In one case, the character's disguise is so thin as to be almost nonexistent: 'Fergusano' stands for an actual person by the name of Ferguson. 'Tomaso' is probably a fictional composite of two historical persons, the Earl of Shaftesbury and Thomas Armstrong.

The protagonists, 'Philander' and 'Silvia', are based on the Whig nobleman Ford Grey, third Baron Grey of Werke, and his sister-in-law, Lady Henrietta Berkeley, who had caused a scandal of great public interest when they eloped together in 1682. Henrietta's abduction led to a trial that caught the public's fascination, leading to booksellers profiting from the publication of the court proceedings under the title *The Trial of Ford Lord Grey of Werk*. Janet Todd (1993, viii) has speculated that both this transcript and Behn's novel may have been published with the government's explicit approval or encouragement in order to weaken support for the Whig cause. Neither Behn, it appears, nor her probable financial backers could allow this opportunity to slip by: to exploit the convergence of politics and sex in order to make the public's enjoyment of a good scandal a useful tool for Tory propaganda.

As regards form and content, the three parts have a number of distinct features. The texts are clearly parts of a trilogy, but the individual instalments have slightly different titles, and each has its own dedication to a supporter of the royalist cause.[98] The parts successively gain in length, from 344 to 401 to 490 pages. The first part begins with an introductory "Argument" (9–10) but then consists exclusively of letters, mainly between Philander (aka Lord Grey) and Silvia (alias Henrietta Berkeley, his lover/sister in law). The story told in the letters is closely based on the documentation of Lord Grey's trial. The second part – relating Silvia's and Philander's "adventures" in the Netherlands and in Cologne – though still consisting mainly of letters, makes increasing use of a third-person narrator. These diegetic passages gradually increase in length, until the third part consists mostly of third-person (and sometimes first-person 'eyewitness') narrative, which comments on and sometimes even appears to ridicule the characters' actions and motivations. Increasingly, letters lose their importance for the story as their reliability in revealing a character's mental state is diminished.[99] In part one, a complex of emotions described as erotic love is to a large extent generated and then maintained by effects of language; here, the epistolary exchanges are directly presented to the reader. The second part, however, teaches the reader to distrust this "lovers' discourse" (Barthes 1990) when Philander uses it to feign being in love in letters addressed to different recipients. Retroactively, these revelations cast doubt on the claims and vows of authenticity in the love letters of part one, allowing the reader to recognise that the code of love has been used (and can be used again, at any time) as a purely mechanical instrument of discourse. There is no necessary correlation between the representamen and the object (in Peirce's terms), between the letter-writer's intense, emotionally charged language of love and his authentic mental state. After this revelation, the language of love is used ironically or even cynically in the novel. Those who take their vows seriously are literally presented as too good for this world when Octavio, Silvia's disappointed Dutch lover, escapes it by taking holy orders. In part three, even Silvia, whom Behn describes in the dedication to part one as "true Tory" (1684, sig. [A7]r), has learnt her lesson and has herself become a successful calculating schemer, using her 'charms' in order to make her 'fortune' (in the dual meaning of good luck and material wealth) by ruining that of others (cf. 1687, 489). As the characters mutate from "amorous" to "diplomatic subjectivity" (Warner 1998, 66–67), their inner lives become increasingly irrelevant. The heterodiegetic narrative configuration of

---

[98] The dedications are to Thomas Condon, Lemuel Kingdon, and, most importantly, Robert Spencer, the second Earl of Sunderland, who "presided over the suppression of Monmouth's rebellion" (Speck 2008, n. p.) and became a close advisor of James II. There is textual evidence that the work was not planned as a series from the start, but that the second part was written after the success of the first. At the end of the second part, the reader is promised "the Third and Last Part of this History" (1685, 401).

[99] For a reading of the novel that relates Behn's shift from epistolarity to narration to "new ideas of the self and the new epistemology based on them", see Gevirtz 2015, 93. More recent readings focused on genre include Villegas López 2015 and Gilbert 2018.

part three observes them from the outside, like a spectator or bystander who watches them from a middle distance. The novel ultimately depicts its characters as roleplayers, fools of fortune propelled through life by their affects and ambitions. They are not envisaged as having a fully 'rounded' character or self.

In the narrator's final comments on the main characters, any claim to depict their interiority has disappeared. In its place, we find a judgemental narrator delivering the moral of the story in an elevated tone, speaking as if on higher historical ground: "So ended the Race of this glorious Youth, who was in his time the greatest Man of a Subject in the World, and the greatest Favourite of his Prince, happy indeed above a Monarch, if Ambition and the Inspiration of Knaves and Fools had not led him to Destruction, and from a Glorious Life brought him to a Shameful Death" (1687, 487–88). But that does not mean that there is no longer room for irony. Concerning Silvia, we are told that she has "ruin'd the Fortune of that young Nobleman [Don Alonzo], and became the Talk of the Town, insomuch that the Governour not permitting her stay there, she was forced to remove for new Prey, and daily makes considerable Conquests where e'er she shows the Charmer" (489). Silvia, having chosen a life of surfaces, appears to have shed any pretense to an authentic emotional identity. She has become a female Machiavel – the personification of "a radical, unprincipled estrangement of internal truth from external manifestation" (Maus 1995, 35) – using her beauty ("show[ing] the Charmer") for profitable "Conquests". Some feminist critics have admired what they take to be Behn's depiction of an autonomous woman in Silvia,[100] though there is little evidence to support this. Where is Silvia's autonomy when she is "*forced* to remove for new Prey" (my italics)? Reading the novel as a work of Tory propaganda, intended primarily to undermine the Whigs' moral authority, further undermines such an argument. Behn may well have had a few sympathies for Silvia, who is without doubt an impressive fictional character, but "show[ing] the Charmer" and living the life of a courtesan is ultimately not commendable in the novel's moral conclusion.

Behn distributes her irony equally between genders. At the very end, she connives, or pretends to connive, with a male chauvinist view: Philander, who decides to turn his coat after the rebellion is crushed, "was at last pardoned, kiss'd the King's Hand, and came to Court in as much Splendor as ever, being very well understood by all good Men" (1687, 490). This all-male 'understanding' obviously refers to Philander's submission to royal authority; his return to the fold is an act of political opportunism, "very well understood". On the other hand, it can also be read as referring to his involvement with Silvia. His rebellion – like Adam's submission to Eve (in Dryden's version) – is presented as an effect, a mere outgrowth, of

---

[100] See, for example, Gardiner 1980, Pearson 1991, Gallagher 1994, Todd 1996. By contrast, Bowers 1999 declares that "every page of the *Love Letters* is constructed to frustrate attempts to locate stable sexual agents and agencies, and to give the lie to the assumptions from which such attempts proceed" (145).

his transgressive sexuality and libertinism. The phrase serves to downplay the political relevance of oppositional actions by presenting them in terms of excessive sexual desires. A staple of anti-Whig propaganda, this rhetorical strategy of sexualising politics occurs, for instance, in Otway's *Venice Preserv'd* (the lechery of Antonio, who is most likely yet another caricature of Shaftesbury) and, as we have seen, in Dryden's *Absalom and Achitophel*.

Behn's narrative strategies in *Love-Letters* are difficult, indeed impossible to separate from her propagandistic purposes. This is why conventional criticism of her handling of character, point of view, and plot as 'inconsistent' is quite beside the point: this very inconsistency and its progressive unveiling are part of an overall authorial strategy.[101] In this respect, Behn's novel is not only to be read as mere political propaganda with a superficial moral purpose of inculcating obedience to the king and disseminating anti-Whig sentiments. In fact, it is – within and beyond the propaganda – a significant literary experiment as a novel that is, on one level, about the reading of novels, about different representational modes and about the strategies of concealing and revealing inwardness in prose fiction. This metafictional level of the text is also didactic, but it leaves its topical context behind as it envisages a media critique of reading as a cultural technique.

Its three volumes could be described as iterations: algorithmic repetitions of a formula, variations on a single theme. The novel's plot is repetitive to the point of self-parody. As Warner explains (1998, 65), "[b]etween installments, characters such as Philander and Silvia do not so much develop as undergo mutation; the plot does not unfold according to a single linear logic, but instead proliferates as a repetitive but variant ensemble of plots, often with self-parodying resemblance; and, finally, such themes as love and loyalty undergo surprising reversal." These repetitions, mutations, and reversals draw the reader's attention to the artificiality of the text as a fictional construct. By emphasising its constructed nature, the text negates expectations of 'realism' about its structures of representation and also its characters, calling attention to the gaps in its construction and asking readers to reflect on their active participation in the process of fiction-making.

In the 1680s, Behn can still count on the attentiveness of active readers, eager to decipher political, personal, and topical subtexts and aware of the functions of genre as fairly stable horizons of expectation – readers like those who eagerly annotated their copies of *Absalom and Achitophel* with 'keys' to the persons represented as biblical figures in Dryden's satire. In contrast to Dryden, Behn makes use of the romance mode of pleasure and entertainment, modifiyng its aesthetics for the purposes of didactic propaganda. As she translates propaganda into fiction and fiction

---

[101] See Steen 2002, who reads Behn's novel in terms of an "'instructional pact' [. . .] between the writer and the ruling elite" (92) and interprets the conflation of the discourses of love and politics in the *Love-Letters* as a – precarious and incongruous – strategy of Tory propaganda (100–103, 105–108, 112–15).

into propaganda, she draws on two distinct but, at least in the 1680s, still related modes of reading. She can rely on readers capable of recognising the letters of Silvia and Philander as parodies of third-rate French amatory fiction, embellished with stock phrases from heroic and pastoral poetry. She can also count on her readers' ability or even expectation to regard the characters as satirical and their self-presentation as ironic; readers will immediately have recognised the characters' names as those pseudo-antique or Shakespearean fancy names familiar from the romance tradition, in particular from Sidney's *Arcadia*. Few educated readers in the 1680s will have missed the parodic elements of Behn's novel as she mocks Lord Grey and his lover-in-law as characters of romance fiction.

In order to achieve her purposes, Behn engages in a kind of double translation. She translates a political and erotic scandal into fiction, and she translates a well-developed continental genre (the French, Spanish, and Italian romance) into English. Part one of *Love-Letters* may well be the first English epistolary novel written exclusively in letters (Day 1966, 146). The most important paradigms for this undertaking are the *Histoire amoureuse des Gaules* (1665) by Roger de Bussy-Rabutin, translated in 1682 as *Loves Empire; or, The Amours of the French Court*; the *Mémoires de Mme. la Duchesse de Mazarin* (1675) by César Vichard de St.-Réal, translated in 1676; Madame de La Fayette's *Princesse de Monpensier* (1662, transl. 1666) and *Princesse de Clèves* (1678, transl. 1679); and the anonymous *Lettres portugaises* (1669), translated by Sir Roger L'Estrange as *Five Love-letters from a Nun to a Cavalier* (1678) (Ballaster 1992, Todd 1993, viii, xiv n. 1, Warner 1998, 48). Translations of French fiction dominated the English literary market; Paul Salzman (1985, 114) notes that of 450 new works published in England during the seventeenth century, 213 were translations, and 164 of these were originally French. Even among the 'original' productions, some "were patent rip-offs of French novels" (Warner 1998, 48 n. 2; cf. Day 1966, 27–47).

No wonder then that Behn introduces the text as exactly such a translation from the French, with only a little inventive adaptation thrown in:

> Having when I was at *Paris* last Spring, met with a little Book of Letters, call'd *L'Intregue de Philander & Silvia*, I had a particular fancy, besides my inclinations to translate 'em into English, which I have done as faithfully as I cou'd, only where he speaks of the ingratitude of *Cæsario* to the King, I have added a word or two to his Character that might render it a little more parallel to that of a modern Prince in our Age; for the rest I have kept close to the French.
>
> (1684, sig. A2^{r-v})

Like many prefaces, this one serves to distance the author from the text by declaring her book to be the 'faithful' translation of a found "Book of Letters". However, far from avoiding what Spenser famously called "suspition of present time" (1987, 15), it also serves to present a story based on real life as a French work of fiction, while providing readers with a key to decipher the "parallel [. . .] in our Age". The author, who remains anonymous throughout, introduces her text as a fiction and gives her readers a crucial hint how to decipher its allegorical dimension. Nevertheless, she also connects her novel to the political reality of its moment of writing and its early readers in a way that William Warner has dubbed "taking hold of reality with fiction" (2016, 275).

In these prefatory remarks, the novel introduces itself as a simulation: a simulated translation from the French. At the same time, the reader is called upon to draw a "parallel", i.e. to decipher the 'real' content behind the simulated façade. This sequence of simulation and unmasking is mirrored in the novel. The letters in part one are feigned representations of the writers' emotional authenticity. Their addressee is called upon to decipher the object from the representamen to arrive at the truth within the writer's inward core, 'that within which passeth show', as it were. As a communicative form, the letter promises access to the inwardness that has been materialised in it; at the same time, the letter addresses the obstacles to such genuine communication or 'the marriage of true minds' – the letter, as writing, lacks everything that renders mutual understanding feasible in spoken discourse (voice, accent, tone, mood, gestures):

> And I at last have recourse to my kind Pen: For while I Write methinks I'm talking to thee, I tell thee thus my Soul, while thou methinks art all the while smiling and listening by; this is much easier than silent thought, and my Soul is never weary of this converse, and thus I wou'd speak a Thousand things, but that still, methinks words do not enough express my Soul, to understand that right there requires looks; there is a Rethorick [sic] in looks, in Sighs and silent touches that surpasses all! there is an Accent in the sound of words too, that gives a sense and soft meaning to little things, which of themselves are of trivial value, and insignificant; and by the cadence of the utterance may express a tenderness which their own meaning does not bear; by this I wou'd insinuate that the story of the heart cannot be so well told by this way as by presence and conversation [. . .]. (1684, 110–11)

In the first part of this quotation from Silvia's letter to Philander, Silvia pictures writing as "talking", as a simulated form of conversation. This is said to be "much easier than silent thought" because of the imagined presence of the addressee ("thou methinks art all the while smiling and listening by"). The illusory nature of this fiction of the addressee's presence is clearly marked by the twice repeated "methinks". As the letter continues, scepticism as to the expressibility of the "Soul" or the "heart" by means of written "words" gains the upper hand. One cannot understand another's "Soul" without recourse to the physical, to "looks", "Sighs and silent touches", without what Silvia calls "a Rethorick" of visual, acoustic and physical signs belonging to a dimension of communicative immedicacy ("presence and conversation") that is unavailable in writing. Writing is secondary to "presence".

Privileging "presence and conversation" over writing, Silvia is making a Hobbesian argument about language: some forty years earlier, in the *Elements of Law*, Hobbes had declared:

> Though words be the signs we have of one another's opinions and intentions: because the equivocation of them is so frequent, according to the diversity of contexture, and of the company wherewith they go (which the presence of him that speaketh, our sight of his actions,

and conjecture of his intentions, must help to discharge us of): it must be extreme hard to find out the opinions and meanings of those men that are gone from us long ago, and have left us no other signification thereof but their books [. . .]. (1994, 1.13.8)

Language is riddled with ambiguity ("equivocation") and context-dependent meanings. For Hobbes, as for Silvia, such problems of communication are alleviated by "the presence of him that speaketh, our sight of his actions, and conjecture of his intentions" (ibid.). But Hobbes's account of language points to a deficiency in Silvia's argument: the interpretation of utterances and gestures in personal conversation is as subject to "conjecture", to inferential procedures of interpretation and the probabilistic deciphering of external signs (spoken words, gestures, etc.), as is the reading of a written text. The difficulty is merely alleviated, not resolved. Something faked can give rise to 'alternative facts'; even love can be feigned by means of exterior signs. Silvia's own terminology reveals this when she writes of a "Rethorick" of "looks, [. . .] Sighs and silent touches" (1684, 110). Rhetorical techniques are employed in order to persuade and have no necessary connection to the truth. Conventional critiques of rhetoric, including Hobbes's, could imply the logical or moral falsehood of arguments that were 'sexed up' by rhetorical flourishes. We may conclude from this that, in exposing Silvia's privileging of presence over writing as fallacious, Behn aims to undermine the reader's trust in any claims to authenticity that her characters may be making in their letters. Readers are encouraged to extend their suspicion to the wider claims made by the physicalist rhetoric of romance to disclose authentic human inwardness. Despite all hyperbolic claims to the contrary by the letter-writers themselves, exteriority trumps interiority at every point.

"The Rhetorick of Love is half-breath'd, interrupted words, languishing Eyes, flattering Speeches, broken Sighs, pressing the hand, and falling Tears: Ah how do they not perswade; how do they not charm and conquer; 'twas thus with these soft easie Arts, that *Silvia* first was won! for sure no Arts of speaking cou'd have talk'd my heart away, though you can speak like any God!" (1684, 91, Silvia to Philander) These letters, especially in the light of Silvia's later disappointment at Philander's infidelity, expose the rhetoric of disclosure as inherently fraudulent. As she misreads his letters as authentic revelations of his affections for her, Silvia also misreads Philander's behaviour towards her as sincere, even though she writes about it in terms of a rhetoric intended to "charm and conquer" and in terms of an "Art" rather than natural affection ("soft easie Arts", ibid.). Silvia desires herself – at least at the beginning – to be persuaded, bewitched, and seduced by Philander according to the rules of this art. She thus reveals herself as a bad reader: even as she recognises rhetoric for what it is, she remains incapable of seeing through its 'charms' to the calculating libertinism they conceal. The purpose of the "Rhetorick of Love" is to produce particular effects by means of a particular code: to arouse passion in the other person and to trigger a process of inference by which the other person is made to imagine the passionate interiority of the lover. Frequently, the letter-writers encourage one another to "imagine" their situation, both visually or spatially – "imagine me in the Meadow behind the Grove" (1684, 83) – or mentally and emotionally – "cou'd you but imagine how I am tormentingly divided" (55). Silvia at first remains caught in the mechanisms of this code; later she will make cynical use of it herself. But this will turn her into its victim once again because she begins to depend on it, incapable of envisaging a life for herself outside of the code's performance. The code is seen through but not broken.

As is the opportunism of Philander. In him, erotic and political motivations shade off into one another, intermingling for Behn's propagandistic purposes. By exposing his political opportunism in a letter to Silvia, Philander offers the reader a chance to draw similar conclusions about his erotic disloyalty: "for the world judges of nothing but by the success; that cause is always good that's prosperous, that is ill that's unsuccessful" (1684, 143). Behn mercilessly exposes the rhetoric of love in all its moral relativism and its clichés, which conceal rather than reveal a genuine inwardness. She even caricatures the metaphysical appeals to a union of soul and body: "And shall we, can we disappoint our Fate, no my soft Charmer, our souls were touch't with the same shafts of Love before they had a being in our Bodies, and can we contradict Divine Decrees?" (20, Philander to Silvia)

Similar to Dryden's critique of Achitophel and Zimri as sliding, unstable characters, Behn foregrounds the destabilising effects of the rhetoric of love that her letter-writers experience. She thus indirectly repeats the old moralist argument for self-control by showing the dangers of giving rein to passion: "cou'd you but imagine how I am tormentingly divided, how unresolv'd between violent Love, and cruel Honour: You would say 'twere impossible to fix me any where; or be the same thing for a moment together" (1684, 55, Silvia to Philander). For Philander, sexual passion is explicitly opposed to thought and reason: "sure the excess of joy is far above dull sense, or formal thinking, it cannot stay for ceremonious method" (220). Silvia agrees when, overwhelmed by her passion for Philander, she denounces chastity or "innocent Love" as "a fiction", feminine virtue and morality as a sham: "there lyes a Womans Art, there all her boasted Vertue, it is but well dissembling, and no more" (212). The pornographic passages of Behn's novel contain all the clichés of one-handed reading (Turner 1995), but these clichés are made transparent to the reader when they are wielded *against* the characters. Silvia's mistake, in part one, is her failure to distinguish between art and nature: she insists on reading the code as a manifestation of authentic inwardness.

In part two, this changes because Silvia learns to make profitable use of the rhetoric of love, of what the narrator refers to as "all the little Stratagems and artifices of Lovers" (1685, 74). She turns herself into a calculating libertine. The narrator explicitly criticises her for having given in to Philander "by importunity and opportunity" (41). Philander, in a letter to his friend Octavio, exposes the rhetoric of love employed in part one as fraudulent when he comments on the waning of affection "by time and repetition" and says that when "injoyment takes off the uneasie keeness of the passion [. . .], then we grow reasonable, and consider; we love with prudence then; as Fencers fight with foyls" (144). In this situation, he argues for the necessity of artifice: "then we've recourse to all the little Arts, the aids of flatterers, and dear dissimulation (that help meet to the luke warme Lover) to keep up a good Character of constancy and a right understanding" (144–45). Again, Philander exposes his cynical opportunism when he remarks that for him "a good Character of constancy" is merely a façade. What matters to him is the reputation of virtue, not its practice.

From her servant Antonett, Silvia learns an important and influential alternative idiom of love. This alternative idiom, ironically introduced as coming from "*a young Church man*" (1685, 190) once in love with Antonett, is the mercantilist language of interest, credit, and security that presents amorous exchanges in terms of financial transactions and monetary gain:

> *he us'd to say Women were like Misers, tho they had always love in store, they seldom car'd to part with it, but on very good int'rest and security, Cent per Cent, most commonly heart for heart at least, and for security he said we were most times too unconscionable, we ask'd Vows at least, at worst Matrimony* – [. . .] *he said a Woman was like a Gamester, if on the winning hand, hope, int'rest, and vanity made him play on, besides the pleasure of the play it self; if on the losing, then he continu'd throwing at all to save a stake at last, if not to recover all; so either way they find occasion to continue the game.* ([191]–192])[102]

Asked by Silvia what a gambler is to do who "*has already play'd for all she had, and lost it at a cast*" (192) – a question clearly aimed at testing the mercantilist idiom's limits of applicability –, Antonett replies: "*The young and fair find Credit every where* [. . .]. *I am indeed of that opinion, that love and int'rest always do best together, as two most excellent ingredients in that rare Art of preserving of Beauty.* [. . .] *Love wou'd have us appear always new, always gay, and magnificent, and money alone can render us so*" (192–[193]). She replaces the gambling metaphor (which is about uncertainty, risk, and chance) with a language of investment and credit. The imagery of fortune (gambling) is pushed aside by a focus on wealth and its increase. Antonett's rhetoric finds Silvia's approval because of its economic, down-to-earth realism: "*you are a good manager in love*", she exclaims, "*you are for the frugal part of it*" (192).

This exchange between Antonett and Silvia launches Silvia's career as a female Machiavel. In her adoption of a mercantilist rhetoric of love, Silvia resembles the courtesan Angellica in Behn's successful comedy *The Rover* (1677). The male and female libertines in this play have thoroughly adapted the language of interest and trade to their own purposes of sexual exploits, yet Angellica offers a perspective of transcending the narrow boundaries of libertine inauthenticity when she exclaims

---

[102] In the Yale copy of Behn 1685 on EEBO, p. 191 is erroneously numbered 193; regular pagination continues from 195 (which is actually 193). The last page, 405, is designated as 401. I give corrected page numbers in square brackets.

to Willmore "Oh, that thou wert in earnest!" (5.1.309) In contrast to the more superficial and susceptible Silvia, Angellica is fully aware that her "richest treasure" is her "honour" (rather than youth and beauty): "All the remaining spoil could not be worth /The conqueror's care or value" (5.1.289–91; Behn 1995, 77–78). In *The Rover* as in *Love-Letters*, Behn makes calculated use of the mercantile idiom in order to play it off against the conventional language of heroic poetry and heroic drama. In *The Rover*, Angellica becomes a much more sympathetic character, in stark contrast to the male libertines around her, as soon as she transposes the code of mercantile "value" into the code of love and honour, which for contemporary playgoers functions as a dramatic code of personal authenticity and integrity (see Berensmeyer 2011). We first witness the erosion of this heroic idiom in Silvia in part one when she writes that she is "tormentingly divided [. . .] between violent Love, and cruel Honour" (1684, 55); now it completely breaks down in part two and is replaced by calculated inauthenticity. In *The Rover*'s Angellica, Behn had already criticised this ideology of libertinism as at least partly illusory. In *Love-Letters*, we can also read an implicit critique of Antonett's and Silvia's rhetoric of credit in a few comments by the narrator, who continues to prefer the language of gambling and thus emphasises the aspects of uncertainty inherent in a calculating and strategic approach to love: Philander, for example, has occasion to "consider how he had won her, how by importunity and opportunity she had at last yielded to him, and therefore might to some new Gamster, when he was not by to keep her heart in continual play" (1685, 41). At the end of part two, the narrator confirms the authority of the vocabulary of fortune: "But what wretched changes of Fortune she met with after this, and a miserable Portion of Fate was destined to this unhappy Wanderer; the last Part of *Philanders* Life, and the Third and Last Part of this History, shall most Faithfully relate" (404–[405]).

In part three, the vocabulary of gambling returns in a lengthy speech by Octavio to Silvia. Octavio begins with the conventional opposition between love and reason, passion and argument. Love, he argues, is "*an unthinking Motion of the Soul, that comes and goes as unaccountably as changing Moons, or Ebbs and Flows of Rivers, only with far less certainty*" (1687, 307). The ability for one soul to "beget its Likeness" in another's "Heart" is unpredictable. Octavio illustrates this by analogy to a lottery:

> There is a Chance in Love as well as Life, and oft the most unworthy are preferred; and from a Lottery I might win the Prize from all the venturing Throng with as much Reason, as think my Chance should favour me with Silvia; it might perhaps have been, but 'twas a wonderous Odds against me. Beauty is more uncertain than the Dice; and tho' I ventured like a forward Gamester, I was not yet so vain to hope to win, nor had I once complain'd upon my Fate, if I had never hop'd; but when I had fairly won, to have it basely snatch'd from my Possession, and like a bafled Cully, see it seiz'd by a false Gamester, and look tamely on, has show'd me such a Picture of myself; has given me such Idea's of the Fool, I scorn to look into my easy Heart, and loath the Figure you have made me there. (307–308)

The "Picture" that emerges in this painful process of self-analysis is one of self-loathing and self-accusation. With the phrase "I scorn to look into my easy Heart" Octavio condemns his gullibility, but also his reliance on the rhetoric of gambling and chance on which his comparison depended: having won the lottery, the prize is "seiz'd by a false Gamester." It is not only foolish to trust in the outward display of signs of love, Octavio argues, but also to trust in the exclusive validity of a certain kind of figural analogy – in this case, the language of gambling as an analogy for love. What the text appears to imply is that the contingencies of human inwardness are too complicated to allow themselves to be straitjacketed in only *one* rhetorical code (e.g. 'love', 'gambling', or 'capitalism').

In part two, Silvia begins to use the rhetoric of love for her own advancement in the world. In doing so, she manipulates herself as well as others. The narrator reports: "I have heard she said she verily believ'd that acting and feigning the Lover possest her with a tenderness against her knowledge and Will" (1685, 246). Among the techniques of such manipulation is the reading of amatory fiction: "a Book of Amours in her other hand" (ibid.). The reading of letters, in part one, is supplemented in parts two and three by the reading of novels, French novels in particular. In part three, Octavio reads "little *French* Novels" (1687, 101); their fictional, exotic character and their distance from real life are emphasised by mention of "the Indies" in the same sentence (ibid.). The two text types, letters and novels, are even conflated when Philander sends Octavio a long narrative letter about his amorous adventures which he refers to as a "Novel": "Thus, dear *Octavio*, I have sent you a Novel, instead of a Letter of my first most happy adventure" (1685, 372). For the reader, the artificiality effect of the epistolary novel of part one is here increased in retrospect, as is the distance between reader and characters. The boundaries between authenticity and inauthenticity, fictional letter and novelistic narrative are blurred. The illusion of lovers to decipher each other's mental and emotional states is thwarted by the human capacity to feign and dissemble. In commenting on this capacity, Octavio draws a cynical but appropriate parallel to religious equivocation, in terms that are closely modelled on the fictional contract between authors and readers: "'tis in Love as in Religion too, there's nothing makes their voteries truly happy but being well deceiv'd" (320).[103]

In part three, finally, Silvia sheds all claims to authenticity in love: Philander's infidelity has "cur'd *Silvia* of her Disease of Love; and chaced from her Heart all that Softness which once had so much favoured him" (1687, 153). The rules of love are exchanged for the laws of the marketplace. Silvia turns to the wealthy Octavio

---

[103] The phrase echoes Davenant, who had compared the "deceptions of Poesie" to those of a conjurer whose tricks are not examined for their factual truth but whose "feigned motions" are watched with pleasure, the audience being "content [. . .] to pay for being well deceiv'd" (1971, 11). Via Swift, the expression – shorn of its cynical or satirical overtones – can further be traced to Coleridge's 'willing suspension of disbelief' as a prerequisite of aesthetic experience.

because "a million of Money rendered him so charming" (241); her "Head" is "wholly possess'd with a Million of Gold" (244–45), and both Octavio and Silvia are now "very well pleased with the Artifices with which they gilted each other" (245). At one point, the narrator coldly describes Silvia as "a fair vain Woman" (239). Her 'sentimental education' transforms Silvia into a skilled seducer and a wealthy courtesan, but it leaves her inwardly empty and set on a race against time that she can only lose in the end. Silvia spends her beauty as she spends her money: "[B]ut now, that she had lost all for *Philander* and *Octavio*, and had a Heart to cast away, or give to a new Lover; it was like her Money, she hated to keep to it, and lavish'd it on any Trifle, rather than hoard it, or let it lie by: 'Twas a loss of time her Youth could not spare" (1687, 374). Needless to add that this view of Silvia makes her appear rather like a bad economist than a successfully autonomous woman.

Behn's narrator is not free of misogynist affect. Invoking conventional ideas about the debasement of love in a fallen world (cf. Keeble 1994, 1–13, 45–46, 76), she attributes Adam's fall to Eve's curiosity: "whose [i.e. Adam's] Woman for want of other Seducers listen'd to the Serpent, and for the Love of change wou'd give way even to a Devil, this little Love of Novelty and knowledge has been intail'd upon her daughters ever since, and *I* have known more Women rendered unhappy and miserable from this torment of curiosity, which they bring upon themselves, than have ever been undone by less villainous Men" (1685, 210, emphasis original).

In presenting what happens when individualities attempt to translate themselves into textualities, and in pointing out what is lost in such a translation, Behn – similar to Dryden – appears to promulgate a politically conservative ideology. Her language is attuned to the changes that occur not only in politics but also in the private sphere and in the religious discourse of her time, as she applies tropes of mobility, circulation, trade, and contingency (gambling) to the idiom of love. Her characters need to reorient themselves in the empty space between a disintegrated system of order and a new one that is as yet only weakly institutionalised. They have no stable selves but are driven hither and thither by their affects and passions. Behn criticises her characters' use of communication (written, spoken and physical sign language) to feign an inward dimension that is inauthentic and artificial. The 'natural' human condition of these characters is the will to power and domination, sexual as well as political. "She naturally lov'd Power and Dominion" is a characteristic comment of the narrator on Silvia (1687, 59). It is a strikingly Hobbesian psychology and anthropology that Behn appears to follow in her novel; the political message, in Behn as much as in Hobbes, is an argument for the need to control the passions and to institute a strong sovereign in order to keep the centrifugal forces of individual desires in check. At the same time, she argues for the necessity, even as she presents the difficulty, of reading and interpreting external signs for internal conditions: after all, such signs are all the evidence we have about the world and the inner lives of others.[104] But it would be a severe mistake to take signs for realities. In this respect, most of her characters, the men above all, turn out to be bad readers – to their own detriment.[105] Silvia learns her reading lesson, but only to the extent that she becomes as morally depraved as her male counterparts whose strategies of simulation she adopts and imitates. It is left to the reader to draw further conclusions about the characters' behaviour, male as well as female, and to search for alternatives.

As I hope to have shown, *Love-Letters Between a Noble-Man and his Sister* hinges on the impossibility of knowing another person's innermost thoughts and feelings; the novel illustrates this predicament by investigating the practice of writing and reading letters. This impossibility pertains to the relationships among the readers of letters in the novel, who remain intransparent to one another, as well as to the relations between the characters and the narrator. The narrator herself is clearly not as privileged in his or her access to information about the characters as (s)he would like to be (on the question of the narrator's gender, see also Chernaik 1998, 25).

In addition to her more topical propagandistic concerns, what Behn appears to have been after is to teach the reader of her novel to see beyond the duplicity of rhetorical codes, to read ironically, and to read according to the method of probable inference. In the process, the reader is indirectly encouraged to develop a code of moral superiority, a code of politeness and rationality – the Tory rationality of constancy, of keeping one's vows – so as to oppose the destabilising flux of desire embodied in the rhetoric of amatory fiction and the 'enthusiastic' subjectivity that it engenders. This kind of subjectivity, seen and judged from a Tory perspective, can appear in no other terms than those of the religious zealotry of the 1640s and 50s. Later Enlightenment objections to the novel as a form of entertainment are partly prefigured in Behn's early example of the genre, in her ironic combination of

---

104 This didactic purpose of Behn's novel – which is never openly stated as a programme – is well captured in Jagodzinski 1999a, 149: "Silvia's 'discoveries' of herself [. . .] revoke any certainties we might have that what appears in print is 'true,' that what individuals present to the world truly has some correspondence with their inner lives". Yet I would contend, against Jagodzinski's view, that Silvia is not simply "the mouthpiece for the author" (149) because this would make a nonsense of Behn's anti-Whig propaganda. Similarly, I think it is an anachronistic – but typical – modern misunderstanding to miss the ironies in Behn's presentation of Silvia and Philander as "the new Adam and Eve" unconstrained by customary, man-made laws (151) and to read their sexual transgression as "the exercise of personal choice" (150) as if this were a post-1960s novel. Alternatively, Warner suggests to group characters according to their (in)capacity to honour vows (Octavio and Calista vs. Philander and Silvia), the "final assertion of the value of vows" in the novel – Octavio's taking holy orders – conforming to Behn's "royalist argument" (1998, 83).
105 This point is noted by Jagodzinski 1999a, 159, who sees Silvia, in contrast to the men, as "the astute author of her fate, who finally determines their place in her life and the role men should serve for her". For similar 'optimistic' readings of female sexuality in *Love-Letters*, see Pearson 1991; Todd 1996, cf. Wehrs 1992 and Warner 1998, 66–87 for a less rosy view.

sensual titillation and rational critique, pornography and moral censure. *Love-Letters* offers a reflection on reading that has to be enacted by the reader. The novel stops short of preaching a didactic lesson. Instead, it introduces a new and forward-looking literary epistemology. It encourages readers to navigate the text in search of significant signs, to resist identification with the characters, and to see beyond the various codes that the characters and the narrator employ to make, and to make sense of, their world. Readers learn not to trust the asymmetrical correlation between a hermetic interiority and a (compensatory but deceptive) hermeneutics of exteriority. None of these codes are ultimately stable or permanent. Their relativity and volatility are the key findings of a semiotic reading of this novel. They give rise to a structure of perspectival contingency, a literary form that will prove foundational as it develops across subsequent decades, even centuries, and that we recognise as the novel.

'This Deed of Trust': Law, Literature, and the Unbearable Politeness of Being in Congreve's *The Way of the World* (1700)

In *The Human Condition*, Hannah Arendt introduces a useful distinction between two types of society: one that relies on "rule and sovereignty" and one that relies on "contracts and treaties". She elaborates: "The danger and the advantage inherent in all bodies politic that rely on contracts and treaties is that they, unlike those that rely on rule and sovereignty, leave the unpredictability of human affairs and the unreliability of men as they are, using them merely as the medium, as it were, into which certain islands of predictability are thrown and in which certain guideposts of reliability are erected" (Arendt 1958, 245). A society based on contracts accepts as fact that human beings are unreliable and unpredictable, and it uses these imperfections as a sort of unstable but flexible foundation for a commonwealth based on legal (rather than absolute) "predictability". This contractual mindset is also part of the cultural contexture of Congreve's comedy of manners *The Way of the World*, set in London a good decade after the events of the Glorious Revolution of 1688 and the signing of the Bill of Rights in 1689, which introduced a system of constitutional monarchy and empowered the British Parliament. His play explores the elasticity as well as the instability of a world based on legal arrangements.

At least since Richard Kroll's substantial work on Congreve (1986, 2002, 2007), it is something of a truism that "Congreve's comedies of contract speak directly to the fraught relationship between contract theory and social reality" (Caldwell 2015, 188). This section is a further contribution to this topic from the perspective of contingency; I will read Congreve's *Way of the World* as an exploration of social forms – manners – of trust and politeness, which are recognised in this play as media in Arendt's sense for a durable and reliable processing of social disagreements.

As we have seen in the previous section, the genres of Restoration comedy and the early novel focus on problems of contingency in the interaction between individualities and textualities. They encourage audiences or readers to recognise characters' weaknesses and strengths as they become manifest in communication, and to become aware of blind spots in the characters' self-perceptions. Both genres thus engage their readers in practical techniques of self-monitoring and observing others, encouraging readers to question and improve their own behaviour. This is particularly important among members of the upper-middle class, whose social status rests on complex relationships of observation and interaction as well as on the cultivation of a "refined sociability" (Klein 1994, 4). A key demographic of Restoration comedy, this elite reproduces itself according to conspicuous theatrical rituals of mutual exposure, display, and control. This, in turn, is observed, reflected, and intensified on stage.

In Congreve's *The Way of the World* (1700), the interactions of this elite take place in spaces of leisure, recreation, and retreat – but never without being observed by others. Polite society is never absent. Congreve's characters play cards in a chocolate-house (a clear class marker, more elegant and less political than a coffee-house), they promenade in St James's Park, or congregate in the house of Lady Wishfort, the fifty-five-year-old widow of a country knight to whom most of the characters (with the exception of the servants) are in some way related. The softer, more soothing beverages consumed in the play (chocolate, various liqueurs and other alcoholic drinks) equally betoken a more relaxed attitude and belong to a more intimate, 'private' atmosphere of 'refined sociability'. The society presented in *The Way of the World* is a cultured and well-propertied elite, attuned to theatre audiences of the period, twelve years after James II had successfully been removed from the English throne in favour of William and Mary.

The revolution of 1688/89, later apostrophised as 'glorious', imposed constitutional limits on the monarchy and fixed a few central rules of policy (no taxation without representation, no standing army, no Catholic successor) that were to become the cornerstones of a new political settlement in the eighteenth century as well as for a "Whig interpretation of history" (Butterfield 1931, Pocock 1985, 215–310) that saw these developments as a necessary teleological sequence rather than as a haphazard though felicitous series of events. Administrative and economic reforms, begun under Charles II, were continued by William, Mary, and Anne, helping transform England into a commercial society whose goal was economic and territorial expansion (witness the foundation of the Bank of England, 1694, and union with Scotland, 1707). This was only possible because the fundamental internal divisions and religious differences of the seventeenth century – now embodied by the Jacobites, loyal supporters of the Stuart claim to the throne – could be contained. Relative political stability meant that material, intellectual, and administrative resources were set free for other pursuits (Spurr 1998).

Without a doubt, newly won freedoms also entailed new problems. Congreve, even though he approves of the improved social and political conditions after 1688, does not harbour illusions about this. What he emphasises in *The Way of the World* is a distinct difference in *style* and social *tact* between an older way of brutal and exploitative acquisitiveness and a new, more refined, more polite, and, above all, legally legitimised form of acquisitiveness that is instituted in the new political order. The old and new style both belong to the complex of "possessive individualism" that Macpherson discerned in Locke's political thought (1962), but they articulate and practice this strategic positioning of the individual in the social game in radically different ways.[106] Both styles are portrayed in the play: Fainall is the old-style rake and libertine whose name indicates his acquisitiveness (he 'would fain have all') as well as his readiness to resort to tricks and lies (not shunning to 'feign all'). He relies on methods of extortion and blackmail that curiously resemble the political intrigues of the Stuart court. His opponent, the admirable Mirabell, makes clever but not illegal use of the loopholes of the law to achieve his goals: to secure both a wife and a fortune for himself. The manipulations that Mirabell engages in (passing off his servant as 'Sir Rowland', a potential noble husband, to Lady Wishfort) are comic and revelatory, even in an Enlightenment sense of critically exposing the intellectual and moral shortcomings of others, whereas the machinations of Fainall and his mistress Mrs Marwood – which fail in the end – are depicted as more sinister and tragic.

Political readings of *The Way of the World* have concentrated on Fainall and Mirabell as allegories of James II and William III, respectively – without stating this hypothesis quite so bluntly. If one takes these names as standing not for individual monarchs but for the more general social trends and mentalities they have come to represent, such a reading can still shed a useful light on the play (see, e. g., Braverman 1993). But *The Way of the World* is more than mere propaganda for the new regime. It plays very subtly with different forms of attitude and behaviour in society, different orientations towards concepts of trust, consent, and contract; in this way, it addresses the constitutional foundations of Williamite England on the threshold of the eighteenth century. As a personification of Protestant England's darkest fears, James II was still alive at the time, and fears of his return, although diminished, may still have been present enough to imbue the rivalry between Fainall and Mirabell (between the duplicitous and the miraculous) with added political significance.

Earlier readings of *The Way of the World* have emphasised the subtlety and care with which Congreve presents and arranges the "contradictory pressures of affection, kinship and law" in the play (Love 1974, 106). Its social world consists of a

---

106 The pervasiveness of gambling metaphors in *The Way of the World* has often been commented upon. See, e g., Wagoner 1968, Kimball 1977.

complex network of kinship ties; conflicts arise between private inclinations and dynastic obligations. These conflicts are complicated by the necessity of acting in accordance with legal constraints imposed on individual passions and desires – a necessity that is accepted even by the plotters. The characters' life choices are encompassed by a complex network of legal documents: wills, deeds, entails, and marriage contracts. The level on which *The Way of the World* most poignantly registers the political and constitutional changes after 1688 is less the potentially allegorical contrast between two types of rake but the observation to what extent legal and contractual arrangements pervade human lives. Like the political world of Locke, Congreve's society is based on the institutional and instrumental foundations of the law.

This foundation has a number of consequences for the ways in which conflicts can be acted out on stage. Legal arrangements are in principle open to revision and do not always provide sufficient protection from what Hannah Arendt (1958, 245) calls "the unreliability of men" (and women). The law in *The Way of the World* is no longer, as in Dryden's *Absalom and Achitophel*, of divine origin and a guarantee of eternal stability but is subject to the contingency vectors of human behaviour. That said, contracts and deeds do enjoy a binding force that is widely accepted (and whose breach would have severe consequences). The legitimacy of the law is secured no longer by theology but by society. The world of Congreve's play is utterly "post-godly" (Klein 1994, 9; cf. Palmes 1990, 78). The Church is only mentioned in connection with obtaining a marriage certificate (until 1754, marriages could only be solemnised according to canon law). The description of the wedding ceremony is devoid of any festive character:

> Sir, there's such a Coupling at *Pancras*, that they stand behind one another, as 'twere in a Country Dance. Ours was the last Couple to lead up; and no hopes appearing of dispatch, besides, the Parson growing hoarse, we were afraid his Lungs would have fail'd before it came to our turn; so we drove round to *Duke's Place*; and there they were riveted in a trice.
> (Congreve 1967, 1.113–19)

Significantly, the term "Christian Commonwealth" is used (apparently without any memory of its political history) by Lady Wishfort to contrast her social ideals of civility and good breeding to the graceless behaviour of her nephew Sir Wilfull Witwoud, whom she calls a "beastly Pagan" (4.440–41). Religion is now clearly subservient to the "dominant paradigm" of gentlemanly politeness as refined sociability (Klein 1994, 9). Hence, the characters' impulses towards morally correct behaviour spring from what they perceive as *social* rather than religious necessities, from what Lady Wishfort calls "Decorums" (3.158) – above all, from the pressure of being observed and morally judged by other people, a pressure that is articulated in terms of virtue, reputation, and 'good breeding'.

The discrepancy between a superficial appearance of respectability and prudence on the one hand and an inward longing for imprudent indulgence is comically explored to great effect in the character of the aging Lady Wishfort ('wish-for-it'), whose mirror scene in Act III is nearly as famous as that in Shakespeare's *Richard II* (of which it might even be an echo):

> *Foible.* Your Ladyship has frown'd a little too rashly, indeed Madam. There are some Cracks discernable in the white Vernish.
>
> *Lady Wishfort.* Let me see the Glass —— Cracks, say's thou? Why I am arrantly flea'd – I look like an old peel'd Wall. Thou must repair me *Foible,* before Sir *Rowland* comes; or I shall never keep up to my Picture. (3.144–50)

As Lady Wishfort has realised, keeping up appearances is what lends stability to images of the self ("my Picture") – a stability that is constantly endangered in the company of other people. Lady Wishfort has forced herself into the role of an actress performing herself. It is highly ironic but also appropriate that we should be confronted with the most poignant analysis of the social constitution of subjectivity only when the scene has finally shifted from the public places of the chocolate house (Act I) and St. James's Park (Act II) to the private boudoir of Lady Wishfort in Act III. In the mirror scene, the public image of Lady Wishfort is contrasted with, and deconstructed by, a scene of intimacy that unmasks the artificiality of Lady Wishfort's public appearance and its complete dependence on her maid's cosmetic skills: "Foible's function is not simply to dress Lady Wishfort, but virtually to put her together, physically and psychically, to meet the world" (Erickson 1984, 344). Congreve's comedy is particularly good at revealing the artificiality of masks and the characters' carefully preserved surfaces, but it also preserves the characters' integrity for the audience, in a manner that points forward to the social comedies of Oscar Wilde two centuries later.

As in Aphra Behn's *Love-Letters Between a Nobleman and His Sister,* the distinction between inwardness and external appearance is vital to this play. Like Behn's novel, *The Way of the World* is also, as we shall see, about reading and about dealing with "linguistic and semiological uncertainties" (Kroll 1986, 731). The dropping of the mask for the sake of authenticity is presented as an ideal but rarely put into practice, because it is based on the precondition of mutual agreement and feeling secure. Even then, full disclosure may not always be desirable. The key scene in this respect is the proviso scene, in which the lovers Mirabell and Millamant, Lady Wishfort's niece, negotiate the rules for their relationship in Act IV. They specify a higher than usual degree of *natural* affection, which is only possible because, through the legal instrument of the nuptial contract, husband and wife become (at least ideally) equal partners. There is some critical debate about whether the proviso scene really allows Millamant to become Mirabell's equal (Love 1974, 99, 106) or whether it merely ensures her submission to a patriarchal order (Kraft 1989, Gill 1996); the fact that the terms of the contract are being discussed by both in a fairly equal manner seems at least to give Millamant a bigger say in her own destiny than was usually the case at the time. The term 'contract' is used by Millamant herself (4.281); it appears to have been commonly used to refer to the formal act of 'spousals' or betrothal which usually preceded a marriage according to canon law; this ceremony had to take place before witnesses, a fact that Millamant alludes to by enlisting the oncoming Mrs Fainall as "a witness to the Sealing of the Deed" (4.281–82). Whereas an official betrothal would be legally and morally binding, the type of contract Mirabell and Millamant engage in "has no power to compel a marriage" (Alleman 1942, 7; on the need for witnesses, 5; cf. Caldwell 2015).

Beside straight-lacing in pregnancy, close friendships with other women, and the consumption of exotic beverages, Mirabell forbids his future wife the use of masks, excessive theatricals, and cosmetics (in direct but implicit contrast to Millamant's aunt Wishfort):

> Mirabell. Item, I Article, that you continue to like your own Face, as long as I shall. And while it passes Current with me, that you endeavour not to new Coin it. To which end, together with all Vizards for the day, I prohibit all Masks for the Night, made of oil'd skins and I know not what [. . .]. (4.245–49)

Mirabell is probably being ironic when he refers to "*Tea, Chocolate* and *Coffee*" as "Native" drinks (4.265–66) as distinct from mostly alcoholic "Foreign Forces" (4.271–72) such as Lady Wishfort is very fond of, or even addicted to. Mirabell's interdiction of female confidants has been explained as a reflex of his fear of female 'same-sex confederacies' generally and because of his treatment at the hands of Lady Wishfort's 'cabal' in particular (see Kraft 1989, 27, 31). Millamant's own proviso, on the other hand, forbids excessive familiarity in the company of others:

> Millamant. [. . .] Good *Mirabell* don't let us be familiar or fond, nor kiss before folks [. . .] Nor goe to *Hide-Park* together the first *Sunday* in a New Chariot, to provoke Eyes and Whispers [. . .]. Let us never Visit together, nor go to a Play together. But let us be very strange and well bred: let us be as strange as if we had been married a great while; and as well bred as if we were not marri'd at all. (4.200–209)

These prenuptial conditions demonstrate the pervasiveness of the legal, contractual model of society even in personal relationships of intimacy. Congreve's characters handle this with aplomb and irony. It seems as if it takes an institutionally valid, semi-public form to realise the greater degree of privacy and naturalness that the couple demand of each other. It is the *form* of the contract, not its details, that allows Mirabell and Millamant to become shared sovereigns of their matrimonial existence. Whereas for Lady Wishfort, public façade and private self-care are one and the same, for Mirabell, but even more for Millamant, the gap between intimacy and the public sphere is a life-changing problem that can only be solved by privately appropriating public instruments of law.

Despite the superficial flippancy of their dialogue, Millamant and Mirabell use the proviso scene to employ the binding power of law as a counterweight to human contingency and uncertainty. Legal discourse offers them a middle way between the extremes of excessive artificiality and excessive sincerity, between a Hobbesian and a Puritan model of social behaviour. What, in most of the other characters, is an unsuccessful struggle between nature and art, is here transformed into a mutual acceptance of faults that transcends the narrow terms of the nature/art opposition. Anticipating this solution, Mirabell explains earlier in the play: "I like her [sc. Millamant] with all her Faults; nay, like her for her Faults. Her Follies are so natural, or so artful, that they become her; and those Affectations which in another Woman wou'd be odious, serve but to make her more agreeable" (1.159–63). Mirabell continues by presenting a literally mechanical 'analysis' of his beloved in terms that curiously seem to echo the mechanical materialism of Hobbes in presenting his concept of the "Artificiall Man" in the introduction to *Leviathan* (Hobbes 1996, 9):

> I took her to pieces; sifted her and separated her Failings; I study'd 'em, and got 'em by rote. The Catalogue was so large, that I was not without hopes, one Day or other to hate her heartily: To which end I so us'd my self to think of 'em, that at length, contrary to my Design and Expectation, they gave me every Hour less and less disturbance; 'till in a few Days it became habitual to me, to remember 'em without being displeas'd. They are now grown as familiar to me as my own Frailites; and in all probability in a little time longer I shall like 'em as well.
>
> (1.164–74, 399)

Fainall, however, is the one who more readily and easily identifies himself as a Hobbesian in his dealings with others. Like Valentine in *Love for Love*, he cancels all "Difference between continued Affectation and Reality" (*Love for Love* 3.40–41). Referring to Mirabell's previous attempts to secure Lady Wishfort's fortune, Fainall remarks: "Had you dissembl'd better, Things might have continu'd in the state of Nature" (*Way* 1.66–67). His mistress, Mrs Marwood, equally reveals her absolutist leanings by speaking about love in political language: "Love will resume its Empire in our Breasts, and every Heart, or soon or late, receive and readmit him as its lawful Tyrant" (2.25–27). Her talk of 'readmitting' a "lawful Tyrant" must have had unmistakable Jacobite associations for audiences in the early eighteenth century.

When Mirabell refers to materialist epistemology and psychology in Act I, he is at least partly being witty – he is, after all, speaking to Fainall when he makes these superficially callous remarks about Millamant. In the course of the play, Mirabell takes the opposite trajectory of Fainall, who in the final scene denounces his wife as a "thing" and Millamant's servant Mincing as "an Insignificant thing" (5.492–93). In the proviso scene, Mirabell and Millamant distance themselves from their Hobbesian environment by affirming an almost utopian ideal of a 'natural' (i.e. unconventional) marriage based on mutual affection, as a return to a (Lockean rather than Hobbesian) state of nature. The contract does not transform Millamant and Mirabell into objects; on the contrary, its binding power is the medium for their autonomy.

Yet what precisely is the function of law in this conflict between competing concepts of naturalness and affectation (and not only between concepts, but also between their underlying value systems, the ordering principles of social life)? The law does not provide stability in and of itself; on the contrary, its very regularity, formal closure, and general validity expose the vulnerability of traditional family and class structures. The law can be instrumentalised against the traditional order, its effectiveness can be used as a threat. This is the case when Mrs Marwood (Fainall's cynical lover) warns Lady Wishfort, who values her reputation above anything else, against the dangers of public scandal should Fainall seek legal action against Mirabell on grounds of adultery and file for separation (5.1.208–227).[107] Lady Wishfort is less afraid of the trial itself than of its ugly consequences: public exposure and humiliation, social death. She is particularly sensitive on this point because she likes to see herself, in the words of Robert A. Erickson, as "the head of an upper-class jury of matrons discussing the social deaths they themselves have helped to promote" (1984, 342). This 'cabal' is vividly described by Fainall (at 1. 50–54) as "com[ing] together like the Coroner's Inquest, to sit upon the murder'd Reputations of the Week". In the drastic language of Mrs Marwood, Lady Wishfort is made to imagine such humiliation as a physical and sexual act of violation (Loftis 1996, 573–74). The law thus appears as an instrument that is at least double-edged; cutting both ways, it is an institution whose role in social life remains ambiguous, asymmetrically poised between nature and artifice.

It is important to realise that the power of law in Congreve's play resides not merely in the capacity to preclude Machiavellian manipulations and attempts to secure one's personal advantage over others – a staple of Restoration patterns of comedy that is modified but not abolished in *The Way of the World*. On the contrary, Congreve uses it for another turn of the screw of such comic patterns: the power of law motivates his characters to exploit the conditions and possibilities of *legal* manipulations to the utmost, while being able to trust in the stability granted by legal structures (Hurley 1971, 194). The "deed of trust" (5.618) between Mirabell and Mrs Fainall that decides the conflict between the two male antagonists is a legal conveyance of property but it also serves as a metaphorical reminder of the importance of trust or confidence as a foundation of the modern civil order. The Lockean

---

107 Mrs Fainall, Lady Wishfort's daughter and formerly the widow Languish, had an affair with Mirabell before the events of the play unfold. According to the law, Fainall could consider a suit in an ecclesiastical court, a suit for 'criminal conversation' in either the Court of Common Pleas or the Court of King's Bench, or (if all else failed) a parliamentary divorce – a legal device that had only been introduced in 1698 (Alleman 1942, 121–24, 135–37). Loftis 1996 places Restoration divorce legislation in the context of a 'civilising process' in parallel to the replacement of duelling by monetary compensation as "the currency of honor" (562). Fainall and Mirabell do not fight a duel, they fight in court (at least in the imagination of Fainall and Mrs Marwood). Yet such a trial would have inevitably given rise to a public scandal (see also Stone 1990).

dimension of this concept and its use in Whig ideology as an oppositional term to 'tyranny' again reflects on the play's political stance towards the seismic shifts in late seventeenth-century English society – to 'readmit' tyranny is out of the question.

The double meaning of "deed" as both action and legal document asserts the instrumental power of law in shaping and transforming social reality. It is related to the pun on the word "instrument" as a legal, non-violent parallel to the use of physical force, for example in the duel, as asserted by the aptly named Sir Wilfull Witwoud:

> *Sir Wilfull.* And, Sir I assert my right; and will maintain it in defiance of you Sir, and of your Instrument. S'heart an you talk of an Instrument Sir, I have an old *Fox* by my Thigh shall hack your Instrument of *Ram Vellum* to shreds, Sir. It shall not be sufficient for a *Mittimus* or a *Taylor's* measure; therefore withdraw your Instrument Sir, or by'r Lady I shall draw mine.
> (5.423–29)

The newly affirmed power of legal structures effectively changes the manner in which manipulation and dissimulation can take place. In *The Way of the World*, the successful manipulator Mirabell gains a decisive advantage over his opponent Fainall because he *has already* exploited the lawful boundaries of legal arrangements "with considerable grace and polish, and in a spirit bordering on the aesthetic" (Love 1974, 88) The power of law makes possible a condition of social (and, within the boundaries of the family, political and dynastic) stability; it enforces and rewards the non-violent solution of conflicts. In this dispensation, theological foundations (so prevalent during the Civil War and its aftermath) are no longer important. Instead, we see the rise of a new norm of mandatory communicative behaviour: politeness. Despite their differences, the characters generally treat each other with deference and politeness, and in some cases super-politeness, even though they may despise or hate each other. The play's highly polished linguistic surface reflects the relatively new discursive norm of politeness and conceals the latent presence of a Hobbesian competition of everyone against everyone else.[108]

Congreve's main characters are the children of neoclassical discourse, using manipulative words and (legal) deeds rather than brute force for their own advancement; they accuse each other in the most indirect, polite, and formal language conceivable. In the very first confrontation between Mirabell and Fainall, growing mutual anger is signalled by increasing linguistic formality. This scene of the two antagonists playing cards also registers a shift in the representation of social life and interpersonal competition from the metaphorical framework of physical combat to one of gambling and strategic planning. Instead of a duel at the end, we get to watch a card game at the beginning. In hindsight, the first lines of the play ("*Fainall.* Have we done? / *Mirabell.* What you please. I'll play on to entertain you," 1.2–3) reveal that Mirabell has in fact

---

[108] On the range of meanings of the term 'politeness' in late seventeenth and early eighteenth century English culture, see Klein 1994, 3–8.

already secured his success through a prior legal arrangement with Mrs. Fainall. Thus Fainall's name is ironically turned against himself, as he himself becomes – is, from the outset – the victim of Mirabell's superior strategy. However, not all of Mirabell's stratagems succeed; his most notable failure is the elaborate scheme involving 'Sir Rowland' to make Lady Wishfort agree to his marrying her niece Millamant. What is most impressive about him is not his talent for scheming but his verbal and rhetorical skill in gaining the help of others (Love 1974, 91).

It is a tribute to the stability of the law that Mirabell at the end does not have to fear Fainall's revenge: "his [sc. Fainall's] Circumstances are such, he must of Force comply" (5.614–15). The legal order has a say in people's financial situation. Due to his legal trickery of holding Mrs Fainall's estate in trust, Mirabell is secure in his financial control over Fainall even before the play has begun – indeed, we learn that Mrs Fainall (Lady Wishfort's daughter) has only agreed to become Fainall's wife in the first place because her former lover Mirabell managed to persuade her to do so in order to preserve her reputation (the implication being a suspected pregnancy). Thus, even though the law is not the solution to all problems – it is in fact a crucial part of the problem in those instances where it is used as an instrument of villainy, as in the case of Mrs Marwood's threat to Lady Wishfort – it does function as a regulative resource that introduces a certain amount of reliability and fixity to the contingencies of human nature.

The world depicted in *The Way of the World* is entirely social. Society, also in the more immediate physical sense of company, is its only frame of reference. It is "a world in which characters scrutinize each other unremittingly" (Kroll 1986, 735). As Mrs Foresight remarks in *Love for Love*: "How can any Body be happy, while they're in perpetual fear of being seen and censur'd?" (2.432–33) In this atmosphere of permanent scrutiny, the worst catastrophe that can occur is the loss of reputation or loss of face. The face is the most important body part, the key medium of non-verbal communication in social interaction, a material interface between inward being and outward show. The face is something you 'put on'. When Mirabell reports on his tacit exclusion from Lady Wishfort's all-female cabal, he says "they all put on their grave Faces" (1.29–30); "put not on that strange Face", Mrs Fainall begs Foible (3.188). But the face is also a fragile and volatile medium, subject to involuntary revelations, as when Lady Wishfort's carefully made-up façade, her "Oeconomy of Face" (3.141–42) suddenly 'cracks' or when Millamant's blushes give away her emotion (3.286–89). Blushing is usually deciphered by others as a form of confession. The rather unrefined Petulant "always take[s] blushing either for a Sign of Guilt, or ill Breeding" (1. 536–37). In their crucial dialogue in Act II, Fainall says to Mrs Marwood: "I have seen the warm Confession red'ning on your Cheeks, and sparkling from your Eyes" (2. 140–41). Marwood urges Millamant to "appear bare fac'd" and confess to loving Mirabell (3.314). The face is the exterior manifestation of one's true personality. This physiognomic theory is presented most dramatically in the character of Lady Wishfort, whose servant professes not to recognise her before she has put on her makeup: "Why truly Sir, I cannot safely swear to her Face in a Morning, before she is dress'd. 'Tis like I may give a shrew'd guess at her by this time" (3.461–63).

The face is a text that can be read; its 'hieroglyphs' are a visual language that must be decoded (Novak 1984). The textuality of visible facial signs is as important in social conversation as the spoken word, because it may reveal what words might otherwise obscure or deny. In the social texture of *The Way of the World*, individuality is constantly exposed to acts of deciphering. Social success is therefore defined as the preservation of 'face' (in the sense of preserving one's dignity and reputation); individual success depends on the ability to realise one's goals without loss of face in the sight of others. Wit is the ability to discriminate among different levels of discourse (Kroll 1986, 732) and to use such discrimination effectively, i. e. in a face-saving manner. In order to maintain this precarious balance between individual and social factors, communicative norms like civility, politeness, and tact are of supreme importance because they offer protection from harm.

In *The Way of the World*, all kinds of objects are made subservient to the concerns of refined sociability and social tact. The use of writing, like the use of religious discourse, serves certain social needs and expectations and ultimately has no legitimacy in its own right. Texts are functionalised as 'instruments' whose content is of far less importance than their form and use. This concerns not only the legal documents in the play. "I writ. I read nothing", says Petulant (5.531, 476), who aided Mirabell in drawing up the decisive deed of trust but claims not to remember "any thing of what that Parchment contain'd" (5.528–29, 476). Memory, in any case, is not the strong point of the splenetic minor characters in this play: "No, but prithee excuse me, – my Memory is such a Memory", says Witwoud by way of apology already during the first act (1.273–74). Later on, he attaches some strategic usefulness to forgetting: "The Devil take him that remembers first, I say" (3.447–48).

The characters' weak recollection of past events also extends to cultural memory, as when Lady Wishfort fails to remember any historical political implications of the phrase "Christian Commonwealth" (4.440–41). Similarly, the edifying literature in her closet is not intended for reading but serves to present her façade of pious respectability. Speaking to Mrs Marwood on Millamant's education in a Puritan and antitheatrical spirit, Lady Wishfort remarks: "O, she wou'd have swooned at the sight or name of an obscene Play-Book" (5.201–202). Yet the way she recommends this reading matter to Mrs Marwood perhaps betrays a more recent and fashionable attitude to reading than would have been considered appropriate by the Puritan authors themselves: "There are Books over the Chimney – *Quarles* and *Pryn*, and the *Short View of the Stage*, with *Bunyan's* Works to entertain you" (3.64–67).[109] Here the word 'entertain'

---

[109] Bunyan's *Works* had been published in 1692, Francis Quarles's *Emblems* in 1635; both were highly popular pious literature. William Prynne's *Histrio-Mastix* (1633) and Jeremy Collier's *Short View of the Stage* (1698) were antitheatrical polemics, the latter containing an attack on Congreve's early plays.

is certain to generate some laughter with audiences who know, or at least know of, the pious nature of these works; the joke hinges on the word 'entertain' as meaning 'to provide amusement or enjoyment' (*OED* IV.15a) as well as, more neutrally, 'to occupy the attention of a person' (OED IV.14.a). The joke can be simultaneouly at Lady Wishfort's expense and that of the pious authors mentioned.

The placing of the books in Lady Wishfort's "closet" is significant because it shows that they are not intended to be read but merely for display. In a fashionable household, a 'closet' or 'cabinet' was a very small room adjacent to a 'chamber' or bedroom, which could be used to "house whatever treasures its owner most prized, to be shown off to an audience of, at most, two at a time. [. . .] The overmantel in a cabinet provided the perfect display space for collections of curios and china" (Picard 1997, 37, 46–47). *Books do furnish a room*, to quote the title of a novel by Anthony Powell. Here they are a part of the external projection of Lady Wishfort's self as she wishes herself to be seen: a serious, high-minded person. This façade receives some cracks when, in a situation of crisis, she reveals herself as a reader of pastoral romances: "Dear *Marwood*, let us leave the World, and retire by our selves and be *Shepherdesses*" (5.134–35). Serious reading, on the other hand, has fallen out of fashion in Congreve's polite society. Likewise, a heavily 'literary' style of writing personal letters is denounced as an affectation:

> Witwoud. [. . .] A messenger, a Mule, a Beast of Burden, he has brought me a Letter from the Fool my Brother, as heavy as a Panegyrick in a Funeral Sermon, or a Copy of Commendatory Verses from one Poet to another. And what's worse, 'tis as sure a forerunner of the Author, as an Epistle Dedicatory. (1.243–48)

Witwoud's brother, Sir Wilfull, subsequently accuses him of having changed "the Stile of [his] Letters" as well has his writing paper (now "gilt round the Edges, no broader than a *Subpœna*"), 3.540–42. Letters are also denounced by Millamant: "O, ay, Letters —— I had letters —— I am persecuted with Letters – I hate Letters – No Body knows how to write Letters; and yet one has 'em, one does not know why —— They serve one to pin up one's Hair" (2.359–62). In the following dialogue with Witwoud, Millamant adds that she only pins up her hair with letters written in verse rather than prose: "I fancy ones Hair wou'd not curl if it were pinn'd up with Prose" (2.366). Her remark can be read as a witty and polite rejection of Witwoud's advances (and as a hint at Molière's Mounsieur Jourdain in *Le bourgeois gentilhomme*, 1670); it also underlines the other characters' lack of poetic sensibility and their merely cosmetic use of literature. Millamant, in fact, places great value on language, literacy, and education: "an illiterate Man's my Aversion. I wonder at the Impudence of any Illiterate Man, to offer to make Love. [. . .] Ah! to marry an Ignorant! that can hardly Read or Write" (3.422–27). Petulant's reply is quite typical of the attitude of most other characters:

> *Petulant.* Why shou'd a Man be ever the further from being married tho' he can't Read, any more than he is from being Hang'd. The Ordinary's paid for setting the *Psalm,* and the Parish-Priest for reading the Ceremony. And for the rest which is to follow in both Cases, a Man may do it without Book – So all's one for that. (3.428–33)

Petulant invokes the 'neck verse' (Psalm 51) that saved many a delinquent from the hangman's noose by benefit of clergy; though many an illiterate thug may have saved his or her neck by memorising it. Like most other characters, Petulant is eager to downplay the importance of literacy or education, which have nothing to do with one's social standing or aptitude for marriage. Similarly, in *Love for Love,* education is rejected as "a little too pedantick for a Gentleman" (5.187–88) – an attitude of surprising longevity in Britain. Petulant's attitude corresponds with the pervasive materialism of most characters in *The Way of the World,* for whom marriage is merely a legal act of mechanical coupling or 'riveting' of bodies (1.119). Millamant and Mirabell are the only characters who seem capable of enjoying *belles lettres*, particularly poetry. This enjoyment is associated with their cultivation of a more 'natural' private interiority. Whereas others complain about or take pride in their lack of memory, or use a book of poems instead of the Bible to swear an oath,[110] Mirabell and Millamant can recite poetry by heart. In Act IV, they communicate with each other by reciting and completing fragments of Cavalier poetry by Waller and Suckling. Sir Wilfull thinks Millamant is insulting him when she says: "Natural, easie *Suckling*!" (4.106).

Mirabell's and Millamant's mutual completion of a couplet by Waller opens the proviso scene in which they negotiate the terms of their living together. As in the sonnet spoken by Romeo and Juliet in Shakespeare's play, the rhyme shows from the very beginning their 'fitness' for each other (Bruce 1987). For them, poetry functions as a kind of common code, a 'lovers' discourse' (Barthes 1990), an elaborate form of intimate communication, as it did in many historical cultures, including Heian Japan (most notably in the *Tale of Genji*). In contrast to Behn's *Love-Letters,* this happens in a very controlled and playful manner. The lovers' attitude to literature is neither determined by escapism nor by pretended piety (as it is for Lady Wishfort). Literary communication provides them with a language in which they can recognise each other as equal partners. By means of this idiom, they can unite in shared spiritual distance from the rampant materialism that surrounds them. Cavalier love poetry, taken out of its royalist context, makes possible a utopia of shared individuality that can no longer be observed by others on the outside. In the linguistic universe of *The Way of the World,* literature becomes the medium for an alternative vision of company that is opposed to the unbearable politeness of being

---

[110] "*Foible.* [. . .] *Madam Marwood* took a Book and swore us upon it: But it was a Book of Verses and Poems, – So long as it was not a Bible-Oath, we may break it with a safe Conscience" (5.98–100). The joke is on Mrs Marwood, who appears to have thought a servant would not notice the difference. Again, the material form of the document (here: the codex) is what counts, not its contents.

in a modern, enlightened but progressively disenchanted world. The only way to communicate authentically in this world is by means of poetry.

If this did not sound so joyless as a conlusion, one could argue at the end of this chapter, and this book, that Congreve's play rings down the curtain on the seventeenth century in the way that it outlines a normative distribution of authority among individualities and textualities. *The Way of the World* can stand as exemplary of a highly productive eighteenth-century field of discourse that attempts to maintain a balance between disparate forces in society and the arts through a flexible but nonetheless rigorous poetic order of discourse and its concomitant aesthetic distribution of the senses. This balance includes the acknowledgement of instability and its translation into flexibility, which is far from arbitrary but rather supple and subtle. Acts of writing and reading become a metonymy for a more general epistemological mode of engaging with the world, based on contingency and probability. Literary culture at the end of the seventeenth and beginning of the eighteenth century can thus be understood as a 'medium', *sensu* Arendt, for the sake of combining disparate and disjointed aspects of reality into flexible (but fairly stable), temporary (but not volatile) arrangements of order. Its purpose is to transform pure, raw contingency into manageable procedures based on probabilities, and to gain a higher-order perspective on the randomness of 'things' that transcends differences even as it acknowledges them, without pretending they are not there or not real. This is not the "dissociation of sensibility" that T. S. Eliot lamented (1951 [1921], 288). It is rather a cause for celebration as the beginning of a more democratic modernity; as the beginning, in other words (in fact, Wallace Stevens's), of the realisation that "the imperfect is our paradise" (1990 [1967], 158).

The Augustan Angle: Civilised Contingency and Normative Discourse

The readings of the last chapter have taken us to the threshold of the eighteenth century. By 1700, the neoclassical discourse of contingency and probability had been established as a coherent and dominant cultural programme as part of the general process of political and social consolidation in Britain. Towards the end of the century, the 'Glorious Revolution' implemented a constitutional form of monarchy and a liberal cultural ideology (Whiggism), including – for Protestants, at least – religious toleration. This created the preconditions for a crucial shift of balance between metaphysics, politics, and epistemology. The problems of reconciling their competing claims could now be solved – or at least 'rationalised away' – by funnelling the problematic experiential dimensions of reason, nature, and faith into the philosophical and moral terms of 'common sense' and 'politeness'. The epistemological and political thinking of John Locke is exemplary in this respect. Locke's empirical and practical rationalism allows for those dimensions of reality that, for Browne and others earlier in the century, had formed such a difficult, knotted complex – religion, politics, and secular (individual and social) frames of reference – to be *disentangled*. In contrast to Browne, Locke holds that the human faculties of perception are exactly matched to earthly requirements and that it is therefore meaningless to yearn for knowledge that transcends these faculties. In the *Essay Concerning Human Understanding* (1690), Locke remarks that "[t]he infinite wise Contriver of us, and all things about us, hath fitted our Senses, Faculties, and Organs, to the conveniences of Life, and the Business we have to do here" (2.23.12; 1979, 302). The tensions that had previously led to wars of religion are now relaxed by this deistic interpretation of the *cosmos* and its related view of natural rights, and these Lockean ideas have an impact on many other areas of human life.

As portrayed in Congreve's *The Way of the World*, the elite has become secular and self-supporting, self-reproducing, living according to its own laws. Secular problems are addressed by secular solutions. Although marriages still have to take place in a church, they are no longer made in heaven but on earth, based on mutual interests and agreements (the 'proviso') – not excluding, obviously, love, as passion *and* reason (Luhmann 1987). The books of the Puritans have their backs turned to this society, becoming objects of decoration on the mantelpiece in ironic reminiscence of the *dii familiares*. The competing claims of reason, nature, and faith are defused in the concepts of common sense and gentlemanly politeness. These terms and their implied rules now regulate civil conversation, including knowing where and when to stop or what not to talk about.

As literature (in the sense of *belles lettres*) becomes a part of social conversation, it is increasingly bound by the rules of what is deemed acceptable, and its *decorum* now implies a social and moral correspondence between authors, genres, and readers.

This correlation undergoes a long development throughout the eighteenth century, from Pope, Johnson, and Swift to Sterne and Fielding, and it is still clearly present in the early nineteenth century. One can see this quite well, for instance, in Jane Austen's *Persuasion* (1818). Here, conversation is the judge of a person's character: "He sat down with them, and improved their conversation very much. There could be no doubt of his being a sensible man. Ten minutes were enough to certify that. His tone, his expressions, his choice of subject, his knowing where to stop, – it was all the operation of a sensible, discerning mind" (2006, 155). But the point extends to literature itself, and the interaction between reading and the mind. Reading the wrong kind of literature – in this case, Byron's "impassioned descriptions of hopeless agony" (108) in works like *The Giaour* – may lead to interventions like the one that Anne Elliot attempts with the mournful Captain Benwick: "[. . .] she ventured to hope he did not always read only poetry; and to say, that she thought it was the misfortune of poetry, to be seldom safely enjoyed by those who enjoyed it completely; and that the strong feelings which alone could estimate it truly, were the very feelings which ought to taste it but sparingly" (108). Faced with the possibly damaging effects of excessive passion in poetry, Austen's protagonist recommends "a large allowance of prose in his daily study; and on being requested to particularize, mentioned such works of our best moralists, such collections of the finest letters, such memoirs of characters of worth and suffering, as occurred to her at the moment as calculated to rouse and fortify the mind by the highest precepts, and the strongest examples of moral and religious endurances" (108–109). Obviously, Austen's point here goes beyond a merely generic or moral contrast between different kinds of literature; as Anne realises after lecturing the Captain, "she had been eloquent on a point in which her own conduct would ill bear examination" (109).

After 1688, literature becomes less overtly political and increasingly more self-consciously aesthetic or aestheticised as it is taken out of political and pragmatic concerns and embedded in a new contexture of *polite conversation*. Milton, to name only one example, is "increasingly depoliticized" after the Restoration, "and eventually memorialized at the very centre of the political and cultural establishment, by a bust mounted in Westminster Abbey in 1737" (Zwierlein 2019, 650; see also Zwierlein 2001, Zwicker 2003, 306–307). John Dennis, Charles Gildon, later Addison and Steele further an aesthetic and polite approach to literary writing (Dennis 1939–40, Gildon 1710, Addison 1970; cf. Reiss 1992, 89, 162). There are at least two sides to this process. One is the increasing idealisation of literature as having a 'higher' value, in the way that a work of art not limited by its historical context receives a quasi-timeless stamp of validity. This will lead on to the nineteenth- and twentieth-century (Arnoldian and Eliotian) harnessing of literature for the purposes of education, as a record of "the best which has been thought and said in the world" (Arnold 1971, 6). The other side is the debasement of literature, particularly poetry, as a useless or even dangerous pursuit, which today has made the job of justifying the value of literature (even in education) more and more difficult. This view has an early supporter in John Locke: in *Some Thoughts*

Concerning Education, he advises parents to suppress any poetic inclinations in their children as a waste of time, which could be used for gainful employment (Locke 1989, 230–31).

As we have seen, in *The Way of the World* it is no longer the *meaning* of a text that counts but its *form* and its practical *use*. With regard to poetry, this use is primarily conversational. It is literature, as Kenneth Burke famously called it, "as equipment for living" (1957). When Mirabell and Millamant recite poetry to each other, they open up an escape hatch from convention. Literature in this use offers a view of alternative possibilities of living. It allows readers to *compare* between different modes of seeing and making the world, also in regard to the limits of various frames of reference or social systems (money, love, class, gender, etc.). It allows them to see behind and beyond prevailing norms. Arguably, this is an important aspect of 'culture', understood in an active sense as the cultivation of comparative observations while acknowledging the limitations of one's point of view (Luhmann 1995). *This* kind of literature – realised, above all, in the form of the novel from the eighteenth century onwards – no longer strives to represent an underlying unity as the foundation for any and all aspects of reality (as Davenant's idea of the epic poem still did and his *Gondibert* spectacularly failed to achieve). On the contrary, it recodifies "social and cultural norms", "detach[-ing] prevailing norms from their functional context" and "focusing on their deficiencies" (Iser 2006, 63) in order to show the possibilities and limitations of these norms as they carve up reality into manageable chunks.

However, although this is arguably what works of literature do, it is rarely if ever made explicit by authors and critics in the early modern period. In theory, literary communication is relegated to the sphere of polite conversation. In an increasingly commercial society, poetry begins to lose its former *cachet* of aristocratic patronage; writers like Defoe resort to all sorts of businesses just to be fed. Stylistically, the copious, humanist and Euphuist manner of writing is replaced by one defined by clarity and precision. The new linguistic ideal is "mathematical plainness", as Thomas Sprat explains in 1667 when he drafts his guidelines for the Royal Society (1958, 113):

> to reject all the amplifications, digressions, and swellings of style: to return back to the primitive purity, and shortness, where men deliver'd so many *things*, almost in an equal number of *words*. They have exacted from all their members a close, naked, natural way of speaking; positive expressions, clear senses; a native easiness, bringing all things as near the mathematical plainness as they can; and preferring the language of Artizans, countrymen, and Merchants, before that of Wits and Scholars.

As we have seen, the heterogeneity of writing styles in the seventeenth century can be attributed to competing concepts of language and discourse. These concepts carry social, political, and religious implications that could not be brought to any kind of consensus before the socio-political settlement after the 1688 revolution because, from Bacon to Locke, linguistic thought and stylistic habits were inextricably connected with mutually opposing ideas of society, religion, and politics. Linguistic reform in the context of the Royal Society, for instance, was pursued for a Hobbesian cause: its goal was to achieve the peaceful exchange of knowledge for the benefit of the commonwealth and thereby to avoid "a warlike State of Nature, one against the other" (Sprat 1958, 33; cf. Salmon 1979, Aarselff 1982, Hüllen 1989). Different ideas on the nexus between language and society also have an impact on aesthetic or formal decisions. For example, rhymed heroic couplets were mostly regarded as a royalist and courtly form of discourse appropriate to the high style, as opposed to blank verse or prose. For Dryden, rhyme was "more fit for the ends of government" (Dryden 1967, 7) whereas blank verse for Milton is "an example [. . .] of ancient liberty recover'd [. . .] from the troublesome and modern bondage of rhyming" (Milton 1998, 55). Entire genres stand and fall with their political embedding: the demise of heroic drama, with its elaborately stylised and elevated speeches, occurs in parallel to the crisis of the Stuart monarchy in the 1670s and its loss of power in 1688 (Kamm 1996, 167, 452–53; Berensmeyer 2011, 134).

The cultural locus and socio-spatial model of the neoclassical discursive ideal is no longer the humanist library or the cabinet of wonder but the public coffee-house, which cultivates exactly this "close, naked, natural way of speaking" and "native easiness" among people of different ranks and professions that Sprat seeks to encourage.[111] Furthermore, the new cultural configuration is characterised by a clear hierarchical distinction between cognitive and experiential, mental and physical modes. The ideal of a 'pure' and 'natural' style does not betoken any simple, unproblematic referentiality of language, but is in fact a complex strategic venture, from within a strict hierarchy of communicative levels, of avoiding rhetorical extremes (see Kroll 1992, 21). In this hierarchical distinction, reason in 'plain style' becomes the medium of truth, whereas passion (and, by extension, flowery, figurative, or poetic language) is found to be the medium of deceit. In a chapter on "the Abuse of Words" in the *Essay concerning Human Understanding,* Locke – following Hobbes – undertakes a neat separation of discursive styles, distinguishing between "Discourses, where we seek rather Pleasure and Delight" from those that provide "Information and Improvement". Only in the former type are the "Ornaments" of rhetoric legitimate means of communication; in the latter, rhetoric is nothing but a "powerful instrument of Error and Deceit":

---

[111] Much, perhaps too much, has been made of the impact of coffee-houses on the development of democratic structures and ideas. But their genuine appeal as models of intelligent conversation (and, by extension, an ideal type of literary communication) in *The Spectator* and elsewhere is beyond question. See, for example, Boswell's exercises of recording 'typical' coffee-house dialogues in his London diary – already based on the model of *The Spectator* (Boswell 1950, 74–76, entry for 11 Dec. 1762), and see also a number of observations on coffee (-house) culture in Schivelbusch 1992 and Kroll 2000. Pincus 1995 gives evidence of coffee-houses in the early 1650s, and finds little to support Habermas's claim that the socio-political impact of coffee-houses only began after 1688. Contrary to a number of views on the matter, Pincus asserts the crucial role of coffee-houses for developing a political public sphere in the Restoration period; he also dispenses with the claim that they excluded women.

> But yet, if we would speak of Things as they are, we must allow, that all the Art of Rhetorick, besides Order and Clearness, all the artificial and figurative application of Words Eloquence hath invented, are for nothing else but to insinuate wrong *Ideas*, move the Passions, and thereby mislead the Judgment; and so indeed are perfect cheat[.] (Locke 1979, 508; 3.10.34)

Dryden is particularly explicit on this in his *Religio Laici*, a text that is cast in the mould of 'religio' writing established by Browne and published in the year of Browne's death, 1682. At the end of his preface, Dryden develops a poetics of instructive literary writing along a clear dividing line between plain style/reason/truth and figurative language/passion/deceit:

> The Expressions of a Poem, design'd purely for Instruction, ought to be Plain and Natural, and yet Majestick: for here the Poet is presum'd to be a kind of Law-giver, and those three qualities which I have nam'd are proper to the Legislative style. The Florid, Elevated, and Figurative way is for the Passions; for Love and Hatred, Fear and Anger, are begotten in the Soul by shewing their Objects out of their true proportion; either greater than the Life, or less; but Instruction is to be given by shewing them what they naturally are. A Man is to be cheated into Passion, but to be reason'd into Truth. (Dryden 1972, 109)

Whereas, in Browne, these epistemic levels are layered and context-dependent, in Locke and Dryden they are stratified and systematised according to what Dryden calls "their true proportion" (1972, 109) and what Locke refers to as "Propriety of Speech" (1979, 514; 3.11.11). These comments need to be read in the context of seventeenth-century debates on linguistic refom in relation to political moderation and common sense, as well as the problem of 'enthusiasm'. As Shaftesbury writes in his essay *Sensus communis* (1709): "The only poison to reason is passion" (1999, 43; cf. Heyd 1995). Language, for Locke, is predominantly a *social* and *intersubjective* medium of exchange: "Speech being the great Bond that holds Society together, and the common Conduit, whereby the Improvements of Knowledge are conveyed from one Man, and one Generation to another" (1979, 509; 3.11.1). Browne's cherished *adiaphora* or "points indifferent" can then be disparaged and set aside as "points obscure" that do not serve "the Improvements of Knowledge". For Locke and others, questions of style can be – and indeed have to be – decided according to decorum, propriety, and probability, in accordance with the appropriate rules of genre. In such a decision process, undecidable questions are excluded for the sake of public peace:

> 'Tis some Relief, that points not clearly known,
> Without much hazard may be let alone:
> And, after hearing what our Church can say,
> If still our Reason runs another way,
> That private Reason 'tis more Just to curb,
> Than by Disputes the publick Peace disturb.
> For points obscure are of small use to learn:
> But *Common quiet* is *Mankind's concern*.
> (Dryden 1972, 122, ll. 443–50)

In Dryden's *Religio Laici* (1682), the conflict is no longer one of private peace being disturbed by public war, but one of "publick Peace" potentially disturbed by "private Reason". This rationalist attitude towards religion does not first arise as a Whig concept in the context of the 'Glorious Revolution' but develops gradually in response to the excesses of religious fundamentalism and Puritanism during Civil War and 'Interregnum'. Naturally, Dryden's argument for religious quietism, appearing in the midst of the Exclusion Crisis, is – as usual – not without its own polemical and partisan edge in favour of Stuart crypto-Catholicism (Zwicker 1998a, 194–95). It was a predominant concern of Restoration England to curb extremes for the sake of maintaining public order and political stability.

Compared to this, Sir Thomas Browne indeed appears "like *Janus* in the field of knowledge" (Browne 2012, 78, *Religio* 2.8). He develops an idea of the context-dependent validity of more than one approach to knowing reality but he does not yet think of translating his epistemological programme into a politically viable strategy of social action. For Dryden, Locke, and later the third Earl of Shaftesbury, such a strategy is the goal as they plead for 'common sense' to enlist in the service of 'common quiet'. The 'age of reason' develops a normative account of human psychology and social behaviour: the ideals of civility and sociability and the necessity of 'public peace' for public welfare override 'private reason' in order to manage and accommodate political and religious differences. This new dispensation of 'civic humanism' (Pocock 1975) establishes a new way of dealing with contingency and probability. Politically instituted in the Williamite settlement and its Whig interpretation after 1688, this discourse is codified and popularised in the writings of Locke, Defoe, and Shaftesbury. The discourse of probability and contingency is gradually developed in the post-Interregnum era, performatively embodied in the theatrical practices of Restoration drama and neoclassical poetry, tested in political and economic theory as well as practice, and ultimately established as the widely accepted norm of the age. In this way, 'neoclassicism' (understood as a discourse that connects social, political, and aesthetic developments) becomes a normative and powerful cultural force throughout the eighteenth century (Paulson 1996, xvi), until its homologies are seen as constraining and ready for a radical transformation in the Romantic period.

All this entails significant consequences for the discursive handling of differences between 'individualities' and 'textualities'. In the political sphere, neoclassical discourse promotes non-violence and the use of "degrees of assent" (Locke 1979, 4.16). With regard to language, it establishes an anti-deterministic attitude, for which signs and referents are connected in an arbitrary manner, so that meaning cannot be secured *a priori* but has to be established within discourse itself. Neoclassical poetics comes to "respect the reader's individual integrity" (Kroll 1991, 77) because literary communication can only work under these conditions if the recipient is willing to cooperate. Communication becomes less hierarchical: the reader is no longer seen as a "prisoner" (Davenant 1971, 17) but as a partner, whose contingent individuality is accepted as the norm. Moreover, if no interpretation of a text can be forced upon the reader, this entails a weakening of religious monopolies on meaning. The gradual shift from Scripture to the classics as a high-cultural reference point, from Milton's biblical epic poems at midcentury to Dryden's translation of Virgil in the 1690s, is *one* indicator of this change. The consequences of this non-deterministic attitude towards language and texts can be assessed with particular clarity in nonconformist circles. Struggling for discursive power and for the power of self-definition, these groups – most notably the Dissenters (see Keeble 1987, Achinstein 2003) – learn to accept that a mere counter-discourse, isolated from more widely accepted cultural forms and norms, is not conducive to their aims. Instead, they adopt the (now standard) rhetoric of contingency in order to prevail. In the words of Richard Kroll, these "communities establish their special claims to discursive authority by exploiting possibilities of choice provided by the accepted discourse, though in the process they risk compromising their peculiar and alienated vision" (1991, 78).

Daniel Defoe, for instance, in his anti-deist *Essay upon Literature* (1726), while arguing for the "Proposition" "that Writing and the use of Letters is of divine Original, and that there was no knowledge of Letters, much more of Writing, before that of the two Tables of Stone written by the Finger of God in *Mount Sinai*" (1999, 22), does not simply assert this as a matter of faith, but employs the standard discourse of opinion and probabilistic inference: "This so exactly agrees with what I have already advanc'd from Reason, and the Nature of things, that I think it amounts to as much Confirmation of it, as History can yeild [sic] us" (39); "What is said already, fully confirms me in the Opinion" (40); "*we find reason to believe*" (33); "all Argument from Probability seems to be against them. On the other Hand, there is the highest Probability, that [. . .]" (ibid.), and so on. Although Defoe argues for what he deems to be absolutely certain, he cannot but present his argument in rhetorical terms that are relative, conditional, and limited by the discursive rules of contingency and probability in order to gain authority, legitimacy, and persuasive force with a wider public .

The extent to which the epistemology of neoclassicism is being incorporated even into concepts of authorial self-presentation by radical Protestants in the Restoration period can not only be gauged in Milton's proems to *Paradise Lost*, which emphasise the speaker's insecurity to the point of exaggeration. Something similar happens in Bunyan's preface to *The Pilgrim's Progress* (1678), "The Author's Apology For His Book", where Bunyan anticipates negative responses to his book. He reports on what "others" have said about it, thus frankly and openly admitting divergent opinions:

> Well, when I had thus put mine ends together,
> I shew'd them others, that I might see whether
> They would condemn them, or them justifie:
> And some said, let them live; some, let them die:
> Some said, *John*, print it; others said, Not so:
> Some said, It might do good; others said, No.
> (Bunyan 1975, 2, ll. 5–10)

His solution to this dilemma (the "straight" he is in, l. 11) is publication:

> At last I thought, Since you are thus divided,
> I print it will, and so the case decided.
> For, thought I; Some I see would have it done,
> Though others in that Channel do not run;
> To prove then who advised for the best,
> Thus I thought fit to put it to the test.
> (ll. 13–18)

The public is given the final word on the quality (and not merely the literary quality) of the work. Bunyan's defence of the book's validity and truthfulness ("advance of Truth", 5, l. 32) and his objective as a writer to "Make [Truth] cast forth its rayes as light as day" (6, l. 18) must be cast in a rhetorical mould of uncertainty, probability, and experiment ("test", 2, l. 18). In the "Apology", readers are asked to suspend their judgement until further notice, or until further revelations of truth have occurred: "Forbear to judge, till you do further see. / If that thou wilt not read, let it alone; / Some love the meat, some love to pick the bone" (2, ll. 26–28).

The evolution of early modern literary culture appears as a history of both internal and external contingencies of textual communication. This history is about the emergence of a literary medium of entertainment ('fiction', 'the novel') out of a number of heterogeneous genres, forms, and types of publication; however, these alternative forms of literary communication and their discursive conditions are retrospectively occluded. In this book, I have attempted to outline the complex spectrum of seventeenth-century literary culture without constricting it to a teleological goal 'towards the modern novel'.

The social, economic, and political ramifications of public discourse in seventeenth-century England are complex and manifold, and they forbid simplistic descriptions of a 'from–to' trajectory. Yet, even though scholars have rightly become suspicious of totalising labels, I think the term 'neoclassicism' recommends itself as a description of later seventeenth- and eighteenth-century literature because it is useful in connecting the early efforts of Davenant and Hobbes with the succeeding works of Dryden, Pope, and, to some extent, Johnson in developing a 'modern' literary theory and practice. There is, in other words, a long seventeenth as as well as a long eighteenth century. I have been less interested in neoclassicism as a doctrine or system than as a discourse: as a series of particular moves and engagements in an ongoing argument, a debate about the appropriateness of certain cultural self-representations, and about the modalities of articulating these representations as they evolve over time.

The definition of neoclassicism or neoclassical discourse developed and employed in this study entails a widening of its implications. Neoclassicism is more than a literary trend of emphasising the Aristotelian unities and the distinct requirements ('proprieties') of different genres. It could be argued that, for a while, neoclassicism functioned as a highly successful cultural compromise, the implications of which transcend the boundaries of literary criticism by providing moral as well as aesthetic grounds on which to establish a dominant discourse of politeness, sociability, and civility – a discourse that, as we have seen, pervaded even into those areas of English society that could not claim cultural dominance. Furthermore, neoclassical poetics established a canon of precepts or rules that served to ameliorate the insecurity of reader-writer relations that was frequently diagnosed and experienced in early modern print culture. However, it is important to see this not merely as a literary project but as a wider cultural trend (within which literary questions have an important role to play): as a public debate about how contingency (in questions of knowledge, politics, and individual choices and constraints) can be accommodated and articulated.

Along these lines, neoclassicism anchored literary communication in the context of an emerging civic society. It promoted politeness-oriented, depoliticised discursive norms. It provided a solid groundwork that allowed for more flexibility and variation, more disagreement, more democratic and individual liberties, without risking the breakdown of society into civil war. From Dryden's *Essay of Dramatick Poesie* onwards, one can see how literary politics in the seventeenth century turned away from internecine to more international forms of contest and competition. Within this changing framework, one can observe a whole cluster of functional changes within literary communication (some of them going back to the erosion of late humanist practices of reading and writing):

- an individualisation of readers and readings, presupposing a contingent and irreducible individuality-as-difference that cannot be contained socially and yet is elevated to the position of a social and discursive norm;
- a non-deterministic attitude to language and meaning, including a loss of authority of religious monopolies on interpretation, accompanied by political restraint and the toleration of divergent opinions;
- probability becomes the epistemic norm, verisimilitude the literary norm. The ideal literary style is described by norms of "true proportion" (Dryden) and "propriety of speech" (Locke);
- the introduction of normative distinctions between genres and text types; reflecting and incorporating these distinctions, the novel emerges as a provisional and hybrid literary form that focuses on social and epistemic contingency.

English neoclassicism achieved a successful reduction of social and political complexity – not least by establishing a 'literary culture' along these lines, by means of and in terms of aesthetics and poetics. Its order of discourse remained stable for a fairly long time, at least until the Romantic period, as an "isomorphism of knowledge, literary structure, and implied procedures of interpretation" (Patey 1984, 174).

By the late seventeenth century, knowledge had become a process of continuous revision of prejudices and hypotheses. It had become provisional, falsifiable, subject to the contingency of the individual's limited powers of observation and to experimental empirical testing of its intersubjective validity. More importantly in the context of this study, this development was not confined to science but occurred in English culture as well, and in English literature in particular. Early modern poets, dramatists, and novelists developed new perspectives on the ways in which worlds and selves are being made. As they envisaged contingency from numerous different angles, works of literature had a substantial share in the rise of neoclassical discourse, and thus in the creation of the modern world.

Bibliography

Aarsleff, Hans. 1982. *From Locke to Saussure. Essays on the Study of Language and Intellectual History*. Minneapolis, MN: University of Minnesota Press.
Achinstein, Sharon. 1994. *Milton and the Revolutionary Reader*. Princeton, NJ: Princeton University Press.
Achinstein, Sharon. 2003. *Literature and Dissent in Milton's England*. Cambridge: Cambridge University Press.
Addison, Joseph. 1970. *Critical Essays from the Spectator, with Four Essays by Richard Steele*. Ed. Donald F. Bond. Oxford: Oxford University Press.
Agamben, Giorgio. 1999. *The Man without Content*. Trans. Georgia Albert. Stanford, CA: Stanford University Press.
Alleman, Gellert Spencer. 1942. *Matrimonial Law and the Materials of Restoration Comedy*. Philadelphia, PA: University of Pennsylvania.
Allen, Don Cameron. 1964. *Doubt's Boundless Sea. Skepticism and Faith in the Renaissance*. Baltimore, MD: Johns Hopkins University Press.
Arendt, Hannah. 1958. *The Human Condition*. Chicago: University of Chicago Press.
Arnold, Matthew. 1971. *Culture and Anarchy*. 1869. Ed. John Dover Wilson. Cambridge: Cambridge University Press.
Assmann, Aleida. 1999. *Erinnerungsräume. Formen und Wandlungen des kulturellen Gedächtnisses*. Munich: Beck.
Assmann, Aleida. 2008. "Canon and Archive." *Cultural Memory Studies. An International and Interdisciplinary Handbook*. Ed. Astrid Erll and Ansgar Nünning. Berlin and New York: De Gruyter, 2008. 97–107.
Assmann, Aleida, and Dietrich Harth, eds. 1991. *Mnemosyne. Formen und Funktionen der kulturellen Erinnerung*. Frankfurt am Main: Fischer.
Augustine, Matthew. 2018. *Aesthetics of Contingency. Writing, Politics, and Culture in England, 1639–89*. Manchester: Manchester University Press.
Austen, Jane. 2006. *Persuasion*. Ed. Janet Todd and Antje Blank. Cambridge: Cambridge University Press.
Babb, Lawrence. 1959. *Sanity in Bedlam. A Study of Robert Burton's* Anatomy of Melancholy. East Lansing, MI: Michigan State University Press.
Bacon, Francis. 1965. *Francis Bacon. A Selection of his Works*. Ed. Sidney Warhaft. Toronto: Macmillan.
Bacon, Francis. 1996. "Of the Colours of Good and Evil." 1597. *The Major Works*. Ed. Brian Vickers. Oxford: Oxford University Press. 97–101.
Bakhtin, Mikhail M. 1981. *The Dialogic Imagination. Four Essays*. Ed. Michael Holquist. Trans. Caryl Emerson and Michael Holquist. Austin, TX: University of Texas Press.
Bal, Mieke. 1999 "Introduction." *The Practice of Cultural Analysis. Exposing Interdisciplinary Interpretation*. Ed. Mieke Bal. Stanford: Stanford University Press. 1–14.
Bal, Mieke, Crewe, Jonathan, and Leo Spitzer, eds. 1999. *Acts of Memory. Cultural Recall in the Present*. Hanover, NH: University Press of New England.
Ballaster, Ros. 1992. *Seductive Forms. Women's Amatory Fiction from 1684 to 1740*. New York and Oxford: Oxford University Press.
Bamborough, J. B. 1989. "Introduction." Burton 1989, vol. 1. xiii–xxxvi.
Barbour, Reid. 2013. *Sir Thomas Browne: A Life*. Oxford: Oxford University Press.
Barker, Francis. 1984. *The Tremulous Private Body*. New York: Methuen.

Barker, Francis. 1990. "In the Wars of Truth: Violence, True Knowledge and Power in Milton and Hobbes." *Literature in the English Civil War*. Ed. Thomas Healey and Jonathan Sawday. Cambridge: Cambridge University Press. 91–109.

Barnaby, Andrew, and Lisa J. Schnell. 2002. *Literate Experience. The Work of Knowing in Seventeenth-Century English Writing*. New York and Houndmills: Palgrave Macmillan.

Barthes, Roland. 1990. *A Lover's Discourse*. Harmondsworth: Penguin.

Barthes, Roland. 1994. "L'effet de réel." *Oeuvres complètes*. Ed. Éric Marty. Vol. 2. Paris: Seuil. 479–484.

Battigelli, Anna 1996. "Between the Glass and the Hand. The Eye in Margaret Cavendish's *Blazing World*." *1650–1850. Ideas, Aesthetics, and Inquiries in the Early Modern Era*. Vol. 2. Ed. Kevin L. Cope. New York: AMS Press. 25–38.

Beal, Peter. 1998. *In Praise of Scribes. Manuscripts and their Makers in Seventeenth-Century England*. Oxford: Clarendon Press.

Beasley, Jerry C. 1982. *Novels of the 1740s*. Athens: University of Georgia Press.

Behn, Aphra. 1684. *Love-Letters Between a Noble-Man And his Sister*. London: Printed, and are to be sold by Randal Taylor, near Stationer's Hall. EEBO (Yale University Library copy)

Behn, Aphra. 1685. *Love Letters from a Noble Man to his Sister: Mixt With the History of their Adventures. The Second Part by the same Hand*. London: Printed for the Author, and are to be sold by the Booksellers of London, 1685. EEBO (Yale University Library copy)

Behn, Aphra. 1687. *The Amours of Philander and Silvia: Being the Third and Last Part of the Love-Letters Between a Noble-Man and his Sister*. London: Printed, and are to be Sold by most Book-Sellers, 1687. EEBO (Yale University Library copy)

Behn, Aphra. 1995. *The Rover. The Feigned Courtesans. The Lucky Chance. The Emperor of the Moon*. Ed. Jane Spencer. Oxford: Clarendon Press.

Belsey, Catherine. 1985. *The Subject of Tragedy. Identity and Difference in Renaissance Drama*. New York: Methuen.

Benedict, Barbara M. 1996. *Making the Modern Reader. Cultural Mediation in Early Modern Literary Anthologies*. Princeton: Princeton University Press.

Benjamin, Walter. 2000. "The Storyteller." Trans. Harry Zohn. *Theory of the Novel: A Historical Approach*. Ed. Michael McKeon. Baltimore and London: Johns Hopkins University Press. 77–93.

Bennett, Joan. 1962. *Sir Thomas Browne. 'A Man of Achievement in Literature'*. Cambridge: Cambridge University Press.

Berensmeyer, Ingo. 2003. "No Fixed Address: Pascal, Cervantes, and the Changing Function of Literary Communication in Early Modern Europe." *New Literary History* 34.4: 383–397.

Berensmeyer, Ingo. 2006. "Rhetoric, Religion, and Politics in Sir Thomas Browne's *Religio Medici*". *Studies in English Literature 1500–1900* 46.1: 113–132.

Berensmeyer, Ingo. 2007. *Shakespeare: Hamlet*. Stuttgart: Klett.

Berensmeyer, Ingo. 2011. "Restoration Tragedy and Heroic Drama: John Dryden's *All for Love, or The World Well Lost*". *A History of British Drama. Genres – Developments – Model Interpretations*. Ed. Sibylle Baumbach, Birgit Neumann, and Ansgar Nünning. Trier: WVT. 129–142.

Berensmeyer, Ingo. 2012. "Literature, Politics and Representation in English Neoclassicism: The Hobbes-Davenant Exchange." *philia & filia* 3.1: 4–24.

Berensmeyer, Ingo. 2019. "Introduction." *Handbook of English Renaissance Literature*. Ed. Ingo Berensmeyer. Berlin and Boston: De Gruyter. 1–23.

Berensmeyer, Ingo, Buelens, Gert, and Marysa Demoor. 2012. "Authorship as Cultural Performance: New Perspectives in Authorship Studies". *ZAA* 60.1: 5–29.

Berry, Boyd. 1976. *Process of Speech: Puritan Religious Writing and "Paradise Lost"*. Baltimore: Johns Hopkins University Press.

Blumenberg, Hans. 1979. "The Concept of Reality and the Possibility of the Novel." *New Perspectives in German Literary Criticism*. Ed. Richard E. Amacher and Victor Lange. Princeton, NJ: Princeton University Press. 29–48.

Blumenberg, Hans. 1981. *Wirklichkeiten in denen wir leben. Aufsätze und eine Rede*. Stuttgart: Reclam, 1981.

Blumenberg, Hans. 1991. *The Legitimacy of the Modern Age*. Trans. Robert M. Wallace. Cambridge, MA: MIT Press.

Blumenberg, Hans. 1996. *Shipwreck with Spectator. Paradigm of a Metaphor for Existence*. Trans. Steven Rendall. Cambridge, MA: MIT Press.

Bohannan, Laura. 1966. "Shakespeare in the Bush." *Natural History* 75.7: 28–33.

Bohn, Cornelia: "Schriftlichkeit als Generator für Modernität." *Konzepte der Moderne*, ed. Gerhard von Graevenitz. Stuttgart and Weimar: Metzler, 1999. 27–51.

Borges, Jorge Luis. 1962. "Pierre Menard, Author of the *Quijote*." Trans. James E. Irby. *Labyrinths. Selected Stories and Other Writings* by Borges. Ed. Donald A. Yates and James E. Irby. Norfolk, CN: New Directions. 36–44.

Boswell, James. 1950. *Boswell's London Journal 1762–1763*. Ed. Frederick A. Pottle. New York, London, Toronto: McGraw-Hill.

Bowers, Toni. 1999. "Seduction Narratives and Tory Experience in Augustan England." *The Eighteenth Century* 40.2: 128–154.

Bowers, Toni. 2009. "Behn's Monmouth: Sedition, Seduction, and Tory Ideology in the 1680s." *Studies in Eighteenth-Century Culture* 38: 15–44.

Braga Riera, Jorge. 2009. *Classical Spanish Drama in Restoration English (1660–1700)*. Amsterdam and Philadelphia, PA: John Benjamins.

Brayman Hackel, Heidi. 2005. *Reading Material in Early Modern England. Print, Gender, and Literacy*. Cambridge: Cambridge University Press.

Braverman, Richard. 1993. "Who to Trust? Rewriting the Revolution in Congreve's *The Way of the World*." *Plots and Counterplots. Sexual Politics and the Body Politic in English* Literature, 1660–1730. Cambridge: Cambridge University Press. 211–237.

Bredekamp, Horst. 1999. *Thomas Hobbes Visuelle Strategien. Der Leviathan: Urbild des modernen Staates. Werkillustrationen und Portraits*. Berlin: Akademie Verlag.

Breiner, Laurence A. 1977. "The Generation of Metaphor in Thomas Browne." *MLQ* 38.3: 261–275.

Brekle, Herbert. 1975. "The Seventeenth Century." *Current Trends in Linguistics*, Ed. Thomas A. Sebeok. The Hague: Mouton. Vol. 13. 277–382.

Brown, Homer Obed. 1997. *Institutions of the English Novel: From Defoe to Scott*. Philadelphia: University of Pennsylvania Press.

Browne, Sir Thomas. 1964a. *Religio Medici and Other Works*. Ed. L. C. Martin. Oxford: Clarendon Press.

Browne, Sir Thomas, 1964b. *The Works of Sir Thomas Browne*. Ed. Geoffrey Keynes. London: Faber and Faber.

Browne, Sir Thomas. 1981. *Pseudodoxia Epidemica*. Ed. Robin Robbins. 2 vols. Oxford: Clarendon Press.

Browne, Sir Thomas. 2012. *Religio Medici* and *Hydriotaphia, or Urne-Buriall*. Ed. Stephen Greenblatt and Ramie Targoff. New York: New York Review Books.

Bruce, Donald Williams. 1987. "Why Millamant Studied Sir John Suckling." *Notes and Queries* 34.232: 334–335.

Bubner, Rüdiger. 1984. *Geschichtsprozesse und Handlungsnormen*. Frankfurt am Main: Suhrkamp.

Bunyan, John. 1975. *The Pilgrim's Progress from this World to That which is to Come*. Ed. James Blanton Wharey. 2nd ed. Roger Sharrock. 1960. Oxford: Clarendon Press.

Burke, Kenneth. 1957. "Literature as Equipment for Living". *The Philosophy of Literary Form. Studies in Symbolic Action*. Rev. ed. New York: Vintage. 253–262.

Burke, Peter. 1993. "*Res et verba*: Conspicuous Consumption in the Early Modern World." *Consumption and the World of Goods*, ed. John Brewer. London and New York: Routledge. 148–161.

Burton, Robert. 1989–2000. *The Anatomy of Melancholy*. Ed. Thomas C. Faulkner, Nicolas K. Kiessling, and Rhonda L. Blair. Commentary by J. B. Bamborough with Martin Dodsworth. 6 vols. Oxford: Clarendon Press.

Butterfield, Herbert. 1931. *The Whig Interpretation of History*. London: Bell.

Bylebyl, Jerome J., ed. 1979. *William Harvey and his Age. The Social Context of the Discovery of the Circulation*. Baltimore, MD: Johns Hopkins University Press.

Caldwell, Lauren. 2015. "Drink Up All the Water in the Sea:' Contracting Relationships in Congreve's *Love for Love* and *The Way of the World*." *ELH* 82.1: 183–210.

Cameron, James Munro. 1962. *The Night Battle: Essays*. London: Helicon.

Campbell, Mary B. 1988. *The Witness and the Other World. Exotic European Travel Writing, 400–1600*. Ithaca, NY and London: Cornell University Press.

Canfield, J. Douglas. 1989. *Word as Bond in English Literature from the Middle Ages to the Restoration*. Philadelphia, PA: University of Pennsylvania Press.

Carew, Thomas. 1893. *The Poems and Masque of Thomas Carew*. Ed. Joseph Woodfall Ebsworth. London: Reeves and Turner.

Carroll, Robert, and Stephen Prickett, eds. 1997. *The Bible. Authorized King James Version*. Oxford: Oxford University Press.

Cassirer, Ernst. 1953. *The Platonic Renaissance in England.*. Trans James P. Pettegrove. Austin, TX: University of Texas Press.

Castoriadis, Cornelius. 1998. *The Imaginary Institution of Society*. Malden, MA and Oxford: Blackwell.

Cave, Terence. 1979. *The Cornucopian Text. Problems of Writing in the French Renaissance*. Oxford: Clarendon Press.

Cavendish, Margaret. 1653: *Poems, and Fancies*. London.

Cavendish, Margaret. 1666a. *Observations upon Experimental Philosophy. To which is added, The Description of a New Blazing World*. London. EEBO (Wing N857).

Cavendish, Margaret. 1666b. *The Description of a New World, Called The Blazing World*. London. EEBO (Wing N857).

Cavendish, Margaret. 1666c. *The Second Part of the Description of the New Blazing World*. London. EEBO (Wing N857).

Cavendish, Margaret. 1671. Frontispiece to *The World's Olio*. British Library shelfmark 8407.h.11. https://www.bl.uk/collection-items/margaret-cavendishs-melancholic-frontispiece.

Cavendish, William. 1984. *Ideology and Politics on the Eve of Restoration: Newcastle's Advice to Charles II*. Ed. Thomas P. Slaughter. Philadelphia, PA: American Philosophical Society.

Cervantes Saavedra, Miguel de. 1987. *El ingenioso hidalgo Don Quijote de la Mancha*. Ed. Vicente Gaos. Madrid.

Chalmers, Gordon C. K. 1936. "Sir Thomas Browne, True Scientist." *Osiris* 2. 28–79.

Chartier, Roger. 1994. *The Order of Books: Readers, Authors and Libraries in Europe between the Fourteenth and Eighteenth Centuries*. Trans. Lydia G. Cochrane. Cambridge: Polity Press.

Chernaik, Warren. 1998. "Unguarded Hearts: Transgression and Epistolary Form in Aphra Behn's *Love-Letters* and the *Portuguese Letters*." *Journal of English and Germanic Philology* 97.1: 13–33.

Cicero, Marcus Tullius. 1942. *De oratore*. Trans. E. W. Sutton and H. Rackham. Loeb Classical Library. Cambridge, MA: Harvard University Press; London: Heinemann.

Claessens, Dieter. 1993. *Das Konkrete und das Abstrakte. Soziologische Skizzen zur Anthropologie*. 1980. Frankfurt am Main: Suhrkamp.

Clare, Janet. 2019. "Sir William Davenant, *The Siege of Rhodes* (1656)." *Handbook of English Renaissance Literature*. Ed. Ingo Berensmeyer. Berlin and Boston: De Gruyter. 615–634.

Cochran, Terry. 2001. *Twilight of the Literary. Figures of Thought in the Age of Print*. Cambridge, MA and London: Harvard University Press.

Cohn, Norman. 1970. *Pursuit of the Millennium*. Rev. ed. New York: Temple Smith.

Coleman, D. C. 1958. *The British Paper Industry, 1495–1860: A Study in Industrial Growth*. Oxford: Clarendon Press.

Coleridge, Samuel Taylor. 1955. *Coleridge on the Seventeenth Century*. Ed. Roberta Florence Brinkley. Durham, NC: Duke University Press.

Coleridge, Samuel Taylor. 1965. *Biographia Literaria or Biographical Sketches of My Literary Life and Opinions*. 1817. Ed. George Watson. London: Dent; Vermont: Tuttle.

Colie, Rosalie. 1973. *The Resources of Kind. Genre Theory in the Renaissance*. Berkeley, Los Angeles, London: University of California Press.

Collini, Stefan. 2019. *The Nostalgic Imagination. History in English Criticism*. Oxford: Oxford University Press.

Condren, Conal. 1993. "Casuistry to Newcastle: *The Prince* in the World of the Book." *Political Discourse in Early Modern Britain*, ed. Nicholas Phillipson and Quentin Skinner. Cambridge: Cambridge University Press. 164–186.

Condren, Conal. 2002. "Historicism and the Problem of Renaissance 'Self-Fashioning.'" *The Touch of the Real. Essays in Early Modern Culture in Honour of Stephen Greenblatt*. Ed. Philippa Kelly. Crawley: University of Western Australia Press. 105–124.

Congreve, William. 1967. *The Complete Plays of William Congreve*. Ed. Herbert Davis. Chicago and London: University of Chicago Press.

Conlon, Michael J. 1979. "The Passage on Government in Dryden's *Absalom and Achitophel*." *Journal of English and Germanic Philology* 78: 17–32.

Conway, Anne. 1992. *The Conway Letters*. Ed. Marjorie Nicholson. Rev. ed. Sarah Hutton. Oxford: Clarendon Press.

Cooper, John R. 1968. *The Art of* The Compleat Angler. Durham, NC: Duke University Press.

Corman, Brian. 2000. "Comedy." *The Cambridge Companion to English Restoration Theatre*. Ed. Deborah Payne Fisk. Cambridge: Cambridge University Press. 52–69.

Corns, Thomas N. 1992. *Uncloistered Virtue. English Political Literature, 1640–1660*. Oxford: Clarendon Press.

Cottegnies, Line, and Nancy Weitz, eds. 2003. *Authorial Conquests. Essays on Genre in the Writings of Margaret Cavendish*. Madison and Teaneck, NJ: Fairleigh Dickinson University Press; London: Associated University Presses.

Cowley, Abraham. 1656. *Poems [. . .] Written by A. Cowley*. London: Printed for Humphrey Moseley. EEBO.

Cowley, Abraham. 1660. *Ode, Upon the Blessed Restoration and Returne of His Sacred Majestie, Charls the Second*. London: Printed for Henry Herringman. (EEBO)

Crane, R. S. 1953. *The Languages of Criticism and the Structure of Poetry*. Toronto: University of Toronto Press.

Cressy, David. 1980. *Literacy and the Social Order. Reading and Writing in Tudor and Stuart England*. Cambridge: Cambridge University Press.

Croll, Morris W. 1966. "The Baroque Style in Prose." 1929. *Style, Rhetoric, and Rhythm. Essays by Morris W. Croll*. Ed. J. Max Patrick and Robert O. Evans, with John M. Wallace and R. J. Schoeck. Princeton, NJ: Princeton University Press. 207–233.

Csikszentmihalyi, Mihalyi. 1990. *Flow. The Psychology of Optimal Experience*. New York: Harper and Row.

Culler, Jonathan. 1988. *Framing the Sign. Criticism and its Institutions*. Norman, OK and London: University of Oklahoma Press.

Cunningham, Andrew. 1996. "Sir Thomas Browne and his *Religio Medici*: Reason, Nature and Religion." *Religio Medici: Medicine and Religion in Seventeenth-Century England*. Ed. Ole Peter Grell and Andrew Cunningham. Hants: Scolar Press; Vermont: Ashgate. 12–61.

Daems, Jim, and Holly Faith Nelson, eds. 2006. *Eikon Basilike. The Portraiture of His Sacred Majesty in His Solitudes and Sufferings*. With Selections from *Eikonoklastes*. John Milton. Peterborough, Ontario: Broadview Press.

Darnton, Robert. 1991. "History of Reading." *New Perspectives on Historical Writing*. Ed. Peter Burke. Cambridge: Polity Press. 140–167.

Daston, Lorraine, and Katharine Park. 1998. *Wonders and the Order of Nature, 1150–1750*. New York: Zone Books.

Davenant, William. 1650a. *The Preface to Gondibert, An Heroic Poem written by Sir William D'Avenant: With an Answer to the Preface by Mr Hobbes*. Paris: Matthieu Guillemot.

Davenant, William. 1650b. *A Discourse upon Gondibert. An Heroic Poem written by Sir William D'Avenant with an Answer to it by Mr. Hobbs*. Paris: Matthieu Guillemot.

Davenant, William. 1971. *Sir William Davenant's Gondibert*. Ed. David F. Gladish. Oxford: Clarendon Press.

Davies, Stevie. 1983. *Images of Kingship in Paradise Lost. Milton's Politics and Christian Liberty*. Columbia, MO: University of Missouri Press.

Day, Robert Adams. 1966. *Told in Letters. Epistolary Fiction Before Richardson*. Ann Arbor, MI: University of Michigan Press.

Daybell, James. 2012. *The Material Letter in Early Modern England. Manuscript Letters and the Culture and Practices of Letter-Writing, 1512–1635*. Basingstoke: Palgrave Macmillan.

de Certeau, Michel. 1984. *The Practice of Everyday Life*. Trans. Steven Rendall. Berkeley, Los Angeles, London: University of California Press.

de Certeau, Michel. 1986. "Mystic Speech." *Heterologies. Discourse on the Other*. Trans. Brian Massumi. Minneapolis, MN: University of Minnesota Press. 80–100.

Defoe, Daniel. 1999. *An Essay upon Literature, or, An Enquiry into the Antiquity and Original of Letters, Proving that the Two Tables Written by the Finger of God in Mount Sinai was the First Writing in the World, and that all Other Alphabets Derive from the Hebrew, etc.* 1726. New York: AMS Press.

Dennis, John. 1939–43. *The Critical Works*. Ed. Edward Niles Hooker. 2 vols. Baltimore: Johns Hopkins University Press.

Derrida, Jacques. 1992. "This Strange Institution Called Literature. An Interview with Jacques Derrida." Trans Geoffrey Bennington and Rachel Bowlby. *Acts of Literature*. Ed. Derek Attridge. New York and London: Routledge. 33–75.

Descartes, René. 1953. *Oeuvres et lettres*. Ed. André Bridoux. Paris: Gallimard.

Docherty, Thomas. 1999. "Tragedy and the Nationalist Condition of Criticism." *Criticism and Modernity. Aesthetics, Literature, and Nations in Europe and its Academies*. Oxford: Oxford University Press. 9–38.

Donne, John. 2001. *Complete Poetry and Selected Prose*. Ed. Charles M. Coffin. New York: Modern Library.

Doody, Margaret Anne. 1996. *The True Story of the Novel*. New Brunswick, NJ: Rutgers University Press.

Döring, Tobias. 2006. *Performances of Mourning in Shakespearean Theatre and Early Modern Culture*. London and New York: Palgrave Macmillan.

Douglas, Amy Scott. 2000. "Self-Crowned Laureates: Towards a Historical Revaluation of Margaret Cavendish's Prefaces." *Pretexts. Literary and Cultural Studies* 9.1. 27–49.
Dowlin, Cornell March. 1934. *Sir William Davenant's Gondibert, Its Preface, and Hobbes's Answer. A Study in English Neoclassicism*. Philadelphia, PA: n. p.
Drummond of Hawthornden, William. 1973. *Flowres of Sion to which is adjoyned his Cypresse Grove*. 1623. Rpt. Amsterdam: Theatrum Orbis Terrarum; New York: Da Capo Press.
Dryden, John. 1956. *The Works of John Dryden*. Vol. 1. *Poems 1649–1680*. Ed. H. T. Swedenberg, Jr. Berkeley, Los Angeles, London: University of California Press.
Dryden, John. 1962. *The Works of John Dryden*. Vol. 8. *Plays: The Wild* Gallant, *The Rival* Ladies, *The Indian Queen*. Ed. John H. Smith, Dougald MacMillan, and Vinton A. Dearing. Berkeley, Los Angeles, London: University of California Press.
Dryden, John. 1967. *The Works of John Dryden*. Vol. 9. *Plays: The Indian* Emperour, *Secret* Love, *Sir Martin Mar-all*. Ed. John Loftis and Vinton A. Dearing. Berkeley, Los Angeles, London: University of California Press.
Dryden, John. 1971. *The Works of John Dryden*. Vol. 17. *Prose 1668–1691*. Ed. Samuel Holt Monk and A. E. Wallace Maurer. Berkeley, Los Angeles, London: University of California Press.
Dryden, John. 1972. *The Works of John Dryden*. Vol. 2. *Poems 1681–1684*. Ed. H. T. Swedenberg, Jr. Berkeley, Los Angeles, London: University of California Press.
Dryden, John. 1974. *The Works of John Dryden*. Vol. 4. *Poems 1693–1696*. Ed. A B. Chambers and William Frost. Berkeley, Los Angeles, London: University of California Press.
Dryden, John. 1978. *The Works of John Dryden*. Vol. 11. *Plays: The Conquest of Granada. Marriage A-la-Mode. The Assignation*. Ed. John Loftis and David Stuart Rodes. Berkeley, Los Angeles, London: University of California Press.
Dryden, John. 1987. *The Works of John Dryden*. Vol. 5. *Poems: The Works of Virgil in English, 1697*. Ed. William Frost and Vinton A. Dearing. Berkeley, Los Angeles, London: University of California Press.
Dryden, John. 1995a. *The Works of John Dryden*. Vol. 12. *Plays: Amboyna*, The *State of Innocence, Aureng-Zebe*. Ed. Vinton A. Dearing. Berkeley, Los Angeles, London: University of California Press.
Dryden, John. 1995b. *The Poems of John Dryden*. Ed. Paul Hammond. 2 vols. Harlow: Longman.
Dryden, John. 2001. *Selected Poems*. Ed. Steven N. Zwicker and David Bywaters. Harmondsworth: Penguin.
Dunn, John. 1969. *The Political Thought of John Locke. An Historical Account of the Argument of the 'Two Treatises of Government.'* Cambridge: Cambridge University Press.
Dunn, John. 2003. *Locke*. 1984. Oxford: Oxford University Press.
Dunn, Kevin. 1994. *Pretexts of Authority. The Rhetoric of Authorship in the Renaissance Preface*. Stanford, CA: Stanford University Press.
Dunn, William P. 1950. *Sir Thomas Browne. A Study in Religious Philosophy*. 1926. Minneapolis, MN: University of Minnesota Press.
Eisenstein, Elizabeth L. 1979. *The Printing Press as an Agent of Change: Communications and Cultural Transformations in Early Modern Europe*. Cambridge and New York: Cambridge University Press.
Eliot, T. S. 1951. "The Metaphysical Poets." 1921. *Selected Essays*. 3rd ed. London: Faber and Faber. 281–291.
Elsky, Martin. 1989. *Authorizing Words. Speech, Writing, and Print in the English Renaissance*. Ithaca, NY and London: Cornell University Press.
Empson, William. 1974. *Some Versions of Pastoral*. 1935. New York: New Directions.
Erickson, Robert A. 1984. "Lady Wishfort and the Will of the World." *MLQ* 45.4: 338–349.

Erll, Astrid, and Ansgar Nünning, eds. 2008. *Cultural Memory Studies. An International and Interdisciplinary Handbook*. Berlin and Boston: De Gruyter.

Ezell, Margaret J. M. 2003. *Social Authorship and the Advent of Print*. Baltimore, MD: Johns Hopkins University Press.

Ezell, Margaret J. M. 2018. *The Oxford English Literary History, vol. V: 1645–1700: The Later Seventeenth Century*. Oxford: Oxford University Press.

Fairfax, Nathaniel. 1674. *A Treatise of the Bulk and Selvedge of the World*. London.

Fallon, Stephen M. 2001. "*Paradise Lost* in Intellectual History." *A Companion to Milton*. Ed. Thomas N. Corns. Oxford: Blackwell. 329–347.

Ferry, Anne. 1968. *Milton and the Miltonic Dryden*. Cambridge, MA: Harvard University Press.

Ferry, Anne. 1983. *The "Inward" Language. Sonnets of Wyatt, Sidney, Shakespeare, Donne*. Chicago, IL and London: University of Chicago Press.

Filmer, Sir Robert. 1991. *Patriarcha and Other Writings*. Ed. Johann P. Sommerville. Cambridge: Cambridge University Press.

Finnegan, Ruth. 1988. *Literacy and Orality: Studies in the Technology of Communication*. Oxford: and New York: Blackwell.

Fish, Stanley E. 1980. *Is There a Text in this Class? The Authority of Interpretive Communities*. Cambridge, MA: Harvard University Press.

Foucault, Michel. 1979. *Discipline and Punish. The Birth of the Prison*. Trans. Alan Sheridan. New York: Random House.

Foucault, Michel. 1980. *Power/Knowledge. Selected Interviews and Other Writings*. Ed. Colin Gordon. New York: Vintage.

Foucault, Michel. 2002. *The Order of Things. An Archaeology of the Human Sciences*. London and New York: Routledge.

Fowler, Alastair. 1982. *Kinds of Literature. An Introduction to the Theory of Genres and Modes*. Oxford: Clarendon Press.

Fox, Adam. 1996. "Custom, Memory and the Authority of Writing." *The Experience of Authority in Early Modern England*. Ed. Paul Griffiths, Adam Fox, and Steve Hindle. Houndmills and London: Macmillan. 89–116.

Fox, Ruth A. 1976. *The Tangled Chain. The Structure of Disorder in the* Anatomy of Melancholy. Berkeley, Los Angeles, London: University of California Press.

Frank, Joseph. 1961. *The Beginnings of the English Newspaper 1620–1660*. Cambridge, MA: Harvard University Press.

Frank, Marcie. 1993. "Staging Criticism, Staging Milton: John Dryden's *The State of Innocence*." *The Eighteenth Century* 34.1: 45–64.

Frye, Northrop. 1957. *Anatomy of Criticism*. Princeton, NJ: Princeton University Press.

Fumerton, Patricia. 1991. *Cultural Aesthetics. Renaissance Literature and the Practice of Social Ornament*. Chicago, IL and London: University of Chicago Press.

Funkenstein, Amos. 1992. "History, Counterhistory, and Narrative." *Probing the Limits of Representation. Nazism and the "Final Solution."* Ed. Saul Friedlander. Cambridge, MA: Harvard University Press. 66–81.

Gabel, Tobias. 2016. *Paradise Reframed. Milton, Dryden, and the Politics of Literary Adaptation, 1658–1679*. Heidelberg: Winter.

Gallagher, Catherine. 1994. *Nobody's Story. The Vanishing Acts of Women Writers in the Marketplace, 1670–1820*. Berkeley, Los Angeles, London: University of California Press.

Gardiner, Judith Kegan. 1980. "Aphra Behn: Sexuality and Self-Respect." *Women's Studies* 7: 67–78.

Gascoigne, John. 1989. *Cambridge in the Age of the Enlightenment. Science, Religion and Politics from the Restoration to the French Revolution*. Cambridge: Cambridge University Press.

Geertz, Clifford. 1973. *The Interpretation of Cultures. Selected Essays*. New York: Basic Books.
Gelber, Michael Werth. 1999. *The Just and the Lively. The Literary Criticism of John Dryden*. Manchester and New York: Manchester University Press.
Gelineau, David. 1994. "Allusion, Legitimacy, and Succession: Milton's Hands Suit Ill with Dryden's Voice." *The Eighteenth Century* 35.1: 28–45.
Genette, Gérard. 1997. *Paratexts. Thresholds of Interpretation*. Trans. Jane E. Lewin. Cambridge: Cambridge University Press.
Gevirtz, Karen. 2015. "From Epistle to Epistemology: *Love-Letters* and the Royal Society." *Women's Writing* 22.1: 84–96.
Giesecke, Michael. 1991. *Der Buchdruck in der frühen Neuzeit. Eine historische Fallstudie über die Durchsetzung neuer Informations- und Kommunikationstechnologien*. Frankfurt am Main: Suhrkamp.
Gilbert, Nora. 2018. "'Impatient to Be Gone': Aphra Behn's Vindication of the Flights of Woman." *Eighteenth-Century Life* 42.1 (2018): 1–27.
Gildon, Charles. 1710. "An Essay on the Art, Rise and Progress of the Stage in Greece, Rome, and England". *The Works of Mr. William Shakespear*. Ed. Nicholas Rowe. Vol. 7, ed. Charles Gildon. i–lii.
Gill, Pat. 1996. "The Way of the World: Telling Differences in Congreve's *Way of the World*." *Broken Boundaries. Women and Feminism in Restoration Drama*. Ed. Katherine M. Quinsey. Lexington: University Press of Kentucky. 164–181.
Gilman, Ernest B. 1978. *The Curious Perspective. Literary and Pictorial Wit in the Seventeenth Century*. New Haven, CT and London: Yale University Press.
Gladish, David F. 1971. "Introduction." *Sir William Davenant's Gondibert*. Ed. David F. Gladish. Oxford: Clarendon Press. ix–xlv.
Glanvill, Joseph. 1661. *The Vanity of Dogmatizing*. London.
Goldberg, Jonathan. 1990. *Writing Matter: From the Hands of the English Renaissance*. Stanford, CA: Stanford University Press.
Goodman, Nelson. 1978. *Ways of Worldmaking*. Hassocks: Harvester Press.
Gordon, Scott Paul. 2002. "Endeavouring to Be the King: Dryden's *Astraea Redux* and the Issue of 'Character.'" *Journal of English and Germanic Philology* 101.2: 201–221.
Graevenitz, Gerhart von, and Odo Marquard, eds. 1998. *Kontingenz*. Munich: Fink.
Grabes, Herbert. 2013. "On the Function and Value of Theory." *New Theories, Models and Methods in Literary and Cultural Studies*. Ed. Greta Olson and Ansgar Nünning. Trier: WVT. 39–57.
Grafton, Anthony, and Lisa Jardine. 1986. *From Humanism to the Humanities. Education and the Liberal Arts in Fifteenth- and Sixteenth-Century Europe*. Cambridge, MA: Harvard University Press.
Grant, Patrick. 1985. *Literature and the Discovery of Method in the English Renaissance*. Houndmills and London: Macmillan.
Greenblatt, Stephen. 1980. *Renaissance Self-Fashioning: From More to Shakespeare*. Chicago: University of Chicago Press.
Greenblatt, Stephen. 1988. *Shakespearean Negotiations. The Circulation of Social Energy in Renaissance England*. Berkeley, Los Angeles, London: University of California Press.
Greenblatt, Stephen. 2002. "Racial Memory and Literary History." *The Touch of the Real. Essays in Early Modern Culture in Honour of Stephen Greenblatt*. Ed. Philippa Kelly. Crawley: University of Western Australia Press. 1–21.
Greenblatt, Stephen, and Ramie Targoff. 2012. "Introduction." *Religio Medici* and *Hydriotaphia, or Urne-Buriall*, by Sir Thomas Browne. Ed. Stephen Greenblatt and Ramie Targoff. New York: New York Review Books. ix–xli.

Greiner, Bernhard, and Maria Moog-Grünewald, eds. 2000. *Kontingenz und Ordo. Selbstbegründung des Erzählens in der Neuzeit*. Heidelberg: Winter.

Griebel, Deborah Joanne. 1979. "Contrary Devotion. An Analysis of Binary Structures in the Works of Sir Thomas Browne." Unpublished MA thesis. British Columbia: University of Victoria.

Grose, Christopher. 2002. "Theatrum Libri. Burton's *Anatomy of Melancholy* and the Failure of Encyclopedic Form." *Books and Readers in Early Modern England*. Ed. Jennifer Andersen and Elizabeth Sauer. Philadelphia: University of Pennsylvania Press. 80–96.

Grotius, Hugo. 1977. *The Jurisprudence of Holland*. Ed. and trans. Robert Warden Lee. 2 vols. 2nd ed. Oxford: Clarendon Press, 1953. Rpt. Aalen: Scientia.

Guibbory, Achsah. 1976. "Sir Thomas Browne's *Pseudodoxia Epidemica* and the Circle of Knowledge." *Texas Studies in Literature and Language* 18: 486–499.

Guibbory, Achsah. 1998. *Ceremony and Community from Herbert to Milton. Literature, Religion and Cultural Conflict in Seventeenth-Century England*. Cambridge: Cambridge University Press.

Gumbrecht, Hans Ulrich. 1980. "Literarische Gegenwelten. Karnevalskultur und die Epochenschwelle vom Spätmittelalter zur Renaissance." *Literatur in der Gesellschaft des Spätmittelalters*. Ed. Hans Ulrich Gumbrecht Heidelberg: Winter. 95–144.

Gumbrecht, Hans Ulrich. 1985. "The Body vs. the Printing Press. Media in the Early Modern Period, Mentalities in the Reign of Castile, and another History of Literary Forms." *Poetics* 14.3–4:179–202.

Gumbrecht, Hans Ulrich. 1990. Eine *Geschichte der spanischen Literatur*. Frankfurt am Main: Suhrkamp.

Gunn, J. A. W. 1969. *Politics and the Public Interest in the Seventeenth Century*. London and Toronto: University of Toronto Press.

Habermas, Jürgen. 1989. *The Structural Transformation of the Public Sphere: An Inquiry into a Category of Bourgeois Society*. Trans. Thomas Burger with Frederick Lawrence. Cambridge, MA: MIT Press.

Habermas, Jürgen. 1997. "Modernity: An Unfinished Project." *Habermas and the Unfinished Project of Modernity. Critical Essays on* The Philosophical Discourse of Modernity. Ed. Maurizio Passerin d'Entrèves and Seyla Benhabib. Cambridge, MA: MIT Press. 38–55.

Hack-Molitor, Gisela. 2001. *On Tiptoe in Heaven. Mystik und Reform im Werk von Sir Thomas Browne (1605–1682)*. Heidelberg: Winter.

Hacking, Ian. 1975. *The Emergence of Probability. A Philosophical Study of Early Ideas about Probability, Induction and Statistical Inference*. London and New York: Cambridge University Press.

Hadfield, Andrew. 2017. *Lying in Early Modern English Culture. From the Oath of Supremacy to the Oath of Allegiance*. Oxford: Oxford University Press.

Hahn, Alois. 1998. "Kontingenz und Kommunikation." *Kontingenz*. Ed. Gerhart von Graevenitz and Odo Marquard. Munich: Fink. 493–521.

Hardison, O. B. Jr. 1989. *Prosody and Purpose in the English Renaissance*. Baltimore, MD and London: Johns Hopkins University Press.

Harris, Tim. 1987. *London Crowds in the Reign of Charles II. Propaganda and Politics from the Restoration until the Exclusion Crisis*. Cambridge: Cambridge University Press.

Harth, Philip. 1993. *Pen for a Party. Dryden's Tory Propaganda in its Contexts*. Princeton, NJ: Princeton University Press.

Havenstein, Daniela. 1999. *Democratizing Sir Thomas Browne*. Religio Medici *and its Imitations*. Oxford: Clarendon Press.

Heal, Felicity. 2014. *The Power of Gifts. Gift-Exchange in Early Modern England*. Oxford: Oxford University Press.

Heyd, Michael. 1995. *'Be Sober and Reasonable': The Critique of Enthusiasm in the Seventeenth and Early Eighteenth Centuries*. Leiden: Brill.
Hillman, David. 1997. "Visceral Knowledge. Shakespeare, Skepticism, and the Interior of the Early Modern Body." *The Body in Parts. Fantasies of Corporeality in Early Modern Europe*. Ed. David Hillman and Carla Mazzio. New York and London: Routledge. 81–105.
Hobbes, Thomas. 1646. *A Minute or first Draught of the Optiques*. British Library Harley MS 3360. http://www.bl.uk/manuscripts/Viewer.aspx?ref=harley_ms_3360_fs001r.
Hobbes, Thomas. 1839–1845a. *Thomae* Hobbes *malmesburiensis opera philosophica quae latine scripsit omnia*. Ed. William Molesworth. 5 vols. London: John Bohn.
Hobbes, Thomas. 1839–1845b. *The English Works of Thomas Hobbes*. Ed. William Molesworth. 11 vols. London: John Bohn.
Hobbes, Thomas. 1971a. "The Answer of Mr. Hobbes to Sir William D'Avenant's Preface Before Gondibert." 1650. Davenant 1971. 45–55.
Hobbes, Thomas. 1971b. *A Dialogue between a Philosopher and a Student of the Common Laws of England*. Ed. Joseph Cropsey. Chicago: University of Chicago Press.
Hobbes, Thomas. 1975. *Hobbes's Thucydides*. Ed. Richard Schlatter. New Brunswick, NJ: Rutgers University Press.
Hobbes, Thomas. 1986. *The Rhetorics of Thomas Hobbes and Bernard Lamy*. Ed. John T. Harwood. Carbondale and Edwardsville: Southern Illinois University Press.
Hobbes, Thomas. 1990. *Behemoth or The Long Parliament*. Ed. Ferdinand Tönnies, introd. Stephen Holmes. Chicago and London: University of Chicago Press.
Hobbes, Thomas. 1991. *Man and Citizen*. Ed. Bernard Gert. Indianapolis: Hackett.
Hobbes, Thomas. 1994. *The Elements of Law Natural and Politic*. Ed. J. C. A. Gaskin. Oxford: Oxford University Press.
Hobbes, Thomas. 1996. *Leviathan*. Ed. Richard Tuck. Cambridge: Cambridge University Press.
Hobbes, Thomas. 1998. *On the Citizen*. Ed. and trans. Richard Tuck and Michael Silverthorne. Cambridge: Cambridge University Press.
Hodges, Devon L. 1985. *Renaissance Fictions of Anatomy*. Amherst, MA: University of Massachusetts Press.
Horne, Bernard S. 1970. *The Compleat Angler, 1653–1967: A New Bibliography*. Pittsburgh, PA: The Pittsburgh Bibliophiles.
Howell, Wilbur Samuel. 1956. *Logic and Rhetoric in England, 1500–1700*. Princeton: Princeton University Press.
Hüllen, Werner. 1989. *'Their Manner of Discourse.' Nachdenken über Sprache im Umkreis der Royal Society*. Tübingen: Narr.
Hume, Robert D. 1976. *The Development of English Drama in the Late Seventeenth Century*. Oxford: Clarendon Press.
Hume, Robert D. 1999. *Reconstructing Contexts. The Aims and Principles of Archaeo-Historicism*. Oxford: Oxford University Press.
Hunter, J. Paul. 1990. *Before Novels: The Cultural Contexts of Eighteenth-Century English Fiction*. New York: Norton.
Huntley, Frank L. 1953. "Sir Thomas Browne and the Metaphor of the Circle." *Journal of the History of Ideas* 14: 353–364.
Huntley, Frank L. 1962. *Sir Thomas Browne. A Biographical and Critical Study*. Ann Arbor, MI: University of Michigan Press.
Hurley, Paul J. 1971. "Law and the Dramatic Rhetoric of *The Way of the World*." *South Atlantic Quarterly* 70: 191–202.
Impey, Oliver, and Arthur MacGregor, eds. 1985. *The Origins of Museums: The Cabinet of Curiosities in Sixteenth- and Seventeenth-Century Europe*. Oxford: Clarendon Press.

Iser, Wolfgang. 1992. "Staging as an Anthropological Category." *New Literary History* 23: 877–888.
Iser, Wolfgang. 1993. *Staging Politics. The Lasting Impact of Shakespeare's Histories*. Trans. David Henry Wilson. New York: Columbia University Press.
Iser, Wolfgang. 2006. *How to Do Theory*. Malden, MA and Oxford: Blackwell.
Iser, Wolfgang. 2013. *Emergenz. Nachgelassene und verstreut publizierte Essays*. Ed. Alexander Schmitz. Konstanz: Konstanz University Press.
Jacob, James R., and Timothy Raylor. 1991. "Opera and Obedience: Thomas Hobbes and *A Proposition for Advancement of Moralitie* by Sir William Davenant." *The Seventeenth Century* 6: 205–250.
Jagodzinski, Cecile M. 1999a. "Discovery, Pornography, and the Novel: Aphra Behn's *Love-Letters Between a Nobleman and His Sister*." Jagodzinski, *Privacy and Print* 131–162.
Jagodzinski, Cecile M. 1999b. *Privacy and Print. Reading and Writing in Seventeenth-Century England*. Charlottesville, VA and London: University Press of Virginia.
Jardine, Lisa, and Anthony Grafton. 1990. "'Studied for Action': How Gabriel Harvey Read his Livy." *Past and Present* 129: 30–78.
Jauss, Hans Robert. 1970–1971. "Literary History as a Challenge to Literary Theory." Trans. Elizabeth Bensinger. *New Literary History* 2: 7–37.
Jenkins, Simon. 1975. *Landlords to London. The Story of a Capital and its Growth*. London: Constable.
Johns, Adrian. 1996. "The Physiology of Reading in Restoration England." *The Practice and Representation of Reading in England*. Ed. James Raven, Helen Small, and Naomi Tadmor. Cambridge: Cambridge University Press. 138–161.
Johns, Adrian. 1998. *The Nature of the Book. Print and Knowledge in the Making*. Chicago, IL and London: University of Chicago Press.
Jones, J. R. 1978. *Country and Court. England 1658–1714*. London: Arnold.
Kahn, Victoria. 1985. *Rhetoric, Prudence, and Skepticism in the Renaissance*. Ithaca, NY and London: Cornell University Press.
Kahn, Victoria. 1994. *Machiavellian Rhetoric from the Counter-Reformation to Milton*. Princeton, NJ: Princeton University Press.
Kamm, Jürgen. 1996. *Der Diskurs des heroischen Dramas*. Trier: WVT.
Kantorowicz, Ernst H. 1957. *The King's Two Bodies. A Study in Medieval Political Theology*. Princeton, NJ: Princeton University Press.
Kaufman, Peter Ivor. 1996. *Prayer, Despair, and Drama. Elizabethan Introspection*. Urbana and Chicago, IL: University of Illinois Press.
Keeble, N. H. 1987. *The Literary Culture of Nonconformity in Later Seventeenth-Century England*. Leicester: Leicester University Press.
Keeble, N. H., ed. 1994. *The Cultural Identity of Seventeenth-Century Women. A Reader*. London and New York: Routledge.
Kenyon, J. P., ed. 1986. *The Stuart Constitution 1603–1688. Documents and Commentary*. 2nd ed. Cambridge: Cambridge University Press.
Kermode, Frank. 1975. "Dissociation of Sensibility." *Essential Articles for the Study of John Donne's Poetry*. Ed. John R. Roberts. Hamden, CN: Archon. 66–82.
Keynes, Geoffrey. 1964. "Editor's Preface." *The Works of Sir Thomas Browne*. Ed. Geoffrey Keynes. London: Faber and Faber, 1964. Vol. 3. xi–xvii.
Kimball, Sue L. 1977. "Games People Play in Congreve's *The Way of the World*." *Essays on Fielding and Others in Honor of Miriam Austin Locke*. Ed. Donald Kay. University, AL: University of Alabama Press. 191–207.
Kinsley, James. 1955. "Historical Allusions in *Absalom and Achitophel*," *Review of English Studies* n.s. 6: 291–297.

Klein, Lawrence E. 1994. *Shaftesbury and the Culture of Politeness. Moral Discourse and Cultural Politics in Early Eighteenth-Century England*. Cambridge: Cambridge University Press.

Klein, Lawrence E. 1998. "Sociability, Solitude, and Enthusiasm." *Huntington Library Quarterly* 60: 153–177.

Knachel, Philip A. 1967. *England and the Fronde. The Impact of the English Civil War and Revolution on France*. Ithaca, NY: Cornell University Press.

Knox, Ronald A. 1950. *Enthusiasm. A Chapter in the History of Religion with Special Reference to the XVII and XVIII Centuries*. Oxford: Clarendon Press.

Kolbrener, William. 1997. *Milton's Warring Angel. A Study of Critical Engagements*. Cambridge: Cambridge University Press.

Korkowski, Bud. 1975. "Genre and Satiric Strategy in Burton's *Anatomy of Melancholy*." *Genre* 8: 74–87.

Kraft, Elizabeth. 1989. "Why Didn't Mirabell Marry the Widow Languish?" *Restoration* 13.1: 26–34.

Kroll, Richard W. F. 1986. "Discourse and Power in *The Way of the World*." *ELH* 53.4: 727–758.

Kroll, Richard W. F. 1991. *The Material Word. Literate Culture in the Restoration and Early Eighteenth Century*. Baltimore, MD and London: Johns Hopkins University Press.

Kroll, Richard W. F. 1992. "Introduction." *Philosophy, Science, and Religion in England 1640–1700*. Ed. Richard Kroll, Richard Ashcraft, and Perez Zagorin. Cambridge: Cambridge University Press. 1–28.

Kroll, Richard W. F. 2000. "Pope and Drugs: The Pharmacology of *The Rape of the Lock*." *English Literary History* 67.1: 99–141.

Kroll, Richard W. F. 2002. "Congreve as Whig: The Politics of Equivalence in *The Way of the World*." *REAL: Yearbook of Research in English and American Literature* 18: 21–38.

Kroll, Richard W. F. 2007. *Restoration Drama and 'The Circle of Commerce'. Tragicomedy, Politics and Trade in the Seventeenth Century*. Cambridge: Cambridge University Press.

Kroll, Richard, Ashcraft, Richard, and Perez Zagorin, eds. 1992. *Philosophy, Science, and Religion in England 1640–1700*. Cambridge: Cambridge University Press.

La Fontaine, Jean de. 1991. *Œuvres complètes*. Vol. 1: *Fables, contes et nouvelles*, Ed. Jean-Pierre Collinet. Paris: Gallimard.

Lamb, Charles. 1935. *The Letters of Charles Lamb*. Ed. E. V. Lucas. New Haven, CT: Yale University Press.

Laslett, Peter. 1973. *The World We Have Lost. England Before the Industrial Age*. 2nd ed. New York: Charles Scribner's Sons.

Laslett, Peter. 1988. "Introduction." *Two Treatises of Government*. By John Locke. Ed. Peter Laslett. Cambridge: Cambridge University Press. 3–126.

Lebrun, François. 1989. "The Two Reformations: Communal Devotion and Personal Piety." *Passions of the Renaissance*. Ed. Roger Chartier. Vol. 3 of *A History of Private Life*. Gen. ed. Philippe Ariès and Georges Duby. Trans. Arthur Goldhammer. Cambridge, MA and London: The Belknap Press of Harvard University Press. 69–109.

Leonard, John. 2001. "Self-Contradicting Puns in *Paradise Lost*." *A Companion to Milton*. Ed. Thomas N. Corns. Oxford: Blackwell. 393–410.

Levine, Joseph M. 1991. *The Battle of the Books. History and Literature in the Augustan Age*. Ithaca, NY and London: Cornell University Press.

Lewalski, Barbara K., ed. 1986. *Renaissance Genres. Essays on Theory, History, and Interpretation*. Cambridge, MA and London: Harvard University Press.

Lewalski, Barbara K. 2003. *The Life of John Milton. A Critical Biography*. Rev. ed. Oxford: Blackwell.

Lilley, Kate. 1994. "Introduction." *The Blazing World and Other Writings*, by Margaret Cavendish. Ed. Kate Lilley. Harmondsworth: Penguin. ix–xxxii.

Linden, Stanton J. 2001. "Margaret Cavendish and Robert Hooke: Optics and Scientific Fantasy in *The Blazing World*." *Ésotérisme, Gnoses & Imaginaire Symbolique: Mélanges offerts à Antoine Faivre*. Ed. Richard Caron et al. Leuven: Peeters. 611–623.
Lipsius, Justus. 1594. *Two Bookes of Constancie*. Trans. John Stradling. London. STC 15694.7. EEBO.
Lobsien, Eckhard. 2000. "Kontingenz des Erzählens und Erzählen der Kontingenz in Miltons *Paradise Lost*." *Kontingenz und Ordo. Selbstbegründung des Erzählens in der Neuzeit*. Ed. Bernhard Greiner and Maria Moog-Grünewald. Heidelberg: Winter. 47–57.
Lobsien, Eckhard. 2003. *Imaginationswelten. Modellierungen der Imagination und Textualisierungen der Welt in der englischen Literatur 1580–1750*. Heidelberg: Winter.
Lobsien, Verena Olejniczak. 1999. *Skeptische Phantasie. Eine andere Geschichte der frühneuzeitlichen Literatur*. Munich: Fink.
Locke, John. 1958. *Essays on the Law of Nature*. Ed. W. von Leyden. Oxford: Clarendon Press.
Locke, John. 1979. *An Essay concerning Human Understanding*. Ed. Peter H. Nidditch. Oxford: Oxford University Press.
Locke, John. 1989. *Some Thoughts Concerning Education*. Ed. John W. Yolton and Jean S. Yolton. Oxford: Clarendon Press.
Locke, John. 1993. *Political Writings of John Locke*. Ed. David Wootton. Harmondsworth: Penguin.
Loewenstein, David. 1990. *Milton and the Drama of History. Historical Vision, Iconoclasm and the Literary Imagination*. Cambridge: Cambridge University Press.
Loewenstein, Joseph. 2002. *The Author's Due. Printing and the Prehistory of Copyright*. Chicago: University of Chicago Press.
Löffler, Arno. 1972. *Sir Thomas Browne als Virtuoso. Die Bedeutung der Gelehrsamkeit für sein literarisches Alterswerk*. Nuremberg: Hans Carl.
Loftis, John E. 1973. *The Spanish Plays of Neoclassical England*. New Haven, CT and London: Yale University Press.
Loftis, John E. 1996. "Congreve's *Way of the World* and Popular Criminal Literature." *SEL* 36.3: 561–578.
Love, Harold. 1974. *Congreve*. Oxford: Blackwell.
Love, Harold. 1993. *Scribal Publication in Seventeenth-Century England*. Oxford: Clarendon Press.
Loxley, James. 1997. *Royalism and Poetry in the English Civil Wars. The Drawn Sword*. Houndmills and London: Macmillan.
Luhmann, Niklas. 1978. "Soziologie der Moral." *Theorietechnik und Moral*, by Niklas Luhmann and Stephan H. Pfürtner. Frankfurt am Main: Suhrkamp. 8–116.
Luhmann, Niklas. 1980. *Gesellschaftsstruktur und Semantik. Studien zur Wissenssoziologie der modernen Gesellschaft*. Vol. 1. Frankfurt am Main: Suhrkamp.
Luhmann, Niklas. 1984. *Soziale Systeme. Grundriß einer allgemeinen Theorie*. Frankfurt am Main: Suhrkamp.
Luhmann, Niklas. 1987. *Love as Passion. The Codification of Intimacy*. Trans. Jeremy Gaines and Doris L. Jones. Cambridge, MA: Harvard University Press.
Luhmann, Niklas. 1992. "The Form of Writing." *Stanford Literature Review* 9: 25–42.
Luhmann, Niklas. 1995. "Kultur als historischer Begriff." *Gesellschaftsstruktur und Semantik. Studien zur Wissenssoziologie der modernen Gesellschaft*. Vol. 4. Frankfurt am Main: Suhrkamp. 31–54.
Luhmann, Niklas. 1998. "Contingency as Modern Society's Defining Attribute." *Observations on Modernity*. Trans. William Whobrey. Stanford: Stanford University Press. 44–62.
Luhmann, Niklas. 2000. *Die Religion der Gesellschaft*. Ed. André Kieserling. Frankfurt am Main: Suhrkamp.
Lukács, Georg. 1971. *The Theory of the Novel. A Historico-Philosophical Essay on the Forms of Great Epic Literature*. Trans. Anna Bostock. Cambridge, MA: MIT Press.

McDowell, Nicholas. 2008. *Poetry and Allegiance in the English Civil Wars. Marvell and the Cause of Wit*. Oxford: Oxford University Press.

McKendrick, Neil, Brewer, John, and J. H. Plumb. 1982. *The Birth of a Consumer Society. The Commercialization of Eighteenth-Century England*. Bloomington, IN: Indiana University Press.

Mackenzie, George, and John Evelyn. 1986. *Public and Private Life in the Seventeenth Century: The Mackenzie-Evelyn Debate. 1665–1667*. Ed. Brian Vickers. Delmar, NY: Scholars' Facsimiles & Reprints.

McKeon, Michael. 1987a. *The Origins of the English Novel: 1600–1740*. Baltimore, MD and London: Johns Hopkins University Press.

McKeon, Michael. 1987b. "Politics of Discourses and the Rise of the Aesthetic in Seventeenth-Century England." *Politics of Discourse. The Literature and History of Seventeenth-Century England*. Ed. Kevin Sharpe and Steven N. Zwicker. Berkeley, Los Angeles, London: University of California Press. 35–51.

McKitterick, David. 2003. *Print, Manuscript and the Search for Order, 1480–1830*. Cambridge: Cambridge University Press.

MacLean, Gerald. 1995. "Literature, Culture, and Society in Restoration England." *Culture and Society in the Stuart Restoration. Literature, Drama, History*. Ed. Gerald MacLean. Cambridge: Cambridge University Press. 3–27.

Maclean, Marie. 1991. "Pretexts and Paratexts. The Art of the Peripheral." *New Literary History* 22.2: 273–279.

Macpherson, C. B. 1962. *The Political Theory of Possessive Individualism*. Oxford: Clarendon Press.

Mahler, Andreas. 2019. "New Ways of Worldmaking: English Renaissance Literature as 'Early Modern.'" *Handbook of English Renaissance Literature*. Ed. Ingo Berensmeyer. Berlin and Boston: De Gruyter, 2019. 66–88.

Makropoulos, Michael. 1997. *Modernität und Kontingenz*. Munich: Fink.

Makropoulos, Michael. 1998. "Modernität als Kontingenzkultur. Konturen eines Konzepts." *Kontingenz*. Ed. Gerhart von Graevenitz and Odo Marquard. Munich: Fink. 55–79.

Malcolm, Noel. 1996. "A Summary Biography of Hobbes." *The Cambridge Companion to Hobbes*. Ed. Tom Sorell. Cambridge: Cambridge University Press. 13–44.

Manley, Lawrence. 1999. "Criticism and the Metropolis: Tudor-Stuart London." *The Cambridge History of Literary Criticism*. Vol. 3. *The Renaissance*. Ed. Glyn P. Norton. Cambridge: Cambridge University Press. 339–347.

Marcus, Leah. 1986. *The Politics of Mirth: Jonson, Herrick, Milton, Marvell, and the Defense of Old Holiday Pastimes*. Chicago, IL: University of Chicago Press.

Maresca, Thomas E. 1974. "The Context of Dryden's *Absalom and Achitophel*." *English Literary History* 41: 340–358.

Marotti, Arthur F. 1995. *Manuscript, Print, and the English Renaissance Lyric*. Ithaca and London: Cornell University Press.

Mascuch, Michael. 1996. *Origins of the Individualist Self. Autobiography and Self-Identity in England, 1591–1791*. Stanford, CA: Stanford University Press.

Maus, Katherine Eisaman. 1995. *Inwardness and Theater in the English Renaissance*. Chicago, IL: University of Chicago Press.

Mead, George Herbert. 1934. *Mind, Self and Society from the Standpoint of a Social Behaviorist*. Chicago, IL: University of Chicago Press.

Milhous, Judith. 1984. "The Multimedia Spectacular on the Restoration Stage." *British Theatre and the Other Arts, 1660–1800*. Ed. Shirley Strum Kenny. Washington: Folger Shakespeare Library; London and Toronto: Associated University Presses. 41–66.

Miller, Jacqueline T. 1986. *Poetic License. Authority and Authorship in Medieval and Renaissance Contexts*. New York and Oxford: Oxford University Press.

Milton, John. 1953a. *Complete Prose Works of John Milton*. Vol. 1. 1623–1642. Ed. Don M. Wolfe. New Haven, CT: Yale University Press.

Milton, John. 1953b. *Complete Prose Works of John Milton*. Vol. 2. 1643–1648. Ed. Don M. Wolfe. New Haven, CT: Yale University Press.

Milton, John. 1957a. *Complete Prose Works of John Milton*. Vol. 3. Ed. 1648–1649. Ed. Merritt Y. Hughes. New Haven, CT: Yale University Press.

Milton, John. 1957b. *Complete Poems and Major Prose*. Ed. Merritt Y. Hughes. New York: Odyssey Press.

Milton, John. 1966. *Complete Prose Works of John Milton*. Vol. 4. *1650–1655*. Ed. Don M. Wolfe. New Haven, CT: Yale University Press.

Milton, John. 1998. *Paradise Lost*. Ed. Alastair Fowler. 2nd ed. Harlow: Longman.

Miner, Earl, ed. 1977. *Literary Uses of Religious Typology from the Late Middle Ages to the Present*. Princeton, NJ: Princeton University Press.

Morse, David. 1989. *England's Time of Crisis: From Shakespeare to Milton. A Cultural History*. Houndmills and London: Macmillan.

Morton, Charles. 1692. *The Spirit of Man*. Boston: Printed by B. Harris for Duncan Campbell. EEBO.

Mueller, William R. 1949. "Robert Burton's Frontispiece." *PMLA* 64: 1074–1088.

Mulryne, J. R. 1982. "The Play of Mind: Self and Audience in *Religio Medici*." *Approaches to Sir Thomas Browne. The Ann Arbor Tercentenary Lectures and Essays*. Ed. C. A. Patrides. Columbia, MO and London: University of Missouri Press. 60–68.

Nardo, Anna K. 1991. *The Ludic Self in Seventeenth-Century English Literature*. Albany, NY: State University of New York Press.

Nate, Richard. 2001. *Wissenschaft und Literatur im England der frühen Neuzeit*. Munich: Fink.

Nenner, Howard. 1997. "The Trial of the Regicides: Retribution and Treason in 1660." *Politics and the Political Imagination in Later Stuart Britain. Essays Presented to Lois Green Schwoerer*. Ed. Howard Nenner. Rochester, NY: University of Rochester Press. 21–42.

Nietzsche, Friedrich. 1988. *Kritische Studienausgabe*. Ed. Giorgio Colli and Mazzino Montinari. 15 vols. Munich: Deutscher Taschenbuch Verlag; Berlin and New York: de Gruyter.

Norbrook, David. 1994. "*Areopagitica*, Censorship, and the Early Modern Public Sphere." *The Administration of Aesthetics. Censorship, Political Criticism, and the Public Sphere*. Ed. Richard Burt. Minneapolis, MN and London: University of Minnesota Press. 3–33.

Norbrook, David. 1999. *Writing the English Republic. Poetry, Rhetoric and Politics, 1627–1660*. Cambridge: Cambridge University Press.

Norton, Glyn P. 1999. "Introduction." *The Cambridge History of Literary Criticism*. Vol. 3: *The Renaissance*. Ed. Glyn P. Norton. Cambridge: Cambridge University Press. 1–22.

Novak, Maximillian E. 1973. "Some Notes Toward a History of Fictional Forms: From Aphra Behn to Daniel Defoe." *Novel. A Forum on Fiction* 6.2: 120–133.

Novak, Maximillian E. 1984. "Foresight in the Stars and Scandal in London: Reading the Hieroglyphs in Congreve's *Love for Love*." *From Renaissance to Restoration. Metamorphoses of the Drama*. Ed. Lauree Finke and Robert Markley. Cleveland: Bellflower Press. 181–206.

Novak, Maximillian E. 2001. *Daniel Defoe: Master of Fictions. His Life and Ideas*. Oxford: Oxford University Press.

Ogden, C.K., and I. A. Richards. 1927. *The Meaning of Meaning. A Study of the Influence of Language upon Thought and the Science of Symbolism*. 1923. New York: Harcourt Brace.

Olson, David R. 1994. *The World on Paper. The Conceptual and Cognitive Implications of Writing and Reading*. Cambridge: Cambridge University Press.

O'Neill, Eileen. 2001. "Introduction." Margaret Cavendish, *Observations upon Experimental Philosophy*, ed. O'Neill. Cambridge: Cambridge University Press, 2001. x–xxxvi.

Ong, Walter J. 1982. *Orality and Literacy: The Technologizing of the Word*. London and New York: Methuen.
Pacchi, Arrigo. 1968. "Una 'Biblioteca Ideale' di Thomas Hobbes: il MS E2 dell' Archivio di Chatsworth." *Acme* 21.1: 5–42.
Palmes, Maria. 1990. "William Congreve: 'The Way of the World.'" *Europäische Komödie*. Ed. Herbert Mainusch. Darmstadt: Wissenschaftliche Buchgesellschaft. 73–97.
Parsons, Talcott. 1968. "Interaction: I. Social Interaction." *International Encyclopedia of the Social Sciences*. Ed. David L. Sills. New York: Macmillan. 7: 429–441.
Parsons, Talcott, and Edward A. Shils, eds. 1951. *Toward a General Theory of Action*. Cambridge, MA: Harvard University Press.
Pascal, Blaise. 1963. *Œuvres complètes*. Paris: Seuil.
Pater, Walter. 1901. *Appreciations, with an Essay on Style*. 4th ed. London; Macmillan.
Patey, Douglas Lane. 1984. *Probability and Literary Form. Philosophic Theory and Literary Practice in the Augustan Age*. Cambridge: Cambridge University Press.
Patterson, Annabel. 1984. *Censorship and Interpretation. The Conditions of Writing and Reading in Early Modern England*. Madison, WI: University of Wisconsin Press.
Patterson, Annabel. 1986. "Pastoral versus Georgic: The Politics of Virgilian Quotation." *Renaissance Genres. Essays on Theory, History, and Interpretation*. Ed. Barbara K. Lewalski. Cambridge, MA and London: Harvard University Press. 241–267.
Paulson, Ronald. 1996. *The Beautiful, Novel, and Strange. Aesthetics and Heterodoxy*. Baltimore, MD and London: Johns Hopkins University Press.
Paulson, William R. 1988. *The Noise of Culture. Literary Texts in a World of Information*. Ithaca, NY and London: Cornell University Press.
Pearson, Jacqueline. 1991. "Gender and Narrative in the Fiction of Aphra Behn." *Review of English Studies* n.s. 42: 40–56, 179–190.
Pearson, Jacqueline. 1996. "Women Reading, Reading Women." *Women and Literature in Britain 1500–1700*. Ed. Helen Wilcox. Cambridge: Cambridge University Press. 80–99.
Pepys, Samuel. 1970–1983. *The Diary of Samuel Pepys*. Ed. Robert Latham and William Matthews. 11 vols. London: Bell.
Perry, Ruth. 1980. *Women, Letters, and the Novel*. New York: AMS Press.
Pfeiffer, K. Ludwig. 2002. *The Protoliterary. Steps toward an Anthropology of Media*. Stanford, CA: Stanford University Press.
Picard, Liza. 1997. *Restoration London*. London: Weidenfeld and Nicolson.
Pincus, Steven. 1995. "'Coffee Politicians Does Create': Coffeehouses and Restoration Political Culture." *Journal of Modern History* 67.4: 807–834.
Plutarch. 1603. *Plutarch's Philosophie, commonlie called, the Morals*. Trans. Philemon Holland. London. EEBO.
Pocock, J. G. A. 1975. *The Machiavellian Moment. Florentine Political Thought and the Atlantic Republican Tradition*. Princeton, NJ: Princeton University Press.
Pocock, J. G. A. 1985. *Virtue, Commerce, and History. Essays on Political Thought and History, Chiefly in the Eighteenth Century*. Cambridge: Cambridge University Press.
Pocock, J. G. A. 1987. *The Ancient Constitution and the Feudal Law. A Study of English Historical Thought in the Seventeenth Century*. 1957. Cambridge: Cambridge University Press.
Pocock, J. G. A. 1998. "Enthusiasm: The Antiself of Enlightenment." *Huntington Library Quarterly* 60: 7–28.
Popkin, Richard H. 1964. *The History of Scepticism from Erasmus to Descartes*. Rev. ed. Assen: Van Gorcum.
Porter, Roy, ed. 1997. *Rewriting the Self. Histories from the Renaissance to the Present*. New York and London: Routledge.

Post, Jonathan F. S. 1985. "Browne's Revisions of *Religio Medici*." *SEL* 25.1: 145–163.
Post, Jonathan F. S. 1987. *Sir Thomas Browne*. Boston: Twayne.
Potter, Lois. 1989. *Secret Rites and Secret Writing: Royalist Literature, 1641–1660*. Cambridge: Cambridge University Press.
Poulet, Georges. 1966. *The Metamorphoses of the Circle*. Trans. Carley Dawson and Elliott Coleman. Baltimore, MD: Johns Hopkins University Press.
Poyet, Albert. 1995. "Contrat et poésie dans *Absalom and Achitophel* et *The Medall* de John Dryden." *Le contrat dans les pays anglo-saxons: théories et pratiques*. Ed. Jean-Louis Breteau. Toulouse: Presses Universitaires du Mirail. 105–116.
Preston, Claire. 2000. "In the Wilderness of Forms: Ideas and Things in Thomas Browne's Cabinets of Curiosity." *The Renaissance Computer. Knowledge Technology in the First Age of Print*. Ed. Neil Rhodes and Jonathan Sawday. London and New York: Routledge. 170–183.
Prins, Jan. 1996. "Hobbes on Light and Vision." *The Cambridge Companion to Hobbes*. Ed. Tom Sorell. Cambridge: Cambridge University Press. 129–156.
Quint, David. 1993. *Epic and Empire. Politics and Generic Form from Virgil to Milton*. Princeton, NJ: Princeton University Press.
Rees, Emma L. E. 2003. "Triply Bound: Genre and the Exilic Self." *Authorial Conquests. Essays on Genre in the Writings of Margaret Cavendish*. Ed. Line Cottegnies and Nancy Weitz. Madison and Teaneck, NJ: Fairleigh Dickinson University Press; London: Associated University Presses. 23–39.
Reik, Miriam M. 1977. *The Golden Lands of Thomas Hobbes*. Detroit, MI: Wayne State University Press.
Reiss, Timothy. 1982a. *The Discourse of Modernism*. Ithaca and London: Cornell University Press.
Reiss, Timothy. 1982b. "Power, Poetry, and the Resemblance of Nature." *Mimesis. From Mirror to Method, Augustine to Descartes*. Ed. John D. Lyons and Stephen G. Nichols, Jr. Hanover, NH and London: University Press of New England. 215–247.
Reiss, Timothy. 1992. *The Meaning of Literature*. Ithaca, NY and London: Cornell University Press.
Reiss, Timothy. 1997. *Knowledge, Discovery and Imagination in Early Modern Europe. The Rise of Aesthetic Rationalism*. Cambridge: Cambridge University Press.
Reiss, Timothy J. 1999. "Cartesian Aesthetics." *The Cambridge History of Literary Criticism*. Vol. 3. *The Renaissance*. Ed. Glyn P. Norton. Cambridge: Cambridge University Press. 511–521.
Reiss, Timothy. 2003. *Mirages of the Selfe. Patterns of Personhood in Ancient and Early Modern Europe*. Stanford, CA: Stanford University Press.
Richetti, John J. 1992. *Popular Fiction Before Richardson. Narrative Patterns: 1700–1739*. Oxford: Oxford University Press.
Rhodes, Neil, and Jonathan Sawday, eds. 2000. *The Renaissance Computer. Knowledge Technology in the First Age of Print*. London and New York: Routledge.
Robbins, Robin. 1981. "Introduction." *Pseudodoxia Epidemica* by Sir Thomas Browne. Ed. Robin Robbins. 2 vols. Oxford: Clarendon Press. 1: xxi–lxi.
Rogers, John. 1996. *The Matter of Revolution. Science, Poetry, and Politics in the Age of Milton*. Ithaca, NY and London: Cornell University Press.
Rosendale, Timothy. 2004. "Milton, Hobbes, and the Liturgical Subject." *SEL* 44.1: 149–172.
Ryle, Gilbert. 1971. "Thinking and Reflecting" and "The Thinking of Thoughts: What Is 'Le Penseur' Doing?". *Collected Essays*. Vol. 2, *1929–1968*. London: Hutchinson, 1971. 465–496.
Saenger, Paul. 1997. *Space Between Words. The Origins of Silent Reading*. Stanford, CA: Stanford University Press.
Salmon, Vivian. 1979. *The Study of Language in Seventeenth-Century England*. Amsterdam: Benjamins.
Salzman, Paul. 1985. *English Prose Fiction, 1558–1700. A Critical History*. Oxford: Clarendon Press.

Sauer, Elizabeth. 2002. "Milton and Dryden on the Restoration Stage." *Fault Lines and Controversies in the Study of Seventeenth-Century English Literature*. Ed. Claude J. Summers and Ted-Larry Pebworth. Columbia, MO and London: University of Missouri Press. 88–110.

Sawday, Jonathan. 1995. *The Body Emblazoned. Dissection and the Human Body in Renaissance Culture*. London and New York: Routledge.

Sawday, Jonathan. 1997. "Shapeless Elegance. Robert Burton's Anatomy of Knowledge." *English Renaissance Prose. History, Language, and Politics*. Ed. Neil Rhodes. Tempe, AZ: Medieval and Renaissance Texts and Studies. 173–202.

Schama, Simon. 2001. *A History of Britain. The British Wars 1603–1776*. London: BBC Worldwide.

Scheibe, Erhard. 1985. "Die Zunahme des Kontingenten in der Wissenschaft." *Neue Hefte für Philosophie* 24/25: 1–13.

Schilling, Bernard. 1961. *Dryden and the Conservative Myth. A Reading of Absalom and Achitophel*. New Haven, CT: Yale University Press.

Schivelbusch, Wolfgang. 1992. *Tastes of Paradise. A Social History of Spices, Stimulants, and Intoxicants*. Trans. David Jacobson. New York: Pantheon.

Schmelzer, Mary Murphy. 1999. *'Tis All One. "The Anatomy of Melancholy" as Belated Copious Discourse*. New York: Peter Lang.

Schmidt, Siegfried J. 1982. *Foundations for the Empirical Study of Literature*. Trans. Robert de Beaugrande. Hamburg: Buske.

Schoenfeldt, Michael G. 1999a. *Bodies and Selves in Early Modern England. Physiology and Inwardness in Spenser, Shakespeare, Herbert, and Milton*. Cambridge: Cambridge University Press.

Schoenfeldt, Michael G. 1999b. "Courts and Patronage," *The Cambridge History of Literary Criticism*. Vol. 3. *The Renaissance*. Ed. Glyn P. Norton. Cambridge: Cambridge University Press. 371–377.

Schütz, Alfred, and Thomas Luckmann. 1973. *The Structures of the Life-World*. Trans. Richard M. Zaner and Tristram Engelhardt. 2 vols. Evanston, IL: Northwestern University Press.

Schwab, Gabriele. 1996. *The Mirror and the Killer-Queen. Otherness in Literary Language*. Bloomington and Indianapolis, IN: Indiana University Press.

Schweikart, Rudolf. 1986. *Der Konstitutionsprozeß von Gesellschaft im vorindustriellen England. Historische Hermeneutik und soziologische Rekonstruktion*. Frankfurt and New York: Campus.

Scodel, Joshua. 2002. *Excess and the Mean in Early Modern English Literature*. Princeton, NJ and Oxford: Princeton University Press.

Scott, Allison V. 2006. *Selfish Gifts. The Politics of Exchange and English Courtly Literature, 1580–1628*. Madison and Teaneck, NJ: Fairleigh Dickinson University Press.

Scribner, R. W. 1988. *For the Sake of Simple Folk*. Cambridge: Cambridge University Press.

Sennett, Richard. 1994. *Flesh and Stone. The Body and the City in Western Civilization*. New York: Norton.

Shaftesbury, Anthony Ashley Cooper, Third Earl of. 1999. *Characteristics of Men, Manners, Opinions, Times*. Ed. Lawrence E. Klein. Cambridge: Cambridge University Press.

Shapin, Steven. 1994. *A Social History of Truth. Civility and Science in Seventeenth-Century England*. Chicago, IL: University of Chicago Press.

Shapin, Steven, and Simon Schaffer. 1985. *Leviathan and the Air Pump. Hobbes, Boyle, and the Experimental Life*. Princeton, NJ: Princeton University Press.

Shapiro, Barbara J. 1983. *Probability and Certainty in Seventeenth-Century England. A Study of the Relationships between Natural Science, Religion, History, Law, and Literature*. Princeton, NJ: Princeton University Press.

Sharpe, Kevin. 1987. *Criticism and Compliment. The Politics of Literature in the England of Charles I*. Cambridge: Cambridge University Press.

Sharpe, Kevin. 1992. *The Personal Rule of Charles I*. New Haven, CT and London: Yale University Press.

Sharpe, Kevin. 2000a. *Reading Revolutions. The Politics of Reading in Early Modern England*. New Haven, CT and London: Yale University Press.

Sharpe, Kevin. 2000b. *Remapping Early Modern England. The Culture of Seventeenth-Century Politics*. Cambridge: Cambridge University Press.

Shawcross, John T. 1989. "The Life of Milton." *The Cambridge Companion to Milton*. Ed. Dennis Danielson. Cambridge: Cambridge University Press. 1–19.

Sidney, Sir Philip. 1973. *A Defence of Poetry. Miscellaneous Prose of Sir Philip Sidney*. Ed. Katherine Duncan-Jones and Jan van Dorsten. Oxford: Clarendon Press. 73–121.

Shifflett, Andrew. 1998. *Stoicism, Politics, and Literature in the Age of Milton. War and Peace Reconciled*. Cambridge: Cambridge University Press, 1998.

Shifflett, Andrew. 2003. "Kings, Poets, and the Power of Forgiveness, 1642–1660." *English Literary Renaissance* 33.1: 88–110.

Silver, Victoria. 1990. "Liberal Theology and Sir Thomas Browne's 'Soft and Flexible' Discourse." *English Literary Renaissance* 20.1: 69–105.

Silver, Victoria. 1996. "Hobbes on Rhetoric." *The Cambridge Companion to Hobbes*. Ed. Tom Sorell. Cambridge: Cambridge University Press. 329–345.

Silver, Victoria. 2001. *Imperfect Sense. The Predicament of Milton's Irony*. Princeton, NJ and Oxford: Princeton University Press.

Simmel, Georg. 1968. "Das Geheimnis und die geheime Gesellschaft." *Soziologie. Untersuchungen über die Formen der Vergesellschaftung*. 5th ed. Berlin: Duncker & Humblot. 256–304.

Simon, Irène. 1971. "Introduction." *Neo-Classical Criticism 1660–1800*. Ed. Irène Simon. London: Arnold. 9–35.

Skinner, Quentin. 1978. *The Foundations of Modern Political Thought*. 2 vols. Cambridge: Cambridge University Press.

Skinner, Quentin. 1981. *Machiavelli*. Oxford: Oxford University Press.

Skinner, Quentin. 1996. *Reason and Rhetoric in the Philosophy of Hobbes*. Cambridge: Cambridge University Press.

Sorell, Tom, ed. 1996. *The Cambridge Companion to Hobbes*. Cambridge: Cambridge University Press.

Speck, W. A. 2008. "Spencer, Robert, second earl of Sunderland (1641–1702)." *Oxford Dictionary of National Biography*. 3 Jan. 2008. Accessed 14 Aug. 2019.

Spenser, Edmund. *The Faerie Queene*. Ed Thomas P. Roche, Jr. Harmondsworth: Penguin, 1987.

Sprat, Thomas. 1958. *The History of the Royal-Society of London, For the Improving of Natural Knowledge*. 1667. Rpt. ed. Jackson I. Cope and Harold Whitmore Jones. St Louis, MO: Washington University Studies.

Springborg, Patricia. 1997. "*Leviathan*, Mythic History, and National Historiography." *The Historical Imagination in Early Modern Britain. History, Rhetoric, and Fiction, 1500–1800*. Ed. Donald R. Kelley and David Harris Sacks. Cambridge: Woodrow Wilson Center Press and Cambridge University Press. 267–297.

Spurr, John. 1998. "England 1649–1750: Differences Contained?" *The Cambridge Companion to English Literature 1650–1740*. Ed. Steven N. Zwicker. Cambridge: Cambridge University Press. 3–32.

Stallybrass, Peter. 1992. "Shakespeare, the Individual, and the Text." *Cultural Studies*, ed. Lawrence Grossberg, Cary Nelson, and Paula A. Treichler. New York and London: Routledge. 593–612.

Steen, Francis F. 2002. "The Politics of Love: Propaganda and Structural Learning in Aphra Behn's *Love-Letters between a Nobleman and His Sister*." *Poetics Today* 23.1: 91–122.

Stevens, Wallace. 1990 [1967]. "The Poems of Our Climate." *The Palm at the End of the Mind: Selected Poems and a Play*. Ed. Holly Stevens. New York: Vintage. 158.

Stone, Lawrence. 1964. "The Educational Revolution in England, 1560–1640." *Past and Present* 28.1: 41–80.

Stone, Lawrence. 1990. *The Road to Divorce*. Oxford: Oxford University Press.

Strachey, Lytton. 1922. *Books and Characters, French and English*. London: Chatto and Windus.

Straznicky, Marta. 1990. "Performing the Self in Browne's *Religio Medici*." *Prose Studies* 13.2: 211–229.

Talmor, Sascha. 1981. *Glanvill. The Uses and Abuses of Scepticism*. Oxford and New York: Pergamon Press.

Taylor, Charles. 1989. *Sources of the Self. The Making of the Modern Identity*. Cambridge: Cambridge University Press.

Todd, Janet. 1993. "Textual Introduction." *Love-Letters Between a Nobleman and His Sister*. Vol. 2 of *The Works of Aphra Behn*. Ed. Janet Todd. London: William Pickering. vii–xiii.

Todd, Janet. 1996. "Who Is Silvia? What Is She? Feminine Identity in Aphra Behn's *Love-Letters Between a Nobleman and His Sister*." *Aphra Behn Studies*. Ed. Janet Todd. Cambridge: Cambridge University Press. 199–218.

Todorov, Tzvetan. 1976–77. "The Origin of Genres." *New Literary History* 8: 159–170.

Tuck, Richard. 1979. *Natural Rights Theories. Their Origin and Development*. Cambridge: Cambridge University Press.

Tuck, Richard. 1993. *Philosophy and Government 1572–1651*. Cambridge: Cambridge University Press.

Tuck, Richard. 1996. "Hobbes's Moral Philosophy." *The Cambridge Companion to Hobbes*. Ed. Tom Sorell. Cambridge: Cambridge University Press. 175–207.

Tuke, Samuel. 1660. *A Character of Charles the Second*. London: Printed for Gabriel Bedell. EEBO.

Tuke, Samuel. 1663. *The Adventures of Five Hours. A Tragi-Comedy*. London: Printed for Henry Herringman. EEBO.

Tulloch, John. 1874. *Rational Theology and Christian Philosophy in England*. 1872. 2nd ed. 2 vols. Edinburgh and London: Blackwood.

Turner, James Grantham. 1995. "Pepys and the Private Parts of Monarchy." *Culture and Society in the Stuart Restoration. Literature, Drama, History*. Ed. Gerald MacLean. Cambridge: Cambridge University Press. 95–110.

Vaihinger, Hans. 1922. *Die Philosophie des Als Ob. System der theoretischen und religiösen Fiktionen der Menschheit auf Grund eines idealistischen Positivismus*. 1911. Leipzig: Felix Meiner.

Vander Motten, J. P., and Katrien Daemen-de Gelder. 2006. "Sir Samuel Tuke (*c*.1615–1674) at the 'Little Court' of Mary Stuart (1631–1660)." *Notes and Queries* 251: 168–170.

van Leeuwen, Henry G. 1963. *The Problem of Certainty in English Thought 1630–1690*. The Hague: Martinus Nijhoff.

Villegas López, Sonia. 2015. "'The Conscious Grove': Generic Experimentation in Aphra Behn's *Love-Letters Between a Nobleman and His Sister* (1684–87)." *Women's Writing* 22.1: 69–83.

Vicari, E. Patricia. 1989. *The View from Minerva's Tower. Learning and Imagination in* The Anatomy of Melancholy. Toronto, Buffalo, London: University of Toronto Press.

Vickers, Brian, ed. 1984. *Occult and Scientific Mentalities in the Renaissance*. Cambridge: Cambridge University Press.

Visser, Colin. 1975. "The Anatomy of the Early Restoration Stage: *The Adventures of Five Hours* and John Dryden's 'Spanish' Comedies." *Theatre Notebook* 29: 56–69, 114–119.

von Maltzahn, Nicholas. 1996. "The First Reception of *Paradise Lost* (1667)." *Review of English Studies* n.s. 47.188: 479–499.

Wagner-Egelhaaf, Martina. 1997. *Die Melancholie der Literatur. Diskursgeschichte und Textfiguration*. Stuttgart and Weimar: Metzler.

Wagoner, Mary. 1968. "The Gambling Analogy in *The Way of the World*." *Tennessee Studies in Literature* 13: 75–80.

Waldenfels, Bernhard. 1990. *Der Stachel des Fremden*. Frankfurt am Main, Suhrkamp.

Walker, William. 2001. "Shaftesbury, Satan, Persuasion, and Whig Ideology." *Dryden and the World of Neoclassicism*. Ed. Wolfgang Görtschacher and Holger Klein. Tübingen: Stauffenburg, 2001. 232–241.

Wallace, John M. 1974–75. "'Examples are Best Precepts': Readers and Meanings in Seventeenth-Century Poetry." *Critical Inquiry* 1: 273–290.

Walton, Izaak. 1983. *The Compleat Angler*. Ed. Jonquil Bevan. Oxford: Clarendon Press.

Warner, William B. 1998. *Licensing Entertainment. The Elevation of Novel Reading in Britain, 1684–1750*. Berkeley, Los Angeles, London: University of California Press.

Warner, William B. 2016. "Reality and the Novel: Latour and the Uses of Fiction." *Eighteenth Century: Theory & Interpretation* 57.2: 267–279.

Warren, Austin. 1970. "The Styles of Thomas Browne." *Connections*. Ann Arbor, MI: University of Michigan Press. 11–23, 186–88.

Watson, George, ed. 1962. *Of Dramatic Poesy and Other Critical Essays*. By John Dryden. 2 vols. London: Dent.

Watt, Ian. 1962. *The Rise of the Novel: Studies in Defoe, Richardson and Fielding*. 1957. Berkeley and Los Angeles: University of California Press.

Watt, Tessa. 1991. *Cheap Print and Popular Piety 1550–1640*. Cambridge: Cambridge University Press.

Wehrs, Donald R. 1992. "Eros, Ethics, Identity: Royalist Feminism and the Politics of Desire in Aphra Behn's Love Letters." *SEL* 32: 461–478.

Wellbery, David. 1992. "The Exteriority of Writing." *Stanford Literature Review* 9: 11–23.

Wheale, Nigel: *Writing and Society. Literacy, Print and Politics in Britain 1590–1660*. London and New York: Routledge, 1999.

Wilden, Anthony. 1987. *The Rules Are No Game. The Strategy of Communication*. London and New York: Routledge and Kegan Paul.

Wilding, Michael. 1987. *Dragons Teeth. Literature in the English Revolution*. Oxford: Clarendon Press.

Wiley, Margaret L. 1952. *The Subtle Knot. Creative Skepticim in Seventeenth Century England*. London: George Allen & Unwin.

Willey, Basil. 1965. *The Seventeenth Century Background. Studies in the Thought of the Age in Relation to Poetry and Religion*. 1934. New York: Columbia University Press.

Williams, Raymond. 1977. "Dominant, Residual, and Emergent." *Marxism and Literature*. Oxford: Oxford University Press. 121–127.

Williams, Raymond. 1983. *Keywords. A Vocabulary of Culture and Society*. New York: Oxford University Press.

Williams, R. Grant. 2001. "Disfiguring the Body of Knowledge: Anatomical Discourse and Robert Burton's *The Anatomy of Melancholy*." *English Literary History* 68.3: 593–613.

Williamson, George. 1970. "Dryden's View of Milton." *Milton and Others*. Chicago: University of Chicago Press, 1970. 103–121.

Wimsatt, W.K. Jr., and Monroe C. Beardsley. 1954. "The Affective Fallacy." *The Verbal Icon. Studies in the Meaning of Poetry*, by W. K. Wimsatt, Jr. Lexington, KY: University of Kentucky Press. 21–39.

Winn, James Anderson. 1987. *John Dryden and His World*. New Haven and London: Yale University Press.

Womersley, David, ed. 2000. *Restoration Drama. An Anthology*. Oxford: Blackwell.
Woolf, Virginia. 1994. "The Elizabethan Lumber Room." 1925. *The Essays*. Vol. 4. 1925–1928. Ed. Andrew McNeillie. London: Hogarth Press. 53–61.
Wootton, David. 1993. "Introduction." *Political Writings*, by John Locke. Ed. David Wootton. Harmondsworth: Penguin. 5–122.
Wordsworth, William. 1977. *Poems*. Vol. 2. Ed. John O. Hayden. Harmondsworth: Penguin.
Wright, Thomas. 1971. *The Passions of the Minde in Generall*. 1604. Ed. Thomas O. Sloan. Urbana, Chicago, London: University of Illinois Press.
Wrigley, E. A., and R. S. Schofield. 1981. *The Population History of England 1541–1871. A Reconstruction*. London: Edward Arnold.
Yates, Frances A. 1977. *Astraea. The Imperial Theme in the Sixteenth Century*. 1975. Harmondsworth: Penguin.
Young, Bruce W. 1986. "Thomas Hobbes versus the Poets: Form, Expression, and Metaphor in Early Seventeenth-Century Poetry." *Encyclia. Proceedings of the Utah Academy of Sciences, Arts and Letters* 63. 151–162.
Zagorin, Perez. 1990. *Ways of Lying. Dissimulation, Persecution, and Conformity in Early Modern Europe*. Cambridge, MA: Harvard University Press.
Zwicker, Steven N. 1988. "England, Israel, and the Triumph of Roman Virtue." *Millenarianism and Messianism in English Literature and Thought 1650–1700. Clark Library Lectures 1981–1982*. Ed. Richard H. Popkin. Leiden and New York: Brill. 37–64.
Zwicker, Steven N. 1993. *Lines of Authority. Politics and English Literary Culture, 1649–1689*. Ithaca, NY and London: Cornell University Press.
Zwicker, Steven N. 1995. "Milton, Dryden, and the Politics of Literary Controversy." *Culture and Society in the Stuart* Restoration. *Literature, Drama, History*. Ed. Gerald MacLean. Cambridge: Cambridge University Press. 137–158.
Zwicker, Steven N. 1997. "Irony, Modernity, and Miscellany: Politics and Aesthetics in the Stuart Restoration." *Politics and the Political Imagination in Later Stuart* Britain. *Essays Presented to Lois Green Schwoerer*. Ed. Howard Nenner. Rochester, NY: University of Rochester Press. 181–195.
Zwicker, Steven N. 1998a. "John Dryden". *Cambridge Companion to English Literature 1650–1740*. Ed. Steven N. Zwicker. Cambridge: Cambridge University Press. 185–203.
Zwicker, Steven N. 1998b. "Reading the Margins. Politics and the Habits of Appreciation". *Refiguring Revolutions. Aesthetics and Politics from the English Revolution to the Romantic Revolution*. Ed. Kevin Sharpe and Steven N. Zwicker. Berkeley, Los Angeles, London: University of California Press. 101–115.
Zwicker, Steven N. 2003. "The Constitution of Opinion and the Pacification of Reading". *Reading, Society and Politics in Early Modern England*. Ed. Kevin Sharpe and Steven N. Zwicker. Cambridge: Cambridge University Press. 295–316.
Zwierlein, Anne Julia. 2001. *Majestick Milton: British Imperial Expansion and Transformations of Paradise Lost, 1667–1837*. Münster: LIT.
Zwierlein, Anne Julia. 2019. "John Milton, *Paradise Lost* (1667/1674)". *Handbook of English Renaissance Literature*. Ed. Ingo Berensmeyer. Berlin and Boston: De Gruyter. 635–659.

Index

Abdera 41, 45
Absalom, *see also* Dryden 167, 169, 171–173, 187
absence 44, 49, 78, 83, 89, 103, 119, 121, 141, 179, 186, 201
absolutism, *see also* monarch 3, 88, 96, 104, 113–114, 119–120, 154, 206
abstraction 18, 63–65, 71, 73, 75, 81, 85, 99, 105, 162, 167, 171
accommodation 80, 83, 153, 176, 219, 222
Achilles 114
Achitophel, *see also* Dryden 167, 169–170, 172–173, 185, 194
action, *see also* theory 15, 24–25, 50, 84, 86, 88, 93, 100, 119, 138, 149, 150, 159, 161, 179–181, 188, 190, 192–193, 203, 208
– human action 88, 91
– legal action 207
– military action 96
– political action 25, 127
– social action 19, 102, 219
actor *or* actress 1, 41–42, 49, 151, 178, 180–181, 204
Adam 64, 70, 80–82, 133, 144, 155–156, 159–160, 167–168, 170, 173, 189, 198–199
adaptation 42, 48, 66, 69, 74–75, 77, 126, 136–137, 149, 156, 160–161, 163, 187, 191, 195
Addison, Joseph 162, 215
adiaphora 218
admiration 6, 30–32, 40, 61, 63, 80, 86, 99, 126, 162, 189, 202
adornment 26, 61, 93, 95, 108
adumbration 66
adventure 42, 154, 156, 188, 197
Aeneas 155, 159
aesthetics 1, 4, 7, 13–14, 17–18, 20, 23, 26, 33, 42, 66, 70–71, 74, 76, 90, 94, 96–99, 108, 137, 144, 151, 154–156, 161–162, 166, 168, 178, 182, 184, 190, 197, 208, 213, 215, 217, 219, 222
affection 39, 54, 85, 94, 141, 193–194, 202, 204, 206
afterlife 62, 95, 119, 125

age, *see also* print, reason 1, 32, 35, 36, 56, 60, 82, 105, 166, 172, 191
– early modern age 76
– Elizabethan age 116, 134, 155
– golden age 155
– iron age 155
Agrippa von Nettesheim 44
– *De occulta philosophia* 44
alchemy 50, 73, 129
alcohol 201, 205
Alexander the Great 90, 113, 114
allegory 11, 56, 63, 104, 116, 124, 135–136, 152, 155, 159, 161–162, 166–168, 171, 191, 202–203
– biblical allegory 167
alliteration 65
allusion 3–4, 28–29, 36, 49–50, 52, 100–101, 104, 136, 139, 141, 152, 154–157, 159, 163, 166–168, 170, 172, 174, 205
– biblical allusion 159
ambiguity 14, 38–39, 50–52, 62, 83, 168, 172, 193, 207
ambivalence 124
America 21, 61, 91
amnesia 144
amnesty 144, 164
amorality, *see also* immorality 117
amphitheatre 90
amplification 216
analogy 2, 31–32, 54, 58, 64, 71, 74–75, 78, 85–86, 98, 115, 131, 152, 157, 163–164, 170, 175, 182, 196–197
anarchy 9, 118, 158, 170–171, 174
anatomy 35–36, 43
angel 62, 80, 112, 172
anger 54, 58, 111, 126, 163, 208, 218
Anglicanism 139
animal 41, 65, 87, 98, 117, 120, 125
– animal metaphors 118–120,
– animal spirits 84–86,
– political animal 118
animus 157, 177
Anne, Queen of England, Scotland and Ireland 201
annotation 6, 190

anonymity 25, 128, 162–163, 187, 191
anthology 72, 139
anthropology 9, 31, 86–87, 89, 117, 121–122, 198
anti-deism 220
anti-democratic 174
anti-determinism 219
anti-Dutch sentiment 152
anti-Puritanism 149, 152, 157, 166
antiquity 60, 184, 191
anti-persuasive attitude 51
anti-republicanism 78, 158
anti-royalism 153, 161
antitheatricalism 210
anti-Whiggism 166, 190, 199
aporia 62
Arcadia 138, 144–145
architecture 4, 132, 157, 177
archive 9, 172
Arendt, Hannah 200, 203, 213
– *The Human Condition* 200
Areopagus 129
Ares 129
aristocracy 78, 129, 138, 216
Aristotle 28, 71, 88, 99, 101, 118, 222
– *Politics* 118
arithmetic 81
Ark of the Covenant 172
Armstrong, Thomas 187
army 60, 74, 100, 102–103, 128, 144, 201
Arnold, Matthew 9, 215
art 32, 37, 47, 60, 65–67, 70–71, 74, 88, 97, 100–101, 111–112, 120, 126–127, 139–140, 147, 157–158, 165, 181, 193–195, 206, 213, 218
– *art de vivre* 134
– artist 94
– freedom of art 9
– visual arts 23
– work of art 9, 215
artificiality 47, 56, 80, 94, 97, 104, 115, 145, 147, 168, 190, 194–195, 197–198, 204, 206–207, 218
Assmann, Aleida 9, 145
assonance 65
Astraea, *see also* Dryden 148, 155
Astragon, court of 140
astrolabe 37
astrology 95 *see also* star
astronomy 156

Athena 130
Athens 127, 129, 133, 172
Atlas 150–151
atom 108, 178
atonement 155, 157
attribution 128, 149, 160, 187, 198
audience 2, 15, 17, 19–21, 25, 33–34, 67, 78, 90, 95–98, 101, 106, 114, 125, 130, 134, 136, 144, 150, 152, 154, 165, 176, 182, 185, 187, 197, 201, 204, 206, 211
aurality 2, 80, 82, 105, 115
Austen, Jane 215
– *Persuasion* 215
authenticity 33, 45, 47, 77, 160, 179, 181, 186, 188–189, 192, 193, 194–198, 204, 213
author, authorship 3–4, 9, 12, 14–15, 17, 22, 24–26, 29, 32–41, 43–48, 51, 53, 67–68, 72–73, 89, 94, 96–97, 106–108, 110, 113–114, 133, 159, 164–165, 178, 184–186, 190–191, 197, 199, 210–211, 214, 216, 220
– author position 35–36, 43, 47, 107
– authorial persona 137
– author-image 28, 37–40, 47
– coauthorship 60
– contingency of authorship 37
authority 18, 25–26, 34–35, 37, 49, 60, 73, 75, 83, 88, 96–97, 100, 102, 120, 122, 127, 136–137, 139, 144, 147–148, 155–156, 159, 161, 173–174, 189, 196, 213, 220, 222
autobiography 127
autonomy 7, 9, 10, 18, 24, 26, 70–72, 74, 89, 106, 179, 183, 189, 198, 206

Bacon, Francis 25, 29, 31, 53–54, 60–61, 87, 101, 108, 131, 178, 216
– *Advancement of Learning* 60–61
– *Novum Organon* 53
– "Of Studies" 131
bagpipe 93
Bakhtin, Mikhail M. 106, 184–185
balance 33, 43, 58–59, 66, 120, 131–132, 163, 168, 182–183, 210, 213–214
Baldwin, William 22
– *Beware the Cat* 22
Bank of England 201
barbarian *or* barbarism 78, 119, 133
Barksdale, Clement 136
– *Nympha libethris, or The Cotswold Muse* 136
baroque 4, 6, 48, 64

Barrow, Isaac 183
Barthes, Roland 138
Barzillai 171
Bate, Henry 61
beast, *see also* bestiality 87, 98, 117, 119, 203, 211
Beatrice (character in Shakespeare's *Much Ado About Nothing*) 180
beauty 78, 90, 102, 106, 108, 189, 195–196, 208, 210
– natural beauty 143, 155
beggar 55, 140–141
Behn, Aphra 11, 26–27, 182, 184–200, 204
– *Love-Letters between a Nobleman and His Sister* 11, 178, 184–200, 204, 212
– *The Rover* 140, 195–196
belief 5, 28, 35, 55, 62, 75, 79, 81, 97, 112, 114, 126, 144, 180–182, 220
Bellarmine, Robert 118
Berkeley, Henrietta 187–188
Berkeley, Robert 161
bestiality, *see also* beast 118
bestseller 77, 134
Bethlehem, Star of 156
Bible, *see also* allusion, interpretation, narrative 25–26, 38, 54, 56, 60, 64, 103, 135, 139, 156, 159–162, 166–167, 171, 190, 212, 220
bildungsroman, *see also* novel 70
black box 197
blackness 62
blending 29, 59, 61, 67–68, 155, 157
– generic blending 144
blindness 70, 80–82, 150, 156, 158
blood, *see also* circulation 8, 19, 112, 149, 151, 169, 171
– royal blood 168
Blumenberg, Hans 2, 7, 16, 20–21, 50, 67, 75
body 57, 64–65, 72, 83–85, 100–101, 160, 164, 177–178, 180–181, 186, 194, 209
– body natural 131, 157, 169, 175
– body politic 3, 55, 74, 131, 148, 157, 163–164, 169, 175
bondage 217
book, *see also* codex 17, 24, 32, 36–42, 44, 46–47, 51–53, 55, 59–61, 77, 79, 88–89, 97, 105–107, 109–111, 127, 129, 131, 134–137, 140, 143–144, 191, 193, 197, 210–212, 214, 220, 221
– *Book of Common Prayer* 139

– bookseller 187
– book trade 73
– courtesy book 99
– how-to-book 29
– printed book 21–22, 25, 34, 84, 123–124, 129
Borges, Jorge Luis 15
Boswell, James 217
Boyle, Robert 29
Bradford (ship) 146
brain 44, 55, 84–86, 91, 107
Brathwait, Richard 142
– *The English Gentleman* 142
Breda *see under* Declaration of Breda
Britain *or* British 200, 212, 214
Broadgates Hall 49
Browne, Thomas 10, 25, 28, 30–33, 47–69, 71–72, 76, 83, 96, 104, 107, 114–115, 119, 134–137, 139, 174, 176–177, 180, 214, 218–219
– *Christian Morals* 66–67, 70
– *The Garden of Cyrus* 32, 48, 63, 65–66, 115
– *Hydriotaphia* 49, 62–66,
– *Pseudodoxia Epidemica* 29, 48, 59–61, 63
– *Religio Medici* 25, 28, 33, 48, 50–60, 62–63, 66, 83, 115, 134–137, 139, 177, 219
Buchanan, George 118, 122
– *De Iure Regni apud Scotos* 118
The Bucolicks of Baptist Mantuan 136
Buckingham, George Villiers, second Duke of 164, 171
Bunyan, John 11, 29, 210, 220–221
– *The Pilgrim's Progress* 220–221
– *Works* 210
Burke, Edmund 105
Burke, Kenneth 9, 216
Burton, Robert 10, 27–48, 50, 55, 59–62, 67–68, 71–73, 76, 96, 104, 106–107, 119, 131, 176, 180
– *The Anatomy of Melancholy* 28, 34–47, 55, 60, 68, 104, 131
Bussy-Rabutin, Roger de 191
– *Histoire amoureuse des Gaules* 191
Byron, George Gordon, Lord 215
– *The Giaour* 215

cabal 205, 207, 209
cabbalism, *see also* Kabbalah 108
cabinet, *see also* wonder 211

Index

Cadmus 129–130
Caesar (Gaius Julius Caesar) 110, 113, 114
calculation 120, 122–123
Calderón de la Barca, Pedro 149
Calvinism 118, 122, 157
Cambridge 23
– Cambridge Platonists 29
– Cambridge School 12
Campanella, Tommaso 42
canon, *see also* law 28, 145, 162, 222
– Canon of Toledo 22, 53
capitalism 4, 72, 140, 197
Carew, Thomas 177
caricature 185, 190, 194
Carolean period 153
Caroline period 150
Cartesianism, *see also* Descartes 81, 85–86, 122
Cary, Lucius, Viscount Falkland 119
Castiglione, Baldassare 137, 182
– *The Book of the Courtier* 182
casuistry 17
Catholicism 4, 78–79, 82, 132, 164, 180, 187, 201, 219
Cavalier 136, 212
– *Five Love-letters from a Nun to a Cavalier* 191
Cavendish, Margaret, first Duchess of Newcastle 11, 26, 76–77, 104–115, 127
– *The Blazing World* 77, 104–115
– *Nature's Pictures drawn by Fancy's Pencil to the Life* 107
– *Observations upon Experimental Philosophy* 104–114
– *Philosophical Letters* 107
Cavendish, William, first Duke of Newcastle 25–26, 127, 144, 157
Cavendish, William, third Earl of Devonshire 127
celebrity 163
celerity 95
Celt 61
censorship, *see also* licensing 9, 22, 44, 52, 115, 124, 129–130, 132, 140, 152
cento 36, 43
century
– eighteenth century 5, 10–11, 17, 27, 69–70, 76, 105, 176, 178, 201–202, 206, 208, 213–216, 219, 221
– fifteenth century 73
– nineteenth century 6, 70, 215
– seventeenth century 2–13, 15, 17, 19, 22–24, 27, 29–30, 32, 47–48, 67–77, 85, 91, 95–96, 99, 104, 106, 114–118, 120–121, 123–124, 134–135, 139–140, 142–144, 146, 155, 160, 163, 165, 175, 177–180, 183–184, 191, 201, 208, 213–214, 216, 218, 220–223,
– sixteenth century 36, 118, 182
– twelfth century 42
– twentieth century 8, 215
ceremony 203, 205, 212
certainty 7, 21, 38, 49, 56, 62, 66, 76, 82, 99, 130, 182, 196
Certeau, Michel de 6–7, 18
Cervantes, Miguel de 15, 22, 53
– *Don Quijote* 15, 22, 53, 90
Cesario 187, 191
chain of being 59
change, *see also* fortune, perspective 14–15, 21, 26, 48, 52, 67, 116, 121, 136, 146, 170, 174, 198, 203, 220
– epistemic change 73, 75–76,
– functional change 20, 73, 222
– media change 22
– regime change 145
– semantic change 179
– structural change 21
chaos 42, 145, 160, 174
chapbook 83
character 56, 112, 138, 142, 150–151, 164, 167–169, 171, 178, 182–191, 193–201, 203–212, 215
– fictional character 90, 185, 189
– flat vs. round character 185
– heroic character 90
characterisation 185–186
charity 58
Charles I, King of England, Scotland and Ireland 77, 83, 91, 96, 118, 146
Charles II, King of England, Scotland and Ireland 25–26, 96, 102–103, 110, 112, 116, 148–149, 151, 153–157, 159, 162, 165–169, 171, 177, 187, 201
Charles, Royal (ship) 146
Charron, Pierre 139
chastity 194
checks and balances 54, 56, 58–59
Cheriton (ship) 146

chess 54
child *or* childhood 22–23, 117, 208, 216
Chillingworth, William 119, 123
 – *The Religion of Protestants a Safe Way to Salvation* 123
china 211
chivalry 116, 165
Christ, *see also* Jesus 139, 155–157, 159, 166
Christianity 30, 55, 58, 62, 79–80, 131, 139, 151–152, 155–157, 159, 203, 210
Christmas 156
Chronicles (biblical books) 172
chronotope 184
church 4, 54, 74, 111, 158, 203, 214, 218
Cicero, Marcus Tullius 30, 117–120, 125, 133, 135, 158
 – *De inventione* 117
 – *De oratore* 117, 125
circulation 6–8, 19–21, 72–74, 76, 131, 178, 182, 198
 – circulation of the blood 19
 – circulation of social energy 19, 72
 – manuscript circulation 9, 21
citizen 45, 115, 119, 125, 127, 147, 157, 176, 179
city 1, 4, 41, 92, 130, 132, 139, 141, 145, 149, 151, 176
Civil War, English 1, 11, 25–26, 29, 51, 69, 74, 96, 115, 118, 120–122, 136, 146–147, 149–150, 153, 157, 208, 219
civilisation 16, 115, 117–119, 121, 123, 132, 170
civility 10–11, 69, 128, 139–140, 143, 165, 182, 203, 210, 219, 222
civitas 116, 122
class, *see also* conflict 9, 95, 137, 201, 207, 216
classicism 71, 136
closet 210–211
code, *see also* honour, love 9, 69, 71, 136, 143, 180, 185, 193–194, 196, 199–200, 210, 212
 – legal code 117
 – rhetorical code 197, 199
 – social code 9
codex, *see also* book 212
codification 20
Coello, Antonio 149
 – *Los empeños de seis horas* 148
coffee 205, 217
 – coffee-house 1, 30, 201, 217
cognition 11, 86, 105
coherence 5, 7–8, 31, 73, 76

Coleridge, Samuel Taylor 28, 50, 97, 105, 143, 197
collaboration 47, 77, 91, 107, 123, 184
collective 1, 25, 165, 180
Collier, Jeremy 210
 – *A Short View of the Stage* 210
Cologne 188
colour 24, 86–87, 89–90, 93, 110, 113, 118, 156
Columbus, Christopher 20
comedy 42, 49–50, 150–151, 166, 195, 200, 202–204, 207
 – Restoration comedy 140, 151, 182–183, 187, 201, 207
commentary 34, 36, 39–40, 45, 48, 146, 155, 163
commerce 1, 5, 58, 182
commoner 97–98, 100
commonplace 14, 49, 61, 91–92, 94
Commons 129, 154
common sense, *see also sensus communis* 30, 140, 183, 214, 218–219
commonwealth 1, 5, 11, 54–58, 72, 74, 95, 98, 111, 125–126, 130–131, 144–145, 176, 200, 203, 210, 217
Commonwealth 83, 142, 146, 203, 210
communication 1, 5, 8, 10–11, 13–18, 20–21, 23–26, 30, 32–34, 37, 40, 43–44, 47–50, 55, 57, 61, 64, 67–69, 71–73, 75–76, 78, 84–85, 87–88, 94, 96–97, 106, 108–109, 111, 114–115, 124–126, 140–141, 143, 151, 176, 178, 180–184, 186, 192–193, 198, 201, 212–213, 217, 219
 – aesthetic communication 7, 26
 – communicative behaviour 208
 – communicative situation 92, 106
 – cultural communication 123
 – epistolary communication 185, 192
 – intimate communication 212
 – literary communication 6–7, 10, 13–15, 17–18, 20–21, 24, 26, 33–34, 40, 67–69, 71, 73, 75–77, 89, 98, 113–114, 116, 136, 212, 216, 219, 221–222,
 – meta-communication 10
 – non-verbal communication 209
 – poetic communication 89, 97, 165, 213
 – print communication 22, 24, 67, 131
 – rational communication 79
 – scientific communication 75, 137
 – textual communication 7, 13–14, 34, 72, 94, 221

community 72, 122, 125, 130, 220
- reading community 73
- royalist community 96
- utopian community 42
comparison 32, 34, 63–64, 67, 78, 95, 98, 102, 127, 133, 149, 197, 216
complexity 6, 18, 21, 29, 32–34, 37, 43, 48, 55, 67–68, 72, 75, 79, 83, 90, 96, 99, 101, 105, 134, 141–143, 152, 163, 174, 180, 201, 203, 214, 217, 221–222
compromise 17, 54, 153, 159, 162, 222
concordia discors 132
concreteness 50, 63–66, 72, 75, 105, 149, 171
Condon, Thomas 188
confession 35, 43, 50, 52, 103, 153, 163, 209
configuration 7, 20, 28, 32, 35, 73–74, 102, 116, 179, 182, 188, 217
- media configuration 34, 72, 124
conflict, *see also* norm 5–8, 13, 25, 48, 51, 56, 58, 60, 69, 74–75, 79, 84, 86, 88, 95–96, 114–116, 121, 123, 130–131, 138–139, 142, 144, 146, 156–157, 161, 165, 175, 178, 180–181, 183, 203, 207–208, 219
- armed conflict 130
- class conflict 9
- internecine conflict 152
- literary conflict 186
Congreve, William 11, 26, 117, 144, 178, 182, 200–214
- *Love for Love* 206, 209, 212
- *The Way of the World* 11, 117, 144, 178, 182, 200–214, 216
conjecture 17, 65–66, 159, 183, 185–186, 193
conscience 58–59, 122, 130, 134, 141, 181, 212
consensus 88, 161, 174, 216
conspiracy, *see also* plot 187
constancy 99, 121, 168, 185, 195, 199
constitution, *see also* monarchy 122, 131, 146, 148, 154, 173, 201–204
- ancient constitution 173
- constitutionalism 118
construction 48, 81, 101, 119, 120, 163, 168, 190
constructivism 16, 21
consumerism 4
consumption 4, 31, 36, 72, 205
content 18, 41, 94, 135, 158, 186–187, 192, 210, 212
- world-content 31
context 6, 8, 10, 14–15, 18–20, 26, 31–32, 51, 64, 88, 90, 106, 108, 190, 193, 212, 216, 218–219
- historical context 11, 15, 48, 96, 142, 149, 155, 215
- open context 20–21, 67, 75
- political *or* social context 15, 96, 149
contexture 5, 8, 13, 18–19, 30, 71–72, 89, 116, 177, 192, 200, 215
contingency, *see also* authorship, perspective, reading, writing 7–8, 10–11, 15–18, 20, 28–30, 32–34, 38, 47–50, 56, 62–64, 66–69, 71–76, 82, 88, 94, 97, 100, 104, 111, 114–116, 134, 139, 142, 145, 159–161, 163, 165–166, 168, 174–175, 178, 183–184, 197–198, 200–201, 213, 219–223
- angle(s) of contingency 8, 11, 27, 49, 62, 68, 178
- contingency vector 203
- culture of contingency 16, 61
- discourse of contingency 214, 220
- double contingency 42–43,
- epistemic contingency 11, 109, 222
- epistemology of contingency 49, 63, 113
- human contingency 205–206, 209
- material contingency 8
- multiple contingency 43, 100
- perspectival contingency 50, 200
- political contingency 76, 119, 145
- rhetoric of contingency 61, 63, 66, 73, 107, 220
- secular contingency 114
- social contingency 11, 76, 114
- temporality of contingency 161
contract 11, 43, 120, 122–123, 178, 197, 200, 202–206
convention 21, 28, 33–36, 39, 43, 48, 56, 81, 92–93, 104, 108, 136–137, 141, 144, 150, 164, 183, 186, 190, 193, 196, 198, 206, 216
- epic convention 167
- fact convention 13
- social convention 75
conversation 1, 30, 119, 140, 192–193, 210, 214–217
- criminal conversation 207
- polite conversation 30, 215–216
conversion 45, 68

conviviality 136
Conway, Anne 12, 107
Copernicus, Nicolaus 20
copia 28
copy 38, 46, 73, 100, 105, 190, 195, 211
corruption 57–58, 65, 133
cosmopolitanism 139
cosmos 214
coterie 34, 73, 140
counter-discourse 220
counter-fiction 145
counter-image 133–134, 143
counterhistory 145
countermemory 11, 145, 158, 161
counter-movement 134
counter-performance 181
counter-polemic 81
counterpressure 112
counter-public sphere 183
counter-reformation 118
counter-temporality 162
counter-text 166
counter-world 21, 112, 115–116, 142
couplet 127, 157–158, 173, 212
– heroic couplet 23, 160, 217
coupling/uncoupling 20–21, 71, 73, 203, 212
court, *see also* culture, philosophy, poet 26, 92, 95–96, 98, 103, 116, 129, 145, 147–149, 151, 154, 156, 163–164, 187, 189, 202, 217
– courtier 4
– court masque 101, 150, 187
– Court of Common Pleas 207
– Court of King's Bench 207
– ecclesiastical court 207
courtesan 189, 195, 198
covenant, *see also* Ark 119, 171–172
Covent Garden 4
Cowley, Abraham 91, 145–150, 153–154, 156–157
– *The Civil War* 146
– *Poems* 146–147, 157
creation 31, 61, 63, 109–110, 121–122, 223
– literary creation 93
creativity 22, 57, 72, 93, 108, 114, 144, 166
creator 113
credit 195–196
crime 156, 169

crisis, *see also* Exclusion Crisis 11, 20, 34, 67, 121, 160–161, 165, 167, 176–177, 186–187, 211, 217
critic 9, 21, 24, 45, 52, 74, 97, 162, 186, 189, 216
criticism 14, 26, 34–35, 45, 47–48, 52, 91, 103, 105, 106–107, 162, 190, 204
– literary criticism 1, 9, 74, 110, 222
– neoclassical criticism 72, 96, 110
– New Criticism 8, 14
critique 8, 11, 22, 34, 42, 64, 71, 80, 86, 104, 106, 111, 142, 159–160, 183, 190, 193–194, 196, 198, 200, 202
Cromwell, Oliver 83, 103, 118, 136, 143–144, 146–147, 155, 158
crowd 79, 90, 98, 127, 174, 176
crown 77, 83, 127, 161, 164, 168
Cudworth, Ralph 29–30
cultural turn 9
culture 2–4, 6, 8–10, 16–17, 19–20, 22–24, 30, 61, 66–67, 71–72, 76, 104, 120, 136–137, 145, 151, 164, 180–181, 183, 201, 208, 212, 216–217, 223
– court culture 104, 137, 151
– literary culture 7, 10–11, 13, 15, 17, 19–24, 26, 61, 67, 69, 73, 76–77, 95, 104, 113–115, 124, 129, 144, 163, 184, 213, 221–222
– media culture 34
– memory culture 145
– noise of culture 6
– political culture 2, 104
– print culture 21, 25, 28, 31, 33–34, 39–40, 42, 44, 47, 67, 96, 222
– Puritan culture 157
– theatrical culture 2
curiosity 1, 2, 28, 30–32, 38, 41, 61, 83, 86, 111, 198
custom 16, 121, 139–140, 156
cybernetics 9

Davenant, William 11, 19, 23, 26, 59, 69, 74, 76–77, 85, 91–105, 108, 112–116, 131, 140, 144, 149–150, 153, 164–166, 174, 181, 197, 216, 219, 221
– *Gondibert* 91–92, 96–104, 115–116, 140, 145, 165, 216
– *Preface to Gondibert* 59, 77, 91, 96–104, 114
– *Proposition for Advancement of Moralitie* 150

– *The Siege of Rhodes* 103
David 155–156, 159, 166, 168–169, 171, 175, 185
death 46, 49, 52, 59, 62, 64–65, 83, 120, 155, 189, 207, 218
deceit *or* deception 97, 111, 115, 197, 217–218
deciphering 3, 25, 38, 44, 63, 71, 83, 184, 186, 190, 191–193, 197, 209–210
Declaration of Breda 133, 148, 153, 155, 159, 163
deconstruction 72, 77, 204
decorum 26, 71, 93, 111, 152, 161, 203, 214, 218
dedication 17, 25–26, 34, 99, 127, 187–188
Defoe, Daniel 11–12, 26, 139, 186, 216, 219–220
– *Essay upon Literature* 220
deformity 64, 88, 171
deism 157, 214
de la Court, Pierre 122
delectare 137, 163, 184
delight 65–66, 79, 89, 100, 108, 110, 113, 169, 217
demagoguery 89, 127, 172
democracy 4, 110, 126–129, 133, 160, 172, 174, 213, 217, 222
democratisation 101, 137
Democritus of Abdera 41–42, 45–46
Democritus Junior 33, 35, 37–38, 40–42, 44–46
Dennis, John 105, 162, 215
depersonalisation 25
depoliticisation 162, 222
Descartes, René, *see also* Cartesianism 81, 84, 101, 178
– *Passions de l'Ame* 101
desire 1, 26, 36, 40–42, 52, 86, 90, 99, 103, 106, 108–109, 111, 113, 125, 127, 140, 147, 169–170, 172, 174–177, 193, 198–199, 203
– sexual desire 168–170, 190
description 6–7, 12, 16, 19–20, 50, 55–56, 63, 69–70, 86, 95, 101, 105, 110, 113, 123, 138, 169, 171, 203, 215, 221
– thick description 20
determinism 19, 69, 73, 219–220, 222
deus ex machina 175
devil, *see also* Satan 54, 57–59, 137, 144, 152, 167, 198, 210
Devonshire *see under* Cavendish
dialectic 76, 106

dialogue 2, 4, 40, 106–107, 137–138, 141, 152, 173, 205, 209, 211, 217
– epistolary dialogue 107
diary 146, 180, 217
didacticism 97, 99, 151, 184, 186, 190, 199–200
differentiation 5, 26, 33, 63, 67–68, 71, 111, 126
Digby, Kenelm 24, 31, 51–52, 115
digestion 36, 40, 73, 97, 131
Digges, Dudley 119, 123
– *The Unlawfulnesse of Subjects* 119
digression 216
disbelief, suspension of 97, 197
discourse, *see also* order 5–8, 10–11, 13–14, 18–19, 21–23, 26–30, 42–44, 49, 51, 55–56, 63–65, 67–68, 71–75, 91, 104–105, 107–109, 111, 115, 124, 128, 132, 134–135, 137–138, 140, 143, 157, 160–164, 180–183, 188, 190, 192, 208, 210, 213, 216–217, 219–223
– analytico-referential discourse 69, 75–76, 182
– history of discourse 13
– ironic discourse 44
– legal discourse 206
– literary discourse 26, 184
– lovers' discourse 188, 212
– neoclassical discourse 11, 29–30, 115, 208, 214, 219, 221, 223
– normative discourse 178, 183, 214–223
– oral discourse 34
– order of discourse 69, 136, 213, 222
– political discourse 166, 174, 178
– religious discourse 198, 210
– universe of discourse 14
– world of discourse 29
– zero point of discourse 37
discovery 20–21, 32–33, 41, 61–62, 64, 71, 73, 76, 89, 111, 118, 131, 138, 199
disease, *see also* writing 35, 50, 107, 163–164, 174, 197
disguise 187
disgust 119
disintegration 1, 3, 19, 21, 35, 72, 132–133, 171, 175, 198
disorder 6, 20, 54, 58, 113, 117, 132, 154, 171
dissent 7, 11, 51, 54, 130, 132, 145, 147, 158, 161–162, 184

Dissenter 11, 220
dissimulation 181, 195, 208
dissociation 1–2, 5–8, 20, 213
dissolution 4, 20–21, 118, 122, 136, 171
distancing 5, 32–33, 38, 50–51, 80, 103, 105–106, 116, 143, 145, 191, 197, 206, 212
distinction 4–5, 7, 10–11, 18, 19, 36, 53, 55–56, 62, 71, 73–74, 83, 89, 92–93, 101, 105, 109, 111, 127, 137, 140–142, 158, 165–166, 176–183, 185, 200, 204, 217, 222
distribution 17, 25, 34, 94, 114, 141, 189, 213
divinity, see also theology 54, 60, 111
division 2–3, 23, 30, 35–36, 62, 78, 98, 102, 112, 115, 145–147, 150, 165, 201
divorce 207
docere et delectare 163
doctrine 55, 60, 89, 135–136, 139, 151, 157, 163, 180, 221
Donne, John 12, 29, 139, 180
– *The First Anniversary* 180
Dorset Garden Theatre 150
doubling 34, 36, 40, 44, 46, 57
doubt 32, 54, 57, 61, 82, 125, 144, 156, 188
Dover 146, 154
dragon 129–130
drama, see also illusion, play, unity 2, 4, 6, 23, 28, 32, 50, 56, 81–82, 90, 92, 124, 149, 160, 162, 181, 184–185, 223
– heroic drama 99, 101, 118, 151, 162, 196, 217
– Restoration drama 103, 150, 162, 219
– Shakespearean drama 6
dream 56–57, 161, 167, 170, 180
drug 44, 131
Dryden, John 1–4, 11, 19, 22–23, 26, 59, 73, 92, 97, 99, 102, 105, 114, 116–117, 124, 133, 141, 145, 150–152, 154–177, 182, 184–185, 187, 189–190, 194, 198, 203, 217–222
– *Absalom and Achitophel* 11, 118, 156, 158, 160–177, 182, 185, 187, 190, 203
– *Annus Mirabilis* 92, 151
– *The Assignation* 150
– *Astræa Redux* 11, 19, 133, 144, 151, 154–161, 165–166, 167–168
– *Aureng-Zebe* 162
– *The Conquest of Granada* 99
– "Discourse concerning the Original and Progress of Satire" 160, 164
– *Essay of Dramatick Poesie* 1–4, 19, 59, 74, 222
– *An Evening's Love* 150

– *The Medal* 124
– "Of Heroique Playes" 97
– *Religio Laici* 218–219
– *The Rival Ladies* 92, 117, 150
– *The State of Innocence* 162, 182, 189
Duchess (character in Cavendish's *The Blazing World*) 112–113
Duke's Company 103
Dunbar (ship) 146
duopoly 103
duplicity 44, 151, 199, 202
Dutch, see also Netherlands 1–2, 152–153, 188
– Dutch host 40
– Dutch Wars 3
dysfunctionality 65
dystopia 33

economics 7, 10, 20
economy
– figural economy 168, 170, 173
– gift economy 24
– political economy 6
– rhetorical economy 169
écriture 19
edition 24, 28–29, 33–38, 41, 44–46, 51–52, 59–60, 77, 105–106, 117, 134–135, 138–143, 147, 150
education 23, 88, 95, 99–101, 106, 112, 123, 125, 127–129, 198, 210–212, 215–216
egoism or egotism 98, 103, 120
eidology 78
ekklesia 129
Eliot, T.S. 7–8, 213, 215
elite 31, 140, 190, 201, 214
Elizabeth I, Queen of England and Ireland 148
Elizabethan period 6, 72, 116, 134, 141, 145, 155, 157
eloquence, see also rhetoric 30, 84, 88–89, 117, 119, 125, 126, 133, 218
– power of eloquence 119
emblem 4, 45, 65, 77, 210
emergence 1, 5, 8, 10, 17, 20, 23, 26–27, 70, 72, 131–132, 165, 176, 179, 186, 221–222
emotion 14, 33, 39–40, 86, 101, 104, 110, 185–186, 188–189, 192, 194, 197, 209
empire, see also imperialism 19, 158, 173, 191, 206
empiricism 26, 61, 71–72, 75, 77, 93, 108, 110, 183, 214, 223

Empress (character in Cavendish's *The Blazing World*) 111–113, 115
encomium 142
encyclopedia 31–32, 34–35, 60, 63
endeavour 54, 60–61, 88, 97, 108, 110, 150
England, merry (old) 143–144, 148, 155
Englishness 2
engraving 37, 39–41, 83

enjambment 80
Enlightenment 6, 10, 26, 71, 123, 178, 183, 199, 202
entertainment 6, 21, 26, 29, 61, 66, 74, 78, 135–137, 142–143, 149, 151, 153, 186, 190, 199, 208, 210–211, 221
enthusiasm 93, 161, 218
environment 116, 139, 206
epideixis 89
epidemiology 131
epigonality 35–36
epilogue 17, 113, 115, 153–154
epistemology 7, 16, 18, 29–30, 33–35, 40, 47, 49–51, 60, 63, 66–76, 80, 85–86, 88–89, 109, 111, 113, 115, 178, 182, 188, 206, 213–214, 219–220
– literary epistemology 27–28, 200
epistle, *see also* dialogue, letter 65, 92, 99, 117, 188, 211
Erasmus of Rotterdam, Desiderius 28, 67, 137
eroticism 7, 138, 169, 170, 172, 186, 194
errata 17, 46
error 29, 31, 42, 46, 60–62, 79, 84, 87, 101, 109, 130, 167, 174, 217
eschatology 115
essay 1–4, 19, 49, 59, 74, 102, 105–106, 127, 131, 136, 184, 214, 217–218, 220, 222
estate 119, 141, 209
Etherege, George 182
ethics 58, 69, 113, 120
etymology 36
Euclid 126
Euphuism 216
Europe 6, 10, 12, 22, 24, 26, 32, 64, 71, 76–77, 138
Eve 81, 133, 160, 173, 189, 198–199
Evelyn, John 31, 136, 178
– *Essay on . . . Lucretius* 136

event 1–2, 4, 15, 19, 25, 42, 64, 71, 80, 96, 115, 118, 132, 138, 144–146, 147–148, 155, 157, 159, 185, 187, 200–201, 207, 210
– event horizon 20
– world event 42
evolution 5, 11, 16–17, 69, 71, 75, 221
Exclusion Crisis 4, 134, 162, 164, 176, 186, 219
execution 52, 77, 91, 96, 118, 130, 146, 148, 160, 164, 175
exile 91, 96, 102, 104–105, 161, 187
exorcism 155
exoticism 197, 205
expectation 21, 63, 85–86, 123, 190–191, 206, 210
experience 2, 13–15, 21, 24, 30–32, 36, 45, 50–51, 55–57, 59–60, 73, 75, 84, 114, 116, 121, 127, 143, 145, 152, 155, 180, 183, 184, 197
exteriority 37–38, 109, 115, 144, 185, 193, 209

fable 90, 113, 129
face 25, 37, 53, 58, 66, 83, 167, 171, 205, 209–210
– loss of face 209–210
– Oeconomy of face 209
faction 54–55, 79, 94, 111, 118, 145, 153, 165, 187
factuality, *see also* convention 9, 75, 90, 166, 197
faith 20, 25, 54–59, 66, 79, 82, 112, 134, 137, 140, 144, 169, 214, 220
Fall (of Man) 31, 160, 162
– fortunate fall 156, 170
falsehood 61, 66, 109, 193
fame 36, 72, 103, 106, 137
family 41, 112, 177, 207–208
– royal family 96
fancy 1–3, 56–57, 66, 89, 91–94, 97, 105, 107–111, 114, 134, 176, 191
Fane, Mildmay 136
– *Otia Sacra* 136
fantasy 115–116, 118, 164
fascination 6, 14, 22, 27, 32, 62, 156, 159, 187
fear 26, 33, 43, 86–87, 103, 112, 117, 119–122, 126, 130, 150, 171–172, 176, 202, 205, 209, 218
– fears and jealousies 150

Index —— 259

femininity 115, 194
feminisation 172
feminism 189
feudalism 154
fiction, see also character, counter-fiction, letter, metafiction, nonfiction, power, state 10–11, 13, 14, 34, 74, 90, 93–94, 104–114, 118, 121, 123–124, 144–145, 147, 176, 183–187, 190–192, 194, 221
– amatory fiction 191, 197, 199
– Arcadian fiction 144
– fictionalisation 67, 104–108, 187
– fictionality 21, 22, 24, 62, 66, 90, 106–111, 113, 115–116, 138, 143, 187, 190, 197
– fiction-making 190
– idle fiction 48
– imaginative fiction 111
– literary fiction 105, 118
– lying fiction 22
– modern fiction 33
– narrative fiction 124, 184
– pastoral fiction 142
– poetic fiction 147
– prose fiction 185–186, 190
– romance fiction 191
– work of fiction 14, 34, 191
Fielding, Henry 186, 215
figuration 5, 72, 74, 157, 181
figure, see also economy, speech, language, thought 3, 28, 30–31, 41, 47, 56, 63, 93–95, 113–114, 119, 121, 128, 155, 157, 166, 171–172, 178, 186, 190, 196–197, 218
Filmer, Robert 158, 174
– *Patriarcha* 158
finance 24, 73, 137, 140–141, 152, 187, 195, 209
fish 136–137, 139
fishing 134–140, 142–143
fixity 14, 52, 73, 168, 170, 209
Fletcher, Phineas 12
flow 14, 65, 72–73, 138, 196
flux 62, 168, 170, 199
focalisation 2, 184
folio 38, 61
folk 205
– folk customs 156
– folk tale 61
– folk tradition 159
– gentlefolk 138

folly 33, 42–43, 50, 68, 79
Fontenelle, Bernard Le Bovier 113
– *Entretiens sur la pluralité des mondes* 113
fool *or* foolishness, see also fortune 42–43, 45, 59, 160, 164, 197
– ship of fools 42, 100
foreign(er) 2, 128, 205
forgetting, see also oblivion 116, 144–146, 150, 153–156, 164, 210
forgiveness 153, 155
form, literary 7, 10, 13, 17–19, 23, 29, 33, 47, 67, 72, 80, 82, 105–107, 137, 158, 160, 167, 175–176, 180, 183, 185–187, 192, 199–200, 210, 216, 221–222
Forster, E. M. 185
fortuna 100, 170
fortune, see also fall 16, 43, 110, 156, 170, 172, 185, 188–189, 195–196, 202, 206
– change of fortune 196
– fools of fortune 189
forum 4, 23
fragment *or* fragmentation 2, 7, 86, 88–89, 94–95, 115, 125, 171, 184, 212
frame, see also reference 33, 38, 58, 64, 168, 174
– framework 7, 43, 68, 70, 75, 111, 117, 129, 208, 222
– framing 7, 36, 109
– narrative frame 3
France *or* French 2–3, 24, 71, 90, 96, 105, 154, 187, 191–192, 197
freedom, see also art, liberty, speech 55, 67, 70, 78, 113–114, 120, 123, 134–135, 158, 160, 170, 183, 202
free will 114, 133, 167
Freud, Sigmund 57, 145
friend *or* friendship 31, 45–46, 49, 57, 138, 152, 194, 205
Fronde 96
frontispiece 17, 37, 39, 77–79, 82, 94, 106, 124, 149, 156
fundamentalism 219
future 16, 86, 95, 102, 123, 148, 151, 156, 205

Galen of Pergamon (Aelius Galenus) 35
Galilei, Galileo 137
gambling 123, 195–198, 202, 208
game, see also May 40, 44, 47, 58, 67, 109, 113, 141, 157, 185, 195, 202, 208

garden 4, 65, 115, 150
- Covent Garden 4
- Dorset Garden Theatre 150
- *Garden of Cyrus* (Browne) 32, 48, 63, 65–66, 115
- Garden of Eden, *see also* paradise 65
Geertz, Clifford 9, 20
- *The Interpretation of Cultures* 9
gender 137, 189, 199, 216
Genesis 122, 167
Genette, Gérard 17, 34
genius 74, 106, 163
Genji, Tale of 212
genre, *see also* blending, theory 6, 12, 18–19, 21–22, 24, 67, 90, 92, 102, 105, 108–111, 116, 124, 137, 163, 180, 184, 186–188, 190–191, 199, 201, 214–215, 217, 221–222
- boundaries *or* limits of genre 21, 28–29, 43, 92
- mixture of genres 151
- poetic genre 91
- rules of genre 105, 218
gentleman 30–31, 75, 138–139, 141–142, 183, 203, 212, 214
- *The English Gentleman* (Brathwait) 142
gentry 143
geocentrism 28, 101
geography 9, 15, 20, 61, 139
geometry 81, 123, 126, 128, 182
German *or* Germany 10, 12, 40, 52
giant 64
gift 103, 112, 118
- divine gift 118, 181
- gift economy 24
Gildon, Charles 105, 215
Glanvill, Joseph 29, 61, 136
- *The Vanity of Dogmatizing* 29
glass, *see also* mirror 31, 94, 103–104, 111, 204
- magnifying *or* multiplying glasses 86, 103, 111
- prospective glasses 86, 94
globalisation 2
globe 1, 33
God 45, 52, 57–58, 61–63, 66, 68–69, 80–82, 102, 112, 114, 118, 120–122, 132, 137, 146–147, 152, 155–158, 167–171, 173, 175–176, 193
- finger *or* hand of God 52, 220
- god of war 129

- the godly (Puritans) 123, 136, 149
- house of God 132
- post-godly 203
- work of God 155
government 26, 54, 58–59, 89, 111–113, 127, 133, 146–147, 160, 170–173, 175, 187, 217
- mixed government 59
- *Two Treatises of Government* (Locke) 11, 116, 123, 173
governmentality 99, 152
grace 16, 79, 114, 132, 150–151, 171, 181, 203, 208
Greece 71, 129
Greenblatt, Stephen 8–9, 19, 65, 72
Grey, Ford, third Baron Grey of Werke 187–188, 191
- *The Trial of Ford Lord Grey of Werk* 187
Grotius, Hugo 87, 120, 122–123
- *De iure praedae* 123

Habermas, Jürgen 4–5, 70, 217
habit 6, 14, 20, 37, 40, 42–43, 87, 99, 139, 155, 206, 216
Hamlet (character) 180–181
Hammond, Henry 119
handwriting, *see also* manuscript 52
Happy Return (ship) 146
harmony 31, 58–59, 63, 66, 102
Harrington, James 129
Harpocrates 46
Harvey, Christopher 139
- *The Synagogue* 139
Harvey, William 19, 72–73, 178
- *De Circulatione Sanguinis* 19
- *De Motu Cordis* 19
hatred 86, 154, 206, 208, 211, 218
health 131, 141, 148
heart 19, 55, 85–86, 99, 139, 155, 157, 163, 168–170, 192–193, 195–198, 206, 208, 212
heaven, *see also* war 54, 63, 65, 77, 79–80, 82, 92, 95, 150–151, 157, 168–169, 214
- war in heaven 80
Hector 114
Heian period 212
Helen 114
hell 50, 159
Henrietta (ship) 146
Heraclitus 46
Herbert, George 12, 139

Herbert, Percy 105, 143
- *The Princess Cloria* 105, 143
Hercules 90, 110, 113
heresy 52
hermeneutics 25, 183, 200
hermeticism 63, 95, 101
hero, *see also* character, couplet, drama, imagination, poem, poetry 70, 95, 145
- epic hero 99–100
- heroic deed 167
- heroic epic 82, 105
heroine 110
Hertfordshire 138
heterodiegetic 188
heterogeneity 3, 21, 29, 74, 83, 116, 124, 134, 151, 176, 216, 221
hierarchy 3, 19, 34, 59, 68, 92, 101, 107–109, 114, 141, 158, 165–166, 168, 217, 219
- political *or* social hierarchy 26, 77, 111
hieroglyph 210
Hippocrates 35, 41, 45
historicism 8
- New Historicism 8, 12, 19
- Old Historicism 8
historiographer royal 166
historiography 5, 71
history, *see also* discourse, knowledge, mentality, novel, style 10–11, 13–14, 34, 60–61, 66, 77, 93, 97–98, 119, 127, 138, 143, 145–146, 155, 161, 166, 188, 196, 220
- conceptual 179
- cultural 8, 12
- history of ideas 6, 75
- human history 69, 118, 123, 159
- intellectual history 12, 48
- literary history 5, 7, 9–10, 12, 26–27, 47, 70–71, 180, 221
- media history 15, 20
- political history 162, 203
- Roman history 136
- salvation history 80
- social history 9, 75
- Whig interpretation of history 201
Hobbes, Thomas 3, 5, 6, 11, 24–26, 29, 42, 59, 69, 72–73, 76–78, 84–99, 101–106, 108, 110–115, 118–130, 132–134, 144, 148, 152, 158, 162, 164–165, 170, 172–174, 176, 178, 181, 192–193, 198, 206, 208, 217, 221

- "Answer to the Preface" 91–96, 98, 104
- *De corpore* 85
- *De homine* 87
- *Dialogue between a Philosopher and a Student . . .* 173
- *The Elements of Law* 84–90, 92–93, 119, 122–123, 126, 130, 192
- *Leviathan* 6, 24, 59, 69, 73, 78, 86–89, 91–96, 99, 102–103, 110, 113, 115, 119–121, 123, 126, 130, 133, 206
- *Tractatus Opticus I* 84
- *Verse Life* 127–128
hobby horse 157, 138
Homer 80
homogeneity 72, 74, 180, 183
homology 160, 168, 219
homosociality 138, 141
honesty 42, 114, 135–140, 143, 163, 165, 182
honour 36, 52, 61, 91, 150–151, 153, 194, 196, 207
- code of honour 141, 151, 196
Hooke, Robert 111
- *Micrographia* 111
Hooker, Richard 30
hope 33, 50, 58, 64, 79, 82, 117, 126, 167, 195, 203, 206, 215
Horace (Quintus Horatius Flaccus) 36, 42, 45, 141, 163–164
- *Odes* 45
horror 115, 119
Howard, Robert 151
- *The Committee* 151
Huguenot 118
human being 87, 117–118, 123, 125, 133, 159, 179, 200
humanism 4–7, 10, 21, 26, 28, 30, 32–33, 36, 49, 59, 61, 67, 69, 72–73, 104, 114–115, 120, 122, 125, 131, 136–138, 176, 178, 216–217, 222
- civic humanism 23, 219
humanitas 102, 116
humanity 8, 80, 102, 122, 125
humour 68
hunting 92, 98, 138
Hutchinson, Lucy 12
hybrid 29, 67, 222
Hyde, Edward 102, 119
hyperbole 47, 50, 193

icon 77–78
iconoclasm 77–78, 83
iconography 61, 83, 146, 149
ideal or idealism 4, 8–9, 23, 26, 28–30, 35, 54, 73, 75–76, 81, 94, 99, 121, 125, 132, 137, 139, 142, 142–144, 170, 180, 183, 203–204, 206, 216–217, 219, 222
idealisation 77, 116, 134, 143, 148, 158–159, 165, 215
identification 36–37, 39–40, 43, 80, 90, 104, 133, 172, 187, 200, 206
identity 41, 50, 189
– personal identity 62
– transtemporal identity 50
ideology 8–9, 75, 78, 87, 89, 91, 96, 100, 102, 123, 131, 148, 151, 153, 158, 161, 196, 198
– royalist ideology 144
– Whig ideology 208, 214
idiom 6–7, 11, 22, 49, 118, 140, 149, 161, 174, 195–196, 198, 212
ignorance 52, 59, 63, 76, 79, 87, 104, 133, 144, 211
illegitimacy 159, 167, 169–170
illiteracy 23, 78–79, 211–212
illusion 77, 81, 84, 97–98, 102, 141, 192, 196–197, 202
– dramatic illusion 181
illustration 31, 37, 54, 106, 124, 131, 196, 199
image, see also author-image, counter-image, picture, self-image 7, 23, 26, 36–39, 49–50, 56–59, 63–64, 72, 77–80, 83, 85–86, 90–92, 94, 100–104, 108, 110, 117–118, 124, 131–132, 134, 145, 147, 154, 166, 168, 170–171, 173, 175, 180, 204
– composite image 94–95, 110
– image-breaker, see also iconoclasm 26, 77
– image-concept 63
– image-rhetoric 127
– master image 72, 94
– mirror image 44
– poetic image 8, 111
– power of images 79
imagery 63, 92–93, 118, 131, 154–156, 159, 171, 176, 195
imaginary, see also sovereign, space, world-making 113, 158, 180
– cultural imaginary 117
– political imaginary 115

imagination, see also reading 6, 16, 42, 46, 50, 54–58, 62, 68, 74, 77, 80, 85, 90, 92, 94–95, 97–98, 101, 104, 113–114, 137, 145, 161, 176–177, 185, 192–194, 207
– associative imagination 92
– heroic imagination 113
– imaginative fiction or literature or writing 18, 23, 26, 48, 90, 93, 106, 111, 114
– visual imagination 64
imitation 58, 81, 91, 94, 97, 99–100, 104–105, 129, 199
immorality, see also amorality 142
immortality 129–130
imperialism, see also empire 1–2, 155
impersonality 74
imprinting 52, 73, 94, 101, 126, 128, 132
inauthenticity 195–198
inconstancy 79, 89, 185
indeterminacy 16, 41, 53, 185
individual or individuality 2–3, 11, 15, 17, 20, 22, 30, 48–49, 51, 53, 55, 57, 59, 71–74, 76, 82, 86, 88–91, 93–95, 98–99, 115, 118, 123, 125, 134, 136, 159, 165, 176–185, 198–199, 201–203, 210, 212–214, 219, 222–223
individualisation 1, 4, 73, 222
individualism 5, 120
– possessive individualism 142, 202
inference 13, 17, 76, 84–85, 90, 181, 183, 185–186, 193, 199, 220
information 6–7, 13, 30–31, 42, 61, 63, 65, 83, 111, 132, 135–138, 143, 151, 176, 180, 185, 199, 217
ingenium 53
innocence 89, 135–139, 142, 145, 151, 157, 159, 194
– *The State of Innocence* (Dryden) 162, 182
innovation 174
inscription 47, 60, 66, 83, 99, 106, 143, 172, 175
– reinscription 95, 146
insecurity 24, 30, 35–36, 38, 47, 98, 154, 170, 220, 222
insincerity 161
inspiration 93, 103, 149, 189
instability 35, 40, 63, 70, 144, 159, 168, 170, 172, 200, 213
instinct 170, 172, 175

institution 20, 22, 60, 67, 69, 75–76, 118–119, 121, 129, 184, 198, 203, 205, 207
intellect 89, 129
intention 13, 45, 50–51, 53, 80, 86, 89–91, 96–97, 102, 125, 129, 151, 153, 157, 161, 165–166, 168, 181, 186, 192–193
interaction 10, 14, 15, 17, 20–21, 24, 43, 57, 67, 73, 88–89, 142, 201, 209, 215
interdiscursivity 28
interest, *see also* self-interest 2–3, 85–86, 95, 120, 140, 165, 171, 176, 195, 214
– private interest 176
– public interest 98, 176, 187
interiority, *see also* inwardness 180, 185, 189, 193, 200, 212
internationality 3, 152, 222
interpellation 180
interpersonality 20, 208
interpretation 2, 6, 8–9, 14, 17, 19, 25, 29, 37, 40, 52–54, 56, 60, 63, 68, 78, 80–81, 83, 86–88, 93, 151, 155–156, 159, 161, 180–181, 186, 193, 198, 201, 214, 219, 222
– biblical interpretation 60
Interregnum 105, 115, 143, 146, 158, 219
intersubjectivity 30, 180, 218, 223
intertextuality 29, 32, 35–36, 43, 68
intimacy 50, 73, 186, 201, 204–205, 212
intrigue, *see also* conspiracy, plot 170, 187, 191, 202
in utramque partem 173
inwardness, *see also* interiority 11, 38, 55, 57, 82, 90, 178–186, 190, 192–194, 197–198, 203–204, 209
Ireland *or* Irish 6
irony 4, 32–33, 44–45, 50, 82, 104, 106, 124, 129, 144–147, 149, 151–152, 157, 159–161, 163–164, 166, 168, 174, 188–189, 191, 195, 199, 204–205, 209, 214
Isaac 64
Iser, Wolfgang 41
Isocrates 129
isomorphism 17, 222
Israel 155, 168–169
Italy *or* Italian 4, 24, 101, 191

Jacobean period 6, 150
Jacobite 201, 206
James I, King of England, Scotland and Ireland 177

James II, King of England, Scotland and Ireland 3, 162, 165, 187–188, 201–202
James (ship) 146
Janus 59, 219
Japan 212
jealousy 119, 149–151, 157
Jerusalem 157
Jesus, *see also* Christ 133
Jews 161
Job (biblical book) 103
John of Salisbury 42
Johnson, Samuel 66, 162, 215, 221
Jones, Inigo 4
Jonson, Ben 12, 180
– *Every Man in His Humour* 180
– *Every Man out of His Humour* 180
Jordan (river) 171
judgement 14, 42, 53, 60, 92, 151, 166, 185, 189, 221
– Last Judgement 126
Juliet (character) 212
Jupiter 155, 159, 163
justice 10, 87, 98, 112, 132, 153, 155, 158, 163, 170, 173, 175
justification, *see also* self-justification 63, 82, 96, 109, 165
Juvenal (Decimus Junius Juvenalis) 164

Kabbalah, *see also* cabbalism 50
Kafka, Franz 49
Killigrew, Thomas 103
king *or* kingship, *see also* monarch, monarchy, right 52, 54–55, 59, 77, 79, 83, 102–103, 120, 122, 127, 127, 129, 146–151, 153–158, 161, 167–177, 180, 187, 189–191
– kingdom 28, 36, 61
– King's Company 103
– king's two bodies, theory of 177
Kingdon, Lemuel 188
kinship 202–203
knowledge, *see also* power, self-knowledge 13, 15–18, 20–22, 28, 30–35, 37, 47–50, 53–54, 57, 59–63, 65, 67–68, 71, 73, 75–76, 81–82, 89, 111, 114, 126, 128, 130, 134, 137, 167, 182–183, 185, 197–198, 214, 217–220, 222–223
– book knowledge 88
– esoteric knowledge 50
– history of knowledge 75

264 — Index

- knowledge technology 28, 30, 32, 67
- literary knowledge 49
- order of knowledge 28, 30, 33
- scientific knowledge 101, 137

Kroll, Richard 200, 220

laboratory 75
labour 24, 26, 54, 73, 78, 83, 98, 101, 130, 140–141
Lacan, Jacques 180
La Fayette, Marie-Madeleine de 191
- *La Princesse de Clèves* 191
- *La Princesse de Monpensier* 191
La Fontaine, Jean de 113
Lamb, Charles 143
landscape, see also painting 46, 106, 138, 180
language, see also love, Puritanism 1, 3, 6–8, 14–16, 19, 22–24, 44, 49–50, 53–56, 66, 68–69, 73, 76, 79–80, 87, 89, 92, 98, 112, 114, 117, 125–127, 129, 132–133, 135–136, 140, 151, 157, 159, 163, 180, 182–183, 186, 188, 192–193, 195–198, 204, 207–208, 211, 212, 216–220, 222
- figurative or metaphorical or poetic language 48, 53, 56, 65, 91, 98, 174, 176, 180, 217
- literary language 13, 212
- magical view of language 159
- metaphysical language 62
- political language 55, 58, 169, 206
- postlapsarian language 159
- sign language 198
- visual language 210
latency 145, 208
Latin 23, 45–46, 49, 66, 83, 125, 128, 138, 155
laughter 33, 46, 182, 211
law 71, 74, 88, 98, 100, 111–112, 117–118, 120–123, 125, 128, 140, 148, 153–154, 158, 161, 168–170, 172–177, 197, 199, 200, 202–203, 205, 207–209, 214
- canon law 203, 205
- divine law 172–173
- common law 121
- lawlessness 92, 158, 170–171
- Mosaic law 151
- natural law 98–99, 115–116, 117, 119, 133, 169, 173
- power of law 173, 205, 207–208
- rule of law 153, 158
- universal unmade law 121
Lea (river) 138
learning, see also education, knowledge 17, 23, 31–32, 61, 82, 89, 96, 99, 111, 128, 130, 137, 139
- *Advancement of Learning* (Bacon) 60–61
Le Blon, Christof (the elder) 37
Lee, Nathaniel 12
legitimacy 75–76, 89, 93, 117–118, 143, 159, 161, 172–175, 203, 210, 217, 220
legitimation 98, 121, 128, 159, 163, 174
leisure 26, 45, 137, 140–143, 201
Lepanto, Battle of 58
L'Estrange, Roger 191
letter, see also epistle, writer 25, 36–37, 47–48, 51–52, 61, 85, 92, 96, 107, 115, 120, 185–186, 188, 191–194, 197, 199, 211, 215, 220
- fictional letter 107
- love letter 185–86, 188
- *Five Love-letters from a Nun to a Cavalier* 191
- *Love-Letters Between a Nobleman and His Sister* (Behn) 11, 178, 184–200, 204, 212
- *Philosophical Letters* (Cavendish) 107
- republic of letters 5, 23–24, 29, 72, 124, 178
Lettres portugaises 191
Leveller 118, 122, 129
Leviathan, see also Hobbes 59, 103
liberalism 28, 95, 113, 119–120, 122, 214
libertinism 190, 193–196, 202
liberty, see also freedom 20, 25, 41, 52, 57, 83, 93, 95, 111, 115, 119–120, 129–130, 132, 159–160, 170, 182, 183, 217, 222
library 24, 30–32, 61, 67, 101, 106, 177, 217
licensing, see also censorship 4, 124, 130–131
lie or lying 13, 22, 87, 189, 202
life 5, 9, 13, 18, 28, 32, 42, 44, 47, 49, 52, 59, 64, 67, 73, 91, 94, 99–100, 103, 107, 120–121, 129–130, 137–138, 140–143, 160, 176, 180, 182, 188–189, 191, 194, 196–197, 199, 203, 205, 214, 218
- active life 178
- city life 141
- contemplative life 135, 178
- country life 138, 141
- court life 151
- everyday life 142
- intellectual life 67
- play of life 49

- political *or* social life 23, 57, 87, 116, 122, 207–208
- private life 180
- public life 143, 166, 177–178, 180
- scholarly life 42
- theatre of life 49

lifestyle 4
liminality 34
Lincoln's Inn Fields 150
Lipsius, Justus 36, 122, 139
litaphorisation 64
literacy 2, 20, 23, 26, 85, 211–212
literariness 50
literature 3, 7–10, 13, 15, 18, 20, 22–24, 26, 28, 69–72, 74, 76–77, 85, 90–91, 93, 98, 102–104, 115, 138, 144, 165, 176, 178, 180–181, 184, 210–212, 214–216, 221, 223
- access to literature
- ancient Greek literature 2
- autonomy of literature 70, 72, 74
- *Essay upon Literature* (Defoe) 220
- history of literature, *see also* history 70
- imaginative literature 23, 93, 114
- literature as fictional discourse
- pastoral literature 105, 142
- theory of literature 93
- work of literature 71, 93, 216, 223

litterae humaniores 18
Locke, John 11, 95, 109, 116, 118–119, 121–123, 132–133, 139, 143, 162, 173, 178, 183–184, 202–203, 206–207, 214–219, 222
- *Essay Concerning Human Understanding* 214, 216–218
- *Some Thoughts Concerning Education* 215–216,
- *Two Treatises of Government* 11, 116, 123, 173

logic 16, 18, 48, 62–63, 89, 126–128, 132, 190, 193
Lombardy 105, 116
Lombart, Peter 83
London 1, 4, 23, 46, 79, 91, 129, 132, 154, 157, 187, 200, 217
- Tower of London 187
Lord Protector, *see also* Cromwell 136, 155
Lords, House of, *see also* Commons 129, 154
Louis XIV, King of France 101, 154, 177
Louvre 96, 187
love, *see also* discourse, letter, poetry, plot, self-love 58, 78, 86, 94, 103, 112, 138, 140, 153–154, 157, 172, 188, 190, 193–198, 206, 211–212, 214, 216, 218
- code of love 188, 196
- erotic love 188
- language of love 140, 188
- *Love for Love* (Congreve) 206, 209, 212
- *Loves Empire* 191
- rhetoric of love 186, 193–195, 197

Lovelace, Richard 136
- "The Grasse-hopper" 136
Lowestoft, Battle of 1, 3
Luhmann, Niklas 5, 12–13, 16, 43, 55
Lukács, György 160
Luther, Martin 67, 83, 118
lying *see* lie

macaroni 36
Machiavel 189, 195
Machiavelli, Niccolò 30, 96–98, 100, 112, 122, 170, 173, 181, 207
machine *or* machinery 48, 73, 150
Mackenzie, George 178
McKeon, Michael 18
Macpherson, C. B. 142, 202
Macrobius 36
macrocosm 30, 59, 74
madness 41–44, 55, 86, 106
magazine 24
magic 31, 39, 44, 79, 148, 155, 159
manual 135, 137
Mandeville, Bernard 59
manifesto 91, 144
manipulation 1, 25, 133, 156, 176, 197, 202, 207–208
manuscript, *see also* handwriting 9, 25, 34, 37, 51–52
marginalia 150
market *or* marketplace 41, 47, 197
- literary market *or* marketplace 10, 72, 137, 187, 191
marketing 17, 39, 41, 73
Marlowe, Christopher 139
marriage 117, 151, 192, 203, 205–206, 212, 214
Marshall, William 77–78
- *Eikon Basilike* 77–79, 82, 149, 156, 176
martyr 77, 82, 130, 157–158
Marvell, Andrew 12, 155
Mary II, Queen of England, Scotland and Ireland 201

266 —— Index

Mary (ship) 146
masquerade, *see also* court masque 40, 144
materialism 72, 77, 84, 91, 107, 115, 178, 206, 212
materiality 6, 8, 13, 21, 24, 44, 50, 66, 172, 192, 201, 212
mathematics 42, 63, 65, 102, 216
matter, *see also* reading 2, 21, 34, 36, 40, 54, 61, 109–110, 131, 133
May game 157
May, prince of 157
meaning 8–9, 14–15, 18–19, 21–22, 38, 40, 64–65, 67–68, 73, 80, 82, 88, 90, 107, 116, 121, 125–126, 163, 167, 169, 172, 175, 177–179, 182, 188, 192–193, 208, 211, 216, 219–220, 222
mechanism 9, 73, 84–85, 99, 131, 157, 178, 194
medal 124
- *The Medal* (Dryden) 124
media, *see also* culture, history, mediation, medium, theory 4–5, 9–10, 13–15, 17, 21–22, 30, 32, 42, 44, 71, 76–77, 103, 116, 124, 190, 200
- media arrangement *or* configuration 15, 34, 72
- media change 22
- media experience 15
- media studies 5, 12
- media technology 30
- media upheaval 5
- multi-media 101
- world of media 42
mediation 1, 5, 18, 29, 68, 73, 76, 78, 101, 116, 140, 144, 151, 178, 181, 183
medicine 163–164, 175
medieval, *see also* Middle Ages 20, 28, 30, 73, 100, 105, 121, 177–178, 182
meditation 49, 58, 81, 134–135
medium, *see also* media, mediation 14–15, 20, 24, 26, 41, 50, 73, 76, 80, 84, 104, 108, 171–172, 181, 186, 200, 206, 209, 212–213, 217–218, 221
melancholy, *see also* Burton 32–33, 35–36, 41, 43–45, 68, 107
- love melancholy 45
- religious melancholy 45
memoir 215
memory, *see also* remembering 2, 92, 95, 101, 145, 147, 160–161, 203, 210, 212
- artificial memory 147
- cultural memory 11, 144–146, 155–156, 210
- national memory 148
- working memory 9
mentality 6, 9, 33, 75, 202
- history of mentalities 6, 75
mercantilism 131, 140, 152, 195–196
mercy 158, 167, 169
Messiah 156
metafiction 190
metaphor 19, 36, 40–41, 49, 52, 54–56, 58, 63–66, 72–73, 86, 88–90, 93, 95–96, 103–104, 118–120, 125–126, 128, 131, 195, 202, 207–208
metaphysics 28–29, 50, 62–63, 94, 140, 149–151, 155, 163–164, 171, 174–175, 178, 194, 214
metonymy 52, 74, 213
Michael (archangel) 70, 80
microcosm 30, 33, 58–59, 74
microscopy 111
Middle Ages, *see also* medieval 21, 60
militancy 128
military, *see also* action, army 3, 25, 97, 102, 125, 128, 131, 158
Milton, John 4, 11, 20, 23, 25–26, 29, 44, 54, 69, 72–73, 76–84, 88, 95, 97–98, 104–105, 114–116, 124, 128–134, 142, 145, 151–152, 155–156, 158–162, 164–167, 171–176, 185–186, 215, 217, 220
- *Areopagitica* 4, 20, 44, 54, 73, 77, 80, 98, 114, 128–129, 131–133, 158, 160
- *Defensio Secunda* 81
- *Eikonoklastes* 77, 124
- *Of Education* 128–129, 131, 171
- *Paradise Lost* 11, 20, 69–70, 80–83, 95, 116, 118, 133, 144, 151–153, 156, 158–159, 160–162, 166–167, 170, 172–173, 175, 186, 220
- *Paradise Regained* 80, 133, 159, 162, 167
- *Samson Agonistes* 162
mimesis 50, 96, 99–100, 103
mimus vitae 49
mind 20, 29, 31, 37–38, 55–56, 78–79, 81–82, 85, 87–88, 90–94, 97, 100–101, 103, 107–110, 112, 114, 122–123, 126, 131, 134, 139, 149, 158, 181, 186, 192, 215
- mastermind 91

- mindreading 37
- mindset 116, 200
miracle, see also wonder 155, 157, 202
mirror or mirroring, see also glass 32, 36–38, 44, 50, 52, 55, 57, 103, 110, 136, 158, 192, 204
mirth 45, 135–139, 142
mise en abyme 2
misogyny 198
misreading 193
Misselden, Edward 19f
- *The Circle of Commerce* 19
misunderstanding 13, 81, 87, 104, 151, 199
mixed mode 3, 74
mobility 7, 23, 73–76, 168, 170, 198
mock epic 167
mockshow 56
moderation 54, 99, 102, 113, 125, 151, 153, 218
modernisation 6, 105
modernism 74
modernity 2, 4–8, 10, 13, 16–18, 20, 24, 26, 28, 33, 47–48, 55, 66–68, 70–72, 74–76, 116, 132, 152, 159–161, 178–179, 207, 213, 217, 221
- early modernity 6–7, 17, 20, 22, 25, 33, 44, 55, 83, 87, 124
Moebius strip 35
Molière (Jean-Baptiste Poquelin) 211
- *Le bourgeois gentilhomme* 211
Molina, Luis 118
monarch or monarchy, see also king 3, 36, 54, 77, 91, 96, 98, 102–103, 112–113, 115, 126–127, 144, 146–147, 156–158, 160, 162–163, 168, 170, 172, 174, 189, 201–202, 214, 217
- absolute monarch or monarchy, see also absolutism 113, 121
- constitutional monarchy 200
- hereditary monarchy 173
money 73, 137, 140, 142, 152, 195, 198, 216
monism 133
Monmouth, James Scott, Duke of 167, 169, 187
monologue 107, 138
monopoly 132, 220, 222
monotheism 112
monster 98, 144
- sea-monster 103
monstrosity 35, 59, 103, 174

Montaigne, Michel Eyquem de 28, 72, 139, 177
monument 146
moralising 50, 141
morality 30, 50, 58, 69, 74–75, 86, 88–89, 94, 96, 98, 101, 120, 151, 166, 174, 182, 185–186, 190, 194, 199–200, 202–203, 205, 214–215, 222
More, Alexander 81
More, Henry 29, 107
More, Thomas 42, 67, 72, 112, 137
- *Utopia* 112
Morris dancing 157
mortality 62, 65, 82, 113–114
Morton, Charles 139
Moses, see also law 62, 155, 166
motion 19, 45, 58, 63, 73, 84–86, 88, 91–92, 95, 101, 109, 113, 171, 196–197
movere 184
multi-media 101
multiplicity 6–8, 10, 21, 29, 32, 47–48, 58, 61, 67
multitude 3, 15, 59, 78, 88–89, 93–94, 98–99, 124, 144, 165, 174, 176, 178
multivalence 14
Muse 82, 149–151
mystery 31, 53–54, 66, 83, 152–153, 164
mysticism 28, 50, 65, 81–82, 177–178, 180
myth or mythology 61, 80, 121, 129–130, 154
- Christian myth or mythology 80, 152, 156
- Greek mythology 151
- mythmaking 155
- origin myth 125

narration 90, 126, 138, 188
narrative 5, 8, 11, 17, 70, 82, 92, 98, 113, 119, 121, 124, 159, 161, 166, 174, 184, 187–188, 190, 197
- biblical narrative 160
- narrative situation 112
- political narrative 167
- theological narrative 167
- travel narrative 61
- utopian narrative 112
narrator 22, 34, 188–189, 194, 196–200
Naseby, Battle of 146
Naseby (ship) 146
nation or nationality 1–3, 72, 74, 79, 132, 152–153, 155, 159, 171, 175–176

– nationalism 1
– native 119, 172–174, 205, 216–217
nature 8, 36, 52, 58, 60–63, 65, 69, 82, 87, 91–92, 99, 101–104, 109, 111, 115–119, 124, 127, 133–135, 143–144, 159, 161, 168–170, 173–176, 183, 194, 206–207, 214, 220
– human nature 58, 85–86, 103, 186, 209
– idyllic nature 135
– law of nature 98–99, 173
– nature vs. art 206
– nature vs. nurture 139
– state of nature 11, 115, 117–124, 130, 133–135, 141, 143, 145, 148, 158–159, 162, 170, 174, 176, 206, 217
navy 1, 91, 128
negation 35, 44, 47, 82, 135, 155, 158, 169
negativity 44–45, 47, 68
neoclassicism 4, 6–7, 10–11, 17, 23, 26, 29–30, 67, 69, 70–77, 92–93, 96, 102–104, 107, 109–110, 114–115, 131, 135, 155, 163, 178–180, 182–183, 208, 214, 217, 219–223
neo-Elizabethan 157
neo-paganism 157
Neoplatonism 28, 90, 101, 108, 151
neostoicism 30
Nestor 114
Netherlands, see also Dutch 122, 149, 152, 188
network 2, 32, 75, 178, 182, 184, 203
New Criticism see under criticism
news 1
newspaper 1
Noah 171
Noah's Ark 172
nobility or nobleman 24, 31, 94, 97, 127, 141, 152, 165, 187, 189, 202
noise 1–3, 6–7, 115, 132
non-fiction 10, 24, 28, 106
non-human 10
non-knowledge 17
non-violence 51, 56, 112, 145, 153, 208, 219
norm 9, 69, 71, 75, 92–94, 100, 105, 115, 119, 134, 137, 161, 165, 184, 208, 213, 216, 219, 222
– communicative or discursive norm 26, 30, 69, 208, 210, 222
– conflict of norms 69
– cultural norm 11, 184, 216, 220

– social norm 11, 21, 23, 99, 115, 216, 222
normalcy 49
North pole 110
Norwich 28, 135
nostalgia 26, 69, 116, 134, 141–144, 148, 155
novel, see also bildungsroman, roman à clef, reader, romance 6, 11, 15, 18, 22, 27, 90, 160, 178, 184–192, 194, 197–201, 204, 211, 216, 221–223
– epistolary novel 185–186, 191, 197
– history of the novel 186
novelty 161, 198

obedience 95–96, 98–99, 101, 112, 120, 124, 128, 149–150, 153, 158, 165, 190
object 26, 35, 47, 50, 63–64, 70, 128, 181, 188, 192
– erotic object 138
– written object 7
objectivity 14, 63, 75, 88, 124
oblivion, see also forgetting 11, 60, 147–148, 151, 155, 157–158, 161, 163–164
– Act of Oblivion 148, 163, 16
– politics of oblivion 158
obscenity 210
observation, see also self-observation 1, 5, 7, 16, 18–19, 23, 26, 32–33, 34, 41, 49–50, 60, 63–64, 66–68, 75–76, 93, 99–100, 103–105, 110–111, 118, 126, 165–166, 201, 203, 216–217, 223
– empirical observation 61, 183
– social observation 100
observer 22, 30–32, 68, 73, 101–102, 134, 181
ochlocracy 129, 158
Oedipus 53
office 24, 101–102, 106, 128, 177
oligarchy 119
Olivia (character in Shakespeare's *Twelfth Night*) 180
ontology 44, 59, 62, 85
opera 6, 103, 162
opiate 163–164, 171
opinion 29, 35, 51, 53, 76, 79, 87, 89–90, 99–100, 109–110, 112, 125–127, 130, 132, 148, 165–166, 171, 181, 184, 192–193, 195, 220, 222
– climate of opinions 29, 136
– freedom of opinion 129
– public opinion 2, 4, 25, 53, 124, 166

Index —— 269

opportunism 144, 170, 173, 189, 194–195
optics 77, 84–89, 94, 96, 98, 101, 103, 111
orality 22, 34, 67, 80, 105, 129, 175
orator, *see also* rhetoric 117, 122, 124–127, 133
– *De oratore* (Cicero) 117, 125
– *Institutio oratoria* (Quintilian) 125
order, *see also* discourse, knowledge 14, 16, 30, 32, 55–56, 59, 65, 69, 75, 92–93, 116, 132–134, 155, 160, 165, 167, 170, 174, 178, 198, 207, 213, 218
– civil order 207
– divine order 65, 133
– higher/lower orders 153
– holy orders 188, 199
– legal order 209
– natural order 115, 158
– order of things 72, 141, 158
– patriarchal order 204
– political order 3, 83, 89, 115, 119, 121–122, 133, 169, 171, 176, 202
– public order 74, 124–125, 133, 219
– social order 1, 3–4, 16, 109, 114, 136, 176, 207
originality 36, 51, 55, 106–107, 191
ornatus 93, 125
Orpheus 98
orthodoxy 158
Ottoman (Empire) 58
Otway, Thomas 12, 190
– *Venice Preserv'd* 190
Overton, Richard 122
Ovid (Publius Ovidius Naso) 130, 163–164
– *Metamorphoses* 130, 163
Oxford 23, 28, 46, 49, 122
Oxford English Dictionary 47

paganism 151, 155, 157, 159, 161, 203
page, *see also* title 29, 35, 37–39, 42, 49, 80, 85, 145, 187–189, 195
– literary page 32
– page number *or* pagination 105, 195
– printed page 59
– written page 14, 37
pageant 78, 145
pain 85–86, 177
painter *or* painting 102, 124, 146, 158
– landscape painting 102
palimpsest 32, 147
pamphlet 25, 29, 83, 88, 118, 128–129, 148, 167
panegyric 26, 113, 154–155, 159, 184, 211

panopticon 101
Pantalone 56
paper 24, 28, 73, 211
– writing paper 211
parable 139
Paracelsus 35
paradise 65, 69, 142, 162, 171, 213
– artificial paradise 115
paradox 21, 34–35, 46, 55, 59–60, 62, 75, 80, 111, 113, 175, 181
parallel 1, 35, 93, 115, 151, 153, 156, 167, 191–192, 197, 207–208, 217
parallelism 17
paratext *or* paratextuality 34
Paris 91, 96, 104, 187, 191
Parker, Henry 122–123
– *Observations* 123
parliament 52, 59, 96, 116, 129, 146, 150, 154, 164, 200, 207
– parliamentarianism 116, 120, 128, 157, 167
– Rump Parliament 136
parody, *see also* self-parody 26, 167, 170, 175, 191
Parsons, Talcott 43
party 58, 100, 134, 136, 144, 146–148, 161, 165
Pascal, Blaise 76, 123
passion 3, 25, 54–56, 58–59, 77, 84–90, 98–99, 103, 105, 111, 122, 126, 135, 148, 150–153, 170, 177, 186, 193–194, 196, 198, 203, 214–215, 217–218
past, the 8–9, 34, 63, 65–66, 69, 97, 121, 123–124, 133, 143–148, 156, 167, 176, 210
pasta 36
pastiche 68, 108
pastime 107, 135, 137
pastoral 11, 91, 105, 115, 119, 124, 134–139, 141–144, 187, 191, 211
Il Pastor Fido 136
pathology 107, 111
–humoral 68
pathos 132
patriotism 1–2, 132
Patrizi, Francesco 101
– *Nova de Universis Philosophia* 101
patronage 24, 72, 216
Paul (saint) 80
paysage moralisée 180
peace 26, 54, 79, 87–89, 95, 98, 100, 107, 123, 126, 128, 130, 143, 147–148, 154, 217–219

pedagogy 88, 114, 153
Peele, George 117
– *Titus Andronicus* 117
Peirce, Charles Sanders 188
Pembroke College 49
pen 26, 147–148, 165, 192
Pepys, Samuel 146, 149, 180
perception, *see also* self-perception 1–2, 15, 21, 35, 67, 85–87, 90, 100, 113, 165, 178, 214
– sense perception 1, 68, 77, 84–86
– visual perception 84–85
performance 2, 4, 15, 18, 20, 28, 30, 34, 56, 60, 90, 97, 128, 148–151, 154, 167, 169, 181, 194, 204
– media performance 77
performativity 10, 14, 19, 40, 50, 71–72, 74, 76, 87, 90, 92, 97, 184, 219
periphrasis 56, 66
peritext 17, 34, 47–48, 104, 106–107
person 1–3, 14, 21, 39, 42–43, 48, 50–53, 55, 57, 67, 75, 88, 90, 94, 100, 108, 110, 119, 138, 141, 150, 153, 155, 168–171, 174–175, 178–183, 185–188, 190, 193, 196, 199, 205, 207, 211, 215
– person of quality 83, 115
persona 35, 40–41, 50, 137, 151, 181
personalisation 174
personality 209
personification 44, 189, 202
perspective, *see also* point of view 2, 5–6, 8–10, 12–13, 21–22, 32–33, 40, 49–50, 61–62, 66–68, 75–76, 94–96, 98, 100, 102–103, 106, 115, 119, 159, 162, 165, 171, 174, 179, 184–185, 195, 199–200, 213, 223
– change of perspective 50
– contingency of perspective 33
– perspectivism 102
persuasion, *see also* rhetoric 53, 54, 55–56, 67, 79, 81, 89–90, 93, 95, 97, 101, 112, 120, 124, 126, 128, 133–134, 165–166, 193, 193, 209, 220
– *Persuasion* (Austen) 215
phenomenology 16, 32, 81
philosophy, *see also* secrecy 2, 16, 23, 26, 29–30, 41, 46, 54, 60, 72, 80, 84, 91–92, 94, 96, 105–109, 114, 146, 179, 183–186, 214
– court of philosophy 26
– experimental philosophy 104–105, 111

– moral philosophy 94
– natural philosophy 19, 28–30, 61, 74, 89, 105–109, 183
– political philosophy 94
– skeptic philosophy 59, 72
– stoic philosophy 59
Phoenicia 129
physiognomy 104, 209
physiology 19, 36, 55, 61, 74, 83, 86, 89, 96, 131, 157, 170, 181
piazza 4
picaresque 166
picture, *see also* image, world 6, 31, 39, 41, 79–80, 88, 94, 122, 137, 143, 192, 196–197, 204
– motion picture 101
piety 20, 99, 167–168, 210–212
pilgrimage 157
pity 88, 126
Plato, *see also* Cambridge, Neoplatonism 100
– *Politikos* 100
Plautus, Titus Maccius 120
– *Asinaria* 120
play, *see also* drama, life 1, 11, 21, 29, 148–151, 153–154, 178, 182, 185, 195, 200–210, 212–213
– heroic play 97
– play-book 210
– playgoing 196, 205
– playhouse 90
– playwright 149
pleasure 26, 42, 69, 85–86, 88–89, 94, 108, 137, 142, 172, 184, 187, 190, 195, 197, 217
plot, *see also* conspiracy, intrigue, Popish Plot, Rye House Plot 118, 140, 145, 151, 153, 175, 187, 190, 203
– love-plot 151
plurality 9, 16, 47, 104, 111, 113
Plutarch 94
Pocock, J. G. A. 5, 7, 14–16, 59, 120–121, 170, 173, 183, 201, 219
poem, *see also* poetry 22, 29, 37–40, 45–46, 69, 80, 82–83, 91–95, 103–104, 108, 128, 138–139, 141, 145, 151, 155–157, 159–161, 163–177, 212, 218
– drinking poem 136
– epic poem 77, 80, 91–92, 146, 159–160, 162, 164–167, 216, 220
– heroic poem 94, 99, 103

poet 8, 13, 74, 91–92, 94–95, 97, 99, 101–104, 108, 119, 139, 147, 149, 155, 160, 163, 181, 211, 215–216, 218, 223
– court poet 103
– poet laureate 166
– religious poet 133
poetics 3, 76–77, 92–93, 95, 98, 119, 218–219, 222
poetry, see also poem 18, 74, 89–91, 93, 97–98, 100–103, 110, 115, 131, 147, 155, 163–166, 185, 212–213, 219
– Cavalier poetry 212
– didactic poetry 184
– epic poetry 81–82, 96, 116, 160, 163, 167
– heroic poetry 91–92, 97, 99–101, 165, 182, 191, 196
– lyric poetry 124
– metaphysical poetry 8
– pastoral poetry 191
– satirical poetry 118
– troubadour poetry 21
point of view, see also perspective 16, 33, 44, 50, 113, 146, 159, 184–185, 190, 216
polemic 6, 11, 56, 69, 76, 81, 112, 114, 121, 123, 133, 136, 144, 162, 166–167, 219
– anti-Puritan polemic 152, 166
– anti-theatrical polemic 210
policy 41, 100–112, 146–148, 154, 158, 162, 201
polis 124, 176, 180
politeness 11, 30, 69, 72, 140, 182–183, 199, 200, 202–203, 208, 210–212, 214–215, 222
politicisation 124, 152
politics, see also political thought 1–7, 9–11, 14, 16, 19–20, 23–26, 29–30, 36, 50, 52, 54–56, 58–59, 68–69, 73–74, 76–77, 79, 83, 85, 87–89, 91, 93–96, 100–105, 112–125, 127–131, 133–136, 139–155, 157–169, 171–178, 181, 183–187, 189–192, 194, 198, 201–203, 206, 208, 210, 214–219, 221–222
polity 88, 118, 130, 132
polygamy 168
polyvalence 33, 44
Ponet, John 122
Pope, Alexander 215, 221
popery 52
Popish Plot 4, 134, 143, 162, 187
populace 49
popularity 17–18, 61, 72, 79, 134, 210, 219
pornography 116, 194, 200
poststructuralism 19
poverty 4, 23, 83, 120, 141–142
Powell, Anthony 211
– Books do Furnish a Room 211
power, see also image, law, tradition 5, 26, 39, 43–44, 58, 65, 80, 82–85, 94–97, 100–102, 110, 114, 117, 119, 121–126, 128, 135–136, 148, 155–157, 159, 171–172, 181, 198, 205–206, 217, 220, 223
– political power 4, 96, 113, 141, 143, 163, 181
– power-knowledge 9
– power of eloquence or rhetoric or words 79, 119, 124–128, 134, 217
– power of fiction or literature 70, 110
– power of rational argument or reason or thought 77, 117, 153
– sovereign power 88, 142
– will to power 198
Power, Henry 111
– Experimental Philosophy 111
prayer 157, 177, 181
precept 49, 74, 94, 98, 100, 112, 126, 215, 222
preface 17, 26, 34, 37, 40–45, 51–52, 54, 56, 60–61, 63, 65, 91, 93, 95–96, 102–104, 107–108, 110–111, 115–116, 135, 137, 146, 163–168, 171, 175, 177, 182, 191–192, 218, 220
prefiguration 156, 161, 183, 199
prejudice 125, 165, 223
prerogative, royal 4, 166
presence 11, 21, 40–41, 57, 62, 89, 92, 96, 99, 103, 117–118, 141, 147, 150, 162, 177, 186, 192–193, 202, 208, 215
– co-presence 72
present, the 9, 34, 69, 119, 123–125, 127, 133, 145–146, 156, 167, 191
presentation 17, 21–22, 31, 33–37, 42, 50–51, 61–62, 67, 77, 79–80, 94, 98–102, 108, 112–114, 117–118, 120, 122–123, 127, 129–130, 138, 142–143, 148–149, 154, 156, 160–161, 166, 168, 170–172, 174–176, 183–185, 188–191, 195, 198–199, 201–202, 204, 206, 209–210, 220
pride 39, 59, 62, 212
priesthood 45, 167–168, 212

print, *see also* book, communication, culture, imprinting, publication, text 4–5, 9, 21–22, 24–26, 28, 30, 32, 34, 39, 44, 46, 51–52, 59, 65, 67, 73, 77, 79–80, 88–89, 91, 94, 105, 123–124, 129, 131, 135, 149–150, 158, 160, 199, 220–221
– age of print 22, 28, 124
– printer 24, 37, 39, 46
– printing press 25, 52, 130, 143
privacy 42, 41, 140, 143, 177, 179, 205
– private sphere 51, 57, 177, 198
probability 7, 17, 21, 62–64, 69, 75–76, 93, 98, 109, 121, 123, 178–179, 183, 186, 193, 206, 213–214, 218–222
probity 75
procreation 171
prodesse 137, 184
proem 80–81, 220
professionalisation 10, 23–24
Project Fear 119
prologue 17, 149–151, 153, 156
promiscuity 166, 168
promise 34, 39, 43–45, 63, 70, 73, 87, 102, 119, 153, 188, 192
propaganda 17, 25, 77–79, 93, 124, 127, 132, 184–185, 187, 189–191, 194, 199, 202
property 24, 92, 114, 158, 174, 207
prophecy 14, 81–82, 114
propriety 182, 218, 222
prose 28–29, 48, 50, 81, 83, 108, 163, 185–186, 190, 211, 215, 217
prosody 80
protagonist 22, 167, 180–181, 187, 215
Protectorate 83, 142
Protestantism 5, 51–52, 79, 82, 123, 132, 149, 160, 180–181, 202, 214, 220
providence 81, 157
proviso 204–206, 212, 214
Prynne, William 210
– *Histrio-Mastix* 210
psalm 212
pseudo-antique 191
pseudonym 37–38, 41
pseudo-orality 129
pseudo-statement 13
psyche, *see also* soul 57, 204
psychology 15, 20, 84, 86, 90, 92, 115, 120, 122, 138, 198, 206, 219
psychomachia 180

psychosis 145
publication *or* publishing 6, 25, 44, 52, 75, 102, 105, 107–108, 129, 132, 136, 146, 148, 187, 221
– print publication 24–25
– publishing house 24
– scribal publication 5, 73
– vanity publication 106
public sphere 1, 4–5, 11, 17, 19, 23–24, 52, 88, 116, 124, 179, 205, 217
pun, *see also* wordplay 39, 64, 155, 208
punishment 46, 82, 98, 102, 112, 120, 122–123, 167, 172
purification 131
Puritanism, *see also* God, culture, polemic 119, 135, 149, 153, 155–157, 161–162, 166, 175, 206, 210, 214, 219
– language of Puritanism 157
purity 141, 216

Quarles, Francis 210
– *Emblems* 210
Quarrel of the Ancients and Moderns 161
quarto 38
quatrain 23
quasi-monastic 42
quasi-perfect 151
quasi-theatrical 28
quasi-timeless 215
queen (in chess) 54, 62
quietism 141, 219
Quintilian (Marcus Fabius Quintilianus) 125
– *Institutio oratoria* 125

radicalism 52, 69, 119, 132, 151, 160, 180, 220
Raiders of the Lost Ark (film) 172
Ralegh, Walter 139
Raphael (archangel) 80
rationalism 5, 16, 26, 29, 69, 71, 81, 95, 102, 123, 131–134, 140, 214, 219
– aesthetic rationalism 71, 108
– religious rationalism 132
rationality, *see also* reason 3, 5, 57, 77, 79–81, 86, 88, 92–93, 95, 98–99, 102, 107, 109–111, 113–115, 117–118, 120, 122–123, 147, 159, 178, 199–200
reader 2–4, 12, 14–15, 17, 19, 21–22, 24–26, 28–30, 32–34, 36–48, 50–51, 53–54, 56, 61–63, 66–68, 73, 78–81, 83, 90, 93–97,

102, 104, 106–108, 110, 113, 118–119, 126, 131, 135–137, 143, 155, 162–163, 165, 167–168, 172, 178, 184–188, 190–194, 197, 199–201, 211, 214, 216, 219–222
– novel-reader 187
– reader address 34
– reader response 15, 32, 39
– readership 137, 161, 166
– reader-writer relationship 33, 37, 222
reading 5–9, 11, 13–15, 17–20, 24, 30–32, 34, 36–37, 40–47, 50, 54, 59, 61, 66, 68, 70, 72, 76–77, 79–80, 83–85, 90, 93–94, 96, 103, 108, 110, 127, 131–132, 135, 137, 143, 149, 155, 166, 177–178, 181, 183–186, 188–191, 193–194, 197–200, 202, 204, 210–215, 222
– act of reading 15, 77, 89, 185
– contingency of reading 17
– epistemology of reading 88
– imaginative reading 110
– mindreading 37
– one-handed reading 194
– political reading 162–163, 202
– private rading 181
– reading community 73
– reading experience 143
– right or true reading 83, 93, 186
– reading matter 32, 210
– reading process 108
– situation of reading 33, 137
– silent reading 85
– typological reading 156, 161
realism 63, 69, 97, 138, 141, 144–145, 185, 190, 195
reality 7, 9, 16, 20–21, 30, 34, 50, 56, 63, 65–68, 72–73, 75–76, 81, 85, 87–89, 100–101, 104–105, 109, 111, 114–115, 136, 142–143, 158, 165, 167, 192, 199, 206, 213–214, 216, 219
– historical reality 121, 123
– human reality 182
– political reality 116, 134, 165, 192
– reality effect 138
– social reality 1, 5, 134, 141, 144, 183, 200, 208
reason, see also rationalism, rationality 53, 53–60, 62, 66, 85–88, 90, 98–99, 101, 105, 108–111, 114, 117, 119–120, 122, 126–128, 130–132, 134–135, 139–140, 147, 153, 160, 174, 183, 186, 194, 196, 214, 217–220
– age of reason 26, 219
– right reason 20, 88, 120, 122, 160
rebellion 54–55, 58, 127, 132, 145, 151–152, 165, 167, 169–171, 174–175, 189
– Monmouth rebellion 187–188
reception 18–19, 33, 72, 94, 107, 163, 178
reconciliation 2, 29, 54, 57, 95, 98, 107, 125, 149, 153–154, 157, 167, 169, 174–176, 214
reconstruction 6, 12–15, 19, 31–32, 146
recreation 32–33, 57, 60, 66–67, 110, 134–136, 138–139, 143, 201
Redcrosse (character in *The Faerie Queene*) 180
reference, see also self-reference 14, 18, 32, 35, 42, 51–52, 69, 98, 129, 154–155, 157, 160, 163, 165–167, 172, 177, 180, 182, 220
– frame of reference 43, 209, 214, 216
referent 63, 66, 219
referentiality 65–66, 217
reflection, see also self-reflection 3, 5, 9, 24, 30, 32–33, 39, 47, 49, 69, 71, 76–77, 88, 105, 115, 171, 200
– meta-communicative reflection 10
reform or reformation 67, 113, 132–133, 156–159, 172, 201, 216
Reformation 1
regicide 148, 164
regime, see also change 133, 136, 147, 155, 157, 160, 202
reign 103, 148
Reiss, Timothy 18, 20, 69, 71, 75–76, 91, 119, 155, 177–179, 182–183, 215
relativism 67, 88, 194
relativity 53, 61, 200
relativisation 26, 139
religion or religiosity 7, 10, 20, 28–29, 51, 53, 55–56, 58, 62, 66, 74, 95, 99–100, 111–112, 114, 123, 132, 136, 139–140, 142, 149, 151–152, 158, 177, 181, 183, 197, 203, 214, 216, 219
– war of religion 149, 214
remembering or remembrance, see also memory 46, 116, 144–146, 160, 206, 210
Renaissance 4–6, 26, 32, 71–72, 75, 91, 93, 95, 125, 137, 180
repetition 14–15, 66, 91, 99, 139, 157, 174, 185, 190, 192, 194
representamen 188, 192

representation, *see also* self-representation 3, 5, 9, 22, 29, 31, 39, 50, 54, 66, 75, 83, 88, 90, 92–94, 97, 102–104, 141, 145, 147, 151, 155, 181–182, 185, 187, 190, 192, 201–202, 208, 216, 221
– literary representation 165, 178
– visual representation 90
republic, *see also* letter 83, 91, 98, 127, 128–130, 132–133, 144, 146–147, 171
– English Republic 1, 83, 91, 98, 133, 135, 148, 158
republicanism 4–5, 25, 59, 77–79, 114, 122, 123, 128–129, 133, 143, 158, 162
reputation 73, 77, 127, 195, 203, 207, 209–210
restoration 77, 83, 144, 146–148, 153–154, 156, 158, 163, 175
Restoration 1, 11, 26, 95, 97, 99, 103, 104–105, 112–113, 115–116, 134, 140, 142–151, 154–156, 159, 161–162, 182–183, 187, 201, 207, 215, 217, 219–220
resurrection 62, 64–65
revelation 5, 22, 82, 155, 188, 190, 193–194, 204, 209, 221
revenge *or* vengeance 148–149, 151, 153, 158, 209
revision 7, 11, 30, 35, 50, 52, 59, 82, 145, 151, 162, 203, 223
revisionism 5, 9, 12, 162
revolt 96, 127, 163, 171
revolution 126, 145–146, 148, 155, 171, 201, 216
– Glorious Revolution 186, 200–201, 214, 219
– scientific revolution 105
reward 102, 112, 208
rhetoric, *see also* contingency, eloquence, orator, Satan 2–3, 7, 11, 18, 21, 23, 25–26, 28, 33–34, 43, 48–59, 61, 63–69, 74, 76–78, 83–84, 87–93, 95, 97–98, 101–102, 104–108, 110, 114–117, 124–135, 144–146, 155, 159–161, 164, 168–173, 175, 177, 181, 190, 193, 195–197, 199, 209, 217–218, 220–221
– image-rhetoric 127
– non-deterministic rhetoric 76
– non-persuasive rhetoric 115
– persuasive rhetoric 26, 57, 90, 125
– power of rhetoric 117, 124, 127
rhyme 23, 91, 160, 172–173, 212, 217
rhythm 49, 65, 80

Richard (ship) 146
Richardson, Samuel
Richmond (ship) 146
right, *see also* law 98, 112, 114, 120, 122, 127, 129, 148, 161, 169–170, 174, 208
– Bill of Rights 200
– civic rights 125
– divine right 120–121, 166, 168
– human rights 123
– natural rights 117, 119–120, 214
righteousness 79, 102, 161, 171
ritual 9, 76, 137, 148, 201
Rochester, John Wilmot, Earl of 116, 146, 168
– *The Farce of Sodom* 116
Roi Soleil 101
role-play 40–41, 189
role-taking 43
roman à clef 187
romance 105, 116, 134, 143, 145, 165, 180, 186–187, 190–191, 193, 211
– epic romance 143, 180
– heroic romance 116, 165
Romanticism 26, 63, 70, 74, 135, 143, 155, 219, 222
Rome 54, 117, 128, 132, 136, 150, 161
Romeo (character) 212
Rousseau, Jean-Jacques 118, 134–135, 143
Royal Charles (ship) 146
Royal Exchange 83
Royal Society 28, 60–61, 75, 126, 216–217
royalism 77, 79, 96, 104, 116, 118, 123, 132–136, 139–141, 143–147, 151, 156–159, 162, 165, 188, 199, 212, 217
royalties 24
rule, *see also* law 7, 9, 22, 26, 29, 51, 62, 70, 74, 76, 100, 105, 111, 113, 122, 140, 158, 161, 170, 193, 197, 200–201, 204, 214, 218, 220, 222
– godly rule 136
– parliamentary rule 128
– personal rule 140
– ruler (instrument) 37
– ruler (person) 170
Rye House Plot 187

saint 77, 112, 161
Saint Germain 96
St.-Réal, César Vichard de 191

– *Mémoires de Mme. la Duchesse de Mazarin* 191
Sales, William 105
– *Theophania* 105
Samuel (biblical books) 166
Samuel, William 138
– *The Arte of Angling* 138
Satan, *see also* devil 54, 80–82, 133, 152, 159, 167, 172–173, 185
– rhetoric of Satan 54
satire 26, 37, 41–43, 45, 111, 118, 144–146, 160, 163–164, 166–168, 176, 184, 190–191, 197
– "Discourse concerning . . . Satire" (Dryden) 160, 164
– Menippean satire 35
savage 49, 118, 170
Scaliger, Julius Caesar 60
scandal 168, 187, 191, 207
scepticism, *see also* skepticism 82, 89, 106–107, 166, 192
sceptre 127
Scheveningen 146, 154
scholarship 8, 30–31, 37, 42, 53, 61, 120, 140, 216
scholasticism 28, 61
science 7, 18, 20, 29, 60–61, 75–76, 80, 86–87, 91–93, 104–106, 109, 111, 126, 134, 183, 223
– experimental science 29, 61
– natural science 20
– new science 96, 101
– popular science 61
Scotland *or* Scottish 6, 201
scribe 112
Scripture 25, 50, 54, 83, 161, 167, 181, 220
secrecy *or* secret 30, 101–102, 108, 126, 140, 143, 164
– philosophy of secrecy 140
secretary 24
– Secretary for Foreign Tongues 128
sect 54, 56, 79
sectarianism 29, 152, 162
secularisation 4, 115, 136, 152
secularism 69, 83, 102, 114–115, 122, 128, 155, 173, 175, 214
security 24, 95, 130, 137, 174, 195, 203–204, 209
sedition 90, 111, 126, 130, 152, 165
Selden, John 120–122

– *Table Talk* 120
self *or* selfhood 20, 32–33, 50–51, 55–58, 66, 73, 99, 140, 177, 179–180, 183, 185, 188–189, 204, 211
– self-accusation 196
– self-analysis 196
– self-awareness 179
– self-care 205
– self-concealment 138
– self-consciousness 3, 7, 18, 33, 50, 67, 132, 159, 185, 215
– self-control 56, 99, 142, 176, 180, 194
– self-cultivation 48, 68, 176
– self-deconstruction 72
– self-defence 173
– self-definition 220
– self-deprecation 32, 40
– self-description 50
– self-discovery 138
– self-dissection 32
– self-distancing 33, 50
– self-enclosure 9, 18
– self-exploration 176
– self-fashioning 72, 140
– self-glorification 113
– self-image 66
– self-interest 86
– self-justification 40
– self-knowledge 36, 42, 140
– self-legitimation 183
– self-loathing 196
– self-love 86, 103
– self-magnification 110
– self-monitoring 201
– self-motivation 55
– self-observation 48, 63, 68, 176, 180
– self-parody 175, 190
– self-perception 201
– self-possession 140, 142
– self-presentation 4, 191
– self-preservation 86, 117, 220
– self-promotion 102
– self-questioning 44, 72
– self-reference 43, 66
– self-reflection 1, 4, 32, 43, 49, 57
– self-reflexiveness 35, 63
– self-reliance 55, 160
– self-representation 221
– self-reproduction 214

– self-staging 33
– self-transformation 80, 83, 138
semantics 19–20, 33, 74–75, 79, 163, 178–179, 185
– cultivated semantics 69
– religious semantics 157
semiotics 50, 73, 200
Seneca, Lucius Annaeus 52, 177
– *De clementia* 177
sense, *see also* common sense, meaning, perception 1–2, 7, 14–15, 18, 21, 23–26, 28, 30–33, 44–45, 47, 49, 53, 56–57, 66–68, 70, 80, 82, 84, 87, 106, 135, 137–138, 150, 160, 173, 177, 186, 192, 194, 200, 202, 209–210, 214, 216
– sense impression 145
– sense-making 21, 122, 200
– sense organs 85
– the senses 31, 57, 84–85, 87, 111, 134, 213–214, 216
– visual sense 84–85
sensibility 6–8, 186, 211, 213
sensus communis, *see also* common sense 85
sententiae 94
sermon 29, 45, 141, 211
– Sermon on the Mount 139
Seville 149
sex 187
– same-sex confederacy 205
sexuality 138, 161, 166–169, 189–190, 194–195, 198–199, 207
shadow 66, 99, 143, 158
Shaftesbury, Anthony Ashley Cooper, first earl of 162, 167, 169, 173, 187, 190
Shaftesbury, Anthony Ashley Cooper, third earl of 26, 182, 184, 218–219
– *Sensus communis* 218
Shakespeare, William 6, 12, 16, 21, 42, 64, 117, 149, 180, 191, 204, 212
– *As You Like It* 42
– *Hamlet* 8, 64–65, 116, 180–182
– *Othello* 16, 149
– *Richard II* 204
– *Richard III* 185
– *Romeo and Juliet* 212
– *Titus Andronicus* 117
Shapin, Steven 75
Sharpe, Kevin 9, 17, 25, 83, 91, 140
ship, *see also* fool, state 91, 100, 172

Sidney, Algernon 129
Sidney, Philip 91, 97, 134, 138, 191
– *The Countess of Pembroke's Arcadia* 138, 191
– *The Defence of Poesie* 13, 91
sign, *see also* language 14, 17–18, 25, 38, 66, 73, 80, 82, 169, 171, 181–183, 186, 192–193, 197–200, 209–210, 219
– theory of signs 181
signature 32, 41, 73, 105, 200
signification 7, 9, 22, 73, 89, 168, 182, 193
signifier 119, 182
silence, *see also* reading 1–3, 43, 45, 63, 85, 140, 147–148, 192–193
simile 93, 96, 157
simulation 44, 80, 108, 129, 181, 192, 199
sin 59, 82, 147, 168
Sinai 99, 220
sincerity 182, 193, 206
singularity 51, 68
skepticism 21, 28, 59, 72, 87, 108, 139
Skinner, Quentin 23, 87, 91, 93, 125, 128, 170
slave 46–47, 133, 168–170, 172
Smith, John 29
Smollett, Tobias 186
sociability 10, 30, 123, 136–137, 182–183, 201, 203, 210, 219, 222
society, *see also* Royal Society 4, 16, 57, 59, 68–69, 72, 74, 79, 87–88, 98–99, 109, 111, 114, 117–121, 123–126, 141–143, 145, 163, 176–178, 183, 200–203, 205, 208–209, 211, 213–214, 216–218, 222
– civic society 222
– civil society 174
– polite society 201, 211
sociology 16, 179, 183
song 138, 141
sonnet 143, 180, 212
soul 22, 54–58, 112, 129, 137, 192, 194, 196, 218
– rational soul 177
Southerne, Thomas 182
– *The Wives Excuse* 182
sovereign *or* sovereignty, *see also* power 3, 88–89, 91, 94–101, 112–115, 117, 121–123, 125–128, 149–150, 152, 158, 169–170, 173, 177, 179, 198, 200, 205
– imaginary sovereign 115
Spain *or* Spanish 148–153, 191
spaniel 92

space 25, 29–31, 37–38, 74, 201
– blank *or* empty space 35, 39, 76, 83, 106–107, 198
– conceptual space 116
– display space 211
– imaginary space 32
– infinite space 180
– inner space 57
– interior space 177
– private space 176–177, 179, 186
– shared space 184
– space between 28, 106, 198
– theatrical space 4, 31
Sparta 127, 129, 172
speaker 7, 21, 43–44, 51, 87, 89, 126, 156–157, 163, 170–173, 220
– epic speaker 80–83
– unreliable speaker 173
Speaker (ship) 146
spectacle 72
– multi-media spectacle 101
spectator 1–2, 4, 31, 33, 42, 49–50, 97, 102, 184, 189
– *The Spectator* (periodical) 217
speech, *see also* theory 7, 9, 11, 22, 82, 87–90, 125–127, 129, 132–133, 150–151, 153, 159, 172–173, 175, 183, 193, 196, 217–218
– abuse of speech 88, 127, 133
– figure of speech 93, 103
– freedom of speech 9, 41, 129, 132
– propriety of speech 218, 222
– simulated speech 80, 129
Speedwell (ship) 146
Spencer, Robert, second earl of Sunderland 188
Spencer Brown, George 72
Spenser, Edmund 24, 105, 134, 180, 191
– *The Faerie Queene* 105, 180
Spinoza, Baruch de 122
spirit 32, 42, 57, 84, 113, 132, 134, 181, 208
– animal spirits 84–85
– divine spirit 57, 93
– Holy Spirit 58
spirituality 31, 50, 55–56, 61–62, 82, 115, 131, 144, 156, 177, 212
Sprat, Thomas 126, 216–217
sprezzatura 182
spring 191

stability 7, 56, 76, 79, 89, 98, 114, 126, 129–130, 144, 160, 168, 170, 172, 174, 185, 201, 203–204, 207–209, 219
stage, *see also* Collier, play, theatre 42, 46–47, 56, 97, 124, 148, 153, 175, 182, 201, 203
– London as stage 4
– stage direction 150
– stage machinery 150
– stage set 150
– staging, *see also* self-staging 5, 28, 33–34, 36–37, 40–41, 42, 44, 47, 50, 65, 67–68, 78, 106–107, 135, 149, 156, 175
star, *see also* astrology, astronomy, Bethlehem 95, 154, 156
state, *see also* commonwealth, nature 2, 11, 24, 54–55, 58, 69, 72, 78, 83, 95, 98–100, 111, 113, 125, 127–133, 145–146, 163–164, 169–171, 174, 177–178
– civic state 123
– Council of State 128
– fiction of state 144–145, 168
– mental state 86, 185, 188
– ship of state 172
– state licensing, *see also* censorship, licensing 124
Stationers' company 61
status naturae, *see also* nature, state of 118
Steele, Richard 215
Sterne, Laurence 215
Stevens, Wallace 213
stoicism, *see also* neostoicism 42, 49, 59, 116, 118, 123, 133, 180
Strachey, Lytton 47
strategy 2–3, 6, 10, 14, 16–17, 19, 21, 25–28, 33–34, 36, 39–43, 47, 66–67, 69, 71, 76–78, 90, 96–97, 102, 104, 108–109, 114, 116, 136–137, 141, 143–144, 146, 148, 152, 156–161, 164, 168, 172–174, 185–186, 190, 196, 199, 202, 208–210, 217, 219
Streamer, Gregory 22
structure 7–9, 12, 17, 19–21, 32–33, 54, 59, 61, 73, 75, 92, 94, 124, 131–133, 138, 140, 145, 185, 190, 200
– class structure 207
– democratic structure 217
– legal structure 207–208
– literary structure 17, 222
– rhetorical structure 159

- social structure 16, 176
- super-structure 35
- textual structure 19, 33

Stuart era 4, 134, 145, 152, 160, 201–202, 217, 219

style, *see also* thought 29, 30, 47–50, 53, 60, 64, 66, 75, 92, 96, 98, 101, 132, 153, 202, 211, 216–218
- cognitive style 75–76
- experiential style 75–76
- history of style 48
- unity of style 48

Suárez, Francisco 118
- *Tractatus de Legibus* 118

subject 55, 63, 83–84, 88–89, 97, 99, 113–114, 117, 120, 123, 125, 148–149, 152, 157–158, 176, 179
- subjection 55
- subjectivity 2, 5, 55, 57, 62, 82, 177, 179, 185, 188–189, 199, 204

subscription 37, 73
substance 20, 84, 111, 131, 133, 158
subtext 137, 190
Success (ship) 146
Suckling, John 212
suffering 52, 81, 147–148, 157, 180, 215
summer 1, 138, 140
sun 64, 95, 101–102, 150–151
supernatural 82, 96
superstition 60, 77, 79, 156
surgery 148, 163, 175
Surrey, Henry Howard, Earl of 180
suspense 1, 97
Swift, Jonathan 12, 26, 197, 215
sword 125, 128, 147–148, 174–175
symbol 9, 56, 63, 65
- status symbol 142
- the symbolic 180

symmetry 132
sympathy 73, 135, 189, 196
synecdoche 73, 141, 184
syntax 48, 79–80, 107, 151
system, *see also* theory 20–21, 24, 26, 31, 54, 56, 58–59, 72, 73, 76, 91, 102, 107, 117, 142, 167, 168, 198, 200, 218, 221
- literary system 9–10, 19, 74
- patriarchal system 140
- political system 133, 165, 172, 176
- social system 5, 9, 216
- subsystem 10
- value system 76, 138, 207

tact 202, 210
tactics 6, 51, 77, 102, 157
talent 23, 64, 103, 125, 209
Targoff, Ramie 65
taste 8, 40, 131, 149, 178, 183, 215
Taylor, John 12
teaching 91, 94, 98, 112, 127–128, 149–150, 153, 164
teichoscopy 2
teleology 7–8, 17, 70–71, 201, 221
telescope *or* telescopy 86, 103, 111, 115
temple 133
temporality, *see also* time 11, 137, 161–162
tension 5, 63, 105–106, 214
terror 118
Tew Circle 119, 123
text, *see also* context, intertextuality, paratext, theatre, writing *passim*
- culture as text 19
- printed text 4, 22, 37, 85, 89, 129
- text-context duality 18
- textuality 11, 19, 22, 33–34, 43, 72, 105, 114, 115, 180, 182, 198, 201, 210, 213, 219
- texture 19, 210
- written text 193

theatre, *see also* amphitheatre, anti-theatricalism, life, performance, play, space, stage 2, 4, 34, 41–42, 49, 56, 68, 97, 103, 105, 116, 148, 150, 181, 201, 205, 219
- amphitheatre 90
- anatomical theatre 43
- Dorset Garden Theatre 150
- Elizabethan theatre 72
- textual theatre 41
- theatricality 1–2, 4, 28, 33, 42, 47, 77, 151, 201, 219
- virtual theatre 31

Themistocles 147
theology, *see also* divinity 28, 31, 58, 60–63, 66–68, 81, 82, 114, 119, 121, 137–138, 158, 166–167, 173, 175, 183, 203, 208
theorem 54
theory, *see also* king, literature, sign 5, 7–10, 12–14, 23, 30, 32, 49, 54, 58, 71–72, 74, 77–78, 84, 86, 88, 90–95, 98–99, 103,

105–106, 110, 117–119, 120–125, 128, 162, 165, 169, 174, 216
- action theory 16
- contract theory 200
- divine right theory 168
- economic theory 219
- genre theory 77
- literary theory 3, 14, 19, 26, 71, 74, 77, 91–93, 97, 100, 102, 115, 149, 221
- media theory 14, 77
- medical theory 164
- natural law *or* rights theory 99, 120, 169, 173
- political theory 5, 58–59, 78, 86, 88, 95, 100, 122–124, 142, 165, 168, 171, 173–174, 176, 181, 219
- physiognomic theory 209
- republican theory 5, 129
- resistance theory 118, 122
- social theory 84, 115
- speech act theory 87
- systems theory 9–10, 12–13, 16
thinking *see under* thought
Thomism 118
thought 8, 49, 55–56, 58, 61–62, 66–67, 90, 92, 94–95, 101, 106–107, 116, 118–120, 125–126, 132, 134, 145, 156, 177–178, 182, 186, 192, 194, 199, 216
- economic thought 74
- figure of thought 118, 121
- political thought 4, 19, 59, 74, 116, 117–118, 134, 140, 143, 202, 214
- rational thought 117, 166
- style of thought 29, 56, 62, 75, 92
Thucydides 24, 126–127, 172
- *Eight Bookes of the Peloponnesian Warre* 127
time, *see also* temporality 2–4, 6, 9, 14–15, 18, 20, 25, 52, 54, 95–97, 110, 115–118, 120–121, 137, 141–143, 148–149, 156, 164, 167–168, 175, 177, 185, 189, 191, 194, 198, 206, 210, 215, 221–222
- time-management 137
- waste of time 216
Titans 163
title *or* title page 4, 17, 27, 34, 37–39, 41, 45, 48, 51, 55, 60–61, 70, 78, 86, 91, 95, 111, 127, 135–136, 155, 187, 211
token 73, 136
tolerance *or* toleration 53, 56, 59, 115, 148, 214, 222

Tonson, Jacob 73
topology 57
topos 2, 42, 100, 112
Tory 134, 146, 165–166, 176, 187–190, 199
totalisation 42, 50, 68, 102, 221
totality 29–30, 35–36, 42, 68, 73, 160
Tottel's Miscellany 22
tourism 138
tradition 1, 8, 13, 16, 28, 41, 46, 52, 56–57, 61, 67, 70–71, 76, 83, 95, 121, 125, 129, 131, 142, 155–156, 161, 163, 165, 170, 173–174, 176, 178, 181, 207
- Christian tradition 151
- classical tradition 120, 124, 125, 177–178
- folk tradition 159
- hermeticist tradition 101
- humanist tradition 138
- pagan tradition 151
- power of tradition 173
- rhetorical tradition 92
- romance tradition 191
- stoic tradition 133
tragedy 65, 71, 90, 151, 154, 202
tragicomedy 145
transfiguration 82
transformation 5–7, 20–21, 26, 30, 34, 36, 40–41, 49, 63, 68, 73, 82, 94, 105, 110, 113, 117, 119–121, 126, 130, 134, 155, 162, 198, 201, 206, 208, 213, 219
transgression 111, 190, 199
translation 6, 24, 45–46, 49, 61, 73, 88, 99, 127–128, 141, 149, 164, 172, 181, 186, 190–192, 198, 213, 219–220
travel, *see also* writing 32, 37, 46, 61, 101, 138
treason 148, 164, 173
treatise 29, 43, 46, 55, 105, 107, 111, 118, 133
trial 77, 81, 84, 131, 148, 162, 173, 187–188, 207
- *The Trial of Ford Lord Grey of Werk* 187
triumvirate 54, 55
trope 17, 19, 42, 58, 63, 81, 89, 93, 128, 156, 166, 171, 198
trust 3, 11, 75, 83, 89, 100, 122–123, 154, 173, 193, 197, 200, 202, 207, 209–210
truth 6, 13, 25–26, 29, 46–48, 50, 53, 58, 60–62, 66, 69, 73–75, 77–79, 83, 88, 90, 92–94, 97–98, 102, 108–112, 121, 125–126, 128, 130–132, 135–136, 147, 165–166, 189, 192–193, 197, 217–218, 221
- wars of truth 124, 134

Tuke, Samuel 11, 145, 148–156, 159
- *The Adventures of Five Hours* 11, 145, 149–154, 156, 176
- *A Character of Charles the Second* 148
Turk 58
type 73, 200, 203, 217
- text type *or* type of writing 21–22, 29, 72, 111, 187, 197, 221–222
- unity of type 73
typography 53, 143
typology 155–156, 161
tyranny 52, 78–79, 128, 130, 133, 208
tyrant 77, 83, 118, 206

Ulysses 114
uncertainty 7, 20–22, 32, 50, 59, 61, 63, 66, 73, 75–76, 79, 81, 100, 114, 120, 123, 154, 170, 195–196, 204, 206, 221
unconsciousness 84, 145
understanding 13, 25, 40, 53–55, 70, 80, 84, 97, 104, 108, 125, 189, 192, 195
unicorn 31
uniformity 4, 112
union 3, 148, 151, 153, 155, 158, 170, 176–177, 194
- political union 54
- union of contraries 62
- union of England and Scotland 201
unity, *see also* style, type, worship 3, 5–6, 20, 57–58, 69, 74, 94–95, 99, 103–104, 109–110, 112, 155, 177–178, 180, 185, 216
- God's unity with creation 63
- national unity 1
- ontological unity 62
- social unity 69, 78
- unities in drama (Aristotle) 23, 222
universalism 34, 65, 67–68
universality 74, 79, 81, 95, 101, 119, 162
universe, *see also* discourse 1, 91, 178, 212
university 106
univocality 14
unreliability 65, 81, 173, 180, 186, 200, 203
urbanisation 180
urbanity 161
urban planning 4
urn 31, 63, 65
usefulness 69, 98–99, 110, 184, 210
utopia 33, 42, 70, 112, 132, 134, 143, 206, 212
- pastoral utopia 139

Utopia (More) 112
utterance 7–8, 10, 13–14, 21, 89, 94, 96, 132, 159, 165, 192–193
- politics of utterance 7, 18
Uzza (biblical character) 172

validity 23, 26, 81, 197, 205, 207, 215, 219, 221, 223
value 6, 9, 19, 47, 52, 69, 71, 73, 76, 86, 92, 110, 113, 131, 134, 138, 142, 144, 146, 185, 192, 196, 199, 207, 211, 215
- aesthetic value 7, 18, 215
- cultural value 74, 158, 184
- shared values 2, 5, 137
- truth value 6, 13, 26
- use value 24
van Diepenbeeck, Abraham 106
van Dyck, Anthony 83
vanitas 42
vanity 63, 106, 195
van Velthuysen, Lambert 122
variability 16, 20, 48, 66
variation 100, 186, 190, 222
vengeance *see under* revenge
Venice 58, 190
ventriloquism 40
verisimilitude 17, 69, 98, 222
verse 8, 80, 108, 139, 154, 163, 175, 211–212
- blank verse 23, 160, 217
- neck verse 212
- *Verse Life* (Hobbes) 127–128
vice 42, 58–59, 87, 91, 131, 163–164
Victorian period 135
viewpoint, *see also* perspective, point of view 51, 100
violence 1, 6, 96, 118, 120–121, 125, 155, 157, 164, 194, 196
Virgil 14, 73, 155–156, 160, 220
- *Aeneid* 14, 155
- *sortes Virgilianae* 14
virtù 30, 161, 170
virtuality 21, 31–32, 59, 63, 142
virtue 5, 30, 49, 79, 87–88, 91–92, 94–100, 102, 116, 139, 141–142, 148, 150, 153, 157, 161, 165, 168, 170, 172, 180, 185, 194–195, 203
- civic virtue 125, 128
- feminine virtue 194
- Roman virtue 161

virtus 30
virtuosity *or* virtuoso 30–31, 111, 151
vis verborum 125
vision 68, 70, 80–82, 84, 86, 115, 134, 142, 152, 158, 160, 161, 212, 220
visuality 2, 4, 11, 34, 37–38, 41, 50, 57, 63–64, 66, 69–70, 76–85, 87, 89–90, 93–96, 102–105, 110, 114–115, 124, 127, 181, 192–193, 210
vita activa / vita contemplativa 139
vitalism 73
Vitoria, Francisco de 118
voice 39, 59, 111, 166, 192
Voltaire (François-Marie Arouet) 80
vow 157, 188, 195, 199
vulgar 53–55, 78–79, 83, 99, 101
– *Vulgar Errors* (Browne) 29, 60

Wakefield (ship) 146
Waldenfels, Bernhard 16
Wales *or* Welsh 6
Waller, Edmund 91, 119, 212
Waller, William 134
– *Divine Meditations* 134
Walsingham 63
Walton, Izaak 11, 115–116, 134–144, 146, 152
– *The Compleat Angler* 11, 115, 134–144
war, *see also* Civil War, heaven, religion, truth, word 1, 3, 51, 96–97, 107, 119, 125–126, 128–129, 132, 145, 147, 217, 219
– civil war 125, 130, 132, 148, 161, 165, 176, 222
– warfare 1, 7, 17, 42, 96, 136, 141, 149
Warren, Austin 48
Wats, Gilbert 61
wealth 69, 142, 171, 188, 195, 197–198
weapon 25, 52, 156
– language or words as weapon 44, 89, 97, 100–101, 124–128, 130, 146, 160, 164
– printing press as weapon 52
Westminster Abbey 4, 215
whale 103
Whig *or* Whiggism, *see also* history, ideology 6, 134, 146, 161–162, 165–166, 169, 170, 176, 187, 189, 190, 199, 201, 208
White, Thomas 86
– *De Mundo* 86
Whitehall 78, 187
Wilde, Oscar 204

William III, King of England, Scotland and Ireland 3, 201–202, 219
Winsby (ship) 146
wisdom 30, 33, 35, 42, 45, 61, 78–79, 87, 122, 125–127, 139, 147, 154, 156, 167, 172–173, 214
wit 30, 61, 92–93, 95, 101–102, 107, 112, 124, 127, 147, 149, 151, 159–160, 163–165, 179–180, 182–183, 206, 210–211
witch 28
wolf 59, 113, 119–120, 144
woman, *see also* femininity 85, 101, 106, 142, 151, 167–168, 171, 189, 194–195, 198, 203, 205–206, 217
wonder, *see also* miracle 31, 61, 167, 169, 196
– cabinet of wonder 28, 30–32, 60–61, 67, 217
word 2, 4, 7–8, 14–15, 18, 20, 35–37, 44–45, 47, 49, 51–52, 56, 61, 63–66, 75, 77–78, 82, 85, 87–90, 93, 110, 125–126, 148, 150, 157–158, 165, 169, 172, 177, 179, 182, 186, 191–193, 208, 210–211, 216, 218, 221
– abuse of words 217
– divine word 159
– faith in words 79
– keyword 19–20, 135, 157, 168, 182
– power of words 79
– printed word 26, 79
– spoken word 193, 210
– wordplay, *see also* pun 61, 64, 89
– war of words 167
– word choice 48
– words as weapons 44, 124–125
– written word 21–22
Wordsworth, William 22, 143
– "Written upon a Blank Leaf in 'The Compleat Angler'" 143
work, *see also* art, fiction, God, literature 9, 12, 18–19, 23–25, 28, 29, 34, 37, 42–43, 45, 48–49, 51–52, 71, 73, 82–84, 87, 92, 101, 105–109, 126, 140, 142, 145, 147, 159, 163, 168, 174, 187–189, 191, 200, 210–211, 215, 221
– literary work 71, 74
– poetic work 128, 162
world, *see also* content, counter-world, discourse, event, macro-/microcosm, media 6, 9, 14, 16–18, 20–21, 24–26, 28–31, 33, 35, 37, 41–42, 52, 58, 62, 65–66, 68, 74–75, 83, 87, 95–96, 100–104, 110,

112–115, 119, 121, 132, 138, 142–143, 154, 160, 163–164, 170, 174–175, 184, 188–189, 194, 197, 199–200, 203–204, 209, 211, 213, 215, 223
- Blazing-world 112–113
- celestial world 113
- conceptual world 29
- disenchanted world 213
- enlightened world 213
- experiential world 184
- exterior *or* external *or* outside world 38, 57, 85
- fallen world 198
- fictional world 108, 111, 113, 115–116
- geocentric world picture
- immaterial world 113
- inverted world 112
- modern world 7, 213, 223
- natural world 143
- other world 110
- pastoral world 138
- phenomenal world 32, 81
- postdiluvian world 123
- postlapsarian world 123
- play-world 139
- plurality of worlds 113
- political world 203
- private world 135
- referential world 66
- social world 145, 202
- virtual world 142
- world as book 46, 52
- world as dream 56
- world as stage 42, 56
- worldmaking 68, 110, 114–116, 186, 216, 223
- world picture 20, 28, 157
worship 101, 112, 117, 156–156
- unity of worship 112
wrestling 128
Wright, Thomas 55–56
- *The Passions of the Minde in Generall* 55–56
writer, *see also* author, reader 7, 10, 17, 24–26, 28, 30, 32–33, 36–37, 40, 44, 48, 58, 74, 77, 92–93, 97, 103, 105, 115–116, 120, 137, 148, 185, 190, 192, 216, 221
- letter-writer 188, 193–194
writing, *see also* inscription, paper 6–9, 11, 13, 15, 20–26, 28–37, 40–41, 45, 47–52, 54, 56, 61–63, 65–68, 72–74, 76–81, 90–93, 95–96, 99, 103, 105–108, 114, 116, 119, 123–124, 126–129, 131, 134–135, 137–138, 143, 146, 149, 152–155, 159, 162–164, 166, 172–173, 175, 177, 183, 186–188, 191–193, 198–199, 210–211, 216, 218–220, 222
- act of writing 20, 37, 41–42, 149, 213
- contingency of writing 28
- disease of writing 107
- handwriting 52
- historical writing 18
- imaginative writing 18, 26, 48, 106
- inflationary writing 28
- invention of writing 129
- literary writing 7, 17–18, 23, 183, 211, 215
- multiplicity of writing 47–48
- pastoral writing 143
- philosophical writing 184
- popular science writing 61
- political writing 37, 93
- rewriting 15, 28, 136, 162
- scientific writing 18
- situation of writing 8, 19, 72, 176
- theoretical writing 105, 123–124
- travel writing 61
- writing materials 24
Wyatt, Thomas 180
Wycherley, William 182

Xerxes 60

Yorick 65
York, Duke of *see under* James II

zeal *or* zealotry 79, 149, 199
Zimri 164, 171, 185, 194
Zwicker, Steven N. 144, 164, 168

www.ingramcontent.com/pod-product-compliance
Lightning Source LLC
Chambersburg PA
CBHW070755230426
43665CB00017B/2366